Getting Into Poetry

Getting Into Poetry

Morris Sweetkind

Boston   HOLBROOK PRESS, INC.

The author wishes to thank the following copyright owners and publishers for permission to reprint a number of the poems appearing in this book:

CONRAD AIKEN—"Blind Date," "Discordants—III" from Collected Poems, copyright 1953 by Conrad Aiken, by permission of Oxford University Press.

W. H. AUDEN—"Law Like Love," "Musée des Beaux Arts," "The Unknown Citizen," copyright 1940, renewed 1968 by W. H. Auden, "O What Is That Sound" (formerly titled "The Quarry"), copyright 1937, renewed 1965 by W. H. Auden, "Sonnet XV" (Sonnets from China) (formerly titled "Embassy"), copyright 1945 by W. H. Auden, from Collected Shorter Poems: 1927–1957, by permission of Random House and Faber and Faber.

MARVIN BELL—"The 3 Corners of Reality," which originally appeared in Poetry, from Things We Dreamt We Died For, copyright © 1966 by Marvin Bell, by permission of The Stone Wall Press and the author.

HAROLD BOND—"The Glove," which originally appeared in The New Yorker, from Dancing on Water, copyright © 1969 by Harold Bond, by permission of The Cummington Press and the author; "Museum Tour," which originally appeared in Hearse, from Fragments of an Earlier Life, copyright © 1972 by Harold Bond, by permission of the author.

ARNA BONTEMPS—"Southern Mansion" from Personals, copyright © 1963 by Arna Bontemps, by permission of Harold Ober Associates.

HAYDEN CARRUTH—"The Event Itself," copyright © 1960 by Hayden Carruth, from Nothing for Tigers, by permission of The Macmillan Co. and the author.

HART CRANE—"The Hurricane" from The Complete Poems and Selected Letters and Prose of Hart Crane, copyright © 1966 by Liveright Publishing, by permission of Liveright Publishing.

H. D.—"Helen" from Selected Poems, copyright 1957 by Norma Holmes Pearson, by permission of Grove Press.

WALTER DE LA MARE—"The Happy Encounter" from Collected Poems, by permission of the literary trustees of Walter de la Mare and The Society of Authors as their representative.

JAMES DICKEY—"The Lifeguard," which originally appeared in The New Yorker, from Drowning with Others, copyright © 1961 by James Dickey, by permission of Wesleyan University Press.

EMILY DICKINSON—"After Great Pain a Formal Feeling Comes" from The Complete Poems of Emily Dickinson, copyright 1929, 1957 by Mary L. Hampson, by permission of Little, Brown and Co.

OWEN DODSON—"Guitar" from Powerful Long Ladder, by permission of the author.

RICHARD EBERHART—"Am I My Neighbor's Keeper?," "The Fury of Aerial Bombardment," "The Groundhog" from Collected Poems: 1930–1960, copyright © 1960 by Richard Eberhart, by permission of Oxford University Press, Chatto and Windus and the author.

KENNETH FEARING—"A La Carte" from New and Selected Poems, copyright 1956 by Kenneth Fearing, by permission of Indiana University Press.

Knopf; "Harlem," copyright 1951 by Langston Hughes, from *The Panther and the Leash*, by permission of Alfred A. Knopf; "Same in Blues," "Theme for English B" from *Montage of a Dream Deferred*, copyright 1951 by Langston Hughes, by permission of Harold Ober Associates.

DAVID IGNATOW—"Get the Gasworks," "How Come?" from *Poems: 1934–1969*, copyright 1948, © 1969 by David Ignatow, by permission of Wesleyan University Press.

DONALD JUSTICE—"In Bertram's Garden" from *The Summer Anniversaries*, copyright 1954 by Donald Justice, by permission of Wesleyan University Press.

X. J. KENNEDY—"Down in Dallas" from *Growing Into Love*, copyright © 1964 by X. J. Kennedy, by permission of Doubleday & Co.

STANLEY KUNITZ—"The Approach to Thebes," "Father and Son," "The Waltzer in the House," which originally appeared in *The New Yorker*, from *Selected Poems: 1929–1958*, copyright 1951, 1953, 1954, 1956, 1957, 1958 by Stanley Kunitz, by permission of Atlantic–Little, Brown.

DENISE LEVERTOV—"Merritt Parkway" from *The Jacob's Ladder*, copyright 1958 by Denise Levertov Goodman; "What Were They Like" from *The Sorrow Dance*, copyright © 1966 by Denise Levertov Goodman, by permission of New Directions Publishing.

PHILIP LEVINE—"Sunday Afternoon" from *Not This Pig*, by permission of Wesleyan University Press.

JOHN L'HEUREUX—"A Bat in the Monastery" from *The Young American Poets*, Paul Carroll, ed., copyright © 1968 by Follett Publishing Co.

VACHEL LINDSAY—"General William Booth Enters Into Heaven" from *Collected Poems*, copyright 1913 by The Macmillan Co., by permission of The Macmillan Co.

LOU LIPSITZ—"Skinny Poem" from *Cold Water*, copyright © 1966 by Lou Lipsitz, by permission of Wesleyan University Press.

AMY LOWELL—"The Cyclists" from *The Complete Poetical Works of Amy Lowell*, copyright 1955 by Amy Lowell, by permission of Houghton Mifflin Co.

ROBERT LOWELL—"Christmas Eve Under Hooker's Statue" from *Lord Weary's Castle*, copyright 1946 by Robert Lowell, reprinted by permission of Harcourt Brace Jovanovich, Inc.; "For the Union Dead" from *For the Union Dead*, by permission of Farrar, Straus & Giroux.

ARCHIBALD MacLEISH—"Ars Poetica," "The End of the World," "You, Andrew Marvell," from *Collected Poems*, copyright 1952 by Archibald MacLeish, by permission of Houghton Mifflin Co. and the author; " 'Dover Beach'—A Note to That Poem" from *Public Speech*, copyright 1936, © 1964 by Archibald MacLeish, by permission of Holt, Rinehart and Winston.

LOUIS MacNEICE—"Snow" from *The Collected Poems of Louis MacNeice*, copyright © 1966 by the estate of Louis MacNeice, by permission of Oxford University Press and Faber and Faber.

JOHN MASEFIELD—"Cargoes" from *Poems*, copyright 1912 by The Macmillan Co., copyright 1940 by John Masefield, by permission of The Macmillan Co.

EDGAR LEE MASTERS—"Emily Sparks," "Judge Selah Lively," "Lucinda Matlock," "Reuben Pantier" from *Spoon River Anthology*, by permission of Mrs. Edgar Lee Masters and The Macmillan Co.

THOMAS McGRATH—"Jig Tune: Not for Love" from *New and Selected Poems*, copyright © 1964 by Thomas McGrath, by permission of The Swallow Press.

ROD McKUEN—"Plan," copyright © 1968 by Rod McKuen, from *Lonesome Cities*, by permission of Random House.

ROBERT MEZEY—"My Mother" from *White Blossoms*, copyright © 1966 by Robert Mezey, by permission of The Cummington Press and the author.

OGDEN NASH—"Kindly Unhitch That Star, Buddy" from *Verses from 1929 On*, copyright 1935 by Ogden Nash, by permission of Little, Brown and Co.

HOWARD NEMEROV—"Elegy for a Nature Poet" from *The Next Room of the Dream,* copyright © 1962 by Howard Nemerov, by permission of The University of Chicago Press and Margot Johnson Agency; "Money," "A Way of Life" from *Blue Swallows,* copyright © 1967 by Howard Nemerov, by permission of The University of Chicago Press and Margot Johnson Agency.

JOHN FREDERICK NIMS—"Penny Arcade" from *The Iron Pastoral,* copyright 1947 by John Frederick Nims, by permission of William Morrow & Co.

WILFRED OWEN—"Anthem for Doomed Youth" from *Collected Poems,* copyright 1946, © 1963 by Chatto and Windus, by permission of Harold Owen, New Directions Publishing and Chatto and Windus.

SYLVIA PLATH—"Lady Lazarus" from *Ariel,* copyright © 1963 by Ted Hughes, by permission of Olwyn Hughes, representing the estate of Sylvia Plath, and Harper & Row, Publishers.

DUDLEY RANDALL—"Booker T. and W. E. B." from *Poem Counterpoem,* "The Idiot" from *The Journal of Black Poetry,* copyright © 1968, 1969 by Dudley Randall, by permission of Broadside Press.

JOHN CROWE RANSOM—"Bells for John Whiteside's Daughter," copyright 1924 by Alfred A. Knopf, renewed 1952 by John Crowe Ransom, "Blue Girls," "Janet Walking," copyright 1927, renewed 1955 by John Crowe Ransom, from *Selected Poems* (3d revised edition), by permission of Alfred A. Knopf.

EDWIN ARLINGTON ROBINSON—"Charles Carville's Eyes," "Cliff Klingenhagen," "Richard Cory" from *The Children of the Night,* by permission of Charles Scribner's Sons; "Eros Turannos" from *Collected Poems,* copyright 1916 by Edwin Arlington Robinson, copyright 1944 by Ruth Nivison, by permission of The Macmillan Co.; "How Annandale Went Out" from *The Town Down the River,* copyright 1910, 1938 by Charles Scribner's Sons, by permission of Charles Scribner's Sons.

THEODORE ROETHKE—"Elegy for Jane," copyright 1950 by Theodore Roethke, "The Geranium," copyright © 1963 by Beatrice Roethke as administratrix of the estate of Theodore Roethke, "I Knew a Woman," copyright 1954 by Theodore Roethke, "The Meadow Mouse," copyright © 1963 by Beatrice Roethke as administratrix of the estate of Theodore Roethke, "My Papa's Waltz," copyright 1942 by Hearst Magazines, all from *The Collected Poems of Theodore Roethke,* by permission of Doubleday & Co.

ALAN ROSS—"Radar" from *Something of the Sea,* copyright 1954 by Alan Ross, by permission of Houghton Mifflin Co. and Curtis Brown.

CARL SANDBURG—"Caboose Thoughts" from *Cornhuskers,* copyright 1918 by Holt, Rinehart and Winston, copyright 1946 by Carl Sandburg, by permission of Holt, Rinehart and Winston; "Jazz Fantasia" from *Smoke & Steel,* copyright 1920 by Harcourt Brace Jovanovich, Inc.; copyright 1948 by Carl Sandburg, reprinted by permission of the publisher. "To the Ghost of John Milton" from *Good Morning, America,* copyright 1928, 1956 by Carl Sandburg, reprinted by permission of Harcourt Brace Jovanovich, Inc.

PETER SEEGER—"Waist Deep in the Big Muddy," copyright © 1967 by Melody Trails, by permission of Melody Trails.

KARL SHAPIRO—"Auto Wreck," copyright 1942, renewed 1970 by Karl Shapiro, from *Selected Poems,* by permission of Random House.

LOUIS SIMPSON—"Hot Night on Water Street," "Walt Whitman at Bear Mountain" from *A Dream of Governors,* copyright 1957 by Louis Simpson, by permission of Wesleyan University Press.

GARY SNYDER—"Foxtail Pine" from *The Back Country,* copyright © 1963 by Gary Snyder, by permission of New Directions Publishing.

THEODORE SPENCER—"The Circus; Or One View of It" from *The Paradox in the Circle,* copyright 1941 by New Directions Publishing, by permission of New Directions Publishing.

STEPHEN SPENDER—"The Express," copyright 1934, renewed 1962 by Stephen Spender, "Ultima Ratio Regum," copyright 1942 by Stephen Spender, from *Collected Poems: 1928–1953*, by permission of Random House and Faber and Faber.

KATHLEEN SPIVACK—"Mythmaking," which originally appeared in *Poetry*, from *The Young American Poets*, Paul Carroll, ed., by permission of the author.

WILLIAM STAFFORD—"Travelling Through the Dark" from *Travelling Through the Dark*, copyright © 1960 by William Stafford, by permission of Harper & Row, Publishers.

JAMES STEPHENS—"The Main Deep," copyright 1925, 1926 by The Macmillan Co., copyright 1953, 1954 by James Stephens, "Nora Criona," copyright 1912 by The Macmillan Co., copyright 1940 by James Stephens, both from *Collected Poems*, by permission of Mrs. Iris Wise, The Macmillan Co., Macmillan London & Basingstoke and The Macmillan Co. of Canada.

WALLACE STEVENS—"The Emperor of Ice-Cream," copyright 1923, renewed 1951 by Wallace Stevens, from *The Collected Poems of Wallace Stevens*, by permission of Alfred A. Knopf.

MAY SWENSON—"Landing on the Moon," copyright © 1963 by May Swenson, "Lion," copyright 1951 by May Swenson, "Satanic Form," copyright 1954 by May Swenson, "Southbound on the Freeway," which originally appeared in *The New Yorker*, copyright © 1963 by May Swenson, all from *To Mix with Time*, by permission of Charles Scribner's Sons.

DYLAN THOMAS—"Do Not Go Gentle Into That Good Night," "Ears in the Turrets Hear," "A Refusal To Mourn the Death, by Fire, of a Child in London" from *The Collected Poems of Dylan Thomas*, copyright 1939, 1946 by New Directions Publishing, copyright 1952 by Dylan Thomas, by permission of New Directions Publishing and J. M. Dent & Sons.

MELVIN B. TOLSON—"An Ex-Judge at the Bar" from *Rendezvous with America*, copyright 1944 by Dodd, Mead & Co., by permission of Dodd, Mead & Co.

JOHN UPDIKE—"Ex-Basketball Player," which originally appeared in *The New Yorker*, from *The Carpentered Hen and Other Tame Creatures*, copyright 1957 by John Updike, by permission of Harper & Row, Publishers.

RUDOLPH VON ABELE—"On a Child Burned to Death in Vietnam," by permission of The New Republic.

DAVID WAGONER—"The Apotheosis of the Garbagemen" from *New and Selected Poems*, copyright © 1969 by Indiana University Press, by permission of Indiana University Press.

RICHARD WILBUR—"The Juggler" copyright 1949 by Richard Wilbur, reprinted from his volume *Ceremony and Other Poems*, by permission of Harcourt Brace Jovanovich, Inc. Originally appeared in *The New Yorker*.

WILLIAM CARLOS WILLIAMS—"Dedication for a Plot of Ground," "The Yachts" from *The Collected Earlier Poems*, copyright 1938 by William Carlos Williams, by permission of New Directions Publishing; "The Dance" from *The Collected Later Poems*, copyright 1944 by William Carlos Williams, by permission of New Directions Publishing.

JAMES WRIGHT—"At the Slackening of the Tide" from *Saint Judas*, by permission of Wesleyan University Press.

WILLIAM BUTLER YEATS—"Crazy Jane Talks with the Bishop," copyright 1933 by The Macmillan Co., copyright © 1961 by Bertha Georgie Yeats, "Lapis Lazuli," copyright 1940 by Georgie Yeats, copyright © 1968 by Bertha Georgie Yeats, Michael Butler Yeats and Anne Yeats, "Sailing to Byzantium," copyright 1928 by The Macmillan Co., copyright 1956 by Georgie Yeats, "The Second Coming," copyright 1924 by The Macmillan Co., copyright 1952 by Bertha Georgie Yeats, "To a Friend Whose Work Has Come To Nothing," copyright 1916 by The Macmillan Co., copyright 1944 by Bertha Georgie Yeats, all from *The Collected Poems of W. B. Yeats*, by permission of M. B. Yeats, The Macmillan Co., The Macmillan Co. of Canada and A. P. Watt & Son.

For Betty

Contents

Preface

This book is designed as an introduction to poetry. The enjoyment of poetry is not limited to an intellectual elite. Like music and art it should be part of everyone's cultural heritage, yielding life-long delight and spiritual nourishment. All of us naturally and spontaneously enjoy *some* poetry, whether it be nursery rhymes, limericks, folk ballads, or rock lyrics. All peoples throughout history have expressed the wonder, fear, joy, mystery, and tragedy of human existence in verbal rhythms that we call poetry. That we, as readers, can respond sympathetically to these emotional expressions demonstrates the universality of the poetic experience. However, a knowledge of the essential purpose, language, and techniques of poetry can heighten understanding and appreciation. To present the fundamental formal elements of poetry so that a reader can *recreate* the poem as a personal, emotional, ethical, and aesthetic experience is the primary purpose of this book.

An analytical approach has been employed merely as a means to an end: to develop in the student self-awareness, to heighten his sensitivity to the amazing variety of human experiences, and to involve him in a continual process of emotional, intellectual, and ethical maturity. As John Oliver Perry has stated: "The unexamined life, equally for a man and a poem, is not worth living, or at least we are curious to know how we make poems live." It is the hope here that the modern student living in an age of anxiety, confusion, and changing values will find both relevance and clarification in exploring the world of poetry.

Since every good poem is an individual presentation or interpretation of human experience, there is no set procedure for reading poetry. Some of the approaches suggested have been found meaningful and enjoyable by other students in the past. Other methods equally acceptable are, of course, possible. An effort has been made to avoid dogmatism and to avoid tearing a passion to tatters by overexplication. Throughout the text a representative cross-section of the wide range of poetry has been included: poems simple and complex, old and new, excellent and faulty, traditional and experimental.

In defining the formal elements in poetry the principle of first discussing general concepts familiar to the student before applying them specifically to poetry has been adopted. Thus rhythm is discussed before meter, imagery before figures of speech, form before stanza, and so on. Notes and suggestive questions have been added to some poems. Student and teacher are free to explore the other poems in any way they find suitable to enjoy the total poetic experience. In the final chapter, poems related by theme are included for comparison and contrast. The epigraphs may be used for discussion or composition.

Because there are many conflicting theories as to the nature of poetry, it is important to state the assumptions on which this book is based.

(1) Like a flower or the human body, the nature of poetry is organic. Its elements (form, rhythm, imagery, diction, sound, symbol, tone, emotion, theme) may for convenience and clarification be studied separately, but it is the relationship of all the parts affecting the reader simultaneously that makes the poem come alive.

(2) Form and content are indissoluble.

(3) A prose paraphrase may sometimes aid in grasping the meaning or grammatical structure of a poem, but it is never a substitute for the poem.

(4) Poetry cannot be studied in an intellectual vacuum. Biographical, historical, psychological, philosophical, or linguistic information often contributes to our understanding of a poem.

(5) Every good poem is an original treatment of human experience in artistic form. Poetry not only gives us pleasure, helps us understand ourselves, others, and the world around us, but, in its very diversity, reveals the essential oneness of humanity by combining universality of emotion with concreteness of detail.

(6) The response to a poem is fuller when it is read intelligently aloud.

(7) Within certain limits more than one interpretation of a complex or symbolic poem (if supported by the text) may be valid. A poem can be read on more than one level of meaning. We do not read into a poem but *out from* it.

The annotated bibliography lists those books that have been found to be particularly useful.

For her many helpful suggestions and her accurate typing in preparing the manuscript, I am most grateful to my wife, Betty. Grateful acknowledgment is also made to Harold Bond for his editorial assistance and advice.

MORRIS SWEETKIND
New Haven, Connecticut

Getting Into Poetry

Poetry doesn't tell; it shows. Prose tells.

—May Swenson

1

The Experience of Poetry

Three Dead in Auto Accident

A head-on collision of two cars near the intersection of Jefferson Street and Fourth Avenue claimed three lives last night.

Amy Smith, 16, of 23 Lawncrest Road, Jonathan Caldwell, 17, of 48 Birch Drive, and Mrs. William Simpson, 54, of 36 Jefferson Street were already dead when the ambulance arrived. Mr. William Simpson has been placed on the danger list.

The wrecked cars and curious crowds caused traffic to be re-routed for several hours after the accident. Officers William Mahoney, Daniel Jones, and Ralph Diglio are investigating.

These three paragraphs are a typical newspaper account of death on our highways. Let us see how a poet deals with such an event.

Auto Wreck

Its quick soft silver bell beating, beating,
And down the dark one ruby flare
Pulsing out red light like an artery,
signal light — The ambulance at top speed floating down
Past beacons and illuminated clocks
Wings in a heavy curve, dips down,
And brakes speed, entering the crowd.
The doors leap open, emptying light;
Stretchers are laid out, the mangled lifted
And stowed into the little hospital.
Then the bell, breaking the hush, tolls once,

And the ambulance with its terrible cargo
Rocking, slightly rocking, moves away,
As the doors, an afterthought, are closed.   14

We are deranged, walking among the cops
Who sweep glass and are large and composed.
One is still making notes under the light.
One with a bucket douches ponds of blood
Into the street and gutter.
One hangs lanterns on the wrecks that cling,
Empty husks of locusts, to iron poles.   7

Our throats were tight as tourniquets,
Our feet were bound with splints, but now   *crude, awkward*
Like convalescents intimate and gauche,
We speak through sickly smiles and warn
trite comments With the stubborn saw of common sense,
The grim joke and the banal resolution.   *inspired*
The traffic moves around with care,   *ordinary*
But we remain, touching a wound   *trite*
That opens to our richest horror.   9

Already old, the question Who shall die?
Becomes unspoken Who is innocent?
For death in war is done by hands;
Suicide has cause and stillbirth, logic.
But this invites the occult mind,
Cancels our physics with a sneer,
And spatters all we knew of dénouement   *the final outcome of a complex sequence of events*
Across the expedient and wicked stones.   8

achieving a particular suitable for end   —Karl Shapiro (1913-   )

The newspaper account gives us bare factual information. The poem, on the other hand, involves us in a more complex experience.

In the first stanza the poet describes the "beating, beating" of the ambulance bell, the red-light beacon pulsing through the darkness as the vehicle speeds past "illuminated clocks," the hush of the crowd as the "terrible cargo" is carried through the ambulance doors "emptying light," and the last clang of the bell as "the little hospital" departs. The scene is vividly communicated because the poet forces us to see, hear, feel, and think.

In the second stanza there is an abrupt shift in point of view from the impersonal to the personal. We are made part of the group of spectators and emotionally involved in the aftermath of the accident. "We are deranged" in contrast to the "composed" policemen who, in a routine manner, are cleaning up the mess and trying to establish order in a disordered world. In the third stanza we are shaken by the horror of the event. We try to adjust to a normal, peaceful world by "sickly smiles" and trite comments on the inevitability of accidents. Bewildered and shocked as we are at the disaster, it still holds a strange fascination for us; and we remain to suffer "our richest horror," fear of sudden death.

In the final section the poet shifts our reaction from emotional involvement to philosophical speculation. This auto wreck raises again the age-old questions: Who shall die? At what time? Why? Are the dead guilty or are we? Are they innocent? Are they victims of chance? Carelessness? Faulty cars? Road conditions? Does the event serve God's purpose? To the poet death by war, suicide, or disease has a rational scientific explanation, but accidental tragedy defies logic and can be accounted for only by some baffling, metaphysical interpretation or by mystic faith.

When the poet describes the "ruby flare" on the ambulance as "pulsing out red light like an artery," he not only gives us a vivid picture by a startling but apt comparison; he frightens us by suggesting that the vehicle of mercy is on a gruesome mission and prepares us for the horror of the "ponds of blood" in the gutter. This fear is intensified by comparing the ambulance to a carrion bird ("floating down . . . Wings in a heavy curve, dips down"). In comparing the wrecked cars clinging to the iron poles to "empty husks of locusts," the poet by this concentrated metaphor evokes both our terror at the destructiveness of the vehicles and our pity for the short-lived reckless victims.

To communicate the profound emotional effect of the accident on the bystanders—physically unharmed but psychically wounded— Karl Shapiro uses appropriate and effective medical imagery ("tourniquets . . . splints . . . convalescents . . . sickly smiles . . . wound"). Even the concluding section, which poses philosophical questionings as to the ultimate meaning of the disaster, is phrased in emotional terms. All our scientific knowledge is canceled "with a sneer" and the "expedient stones" (i.e., suitable for auto traffic) have become wicked instruments of destruction to fragile humanity.

The journalist is primarily interested in reporting the simple facts; the poet, in communicating the depth and complexity of his feelings. By vivid images, comparisons, and other figurative terms the resourceful poet utilizes a primary form of communication which bypasses facts and stirs our deepest level of sensibility, our emotions. By using direct comparisons (similes) and indirect comparisons (metaphors) the poet immediately involves us as emotional participants in the action. Our responses are intensified not only by individual vivid images but by their interaction. Simultaneously appealing to our reason and to our senses, his figurative language effectively evokes complex emotions so that we receive a deeper and richer imaginative experience than the prose statement that simply communicates information.

Compare the following account by Dorothy Wordsworth in her journal with her brother's poem on the same experience composed two years later.

When we were in the woods beyond Gowbarrow Park we saw a few daffodils close to the water-side. We fancied that the sea had floated the seeds ashore, and that the little colony had so sprung up. But as we went along there were more, and yet more; and, at last, under the boughs of the trees, we saw there was a long belt of them along the shore, about the breadth of a country turnpike road. I never saw daffodils so beautiful. They grew among the mossy stones, about and above them; some rested their heads on these stones as on a pillow for weariness; and the rest tossed, and reeled, and danced, and seemed as if they verily laughed with the wind that blew upon them over the lake. They looked so gay, ever glancing, ever changing. The wind blew directly over the lake to them.

I Wandered Lonely as a Cloud

I wandered lonely as a cloud
That floats on high o'er vales and hills,
When all at once I saw a crowd,
A host, of golden daffodils;
Beside the lake, beneath the trees,
Fluttering and dancing in the breeze.

Continuous as the stars that shine
And twinkle on the milky way,
They stretched in never-ending line
Along the margin of a bay:
Ten thousand saw I at a glance,
Tossing their heads in sprightly dance.

The waves beside them danced; but they
Out-did the sparkling waves in glee:
A poet could not but be gay,
In such a jocund company:
I gazed—and gazed—but little thought
What wealth the show to me had brought:

For oft, when on my couch I lie
In vacant or in pensive mood,
They flash upon that inward eye
Which is the bliss of solitude;
And then my heart with pleasure fills,
And dances with the daffodils.

—William Wordsworth (1770–1850)

Dorothy's prose account reveals an intelligent, sensitive observer who is impressed by the beauty of the daffodils and who speculates on their botanical propagation. Her brother's account of the experience is far richer in emotional detail and thought.

The wandering poet represents himself in a lonely mood isolated from the fellowship of nature. His loneliness is communicated by comparing himself to a single slow-moving cloud "high o'er vales and hills." The expansion of the landscape vista intensifies the feeling of loneliness, and the interaction of man and nature is at once established. The depth of his joyful emotional reaction to the daffodils is dependent on their numbers, color, and movement, all of which contribute to the beauty of the scene. Their infinite quantity is suggested not only by the general number "ten thousand saw I at a glance," but by comparing them to the countless "stars that shine/and twinkle on the milky way." The latter image also suggests their beauty further intensified by the adjective "golden" and the picture of the swaying daffodils surpassing "the sparkling waves in glee." By giving the daffodils human qualities, that is, by personifying them—"a crowd, a host . . . tossing their heads . . . a jocund company"—the poet feels they are his companions, and he loses his sense of loneliness. Their joyousness, stressed by the recurrent dance image repeated in all four stanzas, is quickly communicated to the poet. As the beauty and joy of earth, water, and sky are revealed to him in a flash, his spirits are lifted and his alienation is dispelled. His communion with living nature is reestablished.

In this poem Wordsworth not only communicates a universal emotional experience but makes a meaningful comment on it. He realizes that such a revelation of the bond between man and nature gives one not momentary joy but, through the power of memory, continual spiritual refreshment. The mind of man can recall from the depths of the past beautiful spontaneous emotions and recollect them in tranquility.

The superiority of the poem to the prose account as an emotional experience depends not only on Wordsworth's use of images to express feeling but on the poet's use of rhythm and rhyme. Unlike

Karl Shapiro's poem, which is written in unrhymed verses in stanzas of varying length, Wordsworth's poem consists of metered six-line stanzas with a definite rhyme pattern. The looser metrical form of "Auto Wreck" is appropriate to the scene of disorder the poet depicts, just as the regular rhythm in Wordsworth's poem and its recurrent melodic rhymes enhance the joyousness of the dance image in each of the stanzas to communicate the central emotion.

Rhythmic variation is an elemental but valuable resource utilized by a skillful poet for the expression of emotion. The slow movement of the two opening lines of Wordsworth's poem helps communicate the loneliness and sadness of the poet. The lines that follow up to the last stanza shift to the rhythmic momentum of a sprightly dance to express his joy. His pensive mood in the first four lines of the last stanza is accentuated by a solemn, retarded rhythm. Then the poem ends in a sudden return to the earlier joyousness.

Let us go on to contrast a historian's and a poet's handling of the sinking of the "Titanic."

On the night of April 14–15, 1912, a White Star Liner struck an iceberg and sank in the North Atlantic south of Newfoundland with a loss of 1,517 lives. The "Titanic," the fastest ship afloat, was on her maiden voyage. Official investigations revealed that warnings were either not received or were ignored. The ship did not carry sufficient lifeboats, and other vessels in the vicinity were slow in responding to the distress signals.

This is how Thomas Hardy treated the same incident.

The Convergence of the Twain

Lines on the Loss of the "Titanic"

I

In a solitude of the sea
Deep from human vanity,
And the Pride of Life that planned her, stilly couches she.

II

Steel chambers, late the pyres
Of her salamandrine fires,
Cold currents thrid,[1] and turn to rhythmic tidal lyres.

III

Over the mirrors meant
To glass the opulent
The sea-worm crawls — grotesque, slimed, dumb, indifferent.

IV

Jewels in joy designed
To ravish the sensuous mind
Lie lightless, all their sparkles bleared and black and blind.

V

Dim moon-eyed fishes near
Gaze at the gilded gear
And query: "What does this vaingloriousness down here?" . . .

VI

Well: while was fashioning
This creature of cleaving wing,
The Immanent Will that stirs and urges everything

VII

Prepared a sinister mate
For her—so gaily great—
A Shape of Ice, for the time far and dissociate.

VIII

And as the smart ship grew
In stature, grace, and hue,
In shadowy silent distance grew the Iceberg too.

IX

Alien they seemed to be:
No mortal eye could see
The intimate welding of their later history,

X

Or sign that they were bent
By paths coincident
On being anon twin halves of one august event,

XI

Till the Spinner of the Years
Said "Now!" And each one hears,
And consummation comes, and jars two hemispheres.

—Thomas Hardy (1840–1928)

---

[1] Thread.

Hardy's primary purpose is to interpret the *meaning* of this
tragic event. The poem is organized around a *theme* which presents
the author's vision of life. Through his use of contrast and irony,
Hardy stresses the differences between the building of the proud

majestic ship by man and the slow growth of the sinister iceberg by nature. He shows how their fusion of "intimate welding" precipitates the catastrophe. It is ironic because the fulfillment of the event turns out to be the opposite of our expectation. Poets use irony as a forceful method of presenting the complexities and contradictions of human experience. Hardy was particularly aware of the incongruities in life and made frequent use of irony.

In the first five stanzas, by a series of powerful contrasts, the poet emphasizes the theme of the vanity of human wishes, the humbling of man's pride in his conflict with nature. Man builds the fastest, the most beautiful, expensive ship in the world; but it lies— helpless, defeated—in the slime at the bottom of the sea. Its hot furnaces are quenched by "cold currents"; its mirrors reflect not the pretty faces of "opulent" passengers but grotesque sea-worms; its once shining "gilded gear" is now "bleared and black and blind." The "dim moon-eyed fishes" mock the "vaingloriousness" of human beings.

In the last six stanzas Hardy amplifies the irony of this event into a broader philosophical concept; there is a universal power, "the Immanent Will," above man and nature that knows and controls all events in space and time. The catastrophe, the poet implies, was not really an accident but fated. Hardy concludes the poem ironically with the powerful image of a bride and a bridegroom, whose marriage brings not happiness but disaster.

The "smart ship" (always referred to as feminine) "gaily great . . . in stature, grace, and hue" is contrasted with her "sinister mate . . . a Shape of Ice." Though different in origin, size, and purpose, the diverse partners are "twin halves of one august event." When "the Spinner of the Years" gives the fatal command "Now!", the strange tragic consummation is effected.

The poet's use of ironical contrasts to develop his theme is further supported by the rhythmic structure of his stanzas. The first two lines of each stanza—short and rapid in movement—contrast sharply with the long, slow rhythm of the last line. For the most part, the first two lines describe the proud ship but ominously suggest its insecurity; the last line refers to its fated destroyers: the iceberg, the sea, and the Immanent Will.

An encyclopedia would describe a lion in the following terms:

A mammal (*Felix leo* or genus *Panthera*) of the cat family found in the open country in Africa, SW Asia, and W India. Most males, measuring from nine to ten feet, weigh up to five hundred pounds. The lion's short-haired coat varies from yellow to brown, and the

tail ends in a dark tuft. The lion hunts antelope, zebra, and other
small and large animals. Lions sometimes travel in groups.

Here is a poet's treatment of the same animal.

Lion

In the bend of your mouth soft murder
   in the flints of your eyes
   the sun-stained openings of caves
Your nostrils breathe the ordained air
   of chosen loneliness

Magnificently maned as the lustrous pampas
   your head heavy with heraldic curls
   wears a regal frown between the brows
The wide bundle of your chest
   your loose-skinned belly frilled with fur
   you carry easily sinuously pacing on suede paws

Between tight thighs
   under the thick root of your tufted tail
   situated like a full-stoned fruit beneath a bough
   the quiver of your never-used malehood is slung

You pace in dung on cement
   the bars flick past your eyeballs
   fixed beyond the awestruck stares of children
Watching you they remember their fathers
   the frightening hairs in their fathers' ears

Young girls remember lovers too timid and white
   and I remember how I played lion with my brothers
   under the round yellow-grained table
   the shadow our cave in the lamplight

Your beauty burns the brain
   though your paws slue on foul cement
   the fetor of captivity you do right to ignore
   the bars too an illusion

Your heroic paranoia plants you in the Indian jungle
   pacing by the cool water-hole as dawn streaks the sky
   and the foretaste of the all-day hunt
   is sweet as yearling's blood
   in the corners of your lips

                     —May Swenson (1919–   )

The first difference we note between the generalized factual prose statements and the poem is that the poet is describing with precise details a particular lion in a particular situation: a powerful male animal pacing his dirty cage in a zoo. We see the murderous bend of his mouth, the gleaming flints of his eyes, his magnificent mane, his "heraldic curls," his broad chest, his "suede paws," his "loose-skinned belly frilled with fur." The concreteness of these details at once communicates to us the beauty and the ferocity of the lion. To see this beautiful, majestic beast confined in a filthy cage arouses in us as spectators the tragic emotions of pity and terror. Our pity is intensified by the glimpse the poet gives us of the free animal in his native habitat "pacing by the cool-water-hole as dawn streaks the sky" in contrast to his confinement in a foul-smelling cage. The "awestruck" children as well as the adults are frightened by the murderous power displayed by the restless lion in captivity. The poet intensifies the difference between the outdoor world of the predatory lion and the indoor world of the innocent child by contrasting "the sun-stained openings of caves" with the shadow of her cave in the lamplight when in the security of her home she played lion with her brothers. By her use of these functional details May Swenson has involved us in a complex emotional experience which is missing in the prose description of the lion.

The poet goes one step further. She poses for herself and the reader the perennial question: What is more real, an immediate present experience or a lasting memory of the past? The lion's empty existence behind bars or his vision of his free natural life in the jungle? The children's visit to the zoo or their memories as adults of the fright of their fathers? The poet's answer is that the life of the imagination is the real life: "the bars too an illusion."

A social historian in describing conditions in a great metropolis would give us a detailed objective account filled with facts and statistics. He would discuss the causes—political, social, and economic —for these conditions and what measures, if any, were taken for their improvement.

William Blake in the following poem follows a different procedure. By taking a personal approach in a concrete situation, by using language with meticulous care for its suggestiveness, and by framing his material into an artistic form, he involves us in a complex emotional and intellectual experience. The short poem becomes a passionate indictment of a whole society. Its concentrated power stirs our imagination and moves us more than a lengthy sociological treatise.

London

I wander thro' each charter'd street,
Near where the charter'd Thames does flow,
And mark in every face I meet
Marks of weakness, marks of woe.

In every cry of every Man,
In every Infant's cry of fear,
In every voice, in every ban,
The mind-forg'd manacles I hear.

How the Chimney-sweeper's cry
Every black'ning Church appalls;
And the hapless Soldier's sigh
Runs in blood down Palace walls.

But most thro' midnight streets I hear
How the youthful Harlot's curse
Blasts the new born Infant's tear,
And blights with plagues the Marriage hearse.

—William Blake (1757–1827)

Like a biblical prophet Blake is condemning the degradation of a great city—London at the end of the eighteenth century—for the commercialistic spirit of the metropolis, its weak, self-enslaved citizens, its exploitation of children, its imperialistic wars, its hypocritical, ineffective religion, and its false morality. This indictment is poetically effective because Blake has organized the material and brought it into focus by a series of climactic images of sight and sound during a walk through the streets of the world's greatest city at midnight. Like all good poets he is meticulously careful in his choice of words, using them not only for their exact, literal meanings (denotation) but also for their multiple meanings (connotation).

The streets of London are *chartered,* that is, laid out on a map, but also hired, bought, and sold for profit. The river Thames with its wharves, polluted waters, and commercial shipping is likewise despoiled by the crass spirit of industrialism. The woebegone inhabitants of the city have mentally enslaved themselves to the false contemporary ideals of rationalism and materialism and have meekly accepted the bans (restrictions) that a political, industrial, religious, and Puritannical tyranny has foisted upon them. The cry of the pathetic chimney-sweeper *appalls* (casts a black pall) over a blackening (literally and figuratively) church which should condemn such child labor instead of condoning it. The hapless soldier's sigh running in blood "down Palace walls" is a powerful example of the poet's use of synesthesia, or the simultaneous mingling of two senses: in this instance, sound and sight. The cry of the drafted soldier is a despairing protest that places a blood guilt on a militaristic state and at the same time acts as a prophetic warning to the aristocracy of a retributive revolution.

Blake's denunciation of this blighted society reaches its climax in the curse of the youthful harlot. Love, the very source of life, is misused, is bought and sold like a commodity. The innocent infant becomes the victim of a venereal infection, and the marriage relationship through denial of sexual fulfillment is corrupted by prostitution; the joyous carriage of matrimony becomes a hearse.

Although it is difficult to draw an exact dividing line between prose and poetry, the preceding discussion of some typical poems suggests some of the important differences. The prose we read in newspapers, scientific magazines, textbooks, and encyclopedias conveys factual information and is addressed primarily to our rational faculties or intellect. Poetry, by evoking emotion and appealing to our imagination, directly involves us in concrete human activities. It gives us direct, felt experience. Indirectly appealing to our mind, it strikes deeper layers of our consciousness—our emotions, imagination, and memories.

To express strong feeling and to involve us directly in human experience, poetry uses some special rhetorical devices: rhythm, sound effects, sensuous appeal, figures of speech, irony, and connotative language. All these characteristics of the art of poetry are organized around a central theme. They are simply means to an end: to convey the richness and depth, the contradictions and the complexities, the infinite variety of the human condition.

For Discussion

> Poetry lifts the veil from the hidden beauty of the world and makes familiar objects be as if they were not familiar.
>
> —Percy Bysshe Shelley

> The proper and immediate object of poetry is the communication of immediate pleasure.
>
> —Samuel Taylor Coleridge

> Poetry *implies* the whole truth; philosophy *expresses* a particle of it.
>
> —Henry David Thoreau

Poetry is the supreme fiction, madame. . . .
Poetry increases the feeling for reality.

—Wallace Stevens

A poet's function is not to experience the poetic state; that is a private affair. His function is to create it in others. . . . He causes his reader to become "inspired."

—Paul Valéry

Poets present for inspection "imaginary gardens with real toads in them."

—Marianne Moore

Poetry is the synthesis of hyacinths and biscuits.

—Carl Sandburg

Poems Related to Chapter 1

Lawrence Thompson in his biography *Robert Frost: The Early Years, 1874–1915* informs us that the following account in *The Littleton Courier* March 31, 1901 was the occasion for Frost's poem " 'Out, Out—.' "

Bad Tragedy at Bethlehem

Raymond Fitzgerald a Victim of Fatal Accident

Raymond Fitzgerald, one of the twin sons of Michael G. and Margaret Fitzgerald of Bethlehem, died at his home Thursday afternoon, March 24, as the result of an accident by which one of his hands was badly hurt in a sawing machine. The young man was assisting in sawing up some wood in his own door-yard with a sawing machine and accidentally hit the loose pulley, causing the saw to descend upon his hand, cutting and lacerating it badly. Raymond was taken into the house and a physician was immediately summoned, but he died very suddenly from the effects of the shock, which produced heart failure. . . .

"Out, Out—"

The buzz-saw snarled and rattled in the yard
And made dust and dropped stove-length sticks of wood,
Sweet-scented stuff when the breeze drew across it.
And from there those that lifted eyes could count
Five mountain ranges one behind the other
Under the sunset far into Vermont.

And the saw snarled and rattled, snarled and rattled,
As it ran light, or had to bear a load.
And nothing happened: day was all but done.
Call it a day, I wish they might have said
To please the boy by giving him the half hour
That a boy counts so much when saved from work.
His sister stood beside them in her apron
To tell them "Supper." At the word, the saw,
Leaped out at the boy's hand, or seemed to leap—
He must have given the hand. However it was,
Neither refused the meeting. But the hand!
The boy's first outcry was a rueful laugh,
As he swung toward them holding up the hand,
Half in appeal, but half as if to keep
The life from spilling. Then the boy saw all—
Since he was old enough to know, big boy
Doing a man's work, though a child at heart—
He saw all spoiled. "Don't let him cut my hand off—
The doctor, when he comes. Don't let him, sister!"
So. But the hand was gone already.
The doctor put him in the dark of ether.
He lay and puffed his lips out with his breath.
And then—the watcher at his pulse took fright.
No one believed. They listened at his heart.
Little—less—nothing!—and that ended it.
No more to build on there. And they, since they
Were not the one dead, turned to their affairs.

—Robert Frost (1874–1963)

1. From what famous speech in *Macbeth* does the title come? What is the relation of the Shakespearean speech to the theme of Frost's poem? Besides the theme what other ideas does Frost suggest?

2. What does the poem contain that is missing in the newspaper account of the accident and death of the boy? What is in the prose account that is omitted in the poem? What generalizations can you draw from the differences of factual prose and poetic communication?

3. To how many senses does the poem appeal? Give concrete illustrations. In what way is the setting (place and time) appropriate to the action? Are the events arranged in any patterned order? Explain. What is the climax?

4. What do you consider to be the most effective figures of speech? Why?

5. Who are *they* in line 10? *They* in next to the last line? Why is there no mention of the parents of the boy and his sister?

6. What is the function of the following concrete details: (a) sweet-scented stuff, (b) five mountain ranges, (c) sunset far into Vermont, (d) "Supper," (e) a rueful laugh.

7. Compare and contrast this poem with Karl Shapiro's "Auto Wreck."

William Booth (1829–1912), an English religious leader, was the founder and first general of the Salvation Army. Converted at 15, he entered the ministry of the Methodist Church, but in 1861 he began independent evangelistic work in Whitechapel, London. His Christian Mission developed in 1878 into the Salvation Army. With his remarkable organizational ability, he built a worldwide organization on military lines to attack "the fortresses of sin" and to carry on social welfare work among the outcasts of society.

The following poem was written by Vachel Lindsay in 1912 shortly after the death of William Booth. The American poet, poverty-stricken in this period of his life, was "bumming" across the country selling his verses for bread and occasionally sleeping in Salvation Army quarters. He considered himself a member of "the submerged tenth of the population" that the Salvation Army was struggling to save.

General William Booth Enters Into Heaven

To be sung to the tune of "The Blood of the Lamb" with indicated instrument

I

(Bass drum beaten loudly.)
Booth led boldly with his big bass drum—
(Are you washed in the blood of the Lamb?)
The Saints smiled gravely and they said: "He's come."
(Are you washed in the blood of the Lamb?)
Walking lepers followed, rank on rank,
Lurching bravos from the ditches dank,
Drabs from the alleyways and drug fiends pale—
Minds still passion-ridden, soul-powers frail: —
Vermin-eaten saints with moldy breath,
Unwashed legions with the ways of Death—
(Are you washed in the blood of the Lamb?)

(Banjos.)
Every slum had sent its half-a-score
The round world over. (Booth had groaned for more.)
Every banner that the wide world flies
Bloomed with glory and transcendent dyes.
Big-voiced lasses made their banjos bang,
Tranced, fanatical they shrieked and sang: —
"Are you washed in the blood of the Lamb?"
Hallelujah! It was queer to see
Bull-necked convicts with that land make free.
Loons with trumpets blowed a blare, blare, blare

On, on upward thro' the golden air!
(Are you washed in the blood of the Lamb?)

II

(Bass drum slower and softer.)
Booth died blind and still by faith he trod,
Eyes still dazzled by the ways of God.
Booth led boldly, and he looked the chief
Eagle countenance in sharp relief,
Beard a-flying, air of high command
Unabated in that holy land.

(Sweet flute music.)
Jesus came from out the court-house door,
Stretched his hands above the passing poor.
Booth saw not, but led his queer ones there
Round and round the mighty court-house square.
Then, in an instant all that blear review
Marched on spotless, clad in raiment new.
The lame were straightened, withered limbs uncurled
And blind eyes opened on a new, sweet world.

(Bass drum louder.)
Drabs and vixens in a flash made whole!
Gone was the weasel-head, the snout, the jowl!
Sages and sibyls now, and athletes clean,
Rulers of empires, and of forests green!

*(Grand chorus of all instruments. Tambourines to
the foreground.)*
The hosts were sandalled, and their wings were fire!
(Are you washed in the blood of the Lamb?)
But their noise played havoc with the angel-choir.
(Are you washed in the blood of the Lamb?)
Oh, shout Salvation! It was good to see
Kings and Princes by the Lamb set free.
The banjos rattled and the tambourines
Jing-jing-jingled in the hands of Queens.

(Reverently sung, no instruments.)
And when Booth halted by the curb for prayer
He saw his Master thro' the flag-filled air.
Christ came gently with a robe and crown
For Booth the soldier, while the throng knelt down.
He saw King Jesus. They were face to face,
And he knelt a-weeping in that holy place.
Are you washed in the blood of the Lamb?

—Vachel Lindsay (1879–1931)

1. What is your reaction to this poem? Do you think it ridicules, presents a realistic picture, or glorifies the Salvation Army? Justify your opinion.
2. How effective are the rhythms and sound patterns as expressions of the designated instruments? (First, read the poem aloud.)
3. How do you account for the vision of heaven as a "mighty courthouse" square where "King Jesus" dwells? What mass miracle does the Master perform?
4. What humorous touches are found in the poem? Are they out of place in a religious poem? If not, what do they contribute? Is the colloquial, slangy diction appropriate to the mood? Discuss.
5. What are the outstanding traits of General William Booth? Of King Jesus?
6. Compare this poem with Carl Sandburg's "Jazz Fantasia" (page 356) and with the popular song "When the Saints Come Marching In." Is the final effect of the poem sentimental (i.e., mawkishly emotional) or sincere? Justify your opinion.

In 1803 William Wordsworth, his sister Dorothy, and Samuel Taylor Coleridge visited Scotland. Dorothy wrote: "It was harvest-time, and the fields were quietly—might I say pensively?—enlivened by small companies of reapers. It is not uncommon in the more lonely parts of the Highlands to see a single person so employed. The following poem was suggested to William by a beautiful sentence in Thomas Wilkinson's *Tour of Scotland.*" Wilkinson's sentence reads: "Passed a female who was reaping alone; she sung in Erse as she bended over her sickle,—the sweetest human voice I ever heard; her strains were tenderly melancholy, and felt delicious, long after they were heard no more."

The Solitary Reaper

Behold her, single in the field,
Yon solitary Highland Lass!
Reaping and singing by herself;
Stop here, or gently pass!
Alone she cuts and binds the grain,
And sings a melancholy strain;
O listen! for the Vale profound
Is overflowing with the sound.

No Nightingale did ever chaunt
More welcome notes to weary bands
Of travellers in some shady haunt,
Among Arabian sands:
A voice so thrilling ne'er was heard
In spring-time from the Cuckoo-bird,

Breaking the silence of the seas
Among the farthest Hebrides.

Will no one tell me what she sings?—
Perhaps the plaintive numbers flow
For old, unhappy, far-off things,
And battles long ago:
Or is it some more humble lay,
Familiar matter of to-day?
Some natural sorrow, loss, or pain,
That has been, and may be again?

Whate'er the theme, the Maiden sang
As if her song could have no ending;
I saw her singing at her work,
And o'er the sickle bending;—
I listened, motionless and still;
And, as I mounted up the hill,
The music in my heart I bore,
Long after it was heard no more.

—William Wordsworth (1770–1850)

1. What sensuous, emotional, and intellectual experience does Wordsworth communicate in this poem?
2. The second stanza consists of two bird images. What similar emotion do they express? What contrasts are there in the images? What is the effect of their *space* expansion?
3. In stanza three what *time* extension do you find? What lines are memorable for capturing the spirit of folk ballads?
4. What effect does the poet create by stressing that the song is "melancholy" and "plaintive"? that the reaper is "solitary"? that the theme of the song is a mystery?
5. In an earlier version of the poem line 13 read "A sweeter voice ne'er was heard" and line 29, "I listened till I had my fill." Did Wordsworth improve the poem by changing these lines? Discuss.
6. What similarities do you find in this poem and "I Wandered Lonely as a Cloud"? What differences?

The Tiger

Tiger! Tiger! burning bright
In the forests of the night,
What immortal hand or eye
Could frame thy fearful symmetry?

In what distant deeps or skies
Burnt the fire of thine eyes?

On what wings dare he aspire?
What the hand dare seize the fire?

And what shoulder, and what art,
Could twist the sinews of thy heart?
And when thy heart began to beat,
What dread hand? and what dread feet?

What the hammer? what the chain?
In what furnace was thy brain?
What the anvil? what dread grasp
Dare its deadly terrors clasp?

When the stars threw down their spears,
And watered heaven with their tears,
Did he smile his work to see?
Did he who made the lamb make thee?

Tiger! Tiger! burning bright
In the forests of the night,
What immortal hand or eye
Dare frame thy fearful symmetry?

—William Blake (1757–1827)

Like all symbolic poems this one can be interpreted in various ways (within certain limits established by the poet's images, rhetorical structure, diction, metrical pattern, etc.). The following questions suggest some of these interpretations.

1. Who is the speaker in the poem? Blake or a persona (i.e., a character he has created, perhaps a perplexed Bard of Experience)? Are the questions which make up the whole poem rhetorical (i.e., the answers are clearly implied) or do the questions really remain unanswered? What is the primary question?

2. Why does Blake use a frame pattern, the last stanza (with the change of one word) repeating the first? What is the significance of *dare* instead of *could*? What effect does the poet achieve by using a stanza consisting of two rhymed couplets, heavy rhythmic stresses, and masculine rhyme (stressed concluding syllables) exclusively? Why does he repeat *what* thirteen times?

3. Explain the appropriateness and significance of the fire image in stanza one. What other fire imagery does the poet use? For what purpose? What does Blake's implied classical and biblical imagery add to the poem (e.g., "distant deeps"—hell; "skies"—heaven; "On what wings dare he aspire?" —Icarus; "What the hand dare seize the fire?"—Prometheus; the immortal blacksmith—Vulcan, Roman god of fire)? What do all these characters have in common?

4. The first two lines in stanza five refer to the first eruption of evil in heaven and the defeat of the rebellious angels as described by Milton in "Paradise Lost." Why did they water heaven with their tears? What does the Lamb symbolize? Gentleness? Innocence? Mercy? Christ? What does the Tiger? Evil? Primal energy in nature? Is he similar to Behemoth and Leviathan mentioned by Jehovah in the Book of Job to humble man's pride and to suggest the inscrutability of God's power and the mystery of His created universe where kindness and wrath, terror and beauty, good and evil, spirit and matter dwell side by side? Are we justified in comparing Blake's tiger to Melville's Moby Dick and to Yeats' "rough beast" slouching toward Bethlehem ("The Second Coming" (page 213).

5. Compare this poem with May Swenson's "Lion."

Composed Upon Westminster Bridge, September 3, 1802

Earth has not anything to show more fair:
Dull would he be of soul who could pass by
A sight so touching in its majesty:
This City now doth, like a garment, wear
The beauty of the morning; silent, bare,
Ships, towers, domes, theatres, and temples lie
Open unto the fields, and to the sky;
All bright and glittering in the smokeless air.
Never did sun more beautifully steep
In his first splendour, valley, rock, or hill;
Ne'er saw I, never felt, a calm so deep!
The river glideth at his own sweet will:
Dear God! the very houses seem asleep;
And all that mighty heart is lying still!

—William Wordsworth (1770–1850)

On Thursday morning, 29th [July, 1802], we arrived in London. Wm. left me at the Sun. . . . After various troubles and disasters, we left London on Saturday morning at half-past five or six, the 31st of July. We mounted the Dover coach at Charing Cross. It was a beautiful morning. The city, St. Paul's, with the river, and a multitude of little boats, made a most beautiful sight as we crossed Westminster Bridge. The houses were not overhung by their cloud of smoke, and they were spread out endlessly, yet the sun shone so brightly, with such a fierce light, that there was even something like the purity of one of nature's own grand spectacles.

—Dorothy Wordsworth's *Journal*

1. Compare Wordsworth's poem with (a) his sister Dorothy's prose account and (b) with Blake's "London" (page 11).

You, Andrew Marvell

And here[1] face down beneath the sun
And here upon earth's noonward height
To feel the always coming on
The always rising of the night

To feel creep up the curving east
The earthy chill of dusk and slow
Upon those under lands the vast
And ever climbing shadow grow

And strange at Ecbatan[2] the trees
Take leaf by leaf the evening strange
The flooding dark about their knees
The mountains over Persia change

And now at Kermanshah[3] the gate
Dark empty and the withered grass
And through the twilight now the late
Few travelers in the westward pass

And Baghdad[4] darken and the bridge
Across the silent river gone
And through Arabia the edge
Of evening widen and steal on

And deepen on Palmyra's[5] street
The wheel rut in the ruined stone
And Lebanon[6] fade out and Crete[7]
High through the clouds and overblown

And over Sicily the air
Still flashing with the landward gulls
And loon and slowly disappear
The sails above the shadowy hulls

And Spain go under and the shore
Of Africa the gilded sand
And evening vanish and no more
The low pale light across that land

For now the long light on the sea
And here face downward in the sun
To feel how swift how secretly
The shadow of the night comes on . . .

           —Archibald MacLeish (1892–   )

¹ Illinois.   ² The capital of ancient Media, founded in 700 B.C., which was later the residence of Cyrus the Great, the founder of the Persian empire; later the residence of Alexander the Great.   ³ Province in West Persia (Iran).   ⁴ In southeast Iraq.   ⁵ Ancient city of Syria, now being excavated; sacked by Tamerlane in 1401.   ⁶ Mountain in Syria.   ⁷ Island in eastern Mediterranean Sea.

The title of the poem refers to these two lines from Andrew Marvell's poem "To His Coy Mistress":

> But at my back I always hear
> Time's wingèd chariot hurrying near.

Archibald MacLeish's poem describes the shadow of night moving over the globe as viewed by a traveler in a plane flying from the Middle East to America.

1.   What do all the geographical references have in common?
2.   What does the creeping shadow symbolize?
3.   Why does the poet use so many *and's* and omit punctuation?
4.   Is this a poem about the past or is it relevant to our country and our time? Discuss.

How Come?

I'm in New York covered by a layer of soap foam.
The air is dense from the top of skyscrapers
to the sidewalk in every street, avenue
and alley, as far as Babylon on the East,
Dobbs Ferry on the North, Coney Island
on the South and stretching far over
the Atlantic Ocean. I wade
through, breathing by pushing
foam aside. The going is slow,
with just a clearing ahead
by swinging my arms. Others are groping
from all sides, too. We keep moving.
Everything else has happened here
and we've survived: snow storms,
traffic tieups, train breakdowns, bursting
water mains; and now I am writing
with a lump of charcoal stuck between my toes,
switching it from one foot to the other—
this monkey trick learned visiting
with my children at the zoo of a Sunday.
But soap foam filling the air,
the bitter, fatty smell of it . . . How come?
My portable says it extends to San Francisco!

Listen to this, and down to the Mexican border
and as far north as Canada. All the prairies,
the Rocky Mountains, the Great Lakes, Chicago,
the Pacific Coast. No advertising stunt
could do this. The soap has welled out of the ground,
says the portable suddenly. The scientists report
the soil saturated. And now what?
We'll have to start climbing for air,
a crowd forming around the Empire State Building
says the portable. God help the many
who will die of soap foam.

—David Ignatow (1914–   )

Sunday Afternoon

At first when we saw a girl
hit with a beer can and saw
one so drunk he wet his pants,
we moved back and gave them room,
and what mattered was to be
unnoticed.
                          On the body
of the Angel without teeth
I counted seventeen welts
scored with a bicycle chain.
Another was hunched into
the shape clay might take if it
were battered with pine boughs,
and the third who ran off down
a fire trail crying, "I am King
of Richmond," returned like dirt
in the bed of a pick-up.

This was Sunday afternoon
in America, the quiet
daydream of the Sierras,
the celebrations the land
demands. We left the cold fires
of the barbecue, we left
our homes grumbling in the heat
like beached U-Boats and came by two's
or with the kids up the long
black cut of highway to see
the first great movies made flesh.

—Philip Levine (1928–   )

Book Buying in the Tenderloin

A statuary Christ bleeds sweating grief
In the Gethsemane garden of St. Boniface Church
Where empurpled Irish winos lurch
To their salvation. When incense and belief
Will not suffice: ruby port in the storm
Of muscatel-made images of hell
The city spews at their shuffling feet.
In the Longshoremen's Hall across the street,
Three decades have unloaded since the fight
To oust the manic Trotskyite
Screwballs from the brotherhood. All goes well
Since the unions closed their ranks,
Boosted their pensions, and hired the banks
To manage funds for the workingman's cartel.
Christ in plaster, the unions minting coin,
Old hopes converge upon the Tenderloin
Where Comte, Considerant, Fourier
Are thick with dust in the two-bit tray
Of cavernous second-hand bookstores
And the streets suffuse the ten-cent howl
Of jukebox violence, just this side of blues.
Negro boy-whores in black tennis shoes
Prowl in front of noisy, faggot bars.
Like Samuel Gompers, they want more
On this street where every other whore
Is painfully skinny, wears a bouffant,
And looks like a brown, slow-blooming annual flower.
In the places that I haunt, no power
To transform the universal squalor
Nor wisdom to withstand the thin wrists
Of the girls who sell their bodies for a dollar
Or two, the price of a Collected Maeterlinck.
The sky glowers. My God, it is a test,
This riding out the dying of the West.

—Robert Hass (1941–   )

The Apotheosis of the Garbagemen

And they come back in the night through alleys to find us
        By the clashing of raised lids,
By garage doors' lifted heads, the swung gates, the bottomless
        Galvanized cans on their shoulders,
            In luminous coveralls

They follow the easy directions on boxes, scattering
Bushels of brown grass and apple cores,
Old candy wrappers folded around sweet nothings,
And sacks with their stains on fire,
They are coming through hedges, dragging geometry
In a dark clutch of rainbows,
See, the smashed jars
Prinked out with light, and the vacuum bags
Bursting their dust in the night like the phantasms of horseflies,
Through the burning bacon fat
Their baseball caps go flying, their feet
As solid as six packs on the lawn, the slam-bang of their coming
Sending the lettuce leaves against our windows
Like luna moths, the marrow whistling
Out of the wishbones of turkeys, the husks and rinds,
The lost-wax castings of corncobs and teabags,
The burnt-out lightbulbs pulsing in midair,
The coupons filled out
With our last names for all the startling offers,
Oh see, their hands are lifted by the gloves
Untying the knots in plastic bags, to catch
The half-burnt ashes raining around their heads,
The crusts and empties.
As the skeletons of lampshades catch at the first light,
They are going back in their empty trucks and singing
To the dump, to the steaming rust
In the rolling, hunch-backed, beckoning earth,
The sea of decay where our foundering fathers
Rubbled their lives,
They have found the way
Back to God's plenty, to rags and riches,
But will come back to us with all we could wish for
In the darkness, singing love and wild appetite,
The good rats and roaches,
The beautiful hogs and billygoats dancing around them.

—David Wagoner (1926–   )

Rhythms in poetry imitate and express; they are the muscles
and nerves of the poetic organism.

—*Harvey Gross*

2

The Function of Rhythm

One element common to all poetry from the most primitive to the
most sophisticated is rhythm. The earliest literary expression of any
cultural group is always poetry, not prose. Even before the great
Homeric epics were written in the ninth century B.C., legendary bards
were reciting their poems in ancient Greek cities. Even earlier Egyptian,
Babylonian, Chinese, Indian, and Hebrew poets were composing
rhythmic chants for religious, martial, hunting, and entertainment
purposes. The history of all societies down to present time reveals
that rhythmic expression in language has an unbroken continuity
and importance as a civilizing force.

Whether man lives in a primitive state of nature or in a highly
organized society, he lives in a world in which rhythm dominates his
existence. The revolution of the earth around the sun creates the
recurrent cycle of the seasons as well as the alternation of day and
night. The phases of the moon and the rise and fall of the tides follow
a rhythmic pattern. Every flower, tree, insect, fish, and bird follows its
own rhythmic cycle of life—birth, maturity, and death.

Man, too, is a living aggregation of rhythms: he inhales and ex-
hales; his heart beats regularly; he walks, swims, and dances. Thus
rhythmic man living in a rhythmic universe hears the song of birds,
the sound of flowing water, the pattering of rain, the cadenced
pounding of waves. When he wishes to express in language his
prayers, hopes, fears, and desires, his most spontaneous form of expression is rhythmic.

Since poetry is an art of rhythmically *uttered* sounds moving
consecutively in time, the flow of sound—loud or soft, slow or fast,

choppy or smooth—naturally plays an important part in determining our response to a poem and reinforces its diction, images, emotions, and thought.

It is difficult to draw an exact defining line between prose and poetry. Almost all prose, especially of a literary nature, contains some rhythm, but it is not always regularized or continuous. Poetry possesses a higher degree of sustained concentration and conscious rhythmic patterning than prose. The unit of prose expression is the sentence; the unit of poetic expression is the line, which permits a more varied and higher degree of rhythmic organization.

The following selections will illustrate the difference in degree in the rhythmic organization of language from the factual to the metrical.

1. Factual Prose, found in encyclopedias, textbooks, etc.

The mean distance between the center of the earth and that of the moon is 238,857 miles. The moon revolves around the earth in an orbit that is elliptical, not circular.

2. Logical Prose

I hold very strongly by two convictions:—The first is, that neither the discipline nor the subject-matter of classical education is of such direct value to the student of physical science as to justify the expenditure of valuable time upon either; and the second is, that for the purpose of attaining real culture, an exclusively scientific education is at least as effectual as an exclusively literary education.

—Thomas Henry Huxley (1825–1895)

3. Literary Prose (rhythmic, emotive, oracular)

No man is an island entire of itself; every man is a piece of the continent, a part of the main. If a clod be washed by the sea, Europe is the less, as well as if a promontory were, as well, as if a manor of thy friend's or of thine own were. Any man's death diminishes me, because I am involved in mankind, and therefore never send to know for whom the bell tolls; it tolls for thee.

—John Donne (1573–1631)
Meditation XVII Devotions Upon Emergent Occasions

4. Poetic Prose (biblical rhythm colloquialized)

"Now, my own, own love," she whispered, "you are mine, and on'y mine; for she has forgot 'ee at last, although for her you died. But

I—whenever I get up I'll think of 'ee, and whenever I lie down, I'll think of 'ee. Whenever I plant the young larches I'll think that none can plant as you planted; and whenever I split a gad, and whenever I turn the cider-wring, I'll say none could do it like you. If ever I forget your name, let me forget home and Heaven!—But no, no, my love, I never can forget 'ee; for you was a good man and did good things!"

—Thomas Hardy (1840–1928)
The Woodlanders (Marty South at the grave of Giles Winterborne)

5. Biblical Poetry (parallelism, contrast, sustained, quiet tempo)

The Lord is my shepherd; I shall not want.
He maketh me to lie down in green pastures;
He leadeth me beside still waters.
He restoreth my soul:
He guideth me in the paths of righteousness for his name's sake.
Yea, though I walk through the valley of the shadow of death,
I will fear no evil; for thou art with me;
Thy rod and thy staff, they comfort me.
Thou preparest a table before me in the presence of mine
    enemies:
Thou hast anointed my head with oil;
My cup runneth over.
Surely goodness and mercy shall follow me all the days of
    my life;
And I will dwell in the house of the Lord for ever.

—"Psalm 23"

6. Free Verse (cadenced poetry)

A Noiseless Patient Spider

A noiseless patient spider,
I mark'd where on a little promontory it stood isolated,
Mark'd how to explore the vacant vast surrounding,
It launch'd forth filament, filament, filament, out of itself,
Ever unreeling them, ever tirelessly speeding them.

And you O my soul where you stand,
Surrounded, detached, in measureless oceans of space,
Ceaselessly musing, venturing, throwing, seeking the
    spheres to connect them,
Till the bridge you will need be form'd, till the
    ductile anchor hold,

Till the gossamer thread you fling catch somewhere,
  O my soul.

—Walt Whitman (1819–1892)

7. Metered Verse (traditional poetry which can be scanned.)

Upon Julia's Clothes

Whenas in silks my Julia goes,
Then, then, methinks, how sweetly flows
The liquefaction of her clothes.

Next, when I cast mine eyes, and see
That brave vibration, each way free,
Oh, how that glittering taketh me!

—Robert Herrick (1591–1674)

Poetry permits an infinite variety of rhythms expressing the emotions, movements, thoughts, and moods that are part of human experience. Rhythm should be closely integrated with meaning and emotion. It should issue from the pressure of thought and feeling and at the same time influence them. The fundamental principle is appropriateness and expressiveness. Poetic rhythm should always reinforce sense, emotion, and picture, not call attention to itself. In the following rhythmic lines Shakespeare has captured the joyousness of springtime lovers.

It was a lover and his lass,
  With a hey, and a ho, and a hey nonino,
That o'er the green corn-field did pass
  In the spring time, the only pretty ring time,
When birds do sing, hey ding a ding, ding;
Sweet lovers love the spring.

Tennyson's slow-moving, drowsy lines expressively strengthen our sensory impressions of the tropical landscape where the doped "mild-eyed melancholy" Lotos-eaters dwell.

In the afternoon they came unto a land
In which it seemed always afternoon.
All round the coast the languid air did swoon,
Breathing like one that hath a weary dream.
Full-faced above the valley stood the moon

And, like a downward smoke, the slender stream
Along the cliff to fall and pause and fall did seem.

The swaying rhythm of Burns' drinking song reinforces the tipsy
fancies of the friendly revelers.

Willie Brew'd a Peck o' Maut

Chorus
We are not fou, we're nae that fou,
  But just a drappie in our e'e!
The cock may craw, the day may daw,
  And ay we'll taste the barley-bree!

I
O, Willie brew'd a peck o' maut,
  And Rob and Allan cam to see.
Three blyther hearts that lee-lang night
  Ye wad na found in Christendie.

II
Here are we met three merry boys,
  Three merry boys I trow are we;
And monie a night we've merry been,
  And monie mae we hope to be!

III
It is the moon, I ken her horn,
  That's blinkin in the lift sae hie;
She shines sae bright to wyle us hame,
  But, by my sooth, she'll wait a wee!

IV
Wha first shall rise to gang awa,
  A cuckold, coward loun is he!
Wha first beside his chair shall fa',
  He is the King amang us three!

Chorus
We are na fou, we're nae that fou,
  But just a drappie in our e'e!
The cock may craw, the day may daw,
  And aye we'll taste the barley-bree!

—Robert Burns (1759–1796)

Contrast this cadence with the ringing, defiant rhythm of Robert
Bruce's patriotic address to his soldiers before the battle of Bannock-
burn.

Scots, Wha Hae wi' Wallace Bled

I
Scots, wha hae wi' Wallace bled,
Scots, wham Bruce has aften led,
Welcome to your gory bed
    Or to victorie!

II
Now's the day, and now's the hour:
See the front o' battle lour,
See approach proud Edward's power—
    Chains and slaverie!

III
Wha will be a traitor knave?
Wha can fill a coward's grave?
Wha sae base as be a slave?—
    Let him turn, and flee!

IV
Wha for Scotland's King and Law
Freedom's sword will strongly draw,
Freeman stand or freeman fa',
    Let him follow me!

V
By Oppression's woes and pains,
By your sons in servile chains,
We will drain our dearest veins
    But they shall be free!

VI
Lay the proud usurpers low!
Tyrants fall in every foe!
Liberty's in every blow!
    Let us do, or die!

    —Robert Burns (1759–1796)

Browning uses a steady, heavily accented rhythm to march off the royalist regiment that is to battle the Puritan Roundheads.

Kentish Sir Byng stood for his King,
Bidding the crop-headed Parliament swing:
And, pressing a troop unable to stoop
And see the rogues flourish and honest folk droop,

Marched them along, fifty-score strong,
Great-hearted gentlemen, singing this song.

(from "Cavalier Tunes")

But the poet speeds up the rhythm of the gallant horse Roland
who is carrying the good news to Aix.

I sprang to the stirrup, and Joris, and he;
I galloped, Dirck galloped, we galloped all three;
'Good speed!" cried the watch, as the gate-bolts undrew;
"Speed!" echoed the wall to us galloping through;
Behind shut the postern, the lights sank to rest,
And into the midnight we galloped abreast.

—Robert Browning (1812–1889)
(from "How They Brought the Good News from Ghent to Aix")

The peaceful elegiac movement of the following lines is appropriate to the epitaph structure and mood.

With Rue My Heart Is Laden

With rue my heart is laden
For golden friends I had,
For many a rose-lipt maiden
And many a lightfoot lad.

By brooks too broad for leaping
The lightfoot boys are laid;
The rose-lipt girls are sleeping
In fields where roses fade.

—A. E. Housman (1859–1936)

In a short lyric expressing a single mood the poet usually sustains
a fairly uniform rhythm, but shifts in emotion or meaning require a
change in tempo. Such a modulation is evident in the following
sonnet by Shakespeare.

Sonnet 29

When in disgrace with fortune and men's eyes,
I all alone beweep my outcast state,

And trouble deaf heaven with my bootless[1] cries,
And look upon myself, and curse my fate,
Wishing me like to one more rich in hope,
Featured like him, like him with friends possess'd,
Desiring this man's art, and that man's scope,[2]
With what I most enjoy contented least;
Yet in those thoughts myself almost despising,
Haply I think on thee,—and then my state,
Like to the lark at break of day arising,
From sullen earth, sings hymns at heaven's gate;
    For thy sweet love remember'd such wealth brings
    That then I scorn to change my state with kings.

—William Shakespeare (1564–1616)

---

[1] Useless, futile.   [2] Range of opportunity.

The slow, heavy rhythm of the first nine lines helps communicate the mood of despondency. The rhythm of the last five lines suddenly becomes quick, lively, joyous.

The skillful poet adapts his rhythm to reinforce the expressiveness of different poetic experiences. In the following two passages from Milton's *Paradise Lost,* observe how perfectly the movement of the verse harmonizes with the subject matter to communicate the beautiful peacefulness of the first scene and the horrible violence of the second. This organic interrelationship of rhythm and subject matter to create a unified artistic impression is a characteristic of all good poetry.

Nightfall in Eden

Now came still evening on, and twilight grey
Had in her sober livery all things clad;
Silence accompanied; for beast and bird,
They to their grassy couch, these to their nests,
Were slunk, all but the wakeful nightingale;
She all night long, her amorous descant[1] sung;
Silence was pleased: now glowed the firmament
With living sapphires; Hesperus[2] that led
The starry host rode brightest, till the moon,
Rising in clouded majesty, at length
Apparent[3] queen unveiled her peerless light,
And o'er the dark her silver mantle threw.

---

[1] A song with variations.   [2] The evening star.   [3] Manifest.

War in Heaven

Now storming fury rose,
And clamor such as heard in Heaven till now
Was never; arms on armor clashing brayed
Horrible discord, and the madding wheels
Of brazen chariots raged; dire was the noise
Of conflict; overhead the dismal hiss
Of fiery darts in flaming volleys flew,
And flying, vaulted either post with fire.

—John Milton (1608–1674)

Besides using a sustained or changing rhythm, a poet may, if his subject matter calls for it, utilize a rhythm of acceleration (increase the speed of his lines) or a rhythm of deceleration (retard the movement of his verses). A good example of the first is "The Express" and of the second "I Like to See It Lap the Miles."

The Express

After the first powerful plain mainifesto
The black statement of pistons, without more fuss
But gliding like a queen, she leaves the station.
Without bowing and with restrained unconcern
She passes the houses which humbly crowd outside,
The gasworks and at last the heavy page
Of death, printed by gravestones in the cemetery.
Beyond the town there lies the open country
Where, gathering speed, she acquires mystery,
The luminous self-possession of ships on ocean.
It is now she begins to sing—at first quite low
Then loud, and at last with a jazzy madness—
The song of her whistle screaming at curves,
Of deafening tunnels, brakes, innumerable bolts.
And always light, aerial, underneath
Goes the elate meter of her wheels.
Steaming through metal landscape on her lines
She plunges new eras of wild happiness
Where speed throws up strange shapes, broad curves
And parallels clean like the steel of guns.
At last, further than Edinburgh or Rome,
Beyond the crest of the world, she reaches night
Where only a low streamline brightness
Of phosphorus on the tossing hills is white.
Ah, like a comet through flames she moves entranced

Wrapt in her music no bird song, no, nor bough
Breaking with honey buds, shall ever equal.

—Stephen Spender (1909–   )

In this poem the diction and images play an important part in accelerating the rhythm of the poem. As the train leaves the station, it *glides* like a proud queen past a humble crowd (the houses), *passes* the immobile gas works and tombstones, *gathers speed* like a majestic ocean liner, *screams* at curves as it *plunges* on its clean parallels (tracks) through the night "like a comet through flames." Like the express the poem first moves slowly, gradually increases its tempo, and ends in a dazzling burst of speed. Before we have time to catch our breath, the poet concludes with a joyous affirmation of the superiority of the powerful man-made streamliner—both in wonder and beauty—to nature's handiwork.

Eighty years before Spender wrote his poem, Emily Dickinson was less enthusiastic when the railroad was introduced into her town.

I Like to See It Lap the Miles

I like to see it lap the Miles—
And lick the Valleys up—
And stop to feed itself at Tanks—
And then—prodigious step

Around a Pile of Mountains—
And supercilious peer
In Shanties—by the sides of Roads—
And then a Quarry pare

To fit its Ribs
And crawl between
Complaining all the while
In horrid—hooting stanza—
Then chase itself down Hill—

And neigh like Boanerges—[1]
Then—punctual as a Star
Stop—docile and omnipotent
At its own stable door—

—Emily Dickinson (1830–1886)

---

[1] Christ's nickname, "Sons of Thunder," for his disciples, James and John. Referring to a vociferous preacher or orator.

The poet creates fluidity of movement by composing the poem in a single sentence. Notice how the quick regular rhythm of the first thirteen lines is suddenly retarded by the deceleration of the last three.

In reading a poem we must be careful not to isolate the element of rhythm from the subject matter. The total experience of a poem— its sensuous, emotional, imaginative, and intellectual content—is the primary factor in determining our response to it. Rhythm is only one of the poetic elements and is undoubtedly influenced by other technical considerations such as line lengths, pauses, diction, sound patterns, imagery, rhetorical structure, and rhyme.

Read the following poem aloud.

The Waltzer in the House

A sweet, a delicate white mouse,
A little blossom of a beast,
Is waltzing in the house
Among the crackers and the yeast.

O the swaying of his legs!
O the bobbing of his head!
The lady, beautiful and kind,
The blue-eyed mistress, lately wed,
Has almost laughed away her wits
To see the pretty mouse that sits
On his tiny pink behind
And swaying, bobbing, begs.

She feeds him tarts and curds,
Seed packaged for the birds,
And figs, and nuts, and cheese;
Polite as Pompadour to please
The dainty waltzer of her house,
The sweet, the delicate, the innocent white mouse.

As in a dream, as in a trance,
She loves his rhythmic elegance,
She laughs to see his bobbing dance.

—Stanley Kunitz (1905–   )

The poem moves along gracefully with a light, delicate, lilting rhythm. This is enhanced by the short lines and the stressed rhymes as well as the many short-vowel sounds. The alliterative line "Polite as Pompadour to please" not only is pleasant to the ear but suggests that the blue-eyed lady, beautiful and kind, is as charming and extravagant as the mistress of Louis XV. Lately wed and innocent, she is really the waltzer in the house.

For Discussion

I would define, in brief, the Poetry of words as the Rhythmical Creation of Beauty.

—Edgar Allan Poe

Every good poem that I know I recall by its rhythm also.

—Ralph Waldo Emerson

I believe in an "absolute rhythm," a rhythm, that is, in poetry which corresponds exactly to the emotion or shade of emotion to be expressed.

—Ezra Pound

The rhythm of verse permits the expression of more powerful feeling than is possible in prose when such feeling is needed, and it permits at all times the expression of finer shades of feeling.

—Yvor Winters

Rhythm might be described as, to the world of sound, what light is to the world of sight. It shapes and gives new meaning.

—Dame Edith Sitwell

Rhythm doesn't by its mere presence make interesting verse. It is when the poet puts it to intelligent *use* that torpid words leap.

—*Hugh Kenner*

3
Rhythm and Sound Repetitions

If appropriateness and flexibility of rhythm are important contributory elements to good poetry, the reverse is obviously true. Rhythmic inappropriateness and monotony can destroy the effectiveness of a poem.

Consider the concluding stanza of Poe's famous "Annabel Lee."

> For the moon never beams, without bringing me dreams
> Of the beautiful Annabel Lee;
> And the stars never rise, but I feel the bright eyes
> Of the beautiful Annabel Lee;
> And so, all the night-tide, I lie down by the side
> Of my darling—my darling—my life and my bride,
> In her sepulchre there by the sea—
> In her tomb by the sounding sea.

> —Edgar Allan Poe (1809–1849)

The pleasant, lilting rhythm—reinforced by internal rhymes—(*beams–dreams, rise–eyes, tide–side*)—is inappropriate to the tragic emotion the poet is trying to express. The poem becomes sentimental in mood instead of elegiac.

Swinburne, a magnificent metricist, was sometimes carried away by a torrentlike sweep of melody. The following lines from a chorus in his "Atalanta in Calydon" are intended to express a philosophy of despair; man is the victim and sport of the gods.

> Before the beginning of years,
> There came to the making of man

Time, with a gift of tears;
Grief, with a glass that ran;
Pleasure, with pain for leaven;
    Summer, with flowers that fell;
Remembrance fallen from heaven,
    And madness risen from hell;
Strength without hands to smite;
    Love that endures for a breath;
Night, the shadow of light,
    And life, the shadow of death.

—Algernon Charles Swinburne (1827–1909)

However, the swinging, lively rhythm emphasized by the forceful rhymes does not harmonize with the somber meaning. Here meter and matter unconsciously work at cross purposes; the poet's vision is not reinforced by his rhythm. Sense is drowned by melodic sound. Rhythm should not conspicuously call attention to itself but be a natural adjunct to the emotion, meaning, and sensuous impressions of a poem.

A skillful poet will also avoid a monotonous rhythm, which by its singsong effect dulls the sensibility of the reader. Lines lacking rhythmic variety, such as the following, can bore the reader or listener with their mechanical correctness.

Ode

*To Miss Margaret Pulteney, Daughter of
Daniel Pulteney, Esq., in the Nursery*

Dimply damsel, sweetly smiling,
All caressing, none beguiling,
Bud of beauty, fairly blowing,
Every charm to nature owing,
This and that new thing admiring,
Much of this and that inquiring,
Knowledge by degrees attaining,
Day by day some virtue gaining,
Ten years hence, when I leave chiming,
Beardless poets, fondly rhyming. . . .

—Ambrose Philips (1675–1749)

How does a poet speed up or retard the movement of his verse? Since poetry is primarily an auditory art consisting of the uttering of syllables in a time sequence, the poet utilizes the innumerable variations possible in combining and modulating the sound patterns or tone-color of vowel and consonant combinations. The use and repetition of these voice expressions are important factors in influencing verbal rhythms.

Sound patterns should not be studied in isolation; by themselves it is doubtful that they communicate emotion or meaning. They must be heard as interacting factors influencing and influenced by meaning, imagery, diction, tone, and the like. However, once this important principle of interplay is grasped, it is evident that all good poets are sensitive to the contribution that consonant and vowel sounds make to the communication of mood and meaning. Certainly the explosive sound of the noisy *t's, d's,* and the *g* in the line

> That dolphin-torn, that gong-tormented sea

intensifies the effect of the image of the agitated sea as the turbulence of life. The dissonant harshness, the very difficulty we have in pronouncing these verses, helps communicate the terrible power of the stolid iceberg that wrecks a ship:

> Adrift dissolving, bound for death;
> Though lumpish thou, a lumbering one—
>
> (from Melville's "The Berg")

The nasal sounds *m, n, ng* in Tennyson's famous lines

> The moan of doves in immemorial elms
> And murmuring of innumerable bees

suggest the drone and buzz as does Keats' verse

> The murmurous haunt of flies on summer eves.

Vowel sounds may be long, short, or intermediate; that is, the time span (duration) to pronounce them may vary. Usually a preponderance of one type of vowel sound in a line will influence the rhythm. Contrast the slow tempo of Keats'

> Thou still unravished bride of quietness,
> Thou foster-child of silence and slow time

with these quick-moving song bursts:

> Hedge-crickets sing; and now with treble soft
> The red-breast whistles from a garden croft.

Granting that the different sense content will influence the articulation of the sound patterns, there is no doubt that the many long vowels in the first selection help retard the rhythm and that the short vowel sounds of the second speed up the tempo.

Besides the manipulation and modulation of sound clusters and the difficulty or ease of syllabic enunciation, the poet may control his rhythm by two other important devices: the use of the *caesura* and *end-stopped* or *run-on* *lines*. The caesura is a pause within a line indicated by syntax, phrasing, or a mark of punctuation. To the poet these pauses or silences are as important as rests (long or short) are to the musical composer. The use of frequent pauses tends to slow the movement of a line, and the absence of caesuras (particularly in several consecutive lines) gives a poem fluidity of movement. Milton in his blank verse and Pope in his couplets avoid monotony of rhythm by skillful variations of the caesura. The following lines with their shifting pauses effectively describe the horrible landscape in hell that Satan's followers explore:

> . . . Through many a dark and dreary vale
> They passed,//and many a region dolorous,
> O'er many a frozen,// many a fiery Alp,
> Rocks,// caves,// lakes,// fens,// bogs,// dens,// and
>   shades of death—
> A universe of death,// which God by curse
> Created evil,// for evil only good;
> Where all life dies,// death lives,// and Nature breeds,
> Perverse,// all monstrous,// all prodigious things,
> Abominable,// unutterable,// and worse
> Than fables yet have feigned,// or fear conceived,
> Gorgons,// and Hydras,// and Chimaeras dire.

> (from *Paradise Lost*)

The caesuras in the concluding lines of Tennyson's "Choric Song" retard the tired rhythm of the enervated lotos-eaters.

> Surely,// surely// slumber is more sweet than toil,// the shore
> Than labour in the deep mid-ocean,// wind// and wave// and
>   oar;
> Oh rest ye,// brother mariners,// we will not wander more.

The infrequency of caesuras in the following poem gives it the flowing rhythm of a melodious song.

Go, Lovely Rose!

Go, lovely Rose!
Tell her, that wastes her time and me,
    That now she knows,
When I resemble her to thee,
How sweet and fair she seems to be.

Tell her that's young
And shuns to have her graces spied,
    That hadst thou sprung
In deserts, where no men abide,
Thou must have uncommended died.

Small is the worth
Of beauty from the light retired:
    Bid her come forth,
Suffer herself to be desired
And not blush so to be admired.

Then die! that she
The common fate of all things rare
    May read in thee:
How small a part of time they share
That are so wondrous sweet and fair!

—Edmund Waller (1606–1687)

The poet also achieves fluidity of movement by use of *run-on lines* (enjambment), that is, by continuing the meaning from one line to another without a rhetorical or grammatical pause at the end of the line. The following lines from Wordsworth's "Tintern Abbey" are an example of enjambment.

For I have learned
To look on nature, not as in the hour
Of thoughtless youth, but hearing oftentimes
The still sad music of humanity,
Nor harsh nor grating, though of ample power
To chasten and subdue.

In *end-stopped lines* there is a pause both in meaning and meter at the end of verses, usually indicated by punctuation. This passage from Pope's "Essay on Man" is a typical example of the concentrated meaning a good poet can pack into the closed couplet.

Know then thyself, presume not God to scan:
The proper study of mankind is man.
Placed on this isthmus of a middle state,
A being darkly wise and rudely great;
With too much knowledge for the sceptic side,
With too much weakness for the stoic's pride,
He hangs between; in doubt to act, or rest;
In doubt to deem himself a god or beast;
In doubt his mind or body to prefer;
Born but to die, and reasoning but to err;
Alike in ignorance, his reason such,
Whether he thinks too little or too much;
Chaos of thought and passion, all confused;
Still by himself abused, or disabused;
Created half to rise, and half to fall;
Great lord of all things, yet a prey to all;
Sole judge of truth, in endless error hurled;
The glory, jest, and riddle of the world!

—Alexander Pope (1688–1744)

A basic unifying device that poets frequently use is *repetition of sound patterns*—the repetition of consonant or vowel sounds, of words, phrases, lines, or stanzas. The use of recurring sounds in poetry is an important factor in controlling form and communicating emotion and meaning. The earliest primitive and the most sophisticated modern poets utilize it for expressiveness of sense and feeling or for musical embellishment. Some of the most common repetition devices are alliteration, assonance, and rhyme (the functions of the last will be discussed in Chapter 5).

Alliteration is the repetition of identical consonant sounds (usually the initial one of a word or syllable) in a line or stanza. Alliteration gives added emphasis to these words and helps create a pleasant sound (euphony) or a dissonant effect (cacophony) to suggest desired descriptive, emotional, or intellectual effects. Following are some examples from different poems.

Fair is *f*oul and *f*oul is *f*air
.   .   .   .

*S*udden *s*uccessive flights of bullets *s*treak the *s*ilence.
.   .   .   .

The horrid *c*rags, by toppling *c*onvent *c*rown'd,
The *c*ork-trees hoar that *c*lothe the shaggy steep.

Earlier English poets have frequently used alliteration to enhance the musicality of their verse or for rhetorical emphasis. In the main, modern poets have used it sparingly, for unless it is employed with subtlety, it can degenerate into a melodic mannerism that swamps meaning, as it often does in Spenser, Poe, and Swinburne.

A subtler aural repetitive device is *assonance*, the repetition of similar or identical vowel sounds. In identifying assonance the reader must be careful *not to look* for identical vowels but *to listen* to similar sounds. The long e sound may be heard in such words as beauty, rece*i*ve, sheen but not in wren or been. Some examples of assonance follow.

> When I have f*ea*rs that I may c*ea*se to be
> Before my pen has gl*ea*ned my t*ee*ming brain
> .   .   .   .
>
> As a d*a*re-g*a*le skylark scanted in a dull c*a*ge
> .   .   .   .   .   .
> The l*i*ne of festal l*i*ght in Chr*i*st-Church hall.

The effectiveness of combining alliteration and assonance is well illustrated by Coleridge's melodic flowing lines in "Kubla Khan":

> In Xanadu did Kubla Khan
>   A stately pleasure-dome decree:
> Where Alph, the sacred river, ran
> Through caverns measureless to man
>   Down to a sunless sea.

and in Shakespeare's line

> Full fathom five thy father lies.

in which we find an alliterative pattern in the iteration of f sounds and an assonantal one in the i's.

The use of repetition—word, phrase, line, or stanza—as a cohesive device to pattern a poem is as old as poetry itself. The use of a line or lines usually at regular intervals constitutes a *refrain*. It is a universal feature of tribal chants, primitive poetry, religious incantations, and folk ballads. We find it in the Egyptian *Book of the Dead* (3500 B.C.), in the Indian *Vedas* (2,000–800 B.C.), in the Psalms of the Hebrew Bible, and in the lyrics of ancient Greece. Repetition (and its variations), both as an auditory and emotional appeal and as a unifying device, has never lost its popularity, for it is as prevalent in poetry today as in the past.

The musical content of some folk ballads and songs is emphasized by the frequent use of a rhythmic meaningless phrase, such as *Fa la la* or *hey nonny no,* but other repetitive phrases give us the scene of the action, establish tone, evoke emotion, or suggest the theme. In the famous ballad "Edward," the poet structures his dramatic poem by a complex combination of repetitions.

> "Why dois your brand sae drap wi' bluid,
>   Edward, Edward,
> Why dois your brand sae drap wi' bluid,
>   And why sae sad gang ye O?"
> "O I hae killed my hawk sae guid,
>   Mither, Mither,
> O I hae killed my hawk sae guid,
>   And I had nae mair but he O."

The use of a changing refrain to advance the story is called *incremental repetition.* A good example from folk balladry is the popular "The Cruel Brother," which begins as follows:

> A gentleman came oure the sea,
>   Fine flowers in the valley
> And he has courted ladies three
>   With the light green and the yellow.
>
> One o' them was clad in red:
> He asked if she wad be his bride.
> One o' them was clad in green:
> He asked if she wad be his queen.
>
> The last o' them was clad in white:
> He asked if she wad be his heart's delight.

The ballad continues with the bridegroom asking the consent of all the relatives except the brother, who avenges the slight by killing the bride with "his little penknife."

The repetition of a line at the beginning and end of a stanza or a poem may serve as an effective structural device to achieve a *frame (or envelope) pattern.* The following poem is a good example.

John Anderson My Jo

I

> John Anderson my jo[1], John
>   When we were first acquent,

Your locks were like the raven,
Your bonie brow was brent;[2]
But now your brow is beld, John,
Your locks are like the snaw,
But blessings on your frosty pow[3]
John Anderson my jo!

II
John Anderson my jo, John,
We clamb the hill thegither,
And monie a cantie[4] day, John,
We've had wi' ane anither;
Now we maun totter down, John,
And hand in hand we'll go,
And sleep thegither at the foot,
John Anderson my jo!

—Robert Burns (1750–1796)

---

[1] Sweetheart.   [2] Steep (i.e., not sloping from baldness).   [3] Head.
[4] Merry.

The repetition (or with slight variation) of a whole stanza at beginning and end of a poem to give it a frame structure is illustrated by Blake's "The Tiger" (page 18). The dramatic impact of the repetition is powerful, for there has been both clarification and a shift in our emotional and imaginative response between reading the initial stanza and the concluding one.

Closely related to repetition and as universal a principle of poetic utterance is *parallelism,* a similarity or correspondence of phrases or clauses. Like repetition it was one of the basic elements of primitive poetry and is still found in the cadenced verse of Walt Whitman and in the metered poetry of today. Parallelism—based on similarity or contrast—is the central organizing principle of biblical verse. It sets up a pleasing recurrent rhythm and by repetition focuses our attention on a dominant feeling or idea. A sudden departure from the parallel structure shocks us into awareness. Here is an example taken from an ancient Vedda song expressing a man's love for his wife.

For want of gruel or food, life will not depart;
Owing to cold or wind, life will not depart;
Owing to rain or dew, life will not depart.
If there be no wife, life will depart.[1]

---

[1] See C. M. Bowra's *Primitive Song* (Cleveland: World Publishing Co., 1962), pp. 78–81.

In addition to using repetition of sound for aesthetic purposes, a poet may use imitation of sounds, or *onomatopoeia*. The term applies not only to individual words such as *buzz, hiss, crackle,* and *bang,* but to phrases or lines that suggest or symbolize by auditory images sounds or movements. Here again we must remember that the *meaning* of the words is all important in creating an effect; the sounds are simply contributory factors that support the sense. Vachel Lindsay's poem "General William Booth Enters Into Heaven" (page 15) contains many onomatopoetic effects. Some other examples follow.

>   . . . he hears,
> On all sides, from innumerable tongues
> A dismal universal hiss the sound of public scorn.

>   .   .   .   .

> When the hounds of spring are on winter's traces,
>   The mother of months in meadow or plain
> Fills the shadow and windy places
>   With lisp of leaves and ripple of rain.

>   .   .   .   .

> And the silken, sad, uncertain rustling of each purple curtain

>   .   .   .   .

>   The wave withdrawing
> Withers with seaward rustle of flimsy water
> Sucking the sand down: dragging at empty shells:
> The roil after it settling: too smooth: smothered . . .

>   .   .   .   .

> Chieftain Iffucan of Azcan in caftan
> Of tan with henna hackles, halt!

For Discussion

Recurrence is a structural principle of all art, whether temporal or spatial in its primary impact.

—Northrop Frye

As regarding rhythm: to compose in the sequence of the musical phrase, not in sequence of a metronome.

—Ezra Pound

Poems Related to Chapters 2 and 3

Break, Break, Break

Break, break, break,
    On thy cold gray stones, O Sea!
And I would that my tongue could utter
    The thoughts that arise in me.

O well for the fisherman's boy,
    That he shouts with his sister at play!
O well for the sailor lad,
    That he sings in his boat on the bay!

And the stately ships go on
    To their haven under the hill;
But O for the touch of a vanish'd hand,
    And the sound of a voice that is still!

Break, break, break,
    At the foot of thy crags, O Sea!
But the tender grace of a day that is dead
    Will never come back to me.

—Alfred, Lord Tennyson (1809–1892)

This poem was inspired by the death of Tennyson's closest friend Arthur Hallam. In what way does the rhythm of the poem enhance the elegiac mood? Why does the poet repeat the first line in the last stanza?

The following two poems attempt to communicate a musical experience in terms of a love relationship.

When to Her Lute Corinna Sings

When to her lute Corinna sings,
Her voice revives the leaden strings,
And doth in highest notes appear,
As any challenged Echo clear;
But when she doth of mourning speak,
E'en with her sighs the strings do break.

And as her lute doth live or die,
Led by her passion, so must I!
For when of pleasure she doth sing,

My thoughts enjoy a sudden spring;
But if she doth of sorrow speak,
E'en from my heart the strings do break.

—Thomas Campion (1567–1620)

To Jane

The keen stars were twinkling,
And the fair moon was rising among them,
Dear Jane!
The guitar was tinkling,
But the notes were not sweet till you sung them
Again.

As the moon's soft splendour
O'er the faint cold starlight of Heaven
Is thrown,
So your voice most tender
To the strings without soul had then given
Its own.

The stars will awaken,
Though the moon sleep a full hour later,
Tonight;
No leaf will be shaken
Whilst the dews of your melody scatter
Delight.

Though the sound overpowers,
Sing again, with your dear voice revealing
A tone
Of some world far from ours,
Where music and moonlight and feeling
Are one.

—Percy Bysshe Shelley (1792–1822)

1. How successful have Campion and Shelley been in capturing the lyrical mood of a love song?
2. Which poem depends on contrast for its effect? Explain the contrast.
3. Which uses more run-on lines? Why?
4. Are the two poets interested only in melody, or do they express ideas as well? Justify your answer.

Song

Why so pale and wan, fond[1] lover?
　Prithee, why so pale?
Will, when looking well can't move her,
　Looking ill prevail?
　Prithee, why so pale?

Why so dull and mute, young sinner?
　Prithee, why so mute?
Will, when speaking well can't win her,
　Saying nothing do't?
　Prithee, why so mute?

Quit, quit, for shame, this will not move,
　This cannot take her.
If of herself she will not love,
　Nothing can make her.
　The devil take her!

　　　—Sir John Suckling (1609–1642)

_____
[1] Foolish.

1. Discuss the poet's use of the refrain in stanzas one and two. Are the variations justified?
2. What syntactical shift is there in the last stanza? How does this affect the rhythm and influence the meaning?

⌈God's Grandeur⌋

The world is charged with the grandeur of God.
　It will flame out, like shining from shook foil;
　It gathers to a greatness, like the ooze of oil[1]
Crushed. Why do men then now not reck[2] his rod?
Generations have trod, have trod, have trod;
　And all is seared with trade; bleared, smeared with toil;
　And wears man's smudge and shares man's smell: the soil
Is bare now, nor can foot feel, being shod.

And for[3] all this, nature is never spent;
　There lives the dearest freshness deep down things;
And though the last lights off the black West went
　Oh, morning, at the brown brink eastward, springs—

Because the Holy Ghost[4] over the bent[5]
World broods with warm breast and with ah! bright wings.

—Gerard Manley Hopkins (1844–1889)

---

[1] Of olives.   [2] Obey.   [3] Despite.   [4] Often represented as a dove in paintings.   [5] Literally curved, but symbolically sinful.

The poem contrasts the drabness and sinfulness of the modern world with the freshness and purity of nature as viewed by a deeply religious person.

1. How does the poet's use of alliteration and assonance reinforce this contrast?
2. How does the rhythm of the second stanza differ from the first? Why?
3. Which part has more caesuras? Why?

These three poems by Wordsworth, Shelley, and Arnold deal with the theme of death.

A Slumber Did My Spirit Seal

A slumber did my spirit seal;
  I had no human fears:
She seemed a thing that could not feel
  The touch of earthly years.

No motion has she now, no force;
  She neither hears nor sees;
Rolled round in earth's diurnal course,
  With rocks, and stones, and trees.

—William Wordsworth (1770–1850)

Death

I

Death is here and death is there,
Death is busy everywhere,
All around, within, beneath,
Above is death—and we are death.

II

Death has set his mark and seal
On all we are and all we feel,
On all we know and all we fear,
.   .   .   .   .[1]

III
First our pleasures die—and then
Our hopes, and then our fears—and when
These are dead, the debt is due,
Dust claims dust—and we die too.

IV
All things that we love and cherish,
Like ourselves must fade and perish;
Such is our rude mortal lot—
Love itself would, did they not.

—Percy Bysshe Shelley (1792–1822)

---

[1] This line has been lost.

Requiescat[1]

Strew on her roses, roses,
  And never a spray of yew!
In quiet she reposes;
  Ah, would that I did too!

Her mirth the world required;
  She bathed it in smiles of glee.
But her heart was tired, tired,
  And now they let her be.

Her life was turning, turning,
  In mazes of heat and sound.
But for peace her soul was yearning,
  And now peace laps her round.

Her cabin'd, ample spirit,
  It flutter'd and fail'd for breath.
To-night it doth inherit
  The vasty hall of death.

—Matthew Arnold (1822–1888)

---

[1] May she rest in peace.

1. Of these three poems, which one has an inappropriate rhythm? Are there any other reasons for its failure as a poem?
2. In the other two poems what do rhythm, repetition, alliteration, assonance, and onomatopoeia contribute to effective expressiveness? Discuss concrete examples.

The Hurricane

Lo, Lord, Thou ridest!
Lord, Lord, Thy swifting heart

Naught stayeth, naught now bideth
But's smithereened apart!

Ay! Scripture flee'th stone!
Milk-bright, Thy chisel wind

Rescindeth flesh from bone
To quivering whittlings thinned—

Swept—whistling straw! Battered,
Lord, e'en boulders now out-leap

Rock sockets, levin-lathered![1]
Nor, Lord, may worm out-deep

Thy drum's gambade,[2] its plunge abscond!
Lord God, while summits crashing

Whip sea-kelp screaming on blond
Sky-seeth, high heaven dashing—

Thou ridest to the door, Lord!
Thou bidest wall nor floor, Lord!

—Hart Crane (1899–1932)

---

[1] *Levin,* archaic word for lightning.   [2] Fantastic caper or frolic.

1. How would you characterize the rhythm of this poem? Is it appropriate to the subject matter? Discuss.
2. What repetition is there in the poem? What is its function?
3. What use does the poet make of alliteration, assonance, and onomatopoeia?

During Wind and Rain

They sing their dearest songs—
He, she, all of them—yes,
Treble and tenor and bass,
    And one to play;
With the candles mooning each face. . . .
    Ah, no; the years O!
How the sick leaves reel down in throngs!

They clear the creeping moss—
Elders and juniors—aye,
Making the pathway neat
    And the garden gay;
And they build a shady seat. . . .
        Ah, no; the years, the years;
See, the white storm-birds wing across!

They are blithely breakfasting all—
Men and maidens—yea,
Under the summer tree,
    With a glimpse of the bay,
While pet fowl come to the knee. . . .
        Ah, no; the years O!
And the rotten rose is ript from the wall.

They change to a high new house,
He, she, all of them—aye,
Clocks and carpets, and chairs
    On the lawn all day,
And brightest things that are theirs. . . .
        Ah, no; the years, the years;
Down their carved names the rain-drop ploughs.

—Thomas Hardy (1840–1928)

The speaker in this poem is in a cemetery during an autumnal storm contemplating the tombstones of a typical family and reminiscing about their life. By a series of ironic contrasts he suggests the destructivenes of time and the inevitability of death.

1. What do the last lines of each stanza have in common? What shift in rhythm is found in each stanza? What is its function?

2. What does the refrain in each stanza add to the poem? How would you justify the variations in the refrain patterns?

3. What do the sound effects contribute to the mood and theme of the poem?

4. Why are the clocks, carpets, and chairs out on the lawn? What is the "high new house" that "he, she, all of them" change to?

Meeting at Night

I

The grey sea and the long black land;
And the yellow half-moon large and low;
And the startled little waves that leap
In fiery ringlets from their sleep,

As I gain the cove with pushing prow,
And quench its speed i' the slushy sand.

II

Then a mile of warm sea-scented beach;
Three fields to cross till a farm appears;
A tap at the pane, the quick sharp scratch
And blue spurt of a lighted match,
And a voice less loud, thro' its joys and fears,
Than the two hearts beating each to each!

Parting at Morning

Round the cape of a sudden came the sea,
And the sun looked over the mountain's rim;
And straight was a path of gold for him,[1]
And the need of a world of men for me.

—Robert Browning (1812–1889)

---

[1] Refers to the sun.

1. In these two dramatic lyrics by Robert Browning, the speaker, a man, does not mention the word *love*. What ideas are *implied* about the experience of love?
2. To how many senses does the first poem appeal? By what images?
3. In the first poem, what shifts in rhythm are there? Can they be justified?
4. What six colors does the poet introduce in the poems? Why? (i.e., what do they contribute?)
5. In what ways is the second poem a contrast to the first?
6. How do you interpret the last line of the second poem? Does it mean that just as it is a natural law for the sun to move through a prescribed course in the sky, so man, the lover, has a natural need to run his circle of duties in the world of men? Or that the world of men needs him and he must fulfill this obligation? Do you think the speaker would agree with Byron's view (expressed in "Don Juan")?

   "Man's love is of man's life a thing apart;
   'Tis a woman's whole existence."

7. What part do sound patterns play in the two poems?

Jig Tune: Not for Love

Where are you going? asked Manny the Mayor.
What are you doing? asked President Jane.

I'll bet you're a bastard, said Daniel the Deacon;
We'll put you away where you'll never be seen.

There won't be no pardon, said Manny the Murderer.
There won't be no stay, said Tommygun Jane.
Said Daniel McBedlam, You won't go no farther;
My father won't even declare you insane.

For a Madman's Way, intoned Manny the Magnate.
The Public Good, shouted Editor Jane.
I think he's a Commie, cried Danny O'Garrote;
If he won't do murder, I call it a crime.

It's not a long drop, sang Manny the Hangman.
The rope will stop you, crooned Juryman Jane.
In a box long and black, chanted Danny Le Flack,
We'll suit you warm to keep out the rain.

All flesh is grass, sighed Manny the Mourner.
The handsome young man, wept Sob-sister Jane.
R.I.P., prayed Capital Daniel;
If he were alive we could kill him again.

> —Thomas McGrath (1916–   )

My Papa's Waltz

The whiskey on your breath
Could make a small boy dizzy;
But I held on like death:
Such waltzing was not easy.

We romped until the pans
Slid from the kitchen shelf;
My mother's countenance
Could not unfrown itself.

The hand that held my wrist
Was battered on one knuckle;
At every step I missed
My right ear scraped a buckle.

You beat time on my head
With a palm caked hard by dirt,
Then waltzed me off to bed
Still clinging to your shirt.

—Theodore Roethke (1908–1963)

The Main Deep

The long-rólling,
  Steady-póuring,
    Deep-trenchéd,
      Green billow.

The wíde-topped,
  Unbróken,
    Green-glacid,
      Slów-slíding,

Cóld-flushing,
  —On-on-on—
    Chill rushing,
      Hush-hushing,
—Hush-hushing—

—James Stephens (1882–1950)

The Emperor of Ice-Cream

Call the roller of big cigars,
The muscular one, and bid him whip   *ardent desire (sexual)*
In kitchen cups concupiscent curds.
Let the wenches dawdle in such dress
As they are used to wear, and let the boys
Bring flowers in last month's newspapers.
Let be be finale of seem. *What seems is.*
The only emperor is the emperor of ice-cream.

Take from the dresser of deal,
Lacking the three glass knobs, that sheet
On which she embroidered fantails once
hard, callous And spread it so as to cover her face.
If her horny feet protrude, they come
To show how cold she is, and dumb.
Let the lamp affix its beam.
The only emperor is the emperor of ice-cream.

  —Wallace Stevens (1879–1955)

The Juggler

A ball will bounce, but less and less. It's not
A light-hearted thing, resents its own resilience.

Falling is what it loves, and the earth falls
So in our hearts from brilliance,
Settles and is forgot.
It takes a skyblue juggler with five red balls

To shake our gravity up. Whee, in the air
The balls roll round, wheel on his wheeling hands,
Learning the ways of lightness, alter to spheres
Grazing his finger ends,
Cling to their courses there,
Swinging a small heaven about his ears.

But a heaven is easier made of nothing at all
Than the earth regained, and still and sole within
The spin of words, with a gesture sure and noble
He reels that heaven in,
Landing it ball by ball,
And trades it all for a broom, a plate, a table.

Oh, on his toe the table is turning, the broom's
Balancing up on his nose, and the plate whirls
On the tip of the broom! Damn, what a show, we cry:
The boys stamp, and the girls
Shriek, and the drum booms
And all comes down, and he bows and says good-bye.

If the juggler is tired now, if the broom stands
In the dust again, if the table starts to drop
Through the daily dark again, and though the plate
Lies flat on the table top,
For him we batter our hands
Who has won for once over the world's weight.

—Richard Wilbur (1921–   )

The line will have the more charm for not being mechanically straight. We enjoy the straight crookedness of a good walking stick.

—*Robert Frost*

4
The Meaning of Meter

Rhythm—whether appealing to the eye or ear—is present in all art forms: music, the dance, painting, sculpture, architecture, and poetry. When poetic rhythm can be measured with sufficient regularity and predictability, it becomes meter. Whenever colloquial speech becomes heightened by emotion, it tends to fall into a fairly regular pattern which is pleasurable to hear. All the games of children tend to fall into rhythmic movements and, when oral in expression, into metrical patterns of song and speech. The rhythmic swing of Mother Goose verses which children enjoy and the steady beat of rock and roll music that delights today's youth are physically exhilarating. The emotional stimulation is evident by the frequent foot-tapping, hand-clapping, and head-nodding in a musical or poetic performance.

The universal appeal of poetry through the ages is due, to a large extent, to the pleasure we derive from having the chaos of daily experience patterned into metrical form. The regular beat of uttered human sounds probably originated as an instinctive expression or an imitation of the manifold rhythms heard in nature and in the human body, such as breathing and the heart beat. Whether hypnotic or stimulating, poetic meter as a rhythmic beat or spoken stress plays an important part in stirring the imagination, arousing emotion, and emphasizing meaning.

For poetic purposes the unit of speech is the syllable. Since English is a *stressed* language, we give more force (i.e., emphasis or loudness) to some syllables than we do to others when we utter words of more than one syllable. In the two-syllable word *fellow* we stress

59

the first syllable, *fel*-low. In the three-syllable word *surrender* we stress the second syllable, sur-*ren*-der. In the four-syllable word *capitulate* we stress the second syllable, ca-*pit*-u-late. The word *reprehension* is a four-syllable word with a heavy stress on the third syllable, rep-re-*hen*-sion. However, in this word it is obvious that the first syllable *rep* receives more emphatic utterance than *re* and *sion* but less than the main stressed syllable *hen*. The stress on *rep* is called *secondary stress;* the stress on *hen* is called *primary stress.* (When we use the word *stress* alone, we refer to primary stress.)

The fact that English is a stressed language is very important, for stress is one of the basic elements in determining the beat or meter of our poetry. The word *meter* is derived from the Greek term *metron* which means *measure.* Different language groups use different measuring devices to create their own metrical systems.

Meter represents only one aspect of linear rhythm in English poetry. On the opposite spectrum is *free verse,* discussed in Chapter 6, which depends on cadences for its rhythmic patterns but which is otherwise unmeasured. Between the measured regularity of metered poetry and the cadences of free verse are *syllabic poetry* and *accentual poetry.* In syllabic poetry the criterion of line measure is the number of syllables per line. Unlike metered poetry, both the number of stresses (accented syllables) and the position of stresses within a line may vary. Either a constant number of syllables is maintained throughout the poem, or the number of syllables is varied from line to line to create a pattern that is repeated in following stanzas.

Most syllabic poetry is written in odd-numbered line units (five, seven, nine, etc. syllables per line) to avoid the lapse into meter that can happen when the line is measured by an even number of syllables. As in metered poetry, variations in the measure of syllabic poetry are common, especially in the last line of the poem, for emphasis. Marianne Moore has written much of her work in syllabic poetry, and a number of American poets since the 1950s have employed syllabic poetry as an alternative to the regularity of metered poetry and the irregularity of free verse. Examples of syllabic poetry are "The Glove" by Harold Bond (page 178) and "Mother" by Robert Mezey (page 339). Most of these principles apply equally to accentual poetry, except that, instead of syllables, it depends for its measure on the number of stresses per line. Thus, the number of syllables per line may vary, as well as the order of occurrence of stresses—unlike metered poetry. An example of accentual poetry is "God's Grandeur" by Gerard Manley Hopkins (page 50).

The most frequently used method of line measure in the last six hundred years of English poetry, however, is *accentual-syllabic,* or metered poetry. As the name implies, the system takes into account both the number of accents and the number of syllables per line in a fixed order of occurrence. This system combines the advantages of regularity with flexibility. The unit of measure is the *foot*, which consists usually of one accented (stressed) syllable and one or more unaccented (unstressed) syllables. (Exceptions will be explained later.) The line in a metered poem consists of a number of feet ranging from one to eight, with metrical variations commonly employed. The length of the line is indicated by the following terms:

one foot:	*monometer*
two feet:	*dimeter*
three feet:	*trimeter*
four feet:	*tetrameter*
five feet:	*pentameter*
six feet:	*hexameter*
seven feet:	*heptameter*
eight feet:	*octameter*

The most common *poetic feet* in English verse are the following:

iambus (adj. iambic), as in *delay*
anapest (adj. anapestic), as in *intersperse*
trochee (adj. trochaic), as in *river*
dactyl (adj. dactylic), as in *happiness*

Iambic and anapestic feet are called *ascending (or rising) feet:* trochaic and dactylic *descending (or falling) feet.*

Unfortunately we have found no substitute for this complicated-sounding terminology from the Greek, but a term such as iambic pentameter indicates the two essential facts about a line of verse: the kind of foot (two syllables with the accent on the second, ˇ ´) and the number of feet (five).

Once a poet has established a regular base rhythm (i.e., a metrical pattern discernible by scansion), to gain variety, shift tempo, or to reinforce meaning, he will introduce metrical variations or use *substitute feet.* The two often used are the following:

spondee (adj. spondaic): two consecutive accented syllables, as in *day wanes*

pyrrhic: two unstressed consecutive syllables, as in *of the.*

Of course, no poem in English is written in spondaic or pyrrhic meter; rarely do we find even a whole line of such feet.

Because English is a stressed language, it is possible to arrange words that make sense in a definite metrical pattern. To uncover this pattern we first mark with an accent the stressed syllables.

No longer mourn for me when I am dead

The second step in scansion is to mark the remaining syllables as unaccented.

No longer mourn for me when I am dead

The final step is to examine the line to see what pattern of regularity emerges and then to mark off the feet.

No long/er mourn/for me/when I/am dead

This line is *iambic pentameter,* the most common meter in our poetry. Let us scan a few more lines to illustrate the different meters.

For the An/gel of Death/spread his wings/on the blast/

This line is anapestic tetrameter.

Tiger!/Tiger!/burning/bright

This line is *trochaic tetrameter,* with an unaccented syllable omitted at the end of the line. (One or more unstressed syllables may be dropped at the beginning or end of lines.)

This is the/forest pri/meval, the/murmuring/
pines and the/hemlocks

This line is *dactylic hexameter,* also with an unaccented syllable omitted at the end of the line.

In his poem "Ulysses" written in iambic pentameter, Tennyson slows up the movement of a line to express the monotonous passing of time by substituting two spondees in the second and fourth feet.

The long/day wanes:/the slow/moon climbs:/the deep

In another iambic pentameter poem, "The Passing of Arthur," to emphasize an important phrase ("great deep"), he uses two spondaic feet, and to deemphasize the other words he uses two pyrrhic feet.

From the/great deep/to the/great deep/he goes

For purposes of clarity the illustrative examples given above have all been lines of metrical regularity. However, a poem would quickly bore us with a metronomic rhythm; our ears desire variety to sustain our interest. The changes in meter that a poet introduces satisfy this demand, but the variations do not shatter the established pattern whether iambic, dactylic, or whatever. We cannot determine the meter of a poem by simply scanning one line. Usually a definite pattern will emerge only if we analyze the beats and nonbeats of several lines or a whole stanza. A poet will occasionally depart from his adopted meter to indicate a change in tempo or tone or to emphasize meaning, but the predominant meter will quickly reassert itself.

Consider these two stanzas from Coleridge's "The Rime of the Ancient Mariner."

> The fair/breeze blew,/the white/foam flew,
> The fur/row fol/lowed free;
> We were/the first/that ev/er burst
> Into/that si/lent sea.

In this stanza the first two lines set up a regular iambic pattern; movement is accelerated by the alliteration of the *f* sounds. The initial feet in lines 3 and 4 change to trochees. This shift not only adds variety but tends to slow up the movement of the verses and to reinforce meaning.

> Down dropt/the breeze,/the sails/dropt down,
> 'Twas sad/as sad/could be;
> And we/did speak/only/to break
> The si/lence of/the sea.

In the first line of this stanza the spondees, by their two heavy stresses, prepare us for the becalming of the ship. (The fact that the line begins and ends with the word *down* contributes to this effect.) However, the iambic beat quickly reasserts itself in the rest of the stanza. The only other variation is the trochee in the third foot of line 3. Thus, in the twenty-eight feet in these two stanzas, only five are variants of the established iambic meter.

Helpful as a knowledge of scansion is as *one* of the elements in the meaningful organization of a poem, it is not an infallible guide to an oral reading of poetry. Metrical analysis simply presents to *our eyes* the ground plan or blueprint of a poem, not the finished structure in all its detailed complexity. When we read a poem aloud or *hear* it in our imaginative mind, we do not give equal emphasis to the accented syllables. We read for expressive meaning; we do not read mechanically. Some words are more important for sense than others; and these we emphasize more in utterance. Even accented words may receive less sound stress than unaccented ones if meaning is involved. For instance, if we were to read aloud the line

$$\breve{\text{T}}\text{he si/}\acute{\text{le}}\breve{\text{nce}}\ \acute{\text{of}}\text{/}\breve{\text{the}}\ \acute{\text{sea}}$$

we would probably give the unaccented syllable (si)*lence* more sound emphasis than the accented syllable *of* because the meaning requires it.

By simply using two arbitrary symbols for syllable pronunciation, accented or unaccented, scansion is really a crude and inadequate device to measure sound performance. Some consonants have great resonance, some are throaty, some are explosive, some are soft and delicate sounding; in the same way, vowels have different sound effects. Duration and pitch influence the tone-color of sounds. Scansion gives us no help here. Furthermore, what happens to secondary stress? The poet is free to mark these syllables as accented or unaccented.

The inadequacy of conventional metrical analysis is further evident in the handling of the caesura (pause) in the line. In reading a poem intelligently, we realize some pauses should be short and some long. Here punctuation may help us. We naturally would pause longer after a semicolon than a comma. But scansion provides no indication of how long the caesura should be between unpunctuated phrases.

Scansion is helpful in uncovering the basic metrical line measure of a poem. What we must do in reading it for meaning is to find a happy compromise between the prose sense emphasis and the formal metrical pattern. In fact, many readers find the tension—or interplay set up between these two approaches to the *hearing* of a poem and the *seeing* of it—is part of the enjoyment that poetry gives them.

Let us examine a poem and compare the metrical pattern with the prose-sense stress. (The latter will be indicated by italicized syllables that would normally be stressed in an oral performance.)

Composed Upon Westminster Bridge

1. *Earth* has/not *an*/ything/to *show*/more *fair*:
2. *Dull* would/he be/of *soul*/who could/*pass* by

3. A sight/so touch/ing in/its maj/esty:
4. This Ci/ty now/doth, like/a gar/ment, wear
5. The beau/ty of/the morn/ing; si/lent, bare.
6. Ships, tow/ers, domes,/theatres,/and tem/ples lie
7. Open/unto/the fields,/and to/the sky:
8. All bright/ and glit/tering in/the smoke/less air.
9. Never/did sun/more beau/tiful/ly steep
10. In his/first splen/dour val/ley, rock/or hill;
11. Ne'er saw/I, nev/er felt,/a calm/so deep!
12. The riv/er glid/eth at/his own/sweet will:
13. Dear God!/the ver/y hous/es seem/asleep;
14. And all/that might/y heart/is ly/ing still!

—William Wordsworth (1770–1850)

The poem scans as iambic pentameter (of the seventy feet, only seven are variants). If we examine the prose stress, we find, however, considerable variation ranging from three to six stresses in a line. Half the lines of the poem have four voice stresses. The sonnet reaches its emotional climax in the last two lines, and it is interesting to note that here the metrical stress coincides exactly with the voice utterance. Whenever this identity occurs, the lines become unusually emphatic. If this were to happen throughout the poem, the meter would dominate it and create a monotonous, mechanical effect. The poet's problem is to control the meter so as to achieve flexibility and variety to reinforce the communication of emotion and meaning. In this poem, although Wordsworth is "bound/Within the Sonnet's scanty plot of ground," he has found freedom of rhythmic expression within an organic form. The interplay of a fixed pattern with improvisation fulfills one of the fundamental principles of all art, that of unity in variety.

Meter serves other important functions in poetry. By its formalistic structure, it establishes an aesthetic "distance" between the reader and the experience recounted. By framing the material, it focuses our attention so that we read with greater interest and concentration. The ordered pattern of sounds and rhythm makes it easier for us to remember the lines. This mnemonic value of meter explains why we remember and quote poetry more frequently than we do prose or free verse. Because of the complexity of prosody, a poem may be scanned in more than one way, and oral performances may vary. Just as two great pianists may give different interpretations of a Beethoven sonata, so two readers of a poem may differ—within certain limits—in their understanding of its rhythmic nuances.

For various reasons, the most popular meter in English poetry is iambic (ᴗ ⁄). Used in a variety of ways, both in rhymed and un-rhymed poetry, with formal and colloquial language, in lyric and dramatic genres, it has dominated our poetry for more than five hundred years.

Trochaic meter (⁄ ᴗ) is frequently used in short lyrics that need a light, dancelike rhythm, as in Milton's "L'Allegro."

> Come, and trip it as ye go
> On the light fantastic toe.

When the beats are heavily stressed, it is equally adaptable to chant and incantation, as in

> Double, double, toil and trouble;
> Fire burn, and cauldron bubble

> (The witches in *Macbeth* brewing their hell-broth)

and in Burns' "Scots, Wha Hae" (page 31) and Blake's "The Tiger" (page 18). The use of a trochaic meter in a long poem tends to become mechanical and monotonous, as in Longfellow's "Hiawatha."

> I am weary of your quarrels,
> Weary of your wars and bloodshed,
> Weary of your prayers for vengeance,
> Of your wranglings and dissensions:
> All your strength is in your union,
> All your danger is in discord.

Anapestic meter (ᴗ ᴗ ⁄) is usually used by a poet to create movement and speed as in Byron's "The Destruction of Sennacherib"

> The Assyrian came down like a wolf on the fold,
> And his cohorts were gleaming in purple and gold;
> And the sheen of their spears was like stars on the sea,
> When the blue wave rolls nightly on deep Galilee.

and in Browning's "How They Brought the Good News from Ghent to Aix."

I sprang to the stirrup, and Joris, and he:
I galloped, Dirck galloped, we galloped all three.

Dactylic meter ($/\cup\cup$), used most frequently in the nineteenth century, is rarely used today. The falling effect of the dactyl makes it appropriate for elegiac verse as in Hood's "The Bridge of Sighs"

One more Unfortunate,
Weary of breath,
Rashly importunate,
Gone to her death!

but its use in a long poem strikes the ear as artificial and tends to produce a jigging effect.

The preceding discussion of meter is intended to introduce the student to the basic principles of prosody, the rhythmic and sound elements that enter into the composition of a poem. Of course, one can grasp the meaning and feel the emotion of poetry without this knowledge; but the metrical aspect of a good poem, to a greater or lesser degree, always complements the meaning and contributes to the total experience of a particular poem. Does this technical knowledge destroy the appreciation and enjoyment of a poem, or does it enhance one's pleasure? A spectator at a football game who is familiar with the intricacies and strategic possibilities of the different plays certainly enjoys the spectacle more than an uninformed amateur. The same is true of an informed listener at a concert or a knowledgeable viewer in an art museum. When a reader grasps the vital relationship that exists between the semantic content of a poem and its versification, he gains a deeper insight into its meaning and a pleasurable recognition of its artistic unity.

For Discussion

It is not metres, but a metre-making argument that makes a poem—a thought so passionate and alive that like the spirit of a plant or an animal it has an architecture of its own, and adorns nature with a new thing.

—Ralph Waldo Emerson

I believe that the meter-and-meaning process is the organic act of poetry, and involves all its important characters.

—John Crowe Ransom

For rhyme the rudder is of verses,
With which, like ships, they steer their courses.

—Samuel Butler

5
Rhyme and Reason

There is a close relationship between meter and rhyme. Rhyme is a metrical-rhetorical device based on the sound-similarities of words. By so marking the ends of lines and linking them together, rhyme is used by a poet to help organize his material into stanzas. By laying additional stress on sound similarities, rhyme increases the emotional effect in a poem and intensifies experience.

Not all poetry uses rhyme. To a large extent it has been abandoned by contemporary poets. Unrhymed poetry usually written in iambic pentameter is called *blank verse*. Some of the greatest poetry in English is written in blank verse, by Marlowe and Shakespeare in their plays, by Milton in *Paradise Lost*, by Wordsworth in his longer poems, and by Edwin Arlington Robinson in his Arthurian narratives. Even though Milton railed against the troublesome and modern bondage of "riming" and considered it "no necessary adjunct or true ornament of poem or good verse, in long works especially," he used it in many of his poems as have most English poets since Chaucer (1340–1400).

The most extensive type of *rhyme* is terminal (or final) rhyme. This consists of different initial sounds and identical following sounds *(late—mate; greatly—stately; spontaneous—miscellaneous)* used at the end of lines. Usually in strict or full rhyme there is not only correspondence of sound but of accent as well, although good poets have exercised considerable freedom in this respect.

True Wit is Nature to advantage *dress'd*,
What oft was thought, but n'er so well *expressed*.

Rhyme used within a line is called *internal rhyme.*

And ice, mast-*high,* came floating *by.*

.   .   .   .

Making their *tomb* the *womb* wherein they grew.

.   .   .   .

Chilling and *killing* my Annabel Lee.

Rhymes may be masculine or feminine. *Masculine rhyme* con-sists of the rhyming of final stressed syllables. Of course, all mono-syllable rhymes are masculine *(fear—leer).* Rhyming words of two or more syllables are masculine if the final syllables are stressed (un*spent*—re*lent;* unde*filed*—reconc*iled). Feminine rhyme* consists of rhyming words of two or more syllables in which the stressed and rhymed syllables are not the final ones (*sickly—quickly; run-ning—sunning; flourishing—nourishing).* Thus, in feminine rhyme one or more unstressed syllables follow the stressed rhymed syllable.

Now hardly here and there a hackney-*coach* Appearing, show'd the ruddy morn's ap*proach.* Now Betty from her master's bed had *flown,* And softly stole to discompose her *own.*	masculine rhyme
The child's toys and the old man's *reasons* Are the fruits of the two *seasons.*	feminine rhyme
But stood in trembling, patient *tribulation* To be call'd up for her *examination.*	feminine rhyme

Compared to other languages such as French and Spanish, English is deficient in rhymability. For some words there is only a single rhyme (e.g., *mountain—fountain).* Some common words such as *circle* and *wisdom* have no rhymes. To find rhymes for some words, particularly polysyllabic ones, poets (often for comic effect) distort the pronunciation of words. For *rhinoceros* Browning used the bizarre phrase *toss Eros* and Ogden Nash the humorous rhyme *prepoceros.* In *Don Juan* Byron rhymed *intellectual* with *henpecked you all.* To overcome the paucity of rhymes in our language and to make a virtue of necessity, poets have experimented for certain effects (softening sounds, intentional dissonance, variety, and sur-prise) by using slant rhymes and eye rhymes.

Slant rhymes (or near rhymes) are imperfect rhymes created by changing the patterns of consonants or vowels. Emily Dickinson rhymes *time—thine, thing—along, cool—soul.* Hopkins was another nineteenth-century metrical experimenter who widened the range of rhyme. Twentieth-century poets such as Wilfred Owen, W. B. Yeats, and W. H. Auden have enjoyed the freedom of using slant rhymes to supplement conventional full rhyme.

   Eye rhymes by their spelling give our eyes the impression of perfect rhyme but when pronounced turn out not to be identical in sound (*love—prove; cough—plough; keen—been*).

   Recognizing the difficulty of finding exact rhymes in English, today we are more tolerant and understanding of the poet's freedom in the use of rhyme to express emotion and meaning. Just as modern readers reject conformity and rigidity in society, so they reject them in the writing of poetry. Shelley in "To a Skylark," one of our greatest lyrics, rhymes *wert* ("Bird thou never wert") with *heart; higher* (two syllables) with *fire* (one syllable); *daylight* with *delight* (identical syllables, one unstressed, the other stressed); *grass* with *was.* Readers are swept along by the swift, spontaneous rhythm, the ecstatic bursts of melody, and the dazzling images. The variety of rhyme adds to, rather than detracts from, our experiencing the poem.

   The skillful poet uses rhyme not for its own sake but as an adjunct to rhythm for melodic effect, for rhetorical emphasis, and to reinforce meaning. In lyric poems—particularly songs—rhyme plays an important role in creating a musical effect that is evocative of mood. In these two lyrics the mellifluous rhymes combine with the appropriate rhythm—rapid and joyful in the first, slow and quiet in the second—to communicate emotion effectively.

Hark, Hark! the Lark

(From Cymbeline)

Hark, hark! the lark at heaven's gate sings,
   And Phoebus' gins arise,
His steeds to water at those springs
   On chaliced flowers that lies;
And winking Mary-buds begin
   To ope their golden eyes:
With every thing that pretty is,
   My lady sweet, arise!
      Arise, arise!

—William Shakespeare (1564–1616)

Weep You No More, Sad Fountains

Weep you no more, sad fountains;
   What need you flow so fast?
Look how the snowy mountains
   Heaven's sun doth gently waste.
     But my sun's heavenly eyes
      View not your weeping,
      That now lies sleeping
Softly, now softly lies
    Sleeping.

Sleep is a reconciling,
   A rest that peace begets.
Doth not the sun rise smiling
   When fair at even he sets?
     Rest you then, rest, sad eyes,
      Melt not in weeping,
      While she lies sleeping,
Softly, now softly lies
    Sleeping.

           —Anonymous

In an early satirical poem Byron uses a multiplicity of feminine rhymes to create a comic effect.

Why should you weep like Lydia Languish
And fret with self-created anguish
Or doom the lover you have chosen
On winter nights to sigh half-frozen;
In leafless shades to sue for pardon,
Only because the scene's a garden?

The five-line limerick has become a traditional form for light verse. The forceful rhymes play an essential part in communicating the humorous meaning.

An Epicure

An epicure, dining at Crewe,
Found quite a large mouse in his stew.
   Said the waiter, "Don't shout,
   And wave it about,
Or the rest will be wanting one, too!"

           —Anonymous

Faith-Healer

There was a faith-healer in Deal
Who said, "Although pain isn't real,
   If I sit on a pin
   And it punctures my skin,
I dislike what I fancy I feel."

—Anonymous

A Limerick on Limericks

A limerick gets laughs anatomical
Into space that is quite economical.
   But the good ones I've seen
   So seldom are clean,
And the clean ones so seldom are comical.

—Anonymous

Many modern limericks have modified the form by introducing a witty reversal, a pun, or a delayed rhyme in the last line.

Atomic Courtesy

To smash the simple atom
All mankind was intent,
   Now any day
   The atom may
Return the compliment.

—Ethel Jacobson (19 n.d.–   )

A Decrepit Old Gasman

A decrepit old gasman, named Peter,
While hunting around his gas heater,
   Touched a leak with his light;
   He rose out of sight—
And, as everyone who knows anything about
      poetry can tell you, he also ruined the meter.

—Anonymous

Similarly, rhyme in serious poetry can reinforce meaning by emphasizing certain words. In the following poem, based on a public execution, the poet builds up tension to the climactic rhyme "struck."

Eight O'Clock

> He stood, and heard the steeple
>   Sprinkle the quarters on the morning town.
> One, two, three, four, to market-place and people
>   It tossed them down.
>
> Strapped, noosed, nighing his hour
>   He stood and counted them and cursed his luck;
> And then the clock collected in the tower
>   Its strength, and struck.

> —A. E. Housman (1859–1936)

Blake's use of only masculine rhyme in "The Tiger" (page 18) can be justified for several reasons. By setting off two-line thought units connected by rhyme, it unites syntax with meaning. In addition the masculine rhyme hammers out the rhythmic beat of the line. Finally, it strengthens some of the dramatic contrasts: the color-fulness of the tiger and the darkness of the forest (*bright—night)*; the inanimate and the animate (*chain—brain*); violence and pity (*spears—tears*). In good poetry rhyme should be functional, not merely ornamental. Form and content should be one and indivisible.

The end-stopped rhymed couplet in which meter and thought come to a pause at the end of the line is appropriate to the expression of sententious meaning. Eighteenth-century poets found this form the perfect vehicle for communicating epigrammatic truths and pithy maxims such as these couplets of Alexander Pope.

> A little learning is a dang'rous thing;
> Drink deep, or taste not the Pierian spring:
> There shallow draughts intoxicate the brain,
> And drinking largely sobers us again.

> .   .   .   .

> Hope springs eternal in the human breast;
> Man never is, but always to be blest.

If a poet desires the formality of rhyme but wishes to muffle its effect, he uses run-on lines. In "My Last Duchess" Browning's suave Renaissance duke, bound by cruel aristocratic traditions, expresses himself in smooth conversational tones. The poet has subdued the rhymes in the dramatic monologue by the use of enjambment.

> . . . Sir, 'twas not
> Her husband's presence only, called that spot
> Of joy into the Duchess' cheek: perhaps
> Frà Pandolf chanced to say "Her mantle laps
> Over my lady's wrist too much," or "Paint
> Must never hope to reproduce the faint
> Half-flush that dies along her throat"; such stuff
> Was courtesy, she thought, and cause enough
> For calling up that spot of joy. She had
> A heart—how shall I say?—too soon made glad. . .

A resourceful poet will use word, music, meter, and rhyme to embody his imaginative vision. These elements, combined with appropriate imagery and diction, are not isolated in the act of creation but are closely interrelated. Just as a living organism functions through the interplay of its various chemicals, so a poem harmonizes these diverse elements into an effective working unity. By these means a good poem—simple or complex—appeals to our senses, arouses our emotions, and stimulates our minds.

For Discussion

Rhyme is a pretty good measure of the latitude and opulence of a writer. If unskilled, he is at once detected by the poverty of his chimes.

—Ralph Waldo Emerson

Why, why are rhymes so rare to *love*?

—Andrew Lang

A rhyme must have in it some slight element of surprise if it is to give pleasure; it need not be bizarre or curious, but it must be well used if used at all.

—Ezra Pound

Poems Related to Chapters 4 and 5

From Preface to Milton

And did these feet in ancient time
    Walk upon England's mountains green?

And was the holy Lamb of God
    On England's pleasant pastures seen?

And did the Countenance Divine
    Shine forth upon our clouded hills?
And was Jerusalem builded here
    Among these dark Satanic mills?

Bring me my Bow of burning gold!
    Bring me my Arrows of desire!
Bring me my Spear: O clouds, unfold!
    Bring me my Chariot of fire!

I will not cease from Mental Fight,
    Nor shall my Sword sleep in my hand,
Till we have built Jerusalem
    In England's green and pleasant land.

"Would to God that all the Lord's people were Prophets"
                    Numbers, xi Ch., 29v

           —William Blake (1757–1827)

1. What is the prevailing meter of this poem? What variation is there in line two and in stanza three? Can these metrical substitutions be justified?
2. What is the rhyme scheme? Where is there a change? Why? Is the rhyme masculine or feminine? What effect does it create?
3. What is the theme of the poem? Its tone? How do the meter and rhyme reinforce the meaning? What part does repetition play?

Ulysses

It little profits that an idle king,
By this still hearth, among these barren crags,[1]
Match'd with an aged wife,[2] I mete and dole
Unequal laws unto a savage race,
That hoard, and sleep, and feed, and know not me.
I cannot rest from travel: I will drink
Life to the lees: all times I have enjoy'd
Greatly, have suffer'd greatly, both with those
That loved me, and alone; on shore, and when
Thro' scudding drifts the rainy Hyades[3]
Vext the dim sea: I am become a name;
For always roaming with a hungry heart
Much have I seen and known; cities of men
And manners, climates, councils, governments,
Myself not least, but honour'd of them all;
And drunk delight of battle with my peers,
Far on the ringing plains of windy Troy.[4]

I am a part of all that I have met;
Yet all experience is an arch wherethro'
Gleams that untravell'd world, whose margin fades
For ever and for ever when I move.
How dull it is to pause, to make an end,
To rust unburnish'd, not to shine in use!
As tho' to breathe were life. Life piled on life
Were all too little, and of one to me
Little remains: but every hour is saved
From that eternal silence, something more,
A bringer of new things; and vile it were
For some three suns to store and hoard myself,
And this gray spirit yearning in desire
To follow knowledge like a sinking star,
Beyond the utmost bound of human thought.
   This is my son, mine own Telemachus,
To whom I leave the sceptre and the isle—
Well-loved of me, discerning to fulfill
This labour, by slow prudence to make mild
A rugged people, and thro' soft degrees
Subdue them to the useful and the good.
Most blameless is he, centered in the sphere
Of common duties, decent not to fail
In offices of tenderness, and pay
Meet adoration to my household gods,
When I am gone. He works his work, I mine.
   There lies the port; the vessel puffs her sail:
There gloom the dark broad seas. My mariners,
Souls that have toil'd, and wrought, and thought with me—
That ever with a frolic welcome took
The thunder and the sunshine, and opposed
Free hearts, free foreheads—you and I are old;
Old age hath yet his honour and his toil;
Death closes all: but something ere the end,
Some work of noble note, may yet be done,
Not unbecoming men that strove with Gods.
The lights begin to twinkle from the rocks:
The long day wanes: the slow moon climbs: the deep
Moans round with many voices. Come, my friends,
'Tis not too late to seek a newer world.
Push off, and sitting well in order smite
The sounding furrows; for my purpose holds
To sail beyond the sunset, and the baths
Of all the western stars, until I die.
It may be that the gulfs will wash us down:
It may be we shall touch the Happy Isles,[5]
And see the great Achilles,[6] whom we knew.

Tho' much is taken, much abides; and tho'
We are not now that strength which in old days
Moved earth and heaven, that which we are, we are;
One equal temper of heroic hearts,
Made weak by time and fate, but strong in will
To strive, to seek, to find, and not to yield.

—Alfred, Lord Tennyson (1809–1892)

---

[1] Ithaca, a rocky Ionian island of western Greece.   [2] Penelope.   [3] A cluster of stars in the constellation Taurus, believed by the ancient Greeks to indicate the coming of rainy weather.   [4] City in Asia Minor besieged for ten years by the Greeks and finally destroyed.   [5] The Islands of the Blessed identified as the Elysian Fields, where just men went after death.   [6] Greek hero of the Trojan War killed by Paris and immortalized in Homer's *Iliad*.

1. This dramatic monologue is written in iambic pentameter blank verse. By what means has Tennyson achieved flexibility and variety?

2. What examples of functional metrical substitutions can you find?

3. To communicate meaning more effectively where has the poet retarded the rhythm? Where has he accelerated it? What use has he made of onomatopoeia?

4. Although the poem deals with Greek legendary history, does its theme have universality or validity for modern times?

5. What is the speaker's attitude toward his wife? son? his people? his fellow mariners?

6. What is Ulysses' philosophy of life? Is it typically Greek? Victorian? modern?

7. What lines are eminently quotable? Does the meter help make them epigrammatic?

8. "Old age hath yet his honour and his toil." At the age of ninety Sophocles wrote his beautiful play *Oedipus at Colonus;* at eighty-four Hals painted two masterpieces of group portrait art; Yeats wrote his greatest poetry at the end of his life. Can you give other examples of the quoted line?

To the Virgins, to Make Much of Time

Gather ye rosebuds while ye may:
    Old time is still a-flying;
And this same flower that smiles to-day
    To-morrow will be dying.

The glorious lamp of heaven, the sun,
    The higher he's a-getting,
The sooner will his race be run,
    And nearer he's to setting.

That age is best which is the first,
    When youth and blood are warmer;
But being spent, the worse, and worst
    Times still succeed the former.

Then be not coy, but use your time,
    And, while ye may, go marry;
For having lost but once your prime,
    You may forever tarry.

—Robert Herrick (1591–1674)

1. What is the meter of this poem? How do the first two lines differ metrically from the rest of the poem? Why?
2. Is the rhyme masculine or feminine? Or both? Does it follow a regular pattern? Why?
3. The theme of the poem is a very popular one: *carpe diem* (Latin: "seize the day"). What is the tone of the speaker? Angry? Bitter? Friendly? Admonitory? Or what?
4. What rhymes emphasize contrast?

Fear No More

(From Cymbeline)

Fear no more the heat o' the sun
    Nor the furious winter's rages;
Thou thy worldly task hast done,
    Home art gone and ta'en thy wages:
Golden lads and girls all must,
As chimney-sweepers, come to dust.

Fear no more the frown o' the great,
    Thou art past the tyrant's stroke;
Care no more to clothe and eat;
    To thee the reed is as the oak;
The sceptre, learning, physic,[1] must
All follow this, and come to dust.

Fear no more the lightning-flash
    Nor the all-dreaded thunder-stone;[2]
Fear not slander, censure rash;
    Thou hast finished joy and moan:
All lovers young, all lovers must
Consign to thee,[3] and come to dust.

No exorciser harm thee!
Nor no witchcraft charm thee!

Ghost unlaid[4] forbear thee!
Quiet consummation have;
And renownèd by thy grave!

—William Shakespeare (1564–1616)

---

[1] Medicine, i.e., the physician.   [2] Thunderbolt.   [3] Sign the contract, i.e., yield to your condition.   [4] Wandering ghost.

1. How does the last stanza differ in meter and rhyme from the first three? Why? Is there a difference in tone and meaning?
2. What effect does the poet create in the first three stanzas by his repetitive pattern (with variations)?
3. Contrast this elegy with Housman's "With Rue My Heart Is Laden" (page 32). Does the word *golden* mean exactly the same in the two poems? Discuss.
4. Does Shakespeare's use of "chimney-sweepers" have the same connotation as Blake's in "London" (page 11)? Discuss.

Kindly Unhitch That Star, Buddy

I hardly suppose I know anybody who wouldn't rather be a
    success than a failure,
Just as I suppose every piece of crabgrass in the garden
    would much rather be an azalea,
And in celestial circles all the run-of-the-mill angels
    would rather be archangels or at least cherubim and
    seraphim,
And in the legal world all the little process-servers hope
    to grow up into great big bailiffim and sheriffim.
Indeed, everybody wants to be a wow,
But not everybody knows exactly how.
Some people think they will eventually wear diamonds
    instead of rhinestones
Only by everlastingly keeping their noses to their
    grhinestones,
And other people think they will be able to put in more
    time at Palm Beach and the Ritz
By not paying too much attention to attendance at the
    office but rather in being brilliant by starts and fits.
Some people after a full day's work sit up all night getting
    a college education by correspondence,
While others seem to think they'll get just as far by de-
    voting their evenings to the study of the difference in
    temperament between brunettance and blondance.
Some stake their all on luck,
And others put their faith in their ability to pass the buck.

In short, the world is filled with people trying to achieve
   success,
And half of them think they'll get it by saying No and half
   of them by saying Yes,
And if all the ones who say No said Yes, and vice versa,
   such is the fate of humanity that ninety-nine per cent
   of them still wouldn't be any better off than they
   were before,
Which perhaps is just as well because if everybody was a
   success nobody could be contemptuous of anybody
   else and everybody would start in all over again trying
   to be a bigger success than everybody else so they
   would have somebody to be contemptuous of and so
   on forevermore,
Because when people start hitching their wagons to a star,
That's the way they are.

—Ogden Nash (1902–1971)

1. To what extent is the humor of this poem dependent on the unexpected,
    distorted, and delayed rhymes?

A Narrow Fellow in the Grass

A narrow Fellow in the Grass
Occasionally rides—
You may have met Him—did you not
His notice sudden is—

The Grass divides as with a Comb—
A spotted shaft is seen—
And then it closes at your feet
And opens further on—

He likes a Boggy Acre
A Floor too cool for Corn—
Yet when a Boy, and Barefoot—
I more than once at Noon

Have passed, I thought, a Whip lash
Unbraiding in the Sun
When stooping to secure it
It wrinkled, and was gone—

Several of Nature's People
I know, and they know me—
I feel for them a transport
Of cordiality—

But never met this Fellow
Attended, or alone
Without a tighter breathing
And Zero at the Bone—

—Emily Dickinson (1830–1886)

1. What use does the poet make of slant rhyme?
2. Syntactically stanzas three and four as well as five and six are single sentences. Why?
3. What effect does Emily Dickinson create by the use of run-on lines in the last stanza?
4. In her poems—short lyrics—the poet usually speaks in her own person. Why is the persona in this poem a man?
5. Why does the snake stir terror in the speaker? Explain the concluding line of the poem.

The following two poems deal with a common theme, a broken love affair.

When We Two Parted

When we two parted
    In silence and tears,
Half broken-hearted
    To sever for years,
Pale grew thy cheek and cold,
    Colder thy kiss;
Truly that hour foretold
    Sorrow to this.

The dew of the morning
    Sunk chill on my brow—
It felt like the warning
    Of what I feel now.
Thy vows are all broken,
    And light is thy fame;
I hear thy name spoken,
    And share in its shame.

They name thee before me,
    A knell to mine ear;
A shudder comes o'er me—
    Why wert thou so dear?
They know not I knew thee,
    Who knew thee too well: —
Long, long shall I rue thee,
    Too deeply to tell.

In secret we met—
    In silence I grieve,
That thy heart could forget,
    Thy spirit deceive.
If I should meet thee
    After long years,
How should I greet thee?—
    With silence and tears.

—George Gordon, Lord Byron (1788–1824)

Neutral Tones

We stood by a pond that winter day,
And the sun was white, as though chidden of God,
And a few leaves lay on the starving sod;
    —They had fallen from an ash, and were gray.

Your eyes on me were as eyes that rove
Over tedious riddles of years ago;
And some words played between us to and fro
    On which lost the more by our love.

The smile on your mouth was the deadest thing
Alive enough to have strength to die;
And a grin of bitterness swept thereby
    Like an ominous bird a-wing. . . .

Since then, keen lessons that love deceives,
And wrings with wrong, have shaped to me
Your face, and the God-curst sun, and a tree,
    And a pond edged with grayish leaves.

—Thomas Hardy (1840–1928)

1. Contrast the meter in the two poems. Which rhythm do you think more suitable to the dramatic situation? Why? Discuss the meter of the last line of the Hardy poem.

2. Contrast the rhyme patterns of the two poems. Are there any feminine rhymes in the Byron poem? In Hardy's? Which is better adapted to the subject matter? Where does Hardy use an eye rhyme? Where does Byron use identical rhyme? How do these affect your emotional reaction?

3. What part do descriptive details of setting play in the two poems? What is the dominant color in Hardy's poem? Why? What effect does Hardy create by concluding the poem with a series of four images: a face, a white sun, an ash tree, and a "pond edged with grayish leaves"?

4. What is the tone in each poem? Pathetic? Sentimental? Tragic? Or what? Justify your opinion.

5. Characterize the speaker in each poem. Has the experience meant the same to each (i.e., has it influenced his outlook on life)?
6. Which poem do you prefer? Why?

To _____

Music, when soft voices die,
Vibrates in the memory—
Odours, when sweet violets sicken
Live within the sense they quicken.

Rose leaves, when the rose is dead,
Are heaped for the belovèd's bed;
And so thy thoughts, when thou art gone,
Love itself shall slumber on.

—Percy Bysshe Shelley (1792–1822)

1. What do the rhymes contribute to the antithetical meaning of the poem?

The Circus; or One View of It

Said the circus man, Oh what do you like
Best of all about my show—
The circular rings, three rings in a row,
With animals going around, around,
Tamed to go running round, around,
And around, round, around they go;
Or perhaps you like the merry-go-round,
Horses plunging sedately up,
Horses sedately plunging down,
Going around the merry-go-round;
Or perhaps you like the clown with a hoop,
Shouting, rolling the hoop around;
Or the elephants walking around in a ring
Each trunk looped to a tail's loop,
Loosely ambling around the ring;
How do you like this part of the show?
Everything's busy and on the go;
The peanut men cry out and sing,
The round fat clown rolls on the ground,
The trapeze ladies sway and swing,
The circus horses plunge around
The circular rings, three rings in a row;
Here they come, and here they go.
And here you sit, said the circus man,
Around in a circle to watch my show;

Which is show and which is you,
Now that we're here in this circus show,
Do I know? Do you know?
But hooray for the clowns and the merry-go-round,
The painted horses plunging round,
The live, proud horses stamping the ground,
And the clowns and the elephants swinging around;
Come to my show; hooray for the show,
Hooray for the circus all the way round!
Said the round exuberant circus man.
Hooray for the show! said the circus man.

—Theodore Spencer (1902–1949)

Third Avenue in Sunlight

Third Avenue in sunlight. Nature's error.
Already the bars are filled and John is there.
Beneath a plentiful lady over the mirror
He tilts his glass in the mild mahogany air.

I think of him when he first got out of college,
Serious, thin, unlikely to succeed;
For several months he hung around the Village,
Boldly T-shirted, unfettered but unfreed.

Now he confides to a stranger, "I was first scout,
And kept my glimmers peeled till after dark.
Our outfit had as its sign a bloody knout,
We met behind the museum in Central Park.

Of course, we were kids." But still those savages,
War-painted, a flap of leather at the loins,
File silently against him. Hostages
Are never taken. One summer, in Des Moines,

They entered his hotel room, tomahawks
Flashing like barracuda. He tried to pray.
Three years of treatment. Occasionally he talks
About how he almost didn't get away.

Daily the prowling sunlight whets its knife
Along the sidewalk. We almost never meet.
In the Rembrandt dark he lifts his amber life.
My bar is somewhat further down the street.

—Anthony Hecht (1923–   )

"More Light! More Light!"

Composed in the Tower before his execution
These moving verses, and being brought at that time
Painfully to the stake, submitted, declaring thus:
"I implore my God to witness that I have made no crime."

Nor was he forsaken of courage, but the death was horrible,
The sack of gunpowder failing to ignite.
His legs were blistered sticks on which the black sap
Bubbled and burst as he howled for the Kindly Light.

And that was but one, and by no means one of the worst;
Permitted at least his pitiful dignity;
And such as were by made prayers in the name of Christ,
That shall judge all men, for his soul's tranquility.

We move now to outside a German wood.
Three men are there commanded to dig a hole
In which the two Jews are ordered to lie down
And be buried alive by the third, who is a Pole.

Not light from the shrine at Weimar beyond the hill
Nor light from heaven appeared. But he did refuse.
A Lüger settled back deeply in its glove.
He was ordered to change places with the Jews.

Much casual death had drained away their souls.
The thick dirt mounted toward the quivering chin.
When only the head was exposed the order came
To dig him out again and to get back in.

No light, no light in the blue Polish eye.
When he finished a riding boot packed down the earth.
The Lüger hovered lightly in its glove.
He was shot in the belly and in three hours bled to death.

No prayers or incense rose up in those hours
Which grew to be years, and every day came mute
Ghosts from the ovens, sifting through crisp air,
And settled upon his eyes in a black soot.

                     —Anthony Hecht (1923–   )

In Bertram's Garden

Jane looks down at her organdy skirt
As if *it* somehow were the thing disgraced,
For being there, on the floor, in the dirt,

And she catches it up about her waist,
Smooths it out along one hip,
And pulls it over the crumpled slip.

On the porch, green-shuttered, cool,
Asleep is Bertram, that bronze boy,
Who, having wound her around a spool,
Sends her spinning like a toy
Out to the garden, all alone,
To sit and weep on a bench of stone.

Soon the purple dark will bruise
Lily and bleeding-heart and rose,
And the little Cupid lose
Eyes and ears and chin and nose,
And Jane lie down with others soon
Naked to the naked moon.

—Donald Justice (1925–   )

Elegy for a Nature Poet

It was in October, a favorite season,
He went for his last walk. The covered bridge,
Most natural of all the works of reason,
Received him, let him go. Along the hedge

He rattled his stick; observed the blackening bushes
In his familiar field; thought he espied
Late meadow larks; considered picking rushes
For a dry arrangement; returned home, and died

Of a catarrh caught in the autumn rains
And let go on uncared for. He was too rapt
In contemplation to recall that brains
Like his should not be kept too long uncapped

In the wet and cold weather. While we mourned,
We thought of his imprudence, and how Nature,
Whom he'd done so much for, had finally turned
Against her creature.

His gift was daily his delight, he peeled
The landscape back to show it was a story;
Any old bird or burning bush revealed
At his hands just another allegory.

Nothing too great, nothing too trivial
For him; from mountain range or humble vermin
He could extract the hidden parable—
If need be, crack the stone to get the sermon.

And now, poor man, he's gone. Without his name
The field reverts to wilderness again,
The rocks are silent, woods don't seem the same;
Demoralized small birds will fly insane.

Rude Nature, whom he loved to idealize
And would have wed, pretends she never heard
His voice at all, as, taken by surprise
At last, he goes to her without a word.

—Howard Nemerov (1920–   )

Hot Night on Water Street

A hot midsummer night on Water Street—
The boys in jeans were combing their blond hair,
Watching the girls go by on tired feet;
And an old woman with a witch's stare
Cried "Praise the Lord!" She vanished on a bus
With hissing air brakes, like an incubus.

Three hardware stores, a barbershop, a bar;
A movie playing Westerns—where I went
To see a dream of horses called *The Star*. . . .
Some day, when this uncertain continent
Is marble, and men ask what was the good
We lived by, dust may whisper "Hollywood."

Then back along the river bank on foot
By moonlight. . . . On the West Virginia side
An owlish train began to huff and hoot;
It seemed to know of something that had died.
I didn't linger—sometimes when I travel
I think I'm being followed by the Devil.

At the newsstand in the lobby, a cigar
Was talkative: "Since I've been in this town
I've seen one likely woman, and a car
As she was crossing Main Street, knocked her down."
I was a stranger here myself, I said,
And bought the *New York Times,* and went to bed.

—Louis Simpson (1923–   )

Penny Arcade

This pale and dusty palace under the El
The ragged bankers of one coin frequent,
Beggars of joy, and in a box of glass
Control the destiny of some bright event.
Men black and bitter shuffle, grin like boys,
Recovering Christmas and elaborate toys.

The clerk controls the air gun's poodle puff
Or briefly the blue excalibur of a Colt,
Sweeps alien raiders from a painted sky,
And sees supreme the tin flotilla bolt.
Hard lightning in his eye, the hero smiles,
Steady MacArthur of the doodad isles.

The trucker arrogant for his Sunday gal
Clouts the machine, is clocked as "Superman!"
The stunted negro makes the mauler whirl
Toy iron limbs; his wizen features plan
The lunge of Louis, or, no longer black,
Send to the Pampas battering Firpo back.

Some for a penny in the slot of love
Fondle the bosom of aluminum whores,
Through hollow eye of lenses dryly suck
Beatitude of blondes and fallen drawers.
For this Cithaeron wailed and Tempe sighed,
David was doomed, and young Actaeon died.

Who gather here will never move the stars,
Give law to nations, track the atom down.
For lack of love or vitamins or cash
All the red robins of their year have gone.
Here heaven ticks: the weariest tramp can buy
Glass mansions in the juke-seraphic sky.

— John Frederick Nims (1913–   )

No *vers* is *libre* for the man who wants to do a good job.

—*T.S. Eliot*

6

Modern Free Verse

All poets use rhythm, repetition, sound patterns, and parallelism. However, during the last century a number of poets have felt that the use of meter and formal stanzas patterned by rhyme restricts their freedom, and have adopted meterless poetry or *free verse* as a poetic medium of expression. The modern reader, therefore, should understand this type of poetry as well as traditional verse.

Although the King James Version of the Psalms and the Song of Songs as well as the prophetic books of Blake gave impetus to the writing of cadenced verse, the most influential free-verse work was Walt Whitman's *Leaves of Grass*, first published in 1855. In this epochal work Whitman repudiated the traditional bases of poetic form and meter, broadened the subject matter of poetry, and used colloquial speech rhythms.

Further experimentation with free verse was carried out by a group of English and American poets—the Imagists—from 1912 to 1917. Using cadenced verse, rather than regular accentual stresses, and common speech, they concentrated Whitman's expansiveness by building their short poems around concrete images or metaphors which they felt communicated emotion and thought more directly than the formally structured poem expressed in abstract language. By emancipating the twentieth-century poet from the traditional use of meter, rhyme, syntax, and even punctuation, free verse has attracted a majority of contemporary poets.

Instead of writing in uniform metrical feet, a free-verse poet loosens and varies the movement of his lines by using irregular rhythms. He employs these rhythms to reinforce his use of modern—

and particularly American—idioms. He may abandon rhyme or formal stanzaic structure. He varies the lengths of his lines, and may omit or modify punctuation and capitalization to suit his artistic purposes. Possessing a cadenced instead of a regularly stressed pattern, free verse can subtly modulate its rhythm and achieve great flexibility. By its concentration, vivid imagery, and its use of colloquial or sophisticated diction, it is capable of evoking a range of sensory, emotional, and intellectual responses. A poet who uses *cadenced verse*, therefore, occupies the middle ground between conventional scanned verse and the unmetered language of prose.

Free verse permits the writer to utilize the blank page as a painter utilizes his canvas, and to arrange his poem so that its space configuration will appeal to the eye as well as the ear and thus reinforce its mood and meaning. Poets such as e. e. cummings, in addition to creating new word coinages, use typographical devices— broken words, punctuation marks, and the like—for visual emphasis. The free-verse movement in contemporary poetry is part of the widespread experimentation carried on in the other arts—the novel, music, painting, sculpture, the dance—whose purpose is to find expressive new mediums to reinterpret the past and to explore the complexities of modern life.

Let us now read several free-verse poems by successful practitioners.

Helen

All Greece hates
the still eyes in the white face,
the lustre as of olives
where she stands,
and the white hands.

All Greece reviles *regards as vile*
the wan face when she smiles,
hating it deeper still
when it grows wan and white,
remembering past enchantments
and past ills.

Greece sees, unmoved,
God's daughter, born of love,
the beauty of cool feet
and slenderest knees,

could love indeed the maid,
only if she were laid,
white ash amid funereal cypresses. *- evergreen branches or twigs of which are used as a symbol of mourning*

—H.D. (1886–1961)

This poem deals with the hatred of the Greeks toward Helen of Troy, the most beautiful woman of antiquity, when she was returned to her husband after the Greek and Trojan war which her seductive beauty had indirectly precipitated. Lacking a regular meter and symmetrical stanzaic form, the poem still is carefully patterned. The first line of each stanza repeats the word *Greece*. The image of whiteness in the first stanza ("white face," "white hands") is a symbol of physical beauty; it changes in the second ("wan and white" smiling face) to signify an alluring emotional appeal for pardon; it is climactic in the last stanza ("white ash amid funereal cypresses") to symbolize the cold hatred of the Greeks to see her dead. Each stanza contains but two rhyming lines *(stands—hands, reviles—smiles, maid—laid)*, but these appear in different positions. In the last stanza a clash of harsh consonants (*d's, b's*, etc.) and smooth assonance (eight long è sounds) intensifies the paradoxical mood of hate, not love, engendered by faultless beauty. Helen's semidivine face may have "launch'd a thousand ships," but it also "burnt the topless towers of Ilium" and destroyed the manhood of Greece.

In a poem of only twelve lines William Carlos Williams, one of the great masters of free verse, expresses the earthiness and joyousness of life.

The Dance

In Breughel's great picture, The Kermess,
the dancers go round, they go round and
around, the squeal and the blare and the
tweedle of bagpipes, a bugle and fiddles
tipping their bellies (round as the thick-
sided glasses whose wash they impound)
their hips and their bellies off balance
to turn them. Kicking and rolling about
the Fair Grounds, swinging their butts, those
shanks must be sound to bear up under such
rollicking measures, prance as they dance
in Breughel's great picture, The Kermess.

—William Carlos Wiliams (1883–1963)

Like a continuous musical round or circular dance the material is framed in a repetitive pattern. The first and last lines are identical; words such as "bellies" and "round" are repeated. Unbroken fluidity of movement is achieved by omitting capitals at the beginning of lines (eye appeal) and using run-on lines. All the pauses are slight and are contained in the lines. The poem consists of only two sentences. The poet achieves a circular movement by the repetition of *round* and the use of occasional internal rhyme (*round—sound*; *prance—dance*); the lively activity of the peasant dance is suggested by the parallel participles *tripping, kicking, rolling,* and *rollicking.* The festive joyfulness of the music that spurs on the dancers is suggested by the onomatopoetic "squeal and the blare and the/tweedle of bagpipes, a bugle and fiddles."

Summer Remembered

Sounds sum and summon the remembering of summers.
The humming of the sun
The mumbling in the honey-suckle vine
The whirring in the clovered grass
The pizzicato plinkle of ice in an auburn
uncle's amber glass.
The whing of father's racquet and the whack
of brother's bat on cousin's ball
and calling voices call-
ing voices spilling voices. . . .

to pluck strings with fingers instead of a bow (pit' sə kä't'ō)

The munching of saltwater at the splintered dock
The slap and slop of waves on little sloops
The quarreling of oarlocks hours across the bay
The canvas sails that bleat as they
are blown. The heaving buoy bell-
ing HERE I am
HERE you are HEAR HEAR

a u-shaped device for holding oars in place

listen listen listen
The gramophone is wound
the music goes round and around
BYE BYE BLUES LINDY'S COMING
voices calling calling calling
"Children! Children! Time's Up
Time's Up"
Merrily sturdily wantonly the familial voices
cheerily chidingly call to the children TIME'S UP

and the mute children's unvoiced clamor sacks the summer air
crying Mother   Mother   are you there?

—Isabella Gardner (1915–   )

In the first two stanzas the pleasant days of childhood, symbolized by the memories of summer vacations, are recalled by a
series of sounds which are vividly communicated to us by the use
of onomatopoeia, consonance, and assonance. But the irreversible
flow of time destroys the past and its nostalgic recollections. The
children themselves grow up, and their voiceless cry for "Mother
Mother" remains unanswered, the delightful past irrecoverable.

*the formation of a word
by imitating the
natural sound
associated with the
object
i.e. tinkle
buzz*

Landing on the Moon

*a partial rhyme in which consonants in stressed
syllables are repeated but vowels are not
i.e. mocker, maker*

When in the mask of night there shone that cut,
we were riddled. A probe reached down
and stroked some nerve in us,
as if the glint of a wizard's eye, of silver,
slanted out of the mask of the unknown—
pit of riddles, the scratch-marked sky.

*a partial rhyme
in which vowel sounds
are repeated but
consonants are not*

When, albino bowl on cloth of jet,
it spilled its virile rays,
our eyes enlarged, our blood reared with the waves.
We craved its secret, but unreachable
it held away from us, chilly and frail.
Distance kept it magnate. Enigma made it white.

When we learned to read it with our rod,
reflected light revealed
a lead mirror, a bruised shield
seamed with scars and shadow-soiled.
A half-faced sycophant, its glitter borrowed,
rode around our throne.

On the moon there shines earth light
as moonlight shines upon the earth. . . .
If on its obsidian we set our weightless foot,
and sniff no wind, and lick no rain
and feel no gauze between us and the Fire,
will we trot its grassless skull, sick for the homelike shade?

Naked to the earth-beam we will be,
who have arrived to map an apparition,

who walk upon the forehead of a myth.
Can flesh rub with symbol? If our ball
be iron, and not light, our earliest wish
eclipses. Dare we land upon a dream?

—May Swenson (1919–   )

In the first three stanzas the poet depicts the hypnotic fascination the moon has held for mankind through the ages. Its mysterious appeal to primitive man is evident in ancient myth and religious
ritual. When modern scientists with their complex instruments studied
its enigmatic scarred face, it presented a challenge which twentieth-
century astronauts bravely accepted.

In the two concluding stanzas the poet speculates on the possible psychological and physical effects of landing on the moon to
colonize it or to use it as a station for exploring the solar system.
Will man "tranquilized, deserved, desensualized," an automatically
responding "test-subject," have to become a combined rocket and
robot? Will man's relentless quest for knowledge lead to his dehu-
manization?

Walt Whitman at Bear Mountain

*". . . life which does not give the preference to any other life,
of any previous period, which therefore prefers its own
existence . . ."*
—Ortega Y Gasset

Neither on horseback nor seated,
But like himself, squarely on two feet,
The poet of death and lilacs
Loafs by the footpath. Even the bronze looks alive
Where it is folded like cloth. And he seems friendly.

"Where is the Mississippi panorama
And the girl who played the piano?
Where are you, Walt?
The Open Road goes to the used-car lot.

"Where is the nation you promised?
These houses built of wood sustain
Colossal snows,
And the light above the street is sick to death.

"As for the people—see how they neglect you!
Only a poet pauses to read the inscription."

"I am here," he answered.
"It seems you have found me out.
Yet, did I not warn you that it was Myself
I advertised? Were my words not sufficiently plain?

"I gave no prescriptions,
And those who have taken my moods for prophecies
Mistake the matter."
Then, vastly amused—"Why do you reproach me?
I freely confess I am wholly disreputable.
Yet I am happy, because you have found me out."

A crocodile in wrinkled metal loafing . . .

Then all the realtors,
Pickpockets, salesmen, and the actors performing
Official scenarios,
Turned a deaf ear, for they had contracted
American dreams.

But the man who keeps a store on a lonely road,
And the housewife who knows she's dumb,
And the earth, are relieved.

All that grave weight of America
Cancelled! Like Greece and Rome.
The future in ruins!
The castles, the prisons, the cathedrals
Unbuilding, and roses
Blossoming from the stones that are not there . . .

The clouds are lifting from the high Sierras,
The Bay mists clearing.
And the angel in the gate, the flowering plum,
Dances like Italy, imagining red.

—Louis Simpson (1923–   )

This poem, written in colloquial diction and conversational rhythms, is patterned as a dialogue between the personified statue of Whitman and the author. It is a revelatory lyric in which the modern poet discovers the real Whitman and diagnoses the sickness of contemporary America. By gazing at the bronze statue of "the good gray poet" at Bear Mountain State Park in New York State, Louis Simpson tries to identify the authentic Whitman from the mystery and legends that have surrounded him. Was the author of "When Lilacs Last in the Door-Yard Bloom'd," "Song of Myself," and "Song of the Open Road" a superb lyricist, a bombastic poseur, a supreme egoist, or a cosmic prophet proclaiming the triumph of American democracy?

When the modern poet accuses Whitman of being a false prophet in his optimistic vision of the future of America, the old poet is amused at his lack of recognition by the general public, and the misinterpretation of his work by selected readers and disciples. He blandly confesses that he is not a prophet but a poetic creator of many moods: a self-advertising, disreputable egoist and loafer. By an effective, original image Simpson characterizes the poet as "A crocodile in wrinkled metal loafing. . ." (a powerful creature at home on land and sea, relaxed in the sun and deceptive in his moods).

As the modern poet has misread the old poet, the American people have been deceived by the grandiose dreams of unlimited power and world empire. To Simpson this self-aggrandizement, based on materialism and expansion, has not led us into a new Garden of Eden but has infected us with a sickness unto death. Under this "grave (heavy, dangerous, and deadly) weight" America may collapse as ancient Greece and Rome did. We must renounce our arrogance based on affluence and might. We must regain the humility of

> . . . the man who keeps a store on a lonely road,
> And the housewife who knows she's dumb,
> And the earth . . .

Only by curing ourselves of the disease of false "American dreams" and "unbuilding" our castles, prisons, and cathedrals can we really begin to live and find true happiness symbolized by "roses blossoming." In a panoramic Whitmanic vision spanning America from Bear Mountain in New York to the high Sierras in California, the poet sees the clouds lifting and the mists clearing over the Golden Gate Bridge. The magenta-colored flowering plum tree, symbol of the angel of Eden, can help us recapture the joy of Paradise regained.

Although a free-verse poem may eschew regular rhythmical and rhyme patterns and may use contemporary colloquial language, it is not simply prose chopped up and arranged arbitrarily into varied line lengths. A good free-verse poem must be evaluated in terms of its emotional and intellectual expressiveness in the same way that a traditional poem is judged. The effectiveness of a free verse poem is especially dependent on the skill of the poet in handling cadence, repetition, tone, diction, punctuation, and the shape of the poem on the page.

For Discussion

Times change and forms and their meanings alter. Thus new poems are necessary. Their forms must be discovered in the spoken, the living language of their day. . . .

—William Carlos Williams

As regarding rhythm: to compose in the sequence of the musical phrase, not in sequence of a metronome.

—Ezra Pound

Poems Related to Chapter 6

On the Beach at Night

On the beach at night,
Stands a child with her father,
Watching the east, the autumn sky.

Up through the darkness,
While ravening clouds, the burial clouds, in black masses
     spreading,
Lower sullen and fast athwart and down the sky,
Amid a transparent clear belt of ether yet left in the east,
Ascends large and calm the lord-star Jupiter;
And nigh at hand, only a very little above,
Swim the delicate sisters the Pleiades.

From the beach the child holding the hand of her father,
Those burial-clouds that lower victorious soon to devour all,
Watching, silently weeps.

Weep not, child,
Weep not, my darling,
With these kisses let me remove your tears,
The ravening clouds shall not long be victorious,
They shall not long possess the sky, they devour the
     stars only in apparition,
Jupiter shall emerge, be patient, watch again another
     night, the Pleiades shall emerge,
They are immortal, all those stars both silvery and
     golden shall shine out again,
The great stars and the little ones shall shine out again,
     they endure,
The vast immortal suns and the long-enduring pensive
     moons shall again shine.

Then dearest child mournest thou only for Jupiter?
Considerest thou alone the burial of the stars?

Something there is,
(With my lips soothing thee, adding I whisper,
I give thee the first suggestion, the problem and
    indirection,)
Something there is more immortal even than the stars,
(Many the burials, many the days and nights, passing
    away,)
Something that shall endure longer even than lustrous
    Jupiter,
Longer than sun or any revolving satellite,
Or the radiant sisters the Pleiades.

—Walt Whitman (1819–1892)

1. What is the theme of this poem? What contrasts are there? What conflicts? How are they resolved?
2. Is Whitman's handling of free verse effective? What functions do his repetitions serve?

A La Carte

Some take to liquor, some turn to prayer,
Many prefer to dance, others to gamble, and a few resort
    to gas or the gun.
(Some are lucky, and some are not.)

Name your choice, any selection from one to twenty-five:
Music from Harlem? A Viennese waltz on the slot machine
    phonograph at Jack's Bar & Grill? Or a Brahms Concerto
    over WXV?
(Many like it wild, others sweet.)

Champagne for supper, murder for breakfast, romance for
    lunch and terror for tea,
This is not the first time, nor will it be the last time
    the world has gone to hell.
(Some can take it, and some cannot.)

—Kenneth Fearing (1902–1961)

1. How has Fearing imposed a pattern on this free-verse poem?
2. What is its theme?

Ars Poetica (*the art of poetry*)

A poem should be palpable and mute
As a globed fruit,

Dumb
As old medallions to the thumb,

Silent as the sleeve-worn stone
Of casement ledges where the moss has grown—

A poem should be wordless
As the flight of birds.

*

A poem should be motionless in time
As the moon climbs,

Leaving, as the moon releases
Twig by twig the night-entangled trees,

Leaving, as the moon behind the winter leaves,
Memory by memory the mind—

A poem should be motionless in time
As the moon climbs.

*

A poem should be equal to:
Not true.

For all the history of grief
An empty doorway and a maple leaf.

For love
The leaning grasses and two lights above the sea—

A poem should not mean
But be.

—Archibald MacLeish (1892–   )

Although the line lengths vary in the poem, it is artfully shaped into three sections, each consisting of four couplets.

1. What characteristic of poetry is stressed in each section? How do you resolve MacLeish's paradoxes that a poem should be "wordless," "motionless," "not true"?

2. In what sense is MacLeish using the words "mean" and "be" in the last couplet? Is the poem an attack on didacticism in poetry? A plea for concrete images to awaken our deepest emotional memories? A plea for symbolism? Doesn't this poem have "meaning," or does the poet contradict himself?

Skinny Poem

Skinny
poem,
all
your
ribs
showing
even
without
a
deep
breath
thin
legs
rotted
with
disease.

Live
here!
on
this
page,
barely
making
it,
like
the
mass
of
mankind.
—Lou Lipsitz (1938–   )

1. How has the space pattern of this poem reinforced the theme?

Southern Mansion

Poplars are standing there still as death
And ghosts of dead men
Meet their ladies walking

Two by two beneath the shade
And standing on the marble steps.

There is a sound of music echoing
Through the open door
And in the field there is
Another sound tinkling in the cotton:
Chains of bondmen dragging on the ground.

The years go back with an iron clank,
A hand is on the gate,
A dry leaf trembles on the wall.
Ghosts are walking.
They have broken roses down
And poplars stand there still as death.

                    —Arna Bontemps (1902–   )

1. What contrasts are there in this poem?
2. What is the function of the nature images: poplars, a dry leaf, broken roses?

Travelling Through the Dark

Travelling through the dark I found a deer
dead on the edge of the Wilson River road.
It is usually best to roll them into the canyon:
that road is narrow; to swerve might make more dead.

By glow of the tail-light I stumbled back of the car
and stood by the head, a doe, a recent killing;
she had stiffened already, almost cold.
I dragged her off; she was large in the belly.

My fingers touching her side brought me the reason—
her side was warm; her fawn lay there waiting,
alive, still, never to be born.
Beside that mountain road I hesitated.

The car aimed ahead its lowered parking lights;
under the hood purred the steady engine.
I stood in the glare of the warm exhaust turning red;
around our group I could hear the wilderness listen.

I thought hard for us all—my only swerving—
then pushed her over the edge into the river.

                    —William Stafford (1914–   )

1. Why is "Travelling Through the Dark" a better title for this poem than, say, "Driving at Night"?
2. What is the central dilemma faced by the speaker? Why does he hesitate before he resolves it? Is he satisfied with his solution?
3. What emotions does this poem stir in the reader? Pity? Terror? The mysteriousness of life and death? All three?
4. Comment on the poet's use of "still" (line 11) and explain line 17 ("I thought hard for us all—my only swerving—").
5. What does the poet achieve by attributing life to the car and the wilderness?
6. Compare this poem with Karl Shapiro's "Auto Wreck" (page 1) and Richard Eberhart's "The Groundhog" (page 224).

The Geranium

When I put her out, once, by the garbage pail,
She looked so limp and bedraggled,
So foolish and trusting, like a sick poodle,
Or a wizened aster in late September, *[dried, shriveled]*
I brought her back in again
For a new routine—
Vitamins, water, and whatever
Sustenance seemed sensible
At the time: she'd lived
So long on gin, bobbie pins, half-smoked cigars, dead beer,
Her shriveled petals falling
On the faded carpet, the stale
Steak grease stuck to her fuzzy leaves.
(Dried-out, she creaked like a tulip.)

The things she endured!—
The dumb dames shrieking half the night
Or the two of us, alone, both seedy, *[— containing or going to seed, shabby and run-down]*
Me breathing booze at her,
She leaning out of her pot toward the window.

Near the end, she seemed almost to hear me—
And that was scary—
So when that snuffling cretin of a maid *[deficiency of thyroid secretion resulting in deformity and idiocy]*
Threw her, pot and all, into the trash-can,
I said nothing.

But I sacked the presumptuous hag the next week, *[taking undue liberties, proud]*
I was that lonely.

—Theodore Roethke (1908–1963)

The Idiot

"That cop was powerful mean.
First he called me, 'Black boy.'
Then he punched me in the face
and drug me by the collar to a wall
and made me lean against it with my hands spread
while he searched me,
and all the time he searched me
he kicked me and cuffed me and cussed me.

I was mad enough
to lay him out,
and would've did it, only
I didn't want to hurt his feelings,
and lose the good will
of the good white folks downtown,
who hired him."

—Dudley Randall (1914–   )

Popcorn

for Frank O'Hara

it is very late.
my wife and i are sitting around
with nothing to do but watch
the old dead television set
and all the late movies
that were going to be over
are over
and so she says
I have a piece of popcorn
thats as big as a house
in my head, but I want
it to get bigger

and i say because
shes trying so hard,
Can you get it as big as
an old red warehouse
with peeling paint
and dirty trucks inside?

and she says Oh Yeah!

and i say Can you get it
as big as PS 93 on a friday
when all the kids are just
coming out for the weekend?

and she says Oh Yeah, Yeah!

and i give her the final
idea and say Now can you get it
as big as Yankee Stadium
with a capacity crowd,
last of the ninth, two
out, Yanks behind, and Maris
telling everyone hes going
to belt it out of the park?

and she says Oh Yeah, Yeah, Yeah!

But wait, she says.
something's beginning to happen
it's burning

    —Phillip Hey (1942–   )

Dedication for a Plot of Ground

This plot of ground
facing the waters of this inlet
is dedicated to the living presence of
Emily Dickinson Wellcome[1]
who was born in England; married;
lost her husband and with
her five year old son
sailed for New York in a two-master;
was driven to the Azores;
ran adrift on Fire Island shoal,
met her second husband
in a Brooklyn boarding house,
went with him to Puerto Rico
bore three more children, lost
her second husband, lived hard
for eight years in St. Thomas,
Puerto Rico, San Domingo, followed
the oldest son to New York,
lost her daughter, lost her "baby,"
seized the two boys of
the oldest son by the second marriage

mothered them—they being
motherless—fought for them
against the other grandmother
and the aunts, brought them here
summer after summer, defended
herself here against thieves,
storms, sun, fire,
against flies, against girls
that came smelling about, against
drought, against weeds, storm-tides,
neighbors, weasels that stole her chickens,
against the weakness of her own hands,
against the growing strength of
the boys, against wind, against
the stones, against trespassers,
against rents, against her own mind.

She grubbed this earth with her own hands,
domineered over this grass plot,
blackguarded her oldest son
into buying it, lived here fifteen years,
attained a final loneliness and—

If you can bring nothing to this place
but your carcass, keep out.

—William Carlos Williams (1883–1963)

---

[1] Williams' grandmother.

The 3 Corners of Reality

One might speak to great length
of the three corners of reality—
what was seen, what was thought
to be seen, and what was thought
ought to be seen—and forget it.
Or one might argue the relative
merits of looking back, as opposed
to looking ahead or looking in on,
and in no time be willing to end it.
Who has that kind of time to spend?
—they asked when they had the time
to ask; and it seems there was a movie
which flickered successfully
in behalf of these very questions.
Ever, the very very are among us,

appearing to ask for our lives.
Well, I give them the right answers:

"How do you recognize poetry?"
—It looks like poetry.
"How is prose different from poetry?"
—Prose goes by another name.
"Why do you write poetry?"
—Because it feels so good.

And I freely give samples of my pleasing.

—Marvin Bell (1937–   )

A Supermarket in California

What thought I have of you tonight, Walt Whitman, for
I walked down the sidestreets under the trees with a headache
self-conscious looking at the full moon.

In my hungry fatigue, and shopping for images, I went
into the neon fruit supermarket, dreaming of your enumerations!
What peaches and what penumbras; Whole families
shopping at night! Aisles full of husbands! Wives in the
avocados, babies in the tomatoes!—and you, Garcia Lorca,
what were you doing down by the watermelons?

I saw you, Walt Whitman, childless, lonely old grubber,
poking among the meats in the refrigerator and eyeing the
grocery boys.
I heard you asking questions of each: Who killed the
pork chops? What price bananas? Are you my Angel?
I wandered in and out of the brilliant stacks of cans
following you, and followed in my imagination by the store
detective.
We strode down the open corridors together in our
solitary fancy tasting artichokes, possessing every frozen
delicacy, and never passing the cashier.

Where are we going, Walt Whitman? The doors close in
an hour. Which way does your beard point tonight?
(I touch your book and dream of our odyssey in the
supermarket and feel absurd.)
Will we walk all night through solitary streets? The trees
add shade to shade, lights out in the houses, we'll both be
lonely.

    Will we stroll dreaming of the lost America of love past
blue automobiles in driveways, home to our silent cottage?
    Ah, dear father, graybeard, lonely old courage-teacher,
what America did you have when <u>Charon</u> quit poling his ferry
and you got out on a smoking bank and stood watching the
boat disappear on the black waters of <u>Lethe</u>?

River of forgetfulness
in Hades
                                       Berkeley 1955
                      —Allen Ginsberg (1926–   )

What Were They Like?

1)   Did the people of Viet Nam
      use lanterns of stone?
2)   Did they hold ceremonies
      to reverence the opening of buds?
3)   Were they inclined to quiet laughter?
4)   Did they use bone and ivory,
      jade and silver, for ornament?
5)   Had they an epic poem?
6)   Did they distinguish between speech and singing?

1)   Sir, their light hearts turned to stone.
      It is not remembered whether in gardens
      stone lanterns illumined pleasant ways.
2)   Perhaps they gathered once to delight in blossom,
      but after the children were killed
      there were no more buds.
3)   Sir, laughter is bitter to the burned mouth.
4)   A dream ago, perhaps. Ornament is for joy.
      All the bones were charred.
5)   It is not remembered. Remember,
      most were peasants; their life
      was in rice and bamboo.
      When peaceful clouds were reflected in the paddies
      and the water buffalo stepped surely along terraces,
      maybe fathers told their sons old tales.
      When bombs smashed those mirrors
      there was time only to scream.
6)   There is an echo yet
      of their speech which was like a song.
      It was reported their singing resembled
      the flight of moths in moonlight.
      Who can say? It is silent now.

                    —Denise Levertov (1923–   )

Polonius: What do you read, my lord?
Hamlet: Words, words, words.

—William Shakespeare

7
Diction and Tone
as Related to Theme

Degas, the French painter, once remarked to his friend Mallarmé, the poet: "Yours is a hellish craft. I can't manage to say what I want, and yet I'm full of ideas. . . ." Mallarmé replied: "My dear Degas, one doesn't make poetry with ideas, but with words."

What colors are to the painter, notes to the musician, words are to the poet—the basic element of his craft. The ability to use all the resources of language effectively is the aim of any skillful poet. W. H. Auden has suggested that the only right answer that an aspirant to poetry should give to the question, "Why do you want to write poetry?" should be, "I like hanging around words listening to what they say."

A good poet always uses words with precision. Whether he uses archaic words, modern ones, coined words, simple or difficult ones, colloquial or formal diction, his purpose is always to achieve the utmost clarity of expression. What we must understand is that the meaning of a word depends on the poem in which it is used, its relationship to other words, and its appropriateness in context.

When Shakespeare in his "Sonnet 73" (page 145) describes autumn,

> When yellow leaves, or none, or few, do hang
> Upon those boughs which shake against the cold,

he is using simple language but with poetic precision. In autumn some trees still retain their yellow foliage, some have but *few* leaves, and some are stripped bare. The leaves *hang* (word which suggests their lifelessness) and the boughs *shake* (not *tremble,* which would connote life). In "The Sick Rose" Blake does not use the word *bug* to describe the insect destroying the rose but the more powerful word *worm* which carries horrifying implications of death and suggestions of mystery as it flies *invisible* in the night.

Like the scientist, the poet may use words literally, that is, he may limit the meaning of the words to their dictionary definition (*denotation*). Unlike the scientist, however, the poet also uses words for *connotation,* or the emotional associations or overtones of meaning that words have accumulated through usage. *Home* is a more emotionally evocative word than *house; mother,* than *mom; beauty,* than *prettiness.* Sensitive to the response of the reader to a word in a particular context, the poet takes advantage of the clouds of glory that familiar words trail. Sometimes the hidden power within a word is released by its juxtaposition with other words or by its metaphorical use. Consider the beautiful effectiveness of the following stanza through the Elizabethan poet's connotative diction.

> Beauty is but a flower
> Which wrinkles will devour;
> Brightness falls from the air;
> Queens have died young and fair;
> Dust hath closed Helen's eye.
> I am sick, I must die.
> *Lord, have mercy on us!*

(from Thomas Nashe's "In Time of Pestilence")

The poet will always choose words that are appropriate to his material; usually he will combine denotation and connotation. To establish tone and to communicate theme, he must carefully control his diction. In the following poem Melville depicts the execution of John Brown as a symbolic omen of the inevitability of the Civil War. He makes full use of the verbal resources of language by using the denotative capacities of words such as *beam, law,* and *cap,* but liberates the emotional potency contained in the words *Shenandoah, veils,* and *weird.*

The Portent

> Hanging from the beam,
>   Slowly swaying (such the law),
> Gaunt the shadow on your green,
>   Shenandoah!

The cut is on the crown
   (Lo, John Brown),
And the stabs shall heal no more.
Hidden in the cap
   Is the anguish none can draw;
So your future veils its face,
   Shenandoah!
But the streaming beard is shown
   (Weird John Brown),
The meteor of the war.

   —Herman Melville (1819–1891)

For Americans in the North and the South the word *Shenan-doah*—both the river and the valley—is fringed with emotional associations for many reasons: its beautiful scenery and natural wonders, its connection with the raid of John Brown at Harper's Ferry and his execution, its connection with many important battles in the Civil War, its celebration in ballads and songs. Its resonant euphonious sound echoes ironically and portentously in the poem. The hood over John Brown's head as he dangles from the gallows "veils" (covers) not only his anguished face but also the ominous future of the divided nation. The word *weird* has multiple meanings as used in the context of the poem, all relevant to its theme: this irrevocable act will bring on the unavoidable fratricidal conflict. Literally, John Brown was a "weird" (strange) character, an anti-slavery fanatic who in reprisal murdered five people in Kansas but also a courageous martyr who freely gave his life for a noble cause. But the word *weird* also suggests *fateful, prophetic* (cf. with the weird sisters in *Macbeth*) and *inevitable*. Melville intensifies the latter meaning by comparing "the streaming beard" of John Brown to an ominius meteor flashing across the sky. Thus, by using the various resources of language—denotation, connotation, multiple meanings, and metaphor—Melville enriches his diction to make a forceful statement of his theme.

In a similar manner Tennyson handles words effectively in the next poem.

The Eagle

He clasps the crag with crooked hands;
Close to the sun in lonely lands,
Ring'd with the azure world, he stands.
The wrinkled sea beneath him crawls;
He watches from his mountain walls,
And like a thunderbolt he falls.

   —Alfred, Lord Tennyson (1809–1892)

In this succinct descriptive poem Tennyson expresses the power and strength of the bird by the metaphoric phrase "crooked hands." (The harsh alliteration of the four c (k) sounds helps reinforce the concept.) The word *lonely* suggests the proud superiority of the bird, for "close to the sun" he is perched higher than any other bird. The word *ringed* describes him in the center of a vast azure circle of sky, his hunting ground for prey. From his aerial perspective of the mountain walls his keen eyes observe the waves below as "The *wrinkled* sea beneath him crawls." In the last line, with the lightning speed and destructiveness of a thunderbolt, the eagle swoops down upon his prey.

A question frequently raised by poets and critics is whether the language of poetry is essentially different from that of prose. The discussion has sometimes been confused by two different interpretations given to the phrase "poetic diction." To Wordsworth it meant the artificial language popular with neo-classic poets of the eighteenth century who tried to avoid the use of common or "vulgar" words by epithets, circumlocutions, personifications, or elegant classical allusions. In the poetry of Thomson and Pope, sheep became "the bleating kind," "the soft fearful people," or "the harmless race"; fish were "the finny prey" or "the scaly breed"; birds were "the fowls of heaven"; the sun was Sol or Phoebus; wine was "the frantic juice that Bacchus poured." In reaction against this stylized use of language and its degeneration into a set of conventional mannerisms, Wordsworth used the term "poetic diction" in a pejorative sense. By discrediting the concept that a special "elevated" language was needed for poetic expression, he stressed the point that there is no "*essential* difference between the language of prose and metrical composition."

The romantic poets that followed Wordsworth's lead liberated the diction of poetry from this neo-classic bondage. Today we apply the term "poetic diction" (without any disparaging sense attached to it) to any words used in poetry that stir the aesthetic imagination. Modern poets have returned to the tradition of Chaucer, Shakespeare, Blake, Burns, and Whitman that there are no special words suitable for poetry, that all the resources of language are available to the poet. A word is judged by its relationship to other words in a verse, its denotation and connotation, its metaphorical implications, and its suitability to mood and subject matter. All of these factors (including sound and rhythmic appropriateness) must be taken into consideration in evaluating the communicative effectiveness of diction in poetry.

Although Wordsworth's declared purpose, expressed in his rev-

olutionary poetic manifesto, the Preface to the Second Edition of
Lyrical Ballads (1800), "was to imitate, and, as far as possible, to adopt
the very language of men," his actual practice sometimes belied his
aim. Eminently successful in using simple and even colloquial diction
in many of his shorter lyrics, he found himself compelled in his
longer and more philosophical poems to resort to the Latinistic diction and polyphonic harmonies of Milton's style.

The idiom of poetry reflecting the sensibility of an age changes
from period to period. French influences after the Norman conquest
played an important part in influencing the diction of Chaucer. The
Elizabethan poets in the excitement of the Renaissance reveled in
verbal extravagance, coined many new words, and delighted in far-
fetched puns. The metaphysical poets of the seventeenth century
living in a transitional period of new scientific discoveries in many
fields expressed their amorous emotions and even their mystical
religious views in scientific terminology and daring conceits (elaborated metaphors). During the eighteenth century emotional restraint
and poetic decorum became the accepted virtues of poetic expression
in an age of rationalism. Within the confines of the heroic couplet
poets appealed to the mind by writing didactic and satirical poems
replete with personified abstractions and periphrastic epithets. In the
revolutionary nineteenth century subjective, rebel romantic poets such
as Shelley and Byron swept away all this neo-classicism with their
emotional diction which finally degenerated later in the century into
the melodic but often empty flamboyance of Swinburne's language.

Contemporary poets—living in an age of bewildering change,
in an age of anxiety in which traditional values have collapsed—speak
with many voices. Recognizing that the very nature of language is
complex and ambiguous, some modern poets such as T. S. Eliot, W. H.
Auden, and Robert Lowell feel closer to the subtle intellectualities of
the seventeenth-century metaphysical poets rather than the confident
rationalism of the eighteenth century. To express the fragmentation
of the modern world, these poets use contemporary diction, but it
is often dense with complexity because of its overtones of symbolism,
irony, and paradox. Others such as Carl Sandburg, William Carlos
Williams, Allen Ginsberg and the so-called "beat" poets find the
romantic emotionalism and the colloquial American diction that stem
from Walt Whitman suitable mediums of poetic expression. Others
such as Gerard Manley Hopkins, Wallace Stevens, and e. e. cummings
have experimented extensively with language—coining new words,
stretching them into new compounds, truncating them—to achieve
a personal vivid mode of poetic communication.

As the idiom of poetry changes over the years so does the

meaning of individual words. Many words have dropped out of the language, and new ones are continually being added. It is important, then, that the alert reader be sensitive to the meaning and use of particular words in the context of the poem and in the period of its composition. When King Lear refers to himself as a *fond* old man, he does not mean "loveable" but "foolish." In Shakespeare's day a *partisan* is a pike or staff, and *paddock* is a toad. In the opening line of "The Garden," "How vainly men themselves amaze," Marvell uses the word *amaze* to mean "bewilder, perplex, or craze" (from lost in a maze or labyrinth), not to mean "surprise." The modern reader who does not familiarize himself with the seventeenth-century usage of the words in the following poem misses much of the meaning.

Virtue

Sweet day, so cool, so calm, so bright,
  The bridal of the earth and sky,
The dew shall weep thy fall to-night,
  For thou must die.

Sweet rose, whose hue, angry[1] and brave,[2]
  Bids the rash gazer wipe his eye,
Thy root is ever in its grave,
  And thou must die.

Sweet spring, full of sweet days and roses,
  A box where sweets compacted lie,
My music[3] shows ye have your closes[4]
  And all must die.

Only a sweet and virtuous soul,
  Like seasoned timber, never gives;
But though the whole world turn to coal,[5]
  Then chiefly lives.

—George Herbert (1593–1633)

---

[1] Red. [2] Striking. [3] Refers to these verses he has written. [4] Close as used here means the conclusion of a musical phrase or movement. [5] Burn to ashes ("But the day of the Lord will come as a thief in the night . . . the earth also and the works that are therein shall be burned up." 2 Peter 3:10).

A poet not only exploits the potential richness and multiple meanings of words, but also, for a particular aesthetic purpose, resurrects archaic words. Spenser, the Renaissance poet, to give his poetic allegory *The Faerie Queen* the atmosphere of medieval chivalry, used many Middle English words derived from Chaucer. In "The Rime of the Ancient Mariner" Coleridge used such archaic words as *eftsoons* (quickly), *gramercy* (an exclamation of thanks or surprise), *silly* (buckets: empty, useless) to give his poem the flavor of an old folk ballad. Keats followed the same tradition in his "La Belle Dame Sans Merci" (page 316).

By *tone* in poetry we mean the writer's or speaker's attitude toward his material, his audience, or himself. It is the emotional coloring that pervades a poem, sometimes clear, sometimes elusive but important to an understanding of its meaning. In speech we indicate tone usually by pitch or inflection of the voice and sometimes reinforce it by facial expression or gesture. A coach may compliment a player by saying, "That was a great play," in a serious tone. Uttering the same words but stressing *great* in a sarcastic tone, he expresses his scornful criticism. Since poetry is in great measure the communication in language of emotional and intellectual attitudes, the problem of establishing appropriate tone is as important to the poet as understanding it is to the reader. For example, if one were to take W. H. Auden's poem "The Unknown Citizen" (page 192) literally instead of ironically, he would completely misinterpret it.

How does a poet establish tone in a poem? How does a reader determine whether the tone is serious, mocking, reverent, playful, defiant, or philosophic? The poet uses many resources: diction, imagery, metaphor, exaggeration, understatement, and rhythm to suggest tone; and if he is successful, the alert reader will respond to the suggestiveness of the material and its poetic patterning. Tone is the final by-product of the sense content and its organization, the key to an intelligent reading and often an evaluation of a poem.

In considering the question of tone, the reader must take into consideration the speaker in the poem and his voice. Is he the author or a character created, a persona who speaks for the author? What is the attitude of the author and reader toward the speaker? Friendly? Hostile? Sympathetic? To whom is he addressing himself? (That is, what is the dramatic situation?) How does he express himself (in what tone of voice)? Is it intimate, forceful, casual, heroic, indignant? Let us consider two poems that deal with the same theme, the attitude toward death and immortality, to see how a poet manipulates and controls tone.

Although Donne's sonnet "Death, Be Not Proud" (page 163) and Emily Dickinson's "Because I Could Not Stop for Death" both deal with the same subject matter, they are very different in tone. The speaker in Donne's sonnet is a deeply religious and philosophic person (probably the poet himself who was the dean of St. Paul's and one of England's most eloquent preachers). To allay our fears of death, he speaks in a bold, defiant voice to his "mighty and dreadful" adversary in order to deflate him. Like Burns addressing the devil, the speaker even feels sorry for his deluded antagonist, "poor Death." By logic the speaker justifies his attitude of fearless derision. If, after rest and sleep, we rise up refreshed, then after the last "short sleep" when our souls are freed we shall awaken even more pleasurably into eternal life. Death is the slave of fate, chance, war, and sickness, not the master. The challenging tone of the opening line is echoed by the defiant paradox of the conclusion, "Death, thou shalt die."

Because I Could Not Stop for Death

Because I could not stop for Death—
He kindly stopped for me—
The Carriage held but just Ourselves—
And Immortality—

We slowly drove—He knew no haste
And I had put away
My labor and my leisure too,
For His Civility—

We passed the School, where Children strove
At Recess—in the Ring—
We passed the Fields of Gazing Grain—
We passed the Setting Sun—

Or rather—He passed Us—
The Dews drew quivering and chill—
For only Gossamer,[1] my Gown—
My Tippet[2]—only Tulle[3]—

We paused before a House that seemed
A swelling of the Ground—
The Roof was scarcely visible—
The Cornice—in the Ground—

Since then—'tis Centuries—and yet
Feels shorter than the Day
I first surmised the Horses' Heads
Were toward Eternity—

—Emily Dickinson (1830–1886)

---

[1] Gauzelike fabric.   [2] A scarf.   [3] Thin fine net commonly of silk.

Emily Dickinson's poem is in the form of an allegory in which death, personified as a courteous gentleman, takes a lady out for a drive. The tone of the speaker, reinforced by understatement and a chilling irony, is casual and quiet. Her carefully chosen diction and sharp images play an important part in establishing this tone. Too busy with the complex, ambivalent experience of living—"labor" (work and pain) and "leisure" (pleasure)—she did not "stop" (cease her activities), but with civil politeness he "kindly" (ironic understatement) "stopped" (visited, invited her) and ended both pain and pleasure. Donne diminishes the tremendousness of death by deflating a boastful enemy; Emily Dickinson does so by presenting him as a genteel escort with irreproachable manners. By having immortality ride as simply another passenger (the eternal chaperone?) in the coach, she keeps the action in the homely framework of an everyday occurrence, a leisurely ride with a suitor. In the three images of the third stanza she symbolizes the whole cycle ("in the Ring") of human existence from which death separates us: the innocent delights of childhood sports and competition ("strove/at Recess"; in other versions she had used "played" and "at wrestling in a ring"); the ripe experience of maturity and its awareness of mortality ("the Fields of Gazing Grain"); and the approach of death ("the Setting Sun"). With dignified restraint she suggests the horror of death by the damp chill that penetrates her gauzy garments and her glimpse of the strange buried "House," the grave. In the concluding stanza she suggests the modern concept of the relativity of time, which expands or contracts depending upon the significance of human experience. The enormous importance of the day of death is implied by comparing it to the uneventful centuries of Eternity. The philosophic conclusion is toned down by the earthy, domestic image of the rider's last view, "the Horses' Heads." Diction and metaphor have contributed effectively to the establishment of the total tonal pattern.

If the careful control of tone can contribute to the success of a poem, failure in the manipulation of tone can destroy its effectiveness. Again let us consider two poems that deal with a similar theme, that of a rejected lover. The following poem was printed by Tennyson in 1830 but omitted in later editions of his works.

To _____

> Sainted Juliet! dearest name!
> If to love be life alone,
> Divinest Juliet,
> I love thee, and live; and yet
> Love unreturned is like the fragrant flame

Folding the slaughter of the sacrifice
    Offered to gods upon an altar-throne;
My heart is lighted at thine eyes,
Changed into fire, and blown about with sighs.

    —Alfred, Lord Tennyson (1809–1892)

The attempt of the poet to make us share his pangs of unre-
quited love fails and the tone, instead of being tragic, becomes sentimental. The exaggerated epithets he applies to his beloved—
"sainted" and "divinest"—receive no support from the poem; he expects us to take them at their face value. The juxtaposition of the
word *fragrant* with *slaughter* is incongruous. The hackneyed conceit
of the last two lines is mawkish.

Contrast with this failure in handling tone Sir John Suckling's
"Song: Why So Pale and Wan, Fond Lover?" (page 50). Here the poet
creates an intelligent, sophisticated character as the speaker who gives
advice to a rejected lover. The tone is rational, worldly, and witty.
Artfully constructed, colloquial in diction, sustained in tone, the poem
is a complete success.

The alert reader familiar with the poet's use of diction, imagery,
irony, and understatement will usually find little difficulty in accurately
determining tone. However, occasionally he will encounter a poem
which may puzzle him by its ambiguity of tone. If he reads it literally,
he gets one impression; but some subtle suggestions in the poem may
be disturbing and imply a different tone and therefore another meaning. Such a poem is the following.

Holy Thursday—I

'Twas on a Holy Thursday, their innocent faces clean,
The children walking two & two, in red & blue & green,
Grey-headed beadles walk'd before, with wands as white as
    snow,
Till into the high dome of Paul's they like Thames' waters flow.

O what a multitude they seem'd, these flowers of London town!
Seated in companies they sit with radiance all their own.
The hum of multitudes was there, but multitudes of lambs,
Thousands of little boys & girls raising their innocent hands.

Now like a mighty wind they raise to heaven the voice of song,
Or like harmonious thunderings the seats of Heaven among.
Beneath them sit the aged men, wise guardians of the poor;
Then cherish pity, lest you drive an angel from your door.

    —William Blake (1757–1827)

On Ascension Day, the Thursday forty days after Easter commemorating Christ's ascension, it was customary for the charity children in London to be taken to St. Paul's Cathedral in London. Who is the speaker in this poem? Is it the poet speaking ironically or a naive onlooker who is sincerely impressed by the beauty of childhood innocence and the goodness and pity shown by the "wise guardians of the poor"? Both readings are possible. If we accept at face value only the latter reading, we neglect the overtones of irony suggested by the imagery, metaphors, and rhythm as well as Blake's condemnation of the exploitation of England's poor expressed powerfully in other poems. This poem is one of the "Songs of Innocence," not of mature experience. The speaker is probably a sentimental, respectable London citizen who contributes to charity. The cheerful lilting rhythm of the poem, reinforced by the rhyming couplets, aptly expresses his mood of happy benevolence. Even though we view the scene through his sensibility, we sense several jarring details in his idyllic vision. The dirt, poverty, and suffering of the children are not exposed when they are on parade; their faces have been scrubbed clean; they are dressed in cheap, colorful charity garments—red, blue, and green; they walk regimented, two by two, led by "grey-headed beadles" with "white wands," symbols of authority and punishment. The beauty, freedom, and joyousness denied to these institutionalized children is suggested by nature comparisons: a flowing river, flowers, innocent lambs, and a mighty wind. The Christian hymns they sing are not songs of thanks for the kindness of the Church but "thunderings" of (perhaps protesting) angels. Are the aged beadles who sit *below* the innocent children really "wise guardians of the poor"? The didactic tag which completes the poem may express an evangelical truth but may also be bitter irony.

In the companion poem that Blake wrote in "Songs of Experience" there is no ambiguity of tone. In the accents of a biblical prophet the bard denounces the existence of poverty and the suffering of children "in a rich and fruitful land." Believing "in the fatherhood of God" and the equal rights of all to share in the bounties of nature, he is appalled by the sight of destitute children living in the bleak, eternal winter of poverty in the richest nation in the world.

Holy Thursday—II

Is this a holy thing to see
In a rich and fruitful land,
Babes reduc'd to misery,
Fed with cold and usurous hand?

Is that trembling cry a song?
Can it be a song of joy?
And so many children poor?
It is a land of poverty!

And their sun does never shine,
And their fields are bleak & bare,
And their ways are fill'd with thorns:
It is eternal winter there.

For where-e'er the sun does shine,
And where-e'er the rain does fall,
Babe can never hunger there,
Nor poverty the mind appall.

—William Blake (1757–1827)

Tone may be sustained in a poem or it may change. However, a shift in tone must be authentically justified and consciously patterned for purposes of contrast or shock effect. Donne's sonnet "If Poisonous Minerals" (page 169) is organized on a contrast pattern. In the first eight lines the poet establishes a tone of philosophic speculation by his Joblike questioning of God's purpose in punishing rational man and not the lower orders of creation. In the last six lines the tone shifts to an emotional plea for mercy to the confessed sinner. In the following poem the change in tone is manipulated by a shift in point of view from the first-person participant in the action to the sympathetic third-person commentator for the purpose of shocking the surprised reader into an awareness of a domestic tragedy.

Nora Criona

I have looked him round and looked him through,
Know everything that he will do
In such a case, and such a case,
And when a frown comes on his face
I dream of it, and when a smile
I trace its sources in a while.

He cannot do a thing but I
Peep and find the reason why:
Because I love him, and I seek,
Every evening in the week,
To peep behind his frowning eye

With little query, little pry,
And make him if a woman can
Happier than any man.

Yesterday he gripped her tight
And cut her throat—and serve her right!

—James Stephens (1882–1950)

Such shifts in tone are not only justified but essential to the effective communication of meaning.

Let us examine two modern poems that effectively communicate theme by the skillful manipulation of tone.

Janet Waking

Beautifully Janet slept
Till it was deeply morning. She woke then
And thought about her dainty-feathered hen,
To see how it had kept.

One kiss she gave her mother,
Only a small one gave she to her daddy
Who would have kissed each curl of his shining baby;
No kiss at all for her brother.

"Old Chucky, Old Chucky!" she cried,
Running on little pink feet upon the grass
To Chucky's house, and listening. But alas,
Her Chucky had died.

It was a transmogrifying[1] bee
Came droning down on Chucky's old bald head
And sat and put the poison. It scarcely bled,
But how exceedingly

And purply did the knot
Swell with the venom and communicate
Its rigor! Now the poor comb stood up straight
But Chucky did not.

So there was Janet
Kneeling on the wet grass, crying her brown hen
(Translated far beyond the daughters of men)
To rise and walk upon it.

And weeping fast as she had breath
Janet implored us, "Wake her from her sleep!"
And would not be instructed in how deep
Was the forgetful kingdom of death.

—John Crowe Ransom (1888–   )

---

[1] Changing or transforming (a humorous coinage from transmogrify).

A poem dealing with a child's grief at the death of a pet could easily degenerate into sentimentality; but the poet by his objective treatment, careful use of diction, and shifts in tone has avoided this pitfall. The speaker in the poem is a sympathetic (almost doting), intelligent father with a sense of humor. He understands the difference between a child's heartbreaking bewilderment at her first experience with death and the adult's acceptance of mortality. To the innocent romantic child, her brown "dainty-feathered hen" would keep forever, and its sudden death was tragic. To the adult, bald-headed "old Chucky" was comical in life and ridiculous in death.

In the description of the sleeping Janet in stanza one, the beautiful and deep love of the father for his child is established by simple, serious diction. The following two stanzas depict the child's relationship to her family and her pet. In stanzas four and five the tone shifts suddenly to ironic comedy by the use of pompous mock-heroic diction ("a transmogrifying bee") and the humorous contrast of the rising comb and the collapsing hen. In the last two stanzas the Sophoclean grandeur of the diction and the rhythmic sweep of the lines suddenly elevate the tone to one of tragic dignity. We are suddenly reminded that Janet is one of "the daughters of men" who, living in an insecure world, too may unexpectedly enter "the forgetful kingdom of death." Through variations in tone the poet has transformed a trite incident into an effective symbol of human mortality. The title we now realize suggests that the naive child has been awakened from her sleep of innocence and trust and had her first encounter with bitter truth. She has now gained not only a knowledge of the power of imperturbable death but of the helplessness of a loving and "powerful" parent to prevent it. The shattering of her belief in the omnipotence of daddy is her first step toward adulthood.

Father and Son

Now in the suburbs and the falling light
I followed him, and now down sandy road
Whiter than bone-dust, through the sweet
Curdle of fields, where the plums

Dropped with their load of ripeness, one by one.
Mile after mile I followed, with skimming feet,
After the secret master of my blood,
Him, steeped in the odor of ponds, whose indomitable love
Kept me in chains. Strode years; stretched into bird;
Raced through the sleeping country where I was young,
The silence unrolling before me as I came,
The night nailed like an orange to my brow.

How should I tell him my fable and the fears,
How bridge the chasm in a casual tone,
Saying, "The house, the stucco one you built,
We lost. Sister married and went from home,
And nothing comes back, it's strange, from where she goes.
I lived on a hill that had too many rooms:
Light we could make, but not enough of warmth,
And when the light failed, I climbed under the hill.
The papers are delivered every day;
I am alone and never shed a tear."

At the water's edge, where the smothering ferns lifted
Their arms, "Father!" I cried, "Return! You know
The way. I'll wipe the mudstains from your clothes;
No trace, I promise, will remain. Instruct
Your son, whirling between two wars,
In the Gemara[1] of your gentleness,
For I would be a child to those who mourn
And brother to the foundlings of the field
And friend of innocence and all bright eyes.
O teach me how to work and keep me kind."

Among the turtles and the lilies he turned to me
The white ignorant hollow of his face.

—Stanley Kunitz (1905–   )

---

[1] Gemara: the commentary on Jewish canon and civil laws in the Talmud.

The fact that this dramatic lyric was "born of a dream" accounts for the hallucinatory and surrealistic imagery in it as well as the sudden shifts in tone we find in the four parts. In the first section the speaker depicts a universal emotion: the longing of a son for communion and guidance from his father, whose indomitable but inarticulate love kept the son for years in spiritual bondage. The attempt of the son to bridge the generation gap is presented as a frantic quest from city to suburbs to country in a world of autumnal dusk and night. The hectic activity of youth—in a world where space and time are telescoped—is suggested by the movement words "followed," "skimming feet," "strode," "stretched," "raced." The futility of his chase is implied by "the sleeping country" and "the silence unrolling before me."

The casual tone of the second stanza—recounting traditional family troubles, such as financial reverses and the alienation of children from parents—is a direct contrast to the frenetic mood of the first. The intellectual estrangement of the son from the father and his emotional isolation from the real world is recounted in simple, matter-of-fact diction.

The tone of the third stanza is an impassioned prayer of the loyal son living in a tragic era ("whirling between two wars") for a code of conduct based on love and compassion which his gentle father might give him. Ironically the urgent plea is addressed to a parent who drowned himself.

In the final nightmarish confrontation when the son glimpses "the white ignorant hollow" of his father's skull, the tragic shock of existentialist truth finally releases the son from his bondage. In an irrational, destructive world the freedom of the individual begins on the other side of despair.

In "Janet Waking" and "Father and Son" the poets, by employing concrete, dramatic situations, have presented interpretations of life; but the themes have been implied rather than explicitly stated. Since every good poem is a unique, original treatment of human experience, shaped out of the confusion of existence into an artistic form, we are justified in our attempt to apprehend the poet's vision of life. Only after we have achieved a clear understanding of this can we proceed to evaluate it, that is, perhaps accept it as truthful, moral, or significant, or reject it as false, immoral, or trivial. In each of the three steps in reading poetry intelligently and enjoyably—understanding, appreciation, and evaluation—problems arise that need clarification.

To understand a poem we must first consider it as an aesthetic literary creation with an organic life of its own. Formalistic elements such as rhythm, sound patterns, diction, imagery, irony, and paradox interact to create a unified impression. The understanding of the function of these parts to the whole will help us to comprehend the experience in its totality. But, as we have seen, theme in poetry is frequently suggested rather than openly stated. By using dramatic, sensuous, emotional, and imaginative stimuli, the poet communicates meaning by indirection and implication. We are not justified in searching for neat moralistic tags or didactic preachments. The good poet finds life and human experiences too complex for such simplistic pronouncements. What he expects is empathy, or our sympathetic and imaginative projection into the character or situation he is depicting, "that willing suspension of disbelief for the moment, which constitutes poetic faith" (Coleridge).

Message-hunting or the didactic reading of poetry is a constricting and self-defeating activity. Ethical, moral, or philosophical implications engendered by the total aesthetic experience of recreating the poem are legitimate reactions to understanding the central meaning or theme, but a prosaic paraphrase of the content or a glib maxim or platitude extracted is a poor substitute. Furthermore, in poetry, like its sister art, music, a work is judged not solely by its theme but by its treatment and development as well. Bach wrote a magnificent composition using a vulgar tavern tune, and Beethoven wrote his monumental Diabelli Variations using a cheap, popular waltz theme. A poor poet handling a great theme—love, war, or death—produces doggerel; Donne writing about a flea and Burns about a louse produce significant poems.

In understanding a poem through recognition of its theme we must differentiate between a meaningful generalization which emerges naturally and forcefully from the formalistic elements contained in a poem and a moralistic statement gratuitously tacked on. In his "Ode on a Grecian Urn" (page 204) Keats is justified in drawing the philosophical conclusion "Beauty is truth, truth beauty," for it follows logically from the series of effective images and paradoxes he has developed earlier in the poem. However, Bryant blemishes his charming descriptive poem "To a Waterfowl" by the moralistic tag which concludes it, for the idea has already been clearly enunciated in the preceding stanzas.

> He who, from zone to zone,
> Guides through the boundless sky thy certain flight,
> In the long way, that I must tread alone,
> Will lead my steps aright.

The reader who pounces upon the following stanza in "The Rime of the Ancient Mariner" as the central meaning or theme of the poem is being misled.

> He prayeth best, who loveth best
> All things both great and small;
> For the dear God who loveth us,
> He made and loveth all."

This simple Christian message is spoken by the didactic mariner, not by Coleridge. The poem deals with a more complex concept: a sacra-

mental view of the universe, an archetypal experience of crime, suffering and expiation, a transformation of personality through the
awakening of an aesthetic sensibility.

Once we have understood a poem by grasping its formalistic
elements and their relationships to theme, we then can appreciate it
as an emotional, sensuous, and intellectual experience to widen our
sympathies and heighten our sensibilities. Not all poems will interest
us. The world of poetry is broad enough to include all human experiences from the simple to the highly complex, from folk ballads to
metaphysical poetry, from a Burns drinking song to T. S. Eliot's "The
Waste Land." As we grow in emotional and intellectual maturity our
poetic tastes develop, and our enriched comprehension gradually
deepens our appreciation.

In taking the final step of evaluation we must be careful not to
criticize a poem by our prejudices, fixed beliefs, or personal value
judgments but as an artistic expression of a vision of life. Once we
have clearly understood this interpretation of human existence and
given it our sympathetic appreciation, we have a perfect right to reject
it as false, incomplete, or unsatisfactory. This rejection of meaning
does not invalidate the work as an artistic, autonomous, creation of
art. If this were not so, a Jew would not enjoy *The Divine Comedy* of
Dante; a Catholic, the Protestant epic *Paradise Lost;* and an existentialist or atheist, either poem.

For Discussion

The Poet thinks and feels in the spirit of human passions. How, then,
can his language differ in any material degree from that of all other
men who feel vividly and see clearly?

—William Wordsworth

"When *I* use a word," Humpty Dumpty said, in rather a scornful
tone, "it means just what I choose it to mean—neither more nor
less."

"The question is," said Alice, "whether you *can* make words
mean so many different things."

"The question is," said Humpty Dumpty, "which is to be
master—that's all."

—Lewis Carroll

Poetical language should be current language heightened.

—Gerard Manley Hopkins

The fact that the meanings of words change, not only from age to age, but from context to context, is certainly interesting; but it is interesting solely because it is a nuisance.

—Owen Barfield

Poets, we hear languages like the murmuring of bees. Swarm in the head. Where the honey is stored. An instinct for words where, like bees dancing, in language there is a communication below the threshold of language.

—Robert Duncan

The poet and the poet-in-us-all have no business hanging around philosophy.

—Karl Shapiro

Whenever in the course of a poem the poet changes either his tone or his attitude, some change will occur in the handling of the technical elements.

—John Ciardi

Poems Related to Chapter 7

The Fury of Aerial Bombardment

You would think the fury of aerial bombardment
Would rouse God to relent; the infinite spaces
Are still silent. He looks on shock-pried faces.
History, even, does not know what is meant.

You would feel that after so many centuries
God would give man to repent; yet he can kill
As Cain could, but with multitudinous will,
No farther advanced than in his ancient furies.

Was man made stupid to see his own stupidity?
Is God by definition indifferent, beyond us all?
Is the eternal truth man's fighting soul
Wherein the Beast ravens in its own avidity?

Of Van Wettering I speak, and Averill,
Names on a list, whose faces I do not recall
But they are gone to early death, who late in school
Distinguished the belt feed lever from the belt holding pawl.

—Richard Eberhart (1904–   )

1. What is the tone of the first three stanzas? Of the last one? Is the shift justified? Prove.

2. How do the first three stanzas differ from the final one in (a) point of view, (b) diction, (c) use or absence of figurative language, (d) rhyme?
3. What concepts of God, the nature of man, and the causes of war are mentioned? How are these interrelated?
4. Are the three questions in the third stanza rhetorical (i.e., the answers are implied), or does the poet simply ask them without answering them? Discuss.
5. What effect does the poet achieve by mentioning two names and two parts of a bomber machine-gun (belt feed lever and belt holding pawl)? Were Van Wettering and Averill personal friends of the author or simply students in his gunnery class?
6. Is this poem a traditional elegy or a denunciation of twentieth-century mechanized warfare? What is the theme of the poem?

To the Fringed Gentian

Thou blossom bright with autumn dew,
And colored with the heaven's own blue,
That openest when the quiet light
Succeeds the keen and frosty night.

Thou comest not when violets lean
O'er wandering brooks and springs unseen,
Or columbines, in purple dressed,
Nod o'er the ground-bird's hidden nest.

Thou waitest late, and com'st alone,
When woods are bare and birds are flown,
And frosts and shortening days portend
The aged year is near his end.

Then doth thy sweet and quiet eye
Look through its fringes to the sky,
Blue—blue—as if that sky let fall
A flower from its cerulean wall.

I would that thus, when I shall see
The hour of death draw near to me,
Hope blossoming within my heart,
May look to heaven as I depart.

—William Cullen Bryant (1794–1878)

The Last Chrysanthemum

Why should this flower delay so long
       To show its tremulous plumes?
Now is the time of plaintive robin-song,
       When flowers are in their tombs.

Through the slow summer, when the sun
Called to each frond and whorl
That all he could for flowers was being done,
Why did it not uncurl?

It must have felt that fervid call
Although it took no heed,
Waking but now, when leaves like corpses fall,
And saps all retrocede.

Too late its beauty, lonely thing,
The season's shine is spent,
Nothing remains for it but shivering
In tempests turbulent.

Had it a reason for delay,
Dreaming in witlessness
That for a bloom so delicately gay
Winter would stay its stress?

—I talk as if the thing were born
With sense to work its mind;
Yet it is but one mask of many worn
By the Great Face behind.

—Thomas Hardy (1840–1928)

1. Both poems deal with the blossoming of a late autumn flower. What different uses do Bryant and Hardy make of this "objective correlative" (i.e., an object, event, or situation which immediately evokes an emotion)?
2. Contrast the diction and imagery in the two poems. How do they influence the tone of each? What is the relationship of tone to the theme? Do rhythm and rhyme play any part?
3. Discuss the effectiveness of the concluding stanza in the two poems. Which poem do you prefer? Why?

Merritt Parkway

As if it were
forever that they move, that we
keep moving—

Under a wan sky where
as the lights went on a star
pierced the haze and now

follows steadily
               a constant
above our six lanes
the dreamlike continuum . . .

And the people—ourselves!
   the humans from inside the
   cars, apparent
   only at gasoline stops
                    unsure,
     eyeing each other

               drink coffee hastily at the
         slot machines and hurry
     back to the cars
     vanish
     into them forever, to
     keep moving—

Houses now and then beyond the
sealed road, the trees / trees, bushes
passing by, passing
     the cars that
         keep moving ahead of
    us, past us, pressing behind us
                  and
        over left, those that come
      toward us shining too brightly
moving relentlessly

   in six lanes, gliding
   north and south, speeding with
   a slurred sound—

       —Denise Levertov (1923–   )

1. Is this poem simply an objective description of a ride on a modern parkway or does it make some comment on our contemporary civilization? Discuss.
2. Is the diction in the poem appropriate to the theme? Discuss.
3. In what way is the typographical arrangement of the poem an illustration of the following statement by the poet:

I believe every space and comma is a living part of the poem and has its function, just as every muscle and pore of the body has its function. And the way the lines are broken is a functioning part essential to the poem's life.

Consider the following two poems that deal with the same subject: the death of a child.

Dead Cousin

The little cousin now is dead,
　　His spirit's light is quenched;
For him let bitter tears be shed.
　　For him our hearts are wrenched.

His custom was around the home
　　To romp and sing and play,
And with his faithful dog to roam
　　In meadows sweet and gay.

His father's hope, his mother's joy,
　　The last of noble kin,
The trump of death has called our boy
　　To leave a world of sin.

Mournfully jangles the funeral bell,
　　Dolefully knelling his death.
And soon within his gloomy cell
　　He'll know nor light nor breath.

We lift a sad and solemn song
　　As he in earth is laid,
And pray he will not stay for long
　　In Death's eternal shade.

　　　　　　　　—Anonymous

Bells for John Whiteside's Daughter

There was such speed in her little body,
And such lightness in her footfall,
It is no wonder her brown study[1]
Astonishes us all.

Her wars were bruited[2] in our high window.
We looked among orchard trees and beyond,
Where she took arms against her shadow,
Or harried unto the pond

The lazy geese, like a snow cloud
Dripping their snow on the green grass,
Tricking and stopping, sleepy and proud,
Who cried in goose, Alas,

For the tireless heart within the little
Lady with rod that made them rise
From their noon apple-dreams, and scuttle
Goose-fashion under the skies!

But now go the bells, and we are ready;
In one house we are sternly stopped
To say we are vexed at her brown study,
Lying so primly propped.

—John Crowe Ransom (1888–   )

---

[1] Pensive reverie, daydream.   [2] Reported noisily.

1. Contrast the two poems in the following respects: (a) diction, (b) metaphor, (c) tone, (d) rhythm, (e) rhyme, (f) theme.
2. Which do you consider to be the better poem? Why?

A Red, Red Rose

I

O, my luve is like a red, red rose,
   That's newly sprung in June.
O, my luve is like the melodie,
   That's sweetly play'd in tune.

II

As fair art thou, my bonie lass,
   So deep in luve am I,
And I will luve thee still, my dear,
   Till a' the seas gang dry.

III

Till a' the seas gang dry, my dear,
   And the rocks melt wi' the sun!
And I will luve thee still, my dear,
   While the sands o' life shall run.

IV

And fare thee weel, my only luve,
   And fare thee weel a while!
And I will come again, my luve,
   Tho' it were ten thousand mile!

—Robert Burns (1759–1796)

Sonnet XLIII

(Sonnets from the Portuguese)

How do I love thee: Let me count the ways.
I love thee to the depth and breadth and height
My soul can reach, when feeling out of sight
For the ends of Being and ideal Grace.
I love thee to the level of everyday's
Most quiet need, by sun and candle-light.
I love thee freely, as men strive for Right;
I love thee purely, as they turn from Praise.
I love thee with the passion put to use
In my old griefs, and with my childhood's faith.
I love thee with a love I seemed to lose
With my lost saints,—I love thee with the breath,
Smiles, tears, of all my life!—and, if God choose,
I shall but love thee better after death.

—Elizabeth Barrett Browning (1806–1861)

Summum Bonum[1]

All the breath and the bloom of the year in
        the bag of one bee:
All the wonder and wealth of the mine in
        the heart of one gem:
In the core of one pearl all the shade and
        shine of the sea:
Breath and bloom, shade and shine,—wonder,
        wealth, and—how far above them—
            Truth, that's brighter than gem,
            Trust, that's purer than pearl,—
Brightest truth, purest trust in the universe—
        all were for me
            In the kiss of one girl.

—Robert Browning (1812–1889)

---

[1] Highest good.

I Knew a Woman

I knew a woman, lovely in her bones,
When small birds sighed, she would sigh back at them;
Ah, when she moved, she moved more ways than one:

The shapes a bright container can contain!
Of her choice virtues only gods should speak,
Or English poets who grew up on Greek
(I'd have them sing in chorus, cheek to cheek).

How well her wishes went! She stroked my chin,
She taught me Turn, and Counter-turn, and Stand;
She taught me Touch, that undulant white skin;
I nibbled meekly from her proffered hand;
She was the sickle; I, poor I, the rake,
Coming behind her for her pretty sake
(But what prodigious mowing we did make).

Love likes a gander, and adores a goose:
Her full lips pursed, the errant note to seize;
She played it quick, she played it light and loose;
My eyes, they dazzled at her flowing knees;
Her several parts could keep a pure repose,
Or one hip quiver with a mobile nose
(She moved in circles, and those circles moved).

Let seed be grass, and grass turn into hay:
I'm martyr to a motion not my own;
What's freedom for? To know eternity.
I swear she cast a shadow white as stone.
But who would count eternity in days?
These old bones live to learn her wanton ways:
(I measure time by how a body sways).

—Theodore Roethke (1908–1964)

1. Compare these four love poems as to (a) diction, (b) imagery and metaphor, (c) tone, (d) rhythm.

Ode to a Nightingale

I

My heart aches, and a drowsy numbness pains
    My sense, as though of hemlock I had drunk,
Or emptied some dull opiate to the drains
    One minute past, and Lethe-wards[1] had sunk:
'Tis not through envy of thy happy lot,
    But being too happy in thine happiness,—
        That thou, light winged Dryad[2] of the trees,
            In some melodious plot
Of beechen green, and shadows numberless,
    Singest of summer in full-throated ease.

II

O, for a draught of vintage! that hath been
   Cool'd a long age in the deep-delved earth,
Tasting of Flora[3] and the country green,
   Dance, and Provencal song;[4] and sunburnt mirth!
O for a beaker full of the warm South,
   Full of the true, the blushful Hippocrene,[5]
     With beaded bubbles winking at the brim,
       And purple-stained mouth;
   That I might drink, and leave the world unseen,
    And with thee fade away into the forest dim:

III

Fade far away, dissolve, and quite forget
   What thou among the leaves hast never known,
The weariness, the fever, and the fret
   Here, where men sit and hear each other groan;
Where palsy shakes a few, sad, last grey hairs,
   Where youth grows pale, and spectre-thin, and dies;
     Where but to think is to be full of sorrow
       And leaden-ey'd despairs,
   Where Beauty cannot keep her lustrous eyes,
    Or new Love pine at them beyond tomorrow.

IV

Away! away! for I will fly to thee,
   Not charioted by Bacchus[6] and his pards,[7]
But on the viewless wings of Poesy,
   Though the dull brain perplexes and retards:
Already with thee! tender is the night,
   And haply[8] the Queen-Moon is on her throne,
     Cluster'd around by all her starry Fays;[9]
       But here there is no light,
   Save what from heaven is with the breezes blown
    Through verdurous glooms and winding mossy ways.

V

I cannot see what flowers are at my feet,
   Nor what soft incense hangs upon the boughs,
But, in embalmed[10] darkness, guess each sweet
   Wherewith the seasonable month endows
The grass, the thicket, and the fruit-tree wild;
   White hawthorn, and the pastoral eglantine;
     Fast fading violets cover'd up in leaves;
       And mid-May's eldest child,
   The coming musk-rose, full of dewy wine,
    The murmurous haunt of flies on summer eves.

VI

Darkling I listen; and, for many a time
  I have been half in love with easeful Death,
Call'd him soft names in many a mused rhyme,
  To take into the air my quiet breath;
Now more than ever seems it rich to die,
  To cease upon the midnight with no pain,
    While thou art pouring forth thy soul abroad
      In such an ecstasy!
Still wouldst thou sing, and I have ears in vain—
  To thy high requiem[11] become a sod.

VII

Thou wast not born for death, immortal Bird!
  No hungry generations tread thee down;
The voice I hear this passing night was heard
  In ancient days by emperor and clown:[12]
Perhaps the self-same song that found a path
  Through the sad heart of Ruth,[13] when, sick for home,
    She stood in tears amid the alien corn;
      The same that oft-times hath
Charm'd magic casements, opening on the foam
  Of perilous seas, in faery lands forlorn.

IX

Forlorn! the very word is like a bell
  To toll me back from thee to my sole self!
Adieu! the fancy[14] cannot cheat so well
  As she is famed to do, deceiving elf.
Adieu! adieu! thy plaintive anthem fades
  Past the near meadows, over the still stream,
    Up the hill-side; and now 'tis buried deep
      In the next valley-glades:
Was it a vision, or a waking dream?
  Fled is that music—Do I wake or sleep?

—John Keats (1795–1821)

---

[1] Toward oblivion. Souls who drank the waters of the river Lethe gained forgetfulness. [2] Wood-nymph. [3] Goddess of flowers. [4] Provence, in southern France, home of the medieval troubadours. [5] Fountain of the Muses whose waters inspired poets. [6] God of wine. [7] Keats represents Bacchus' coach as drawn by leopards (pards). [8] Perhaps. [9] Fairies. [10] Aromatic. [11] Musical mass for the dead. [12] Rustic. [13] Old Testament heroine. [14] Imagination.

1. In the first stanza what contrast of emotions is presented by the poet in the human world and the nightingale in the world of nature?
2. Which stanza depicts the world of mankind? By what images? Do you

think tragic events in the life of Keats are responsible for this depressing picture, or is it a valid presentation of the universal life of humanity?

3. Which stanzas depict the world of nature? By what images? What are the characteristics of this world? How do they differ from man's?

4. By what two means can the poet escape from his world to nature's? Which one does he choose? Why?

5. Is the "vintage" (sparkling Burgundy?) described in stanza two the product of nature, the work of man, or both? Is it to be taken literally as a drink, or is it used as a symbol of the beauty and joyousness of nature? Or is it a means of entering the world of the nightingale?

6. Does the song of the bird act as an opiate dulling the pain of the poet, as a stimulant to his poetic imagination, or as both?

7. What line in the poem reveals that the poet has successfully escaped from the painful world of mortality into the deathless, beautiful world of nature? Is this escape permanent or transitory? Why? Does this flight give him a deeper glimpse into the nature of reality (i.e., is it a mystic "vision") or simply a reverie or daydream?

8. What is the poet's attitude toward death in stanza six? Is it consistent with his depiction of life? Why or why not? How does its portrayal in this stanza differ from that in stanza three?

9. In what sense is the nightingale an "immortal Bird"? By what images does the poet reinforce this idea? Since this particular flesh and blood, feathered creature like man must die, is the poet inconsistent? Or is the nightingale used as a symbol? If so, of what? What forever alienates man from the world in which the bird lives?

10. What is the meaning of the concluding three lines of stanza seven? What new world is depicted here? How is it related to man and to nature?

11. What word suggests the poet's return to the world of mankind? Why is the fading song of the nightingale described as a "plaintive anthem"? Is the tone of the last stanza similar to the opening one? Why? Why does the poem end with a question? How would you answer it?

12. Compare and contrast this poem with Hardy's "The Darkling Thrush" (page 149).

When I Heard the Learn'd Astronomer

When I heard the Learn'd astronomer,
When the proofs, the figures, were ranged in columns before me,
When I was shown the charts and the diagrams, to add, divide,
    and measure them,
When I sitting heard the astronomer where he lectured with
    much applause in the lecture-room,
How soon unaccountable I became tired and sick,
Till rising and gliding out I wander'd off by myself,
In the mystical moist night-air, and from time to time,
Look'd up in perfect silence at the stars.

—Walt Whitman (1819–1892)

Desert Places

Snow falling and night falling fast, oh, fast
In a field I looked into going past,
And the ground almost covered smooth in snow,
But a few weeds and stubble showing last.

The woods around it have it—it is theirs.
All animals are smothered in their lairs.
I am too absent-spirited to count;
The loneliness includes me unawares.

And lonely as it is, that loneliness
Will be more lonely ere it will be less—
A blanker whiteness of benighted snow
With no expression, nothing to express.

They cannot scare me with their empty spaces
Between stars—on stars where no human race is.
I have it in me so much nearer home
To scare myself with my own desert places.

—Robert Frost (1875–1963)

1.   In these two poems the authors use contrast and a sudden shift in tone.
     How does the diction contribute to establish this contrast? What is the
     difference in attitude toward the stars of Whitman and Frost?
     (1621–1678)   Andrew Marvell : Milton's contemporary, 17th century poet

To His Coy Mistress[1]   *(beloved, sweetheart)*

1. transiency of life
2. shortness of man's allotted span
3. sureness of death
4. urgency of lovers

Ideal situation   Had we but world enough, and time,
                    This coyness, lady, were no crime.
                    We would sit down and think which way
                    To walk, and pass our long love's day;
                    Thou by the Indian Ganges[2] side   *sacred river in India*
                    Shouldst rubies find; I by the tide   *sing sad love songs*
River in   Of Humber[3] would complain.[4] I would
England flowing   Love you ten years before the Flood;[5]   *deluge in time of Noah*
through Hull,   And you should, if you please, refuse
Marvell's home-   Till the conversion of the Jews.   *dull, plant-like, lowest of 3 souls*
town   My vegetable[6] love should grow   *(p. 138)*
                    Vaster than empires, and more slow.
                    An hundred years should go to praise
                    Thine eyes, and on thy forehead gaze;
                    Two hundred to adore each breast,
                    But thirty thousand to the rest;
                    An age at least to every part,

And the last age should show your heart.
For, lady, you deserve this state,
Nor would I love at lower rate.[7]
    But at my back I always hear
Time's wingèd chariot hurrying near;
And yonder all before us lie
Deserts of vast eternity.
Thy beauty shall no more be found,
Nor in thy marble vault shall sound
My echoing song; then worms shall try
That long preserved virginity,
And your quaint[8] honor turn to dust,
And into ashes all my lust.
The grave's a fine and private place,
But none, I think, do there embrace.
    Now, therefore, while the youthful hue
Sits on thy skin like morning dew,
And while thy willing soul transpires[9]
At every pore with instant fires,
Now let us sport us while we may;
And now, like am'rous birds of prey,
Rather at once our time devour,
Than languish in his slow-chapped[10] power.
Let us roll all our strength, and all
Our sweetness, up into one ball;
And tear our pleasures with rough strife
Thorough[11] the iron gates of life.
Thus, though we cannot make our sun
Stand still,[12] yet we will make him run.

—Andrew Marvell (1621–1673)

---

[1] Beloved, sweetheart. [2] Sacred river in India. [3] River in northern England flowing through Hull, Marvell's home town. [4] Sing sad love songs. [5] The great deluge in the time of Noah. [6] The lowest of the three souls (rational, possessed by man; sensitive, by man and animals; vegetable, by plants that unconsciously grow larger). [7] Valuation. [8] Prim. [9] Breathes forth. [10] Chewing with slow chaps (i.e., jaws). [11] Through. [12] Unlike Joshua in the Bible or Zeus in classical mythology.

1. The prose sense of this poem develops a logical argument that falls into three parts: (a) If we had . . . (b) but we haven't . . . (c) therefore, let us . . . Complete the clauses.

2. Discuss the difference in tone in each of the three parts. To what extent do diction, rhythm, and imagery contribute to the establishment of tone?

3. Contrast Marvell's handling of the *carpe diem* ("seize the day") theme with Herrick's in "To the Virgins, to Make Much of Time" (page 77).

Southbound on the Freeway

A tourist came in from Orbitville,
parked in the air, and said:

The creatures of this star
are made of metal and glass.

Through the transparent parts
you can see their guts.

Their feet are round and roll
On diagrams or long

measuring tapes, dark
with white lines.

They have four eyes.
The two in back are red.

Sometimes you can see a five-eyed
one, with a red eye turning

on the top of his head.
He must be special—

the others respect him
and go slow

when he passes, winding
among them from behind.

They all hiss as they glide,
like inches, down the marked

tapes. Those soft shapes,
shadowy inside

the hard bodies—are they
their guts or their brains?

　　　—May Swenson (1919–　　)

Eros Turannos[1]

She fears him, and will always ask
　　What fated her to choose him;
She meets in his engaging mask
　　All reasons to refuse him;

But what she meets and what she fears
Are less than are the downward years,
Drawn slowly to the foamless weirs
    Of age, were she to lose him.

Between a blurred sagacity
    That once had power to sound him,
And Love, that will not let him be
    The Judas that she found him,
Her pride assuages her almost,
As if it were alone the cost. —
He sees that he will not be lost,
    And waits and looks around him.

A sense of ocean and old trees
    Envelops and allures him;
Tradition, touching all he sees,
    Beguiles and reassures him;
And all her doubts of what he says
Are dimmed with what she knows of days—
Till even prejudice delays
    And fades, and she secures him.

The falling leaf inaugurates
    The reign of her confusion;
The pounding wave reverberates
    The dirge of her illusion;
And home, where passion lived and died,
Becomes a place where she can hide,
While all the town and harbor side
    Vibrate with her seclusion.

We tell you, tapping on our brows,
    The story as it should be, —
As if the story of a house
    Were told, or ever could be;
We'll have no kindly veil between
Her visions and those we have seen, —
As if we guessed what hers have been,
    Or what they are or would be.

Meanwhile we do no harm; for they
    That with a god have striven,
Not hearing much of what we say,
    Take what the god has given;
Though like waves breaking it may be,

Or like a changed familiar tree,
Or like a stairway to the sea
    Where down the blind are driven.

—Edwin Arlington Robinson (1865–1935)

---

[1] The tyrant love.

Lady Lazarus

I have done it again.
One year in every ten
I manage it—

A sort of walking miracle, my skin
Bright as a Nazi lampshade,
My right foot

A paperweight,
My face a featureless, fine
Jew linen.

Peel off the napkin
O my enemy.
Do I terrify?—

The nose, the eye pits, the full set of teeth?
The sour breath
Will vanish in a day.

Soon, soon the flesh
The grave cave ate will be
At home on me

And I a smiling woman.
I am only thirty.
And like the cat I have nine times to die.

This is Number Three.
What a trash
To annihilate each decade.

What a million filaments.   *a thread-like conductor made*
The peanut-crunching crowd   *incandescent by the passage*
Shoves in to see   *of an electric current*

Them unwrap me hand and foot—
The big strip tease.
Gentlemen, ladies

These are my hands
My knees.
I may be skin and bone,

Nevertheless, I am the same, identical woman.
The first time it happened I was ten.
It was an accident.

The second time I meant
To last it out and not come back at all.
I rocked shut

As a seashell.
They had to call and call
And pick the worms off me like sticky pearls.
                    maggots

Dying
Is an art, like everything else.
I do it exceptionally well.

I do it so it feels like hell.
I do it so it feels real.
I guess you could say I've a call.

It's easy enough to do it in a cell.
It's easy enough to do it and stay put.
It's the theatrical

Comeback in broad day
To the same place, the same face, the same brute
Amused shout:

"A miracle!"
That knocks me out.
There is a charge

For the eyeing of my scars, there is a charge
For the hearing of my heart—
It really goes.

And there is a charge, a very large charge
For a word or a touch
Or a bit of blood

Or a piece of my hair or my clothes.
So, so, Herr Doktor.
So, Herr Enemy.

I am your opus,
I am your valuable,
The pure gold baby

That melts to a shriek.
I turn and burn.
Do not think I underestimate your great concern.

Ash, ash—
You poke and stir.
Flesh, bone, there is nothing there—

A cake of soap,
A wedding ring,
A gold filling.

Herr God, Herr Lucifer
Beware
Beware.

Out of the ash
I rise with my red hair
And I eat men like air.

—Sylvia Plath (1932–1963)

An image is that which presents an intellectual and emotional complex in an instant of time.

—*Ezra Pound*

8

The Importance of Image and Metaphor in Poetry

Important as rhythm, sound patterns, and rhyme are to poetic communication, these aural elements interact with two other essential components of the art of poetry: imagery and figurative language. An *image* is the reproduction in the mind of a physical sensation by the use of language. An image appeals to one or more of our five senses. It is used in poetry to convey or reinforce a sensory impression or as a figure of speech (generic term *metaphor*). A figure of speech is an unliteral form of expression using comparison, contrast, exaggeration, or personification for the forceful communication of emotion and/or thought. (The use of image as symbol will be discussed in Chapter 10.)

Whenever we strive for vivid and emotional expression we use figurative language, such as similes and metaphors. This is especially true of slang, the poor man's metaphor and the teenager's delight. We hear, "he wolfs his food," "he's an eager beaver," "he's a rat," "she's a wet blanket." Adults are characterized as "squares," "phonies," or "killjoys." New inventions are succinctly described in metaphorical terms. We speak of an automobile as "stream-lined" and of a television "antenna" (a movable segmented organ of sensation on the head of insects); a helicopter is a "whirly-bird," a synchroton is a "nuclear merry-go-round," and an atomic explosion is "a mushroom cloud."

By its very nature poetry is metaphorical. The poet's purpose is not to give us facts but to communicate simple or complex emotional, intellectual, sensory, or imaginative experiences. Imagery clarifies and

144

concretizes the poet's vision and stimulates an appropriate and sympathetic response in the reader. In "Ars Poetica" MacLeish reinforces his statement that a poem should be palpable, mute, dumb, silent, and wordless by using four concrete sensuous images that stir the imagination: a globed fruit, old medallions, the sleeve-worn stone of casement ledges, the flight of birds. The rich emotional associations connected with these images vibrate in our memories.

The concept that the primary purpose of figurative language in poetry is for illustration and embellishment is no longer considered valid. Metaphoric expression—or, as Frost puts it, saying one thing and meaning another, saying one thing in terms of another—is the very essence of poetry. The poet's persistent use of image and metaphor not only satisfies our desire for perceiving resemblances but *evokes* emotional, sensuous, and intellectual impressions that intensify our experience of reality. Poetic metaphor is a form of discourse that overcomes the limitations of literal language. It uncovers and discovers aspects of truth by new juxtapositions which give us "a momentary stay against confusion."

The poet uses figurative language to appeal directly to our emotions and to stimulate psychological reactions. Merely naming an emotion—sadness, joy, or fear—does not make us feel it. By using concrete images and effective metaphors, the poet engages the deepest resources of our being, our feelings and our memories. He alerts our imagination to grasp the relationship of separate images and thus evokes in us a more complete and complex emotional response than a bare prose statement. Consider this sonnet by Shakespeare.

Sonnet 73

That time of year thou mayst in me behold
When yellow leaves, or none, or few, do hang
Upon those boughs which shake against the cold,
Bare ruin'd choirs, where late the sweet birds sang.
In me thou see'st the twilight of such day
As after sunset fadeth in the west;
Which by and by black night doth take away,
Death's second self, that seals up all in rest.
In me thou see'st the glowing of such fire,
That on the ashes of his youth doth lie,
As the death-bed whereon it must expire,
Consumed with that which it was nourisht by.
    This thou perceivest, which makes thy love more strong,
    To love that well which thou must leave ere long.

—William Shakespeare (1564–1616)

The prose meaning, simply stated, is: "Since you perceive that I am growing old, your love should be stronger now because death will soon separate us." The poem, however, involves us in a richer and deeper experience through its suggestive imagery. In the first twelve lines the poet develops three different but related metaphors for death: the dying of the year (late autumn or winter), the dying of a day, and the dying of a fire. The concrete images of the yellow leaves, the bare trees, the cold wind create a mood of desolation. By calling the boughs of the trees "bare ruined choirs" Shakespeare gives the first image a second and deeper level of metaphoric meaning. The word *choirs* calls to mind an English cathedral in ruins and the singers who have vanished. Emotionally we identify with the aging man. The poet reinforces this feeling by appealing to our memories of happier summer days when "the sweet birds sang" and the voices of the cathedral singers were heard. These sight and sound images interact simultaneously to penetrate our deepest consciousness and in their fusion evoke a unified emotional experience.

The second image of the fading sunset, the coming of twilight, and the obliteration of colorful beauty by black night, "Death's second self," enhances the poignancy of the inevitability of death. In the same manner the final image of the last glow of a fire extinguished by the ashes—once the very wood that fed the flames—intensifies our feelings of regretful sadness. By itself the statement of the concluding couplet would be ineffective; but coming after the powerful emotional buildup created by the preceding images, it impresses us with its psychological truth.

The forcefulness of the three images is due not only to their individual vividness but to their coherence and artistic progression. When the dying poet compares himself to autumn, a sunset, and a glowing fire, he presents images that are colorful and pleasurable (like life) but as presented in this context are painful in their emotional impact because of their transitoriness. They not only reinforce each other but are arranged in a climactic order of transience: a year, a day, a moment.

All the beauty of a sun-drenched landscape is communicated to us by Shakespeare's personification of the sun

> Kissing with golden face the meadows green,
> Gilding pale streams with heavenly alchemy.

> ("Sonnet 33")

We are moved by Shakespeare's succinct metaphor in "Sonnet 94," "Lilies that fester smell far worse than weeds," to understand the degradation of a noble character. Coleridge's ancient mariner communicates his sudden terror in the lines

> Fear at my heart, as at a cup,
> My life-blood seemed to sip!

The cosmic sweep of infinite space and time finds effective expression in Henry Vaughan's two similes.

> I saw eternity the other night
> Like a great ring of pure and endless light,
>   All calm as it was bright;
> And round beneath it, time, in hours, days, years,
>   Driven by the spheres,
> Like a vast shadow moved, in which the world
>   And all her train were hurled.

> (from "The World")

The dazzling colorfulness of a bird is captured in Marianne Moore's metaphor "fire in the dove-neck's/iridescence."

In a well-known poem Carl Sandburg brings out the stealthiness, quietness, softness, and transience of fog by comparing it to the arrival and departure of a cat ("Fog"), and he constructs another poem ("Lost") around a single simile comparing a fog-bound boat to a lost child. Andrew Marvell, in a beautifully elaborated simile, compares the human soul to a dewdrop.

On a Drop of Dew

> See how the orient[1] dew,
> Shed from the bosom of the morn
>   Into the blowing roses,
> Yet careless of its mansion new,
> For the clear region where 'twas born
>   Round in itself incloses,
>   And in its little globe's extent
> Frames as it can its native element;
> How it the purple flower does slight,
>   Scarce touching where it lies,
> But gazing back upon the skies,
>   Shines with a mournful light
>   Like its own tear,
> Because so long divided from the sphere.
>   Restless it rolls and unsecure,

Trembling lest it grow impure,
Till the warm sun pity its pain,
And to the skies exhale it back again.
So the soul, that drop, that ray
Of the clear fountain of eternal day,
Could it within the human flower be seen,
Rememb'ring still the former height,
Shuns the sweet leaves and blossoms green;
And recollecting[2] its own light,
Does, in its pure and circling thoughts, express
The greater heaven in an heaven less.
In how coy a figure wound,
Every way it turns away;
So the world excluding round,
Yet receiving in the day;
Dark beneath but bright above,
Here disdaining, there in love;
How loose and easy hence to go,
How girt and ready to ascent;
Moving but on a point below,
It all about does upwards bend.
Such did the manna's[3] sacred dew distil,
White and entire, though congealed and chill;
Congealed on earth, but does, dissolving, run
Into the glories of th' almighty sun.

—Andrew Marvell (1621–1678)

---

[1] Sunrise. [2] Withdrawing. [3] Food miraculously supplied to Israelites in the wilderness (Exodus XVI).

The soul being an abstract entity, Marvell's aesthetic problem is how to objectify the intangible and invisible being during its earthly sojourn in the human body. His solution is to describe with delicate particularity a dewdrop fallen from the morning sky and resting lightly on a purple flower. By suggesting the many resemblances between the pure, restless droplet and the soul, he clarifies the nature of the human soul and its desire to return uncontaminated to its heavenly home. The whole poem is a brilliantly developed simile, the sustained analogy serving as the core of the poem.

Instead of elaborating a single figure of speech, a poet may express his vision of human existence in a series of comparisons. But these must be held together in some meaningful relationship. In this poem all the figures suggest evanescent beauty.

Sic Vita

Like to the falling of a star,
Or as the flights of eagles are,
Or like the fresh spring's gaudy hue,
Or silver drops of morning dew,
Or like a wind that chafes the flood,
Or bubbles which on water stood:
Even such is man, whose borrowed light
Is straight called in, and paid to night.
The wind blows out, the bubble dies;
The spring entombed in autumn lies;
The dew dries up, the star is shot;
The flight is past—and man forgot.

—Henry King (1591–1669)

Finally, to observe the importance of interacting metaphors in creating mood and communicating meaning, let us consider another poem.

The Darkling Thrush

I leant upon a coppice gate[1]
    When Frost was spectre-gray,
And Winter's dregs made desolate
    The weakening eye of day.
The tangled bine-stems[2] scored the sky
    Like strings of broken lyres,
And all mankind that haunted nigh
    Had sought their household fires.

The land's sharp features seemed to be
    The Century's corpse outleant,[3]
His crypt the cloudy canopy,
    The wind his death-lament.
The ancient pulse of germ and birth
    Was shrunken hard and dry,
And every spirit upon earth
    Seemed fervourless as I.

At once a voice arose among
    The bleak twigs overhead
In a full-hearted evensong[4]
    Of joy illimited;

An aged thrush, frail, gaunt, and small,
    In blast-beruffled plume,
Had chosen thus to fling his soul
    Upon the growing gloom.

So little cause for carollings
    Of such ecstatic sound
Was written on terrestrial things
    Afar or nigh around,
That I could think there trembled through
    His happy goodnight air
Some blessed Hope, whereof he knew
    And I was unaware.

—Thomas Hardy (1840–1928)

---

[1] A gate leading to a small wood or grove of trees.   [2] Creeping Vines.
[3] Stretched out.   [4] Vespers of "Evening Prayer" of the Church of
England.

Hardy wrote this poem on December 31, 1900. In the first two
stanzas he represents the speaker (it could be the poet or an imaginary
speaker, a dramatic *persona*) in a desolate wintry landscape. He is
in a state of profound despair as he contemplates the end of the nineteenth century and the woes it has brought to suffering humanity. By
a series of effective somber metaphors the poet brings into harmony
the barren scene and the listless mood of the pessimistic spectator.
The frost, seen through the twilight of a half-closed eye, is a ghostly
gray; the climbing plants, "like strings of broken lyres," scratch the
skies and suggest mournful musical score lines. The preceding century
lies like a stark corpse under a cloudy canopy mourned by a windy
dirge. In the cold and barren earth the eternal cycle of growth seems
suspended. The wine of life has evaporated, and only the desolate
dregs of winter remain. Ghostly humanity "that haunted nigh" has
fled to the shelter of "their household fires." The gloom of the landscape is as profound as the "fervourless" speaker.

Suddenly from this bleak landscape rises the joyous song of a
thrush. The bird—"in blast-beruffled plume"—is not the romantic
songster of a Wordsworth or Shelley but a typical Hardyan bird—old,
frail, and gaunt—like man taking a terrible beating from nature. But
like puny man in his artistic and religious creations defying an immense, meaningless universe, the small bird bursts into a song of
hope which does not convert the speaker to optimism but suggests to
him the mysterious paradox of life, the persistence of joy in a tragic
world of sadness, the survival of life in a universe of death. The

speaker simply admits the possibility that the bird has a vision of a world of happiness denied to man. By this conclusion the poet resolves the emotional tensions set up in the poem by the clash of contrasting metaphors of gloom and joy.

Images and metaphors are not always arranged by the poet in a neat, orderly pattern or in a logical progression. Influenced by photography, the cinema, and the collages of abstract art, modern poets have developed a kind of *verbal montage,* consisting of a series of metaphors flashed before the reader, often without transitions, which he must bring into coherent focus by the use of his own imagination. Images are not only juxtaposed but telescoped and superimposed. Much of the difficulty of reading modern poetry consists of understanding this "dynamics of metaphor," in Hart Crane's phrase. The poet, in attempting to capture some of the complexity of modern man's emotional, spiritual, and intellectual involvement with the world, uses as a means of discourse not the simple logic of reason but the more involved "logic of metaphor" which demands of the reader a refined and alert sensibility to grasp the coherent relationship of the resemblances. In such a metaphorical context words, phrases, and comparisons are used more for their associational rather than their literal meanings.

Dylan Thomas has defined this aspect of modern poetry in these words:

> Out of the inevitable conflict of images—inevitable because of the creative, recreative, destructive and contradictory nature of the motivating centre, the womb of war—I try to make that momentary peace which is a poem.

Let us consider one of his early poems (1936) as an illustration.

Ears in the Turrets Hear

Ears in the turrets hear
Hands grumble on the door,
Eyes in the gables see
The fingers at the locks.
Shall I unbolt or stay
Alone till the day I die
Unseen by stranger-eyes
In this white house?
Hands, hold you poison or grapes?

Beyond this island bound
By a thin sea of flesh

And a bone coast,
The land lies out of sound
And the hills out of mind.
No bird or flying fish
Disturbs this island's rest.

Ears in this island hear
The wind pass like a fire,
Eyes in this island see
Ships anchor off the bay.
Shall I run to the ships
With the wind in my hair,
Or stay till the day I die
And welcome no sailor?
Ships, hold you poison or grapes?

Hands grumble on the door,
Ships anchor off the bay,
Rain beats the sand and slates.
Shall I let in the stranger,
Shall I welcome the sailor,
Or stay till the day I die?

Hands of the stranger and holds of the ships,
Hold you poison or grapes?

—Dylan Thomas (1914–1953)

The poem does not answer but poses the question what kind of a life should one lead: Should one retain his purity and inviolable privacy in a womblike contentment or venture out into the turmoil of a world inhabited by strangers where one may find the joys of life ("grapes") but also risk the dangers of suffering and death ("poison")? The first stanza is an extended metaphor of the isolated person living in a turreted white house (suggestive of innocence) undecided whether he should unbolt the locks to enter the turbulent, dangerous world of experience. Abruptly the second stanza shifts the metaphor of isolation by comparing the body of flesh and bone to an island cut off from the mainland. The ships at anchor in the bay, the stranger knocking at the door, the wind and rain—all the excitement and danger of living tempt the isolated islander to welcome the sailor and run to the ships. The frightened weaklings do not venture forth; the rash Dylan Thomases quickly unbolt the locks and head for the mainland.

The telescoped metaphors of hands grumbling at the door and an island bound by a sea of flesh and a bone coast as well as images of a fiery wind, rain, poison, and grapes are all fused by the imagination of the poet into a coherent emotional experience.

Another type of figurative language that often perplexes poetry readers is the *conceit,* an intricate or far-fetched metaphor consisting of a comparison of incongruous, diverse elements which, however, have some point of resemblance. The effect of bringing together such discordant images in a conceit may be surprise or revelation. If the unusual comparison is used to bring out an emotional or intellectual truth, the conceit becomes a powerful vehicle of poetic communication. The conceit has been popular in fourteenth-century Italian and seventeenth-century Spanish poetry, in Elizabethan poetry and the metaphysical school of Donne and his followers, in nineteenth-century French poetry (Baudelaire, Mallarmé, Laforgue), and in our day in the work of T. S. Eliot, Hart Crane, Dylan Thomas, and W. H. Auden.

Richard Crashaw, a serious religious poet of the seventeenth century, wrote two poems, "The Tear" and "Saint Mary Magdalene, or The Weeper." Following a baroque tradition of decorative imagery, he occasionally lapsed into ludicrous conceits by using inappropriate and fanciful comparisons.

> Fair drop, why quak'st thou so?
>   'Cause thou straight may lay thy head
> In the dust? Oh no;
>   The dust shall never be thy bed:
> A pillow for thee will I bring,
> Stuffed with down of angel's wing.

> (from "The Tear")

In the other poem he compares the tears of Saint Mary Magdalene to

> ". . . two faithful fountains;
> Two walking baths, two weeping motions,
> Portable, and compendious oceans."

The successful utilization of metaphoric communication (including the conceit) can be seen in the following poem by John Donne, which he is said to have given to his wife when he left for the Continent on a diplomatic mission in 1611.

A Valediction[1] Forbidding Mourning

> As virtuous men pass mildly away,
>   And whisper to their souls to go,
> Whilst some of their sad friends do say,
>   "The breath goes now," and some say, "No";

So let us melt, and make no noise,
  No tear-floods nor sigh-tempests move;
'Twere profanation of our joys
  To tell the laity[2] our love.

Moving of the earth[3] brings harms and fears
  Men reckon what it did and meant;
But trepidation of the spheres[4]
  Though greater far, is innocent.[5]

Dull sublunary[6] lovers' love,
  Whose soul is sense, cannot admit
Absence, because it doth remove
  Those things which elemented[7] it.

But we, by a love so much refined
  That ourselves know not what it is,
Inter-assured of the mind,
  Care less eyes, lips, and hands to miss.

Our two souls, therefore, which are one,
  Though I must go, endure not yet
A breach, but an expansion
  Like gold to airy thinness beat.

If they be two, they are two so
  As stiff twin compasses are two;
Thy soul the fixed foot, makes no show
  To move, but doth if the other do.

And though it in the center sit,
  Yet when the other far doth roam,
It leans, and hearkens after it,
  And grows erect as that comes home.

Such wilt thou be to me, who must,
  Like the other foot, obliquely run;
Thy firmness makes my circle just,
  And makes me end where I begun.

—John Donne (1572–1631)

---

[1] Farewell. [2] Laymen, i.e., those not initiated into the mysteries of religion—or of spiritual love. [3] An earthquake (equated with the sensuality of physical love). [4] Vibration of the spheres in the Ptolemaic system (equated with true love). [5] Harmless. [6] Below the moon, i.e., earthly (or sensual). [7] Composed.

Although the metaphors in this poem are drawn from a wide range of experiences and subjects—dying, religion, geology, astronomy, the goldsmith's art, and mathematics—they are all held together in a meaningul relationship by contrasting two types of love: a high spiritual one and a transient sensual one. In the six opening lines the poet suggests that the temporary separation of two people who truly love each other should be as quiet and peaceful as the farewell of sad, pious friends around the death bed of virtuous men. In such a leave-taking hysterical "tear-floods" and sentimental "sigh-tempests" would be a desecration. The poet, in comparing his love and his wife's to the love of high churchmen for God, suggests the profound spiritual nature of their joyful affection which would be profaned by noisy, violent outbursts of emotion.

> 'Twere profanation of our joys
> To tell the laity our love.

In the third stanza Donne develops the paradox that the greater disturbance of the heavenly spheres (like true love) brings harmony and peace while the lesser one of a noisy earthquake (like physical love) "brings harms and fears." The next stanza, defining the nature of this physical love as dull, earthy, and sensuous, states that a separation ("absence") would destroy it. But the poet's spiritual love (really indefinable), including as a subordinate element physical passion, is refined by an intellectual communion of two souls which can never be parted for they form one indissoluble bond. To convey this concept Donne uses the brilliant figure of a lump of gold which can be beaten by a skilled artisan "to airy thinness."

The last three stanzas elaborate with scientific precision the famous conceit comparing the relationship of the poet's soul and his wife's to the two legs of a draughtsman's compass which can circumscribe the perfect mathematical figure, a circle. As the two parts of the compass form one instrument, so their two souls form one entity. So perfectly are they attuned to each other that the "fixed foot" (his wife's soul) only moves when the other one does. Besides resolving the mathematical paradox that one plus one can equal one, Donne suggests another; the farther the distant foot roams, the more the center one leans toward it (i.e., is closer). As the other returns to the center of the circle, the fixed foot "grows erect" and its firmness (faithfulness) permits the circling foot to return to its starting point, thus completing the perfect figure (journey). Despite the disparate elements in the conceit, the exactness with which the details are worked out adds to the forcefulness of the comparison which embodies abstract concepts in concrete mathematical terms.

What does Donne gain by using so many varied and seemingly incongruous images in a love poem? By directing the original metaphors around a central core contrasting concepts of love, he unifies the poem and saves it from falling into sentimentality or triteness. We sense that both a deep emotion and a keen intellect are present, what T. S. Eliot would call a unified sensibility. The metaphors are used functionally, not decoratively. The poem is a good illustration of Laurence Perrine's statement: "Only form makes content memorable; only content makes form meaningful. . . . Form and content are ultimately one."

The conceit, an ingenious discordant analogy, serves several purposes in a poem: It concretizes abstractions, clarifies complexities, and defines the indefinable. A good example of its successful use by a modern poet is this poem by W. H. Auden.

Law Like Love

Law, say the gardeners, is the sun,
Law is the one
All gardeners obey
Tomorrow, yesterday, today.

Law is the wisdom of the old
The impotent grandfathers shrilly scold;
The grandchildren put out a treble tongue,
Law is the senses of the young.

Law, says the priest with a priestly look
Expounding to an unpriestly people,
Law is the words in my priestly book,
Law is my pulpit and my steeple.

Law, says the judge as he looks down his nose,
Speaking clearly and most severely,
Law is as I've told you before,
Law is as you know I suppose,
Law is but let me explain it once more,
Law is The Law.

Yet law-abiding scholars write,
Law is neither wrong nor right,
Law is only crimes
Punished by places and by times,
Law is the clothes men wear
Anytime, anywhere,
Law is Good-morning and Good-night.

Others say, Law is our Fate;
Others say, Law is our State;
Others say, others say
Law is no more
Law has gone away.

And always the loud angry crowd
Very angry and very loud
Law is We,
And always the soft idiot softly Me.

If we, dear, know we know no' more
Than they about the law,
If I no more than you
Know what we should and should not do
Except that all agree
Gladly or miserably
That the law is
And that all know this,
If therefore thinking it absurd
To identify Law with some other word,
Unlike so many men
I cannot say Law is again,
No more than they can we suppress
The universal wish to guess
Or slip out of our own position
Into an unconcerned condition.
Although I can at least confine
Your vanity and mine
To stating timidly
A timid similarity,
We shall boast anyway:
Like love I say.

Like love we don't know where or why
Like love we can't compel or fly
Like love we often weep
Like love we seldom keep.

—W. H. Auden (1907–   )

The first half of the poem suggests the different concepts of law held by various individuals. To the gardener or farmer it is the recurrent, eternal cycle of nature dominated by the sun. To the old it is the accumulated wisdom that age brings; to the young it is the Epicurean enjoyment of the senses. To the religious person it is the precepts found in a divinely revealed book. To the judge it is involved legalistic phraseology in statutes that need interpretation and explanation. To scholars who believe in relativism, law is not immutable but merely the outgrowth of local customs, differing in time and place. To pessimists law is Fate; to totalitarians it is the supremacy of the State. Some say that law has vanished and anarchy reigns. The angry mob makes violence its law; the egoist establishes his own.

Various as the concepts of law are, people still reverence it and feel it is a dominating force in directing and controlling their lives. To give a simple, clear definition seems impossible. Yet Auden, in a mood of humility, concludes the poem by a brilliant conceit suggesting a fourfold similarity between law and love, a conceit that acts as a revealing spotlight of clarification.

For Discussion

The greatest thing by far is to be a master of metaphor. It is the one thing that cannot be learnt from others; and it is also a sign of genius, since a good metaphor implies an intuitive perception of the similarity in dissimilars.

—Aristotle

Imaging is in itself the very height and life of poetry.

—Sir Philip Sidney

Every poem is a new metaphor inside or it is nothing. And there is a sense in which all poems are the same old metaphors always.

—Robert Frost

An effective figure of speech is both a perception of reality and a projection of the imagination. It is a sudden insight into a meaningful relationship between things not often thought to be like.

—*M. L. Rosenthal and A. J. M. Smith*

9
Figures of Speech

Although traditional rhetoricians have classified more than two hundred figures of speech, the modern reader will find that the identification of a few of the most common will be sufficient for his enjoyment and study of poetry. The student should be cautioned that merely identifying or even analyzing an individual figure of speech is not so important as understanding its function and effectiveness in the whole poem. Figures of speech interact with each other and must always be evaluated in the context of the poem. Furthermore, many good poems contain little or no imagery.

Four figures of speech based on the principle of analogy are the simile, metaphor, allegory, and personification. A *simile* is a comparison of two objects, qualities, or actions made explicit by the use of the words *like* or *as*. The terms compared, although different, do resemble each other. An emerald and an iceberg differ in size, temperature, and other respects but resemble each other in shimmering green color. Coleridge stresses this resemblance in his simile describing an iceberg near the south pole.

> And ice, mast-high, came floating by,
> As green as emerald.

An *extended* (or *epic*) simile is elaborated with many descriptive details to emphasize narration, description, emotion, or characterization. Homer, Virgil, Dante, Milton, Keats (in "Hyperion"), and Arnold (in

"Sohrab and Rustum" and "Balder Dead") have made frequent use of the epic simile in their narratives. In the following epic simile, Milton conditions our response to Satan's leap over the wall of paradise.

> . . . As when a prowling wolf,
> Whom hunger drives to seek new haunt for prey,
> Watching where shepherds pen their flocks at eve
> In hurdled cotes amid the field secure,
> Leaps o'er the fence with ease into the fold;
> Or as a thief bent to unhoard the cash
> Of some rich burgher, whose substantial doors,
> Cross-barred and belted fast, fear no assult,
> In at the window climbs, or o'er the tiles:
> So clomb this first grand thief into God's fold.

A *metaphor* is a condensed comparison which omits the *like* or *as*. Following are some examples.

> Love is a sickness full of woes

> *   *   *

> The western wave was all aflame

By a series of powerful metaphors Shakespeare reveals the hopelessness and pessimism of the disillusioned Macbeth at the end of his life.

> To-morrow, and to-morrow, and to-morrow,
> Creeps in this petty pace from day to day,
> To the last syllable of recorded time;
> And all our yesterdays have lighted fools
> The way to dusty death. Out, out brief candle!
> Life's but a walking shadow; a poor player,
> That struts and frets his hour upon the stage,
> And then is heard no more: it is a tale
> Told by an idiot, full of sound and fury,
> Signifying nothing.

Although a simile has the advantage of immediate clarity, a good metaphor, by its brevity and compression, fuses two different objects, qualities, or actions into a new and surprising relationship which sharpens our vision and understanding. The emotional connotation of the words and the quick fusion of diverse elements affect our emotional response and sensibility.

A metaphor extended in the form of a connected narrative to express a writer's view of history, ethics, or philosophy is called an *allegory*. Usually starting with some abstract concept of life, the author embodies his idea in specific events and characters. As in all metaphors, because the comparison is implied rather than explicitly stated, an allegory moves on a double level and must be read with an alert mind to grasp the relationship between the historical (or fictional) characters and the abstract virtues, vices, or ideas implied. An allegory may be short or long, simple or complex. In the most famous poetic allegory in English, Spenser's *The Faerie Queene*, the Red Cross Knight, the defender of the English Reformed Church, represents the virtue of holiness; and Duessa (Mary, Queen of Scots), the rival of Gloriana (Queen Elizabeth), represents the vice of deceit. Coleridge's "The Rime of the Ancient Mariner" is an allegory of sin, alienation, and redemption. A good example of a short poetic allegory is the following poem by Robert Frost.

The Draft Horse

With a lantern that wouldn't burn
In too frail a buggy we drove
Behind too heavy a horse
Through a pitch-dark limitless grove.

And a man came out of the trees
And took our horse by the head
And reaching back to his ribs
Deliberately stabbed him dead.

The ponderous beast went down
With a crack of a broken shaft.
And the night drew through the trees
In one long invidious draft.

The most unquestioning pair
That ever accepted fate
And the least disposed to ascribe
Any more than we had to to hate,

We assumed that the man himself
Or someone he had to obey
Wanted us to get down
And walk the rest of the way.

—Robert Frost (1875–1963)

The narrative content of the poem consists of the mysterious adventure of an incautious couple driving in a frail buggy through a sinister dark wood. A man comes out of the trees and in a ritualistic sacrifice kills the ponderous horse. The perplexed couple is forced to "walk the rest of the way."

We can read the poem as an allegory of vulnerable humanity unprepared to face strange disasters on the journey of life. Three details suggest man's lack of caution in traveling through "a pitch-dark limitless grove": a faulty lantern, a frail buggy, and an unsuitable horse. (Is the couple, like Dante, lost in the gloomy wood?) Does the man kill the horse as a sacrificial scapegoat to preserve the lives of the couple? Out of hatred? Or is he compelled to do so by a superhuman power he must obey? Whatever the answer, the "unquestioning pair" accept their fate with quiet resignation.

A metaphorical device frequently used in allegories and lyric poems is *personification,* which attributes life to inanimate objects or abstractions. Keats personifies autumn as the "close bosom-friend of the maturing sun" and as a gleaner "drows'd with the fume of poppies" who "spares the next swath and all its twined flowers." Milton, in "L'Allegro," personifies loathed melancholy as the child of blackest midnight, mirth as a fair goddess, and liberty as a mountain nymph. Stephen Spender's "Express" sings with "a jazzy madness."

We find this rhetorical figure in the oldest poems. Primitive man believed in the existence of life and spirit in all forms of nature. Early religious poems and hymns expressed this animism imaginatively by using personification. In eighteenth-century English poetry personification lost its emotional impact and degenerated into vague intellectual abstractions as in Alexander Pope's couplets from "Windsor Forest."

> See Pan with flocks, with fruits Pomona crowned;
> Here blushing Flora paints th' enamelled ground;
> Here Ceres' gifts in waving prospect stand,
> And nodding, tempt the joyful reaper's hand;
> Rich Industry sits smiling on the plains,
> And peace and plenty tell a Stuart reigns.

Romantic poets such as Wordsworth, Shelley, and Keats reestablished a strong identification with nature and revived its poetic effectiveness. Shelley's "A Dirge" is an example.

A Dirge

> Rough wind, that moanest loud
> Grief too sad for song;

Wild wind, when sullen cloud
Knells all the night long;
Sad storm, whose tears are vain,
Bare woods, whose branches strain,
Deep caves and dreary main,—
    Wail, for the world's wrong.

—Percy Bysshe Shelley (1792–1822)

Often closely associated with personification is *apostrophe,* whereby the poet addresses a dead or absent person directly as living or present or addresses an inanimate thing or abstract quality as if alive and capable of understanding. Its purpose is to focus attention on the person or thing addressed, to dramatize a situation, or to establish an intimate, emotional relationship between poet and his audience. Donne opens one of his love poems with this startling apostrophe (combined with personification).

    Busy old fool, unruly sun,
    Why dost thou thus
Through windows and through curtains call on us?

In his famous "Holy Sonnet X," he frames the poem by apostrophizing death in the first and last lines, setting him up as a boastful but deflated antagonist in a dramatic David and Goliath conflict.

Holy Sonnet X

Death be not proud, though some have callèd thee
Mighty and dreadful, for thou art not so;
For those whom thou think'st thou dost overthrow
Die not, poor Death, nor yet canst thou kill me.
From rest and sleep, which but thy pictures be,
Much pleasure; then from thee much more must flow,
And soonest our best men with thee do go,
Rest of their bones, and soul's delivery.
Thou art slave to fate, chance, kings, and desperate men
And dost with poison, war, and sickness dwell;
And poppy or charms can make us sleep as well
And better than thy stroke; why swell'st thou then?
One short sleep past, we wake eternally,
And death shall be no more; Death, thou shalt die.

—John Donne (1573–1631)

Related to these figures of comparison is *metonomy* which is based on the close association of ideas so that a part may stand for the whole ("Arthur with a hundred spears rode far"), the whole for the part ("the smiling year," for spring), the instrument for the agent ("the pen is mightier than the sword"), the container for the thing contained ("the kettle boils"), the material for the object ("pigskin" for football). Based on substitution, this figure is helpful to the poet for it serves as an imagistic shorthand to emphasize concrete detail.

Yeats opens his *"Lapis Lazuli"* with the lines

> I have heard that hysterical women say
> They are sick of the palette and fiddle-bow.

Palette is a metonymic substitute for the art of painting and *fiddle-bow* for the art of music. Emily Dickinson uses a single color to stand for a whole glowing sunset.

> The red upon the hill
> Taketh away my will.

A forceful figure of speech that is the opposite of figures of comparison and association is *antithesis* which places two items in juxtaposition in order to emphasize contrast. Antithesis, particularly effective in satirical verse, was exploited by eighteenth-century neo-classic poets who found in the balanced phrasing an ideal resource appropriate to the pattern of the closed couplet. Alexander Pope concludes his attack on a court favorite whom he detested in these vigorous contrasts.

> Amphibious thing! that acting either part,
> The trifling head, or the corrupted heart;
> Fop at the toilet, flatt'rer at the board,
> Now trips a lady, and now struts a lord.
> Eve's tempter thus the Rabbins have expresst,
> A cherub's face, a reptile all the rest;
> Beauty that shocks you, Parts that none will trust,
> Wit that can creep, and Pride that licks the dust.

Two contrasting figures, hyperbole and understatement, have been used by poets in all ages. *Hyperbole* is an exaggeration or conscious overstatement of literal truth to create a desired effect. It may be used for descriptive emphasis, for the expression of strong emotion, or for comic purposes. To impress the reader with the majesty, size, and power of Satan, Milton tells us that Satan's massive round shield was as large as the moon seen through Galileo's telescope, and that his spear, equal to the tallest Norwegian pine and fit to be the mast of a great ship, was handled by Satan as if it were but a wand.

Shakespeare uses a powerful hyperbole to express the tragic horror of Macbeth after the murder of King Duncan.

> What hands are here? they pluck out mine eyes.
> Will all great Neptune's ocean wash this blood
> Clean from my hand? No; this my hand will rather
> The multitudinous seas incarnadine,
> Making the green one red.

The comic use of hyperbole is illustrated by Sir John Suckling's description of the bride's ring in "A Ballad Upon a Wedding."

> It looked like the great collar (just)
>   About our young colt's neck.

The reverse of hyperbole (overstatement) is *understatement,* which achieves intensification of emotion by restraint or is used for ironic effect. Wordsworth concludes one of his Lucy poems with the *suggestion* of profound grief.

> She lived unknown, and few could know
>   When Lucy ceased to be;
> But she is in her grave, and, oh,
>   The difference to me!

In his famous love poem "To His Coy Mistress" Marvell creates an ironic effect by the "I think" in the following understatement.

> The grave's a fine and private place,
> But none, I think, do there embrace.

For Discussion

The moment our discourse rises above the ground line of familiar facts, and is inflamed with passion or exalted by thought, it is clothed in images. . . . This imagery is spontaneous.

—Ralph Waldo Emerson

What really matters in a metaphor is the psychic depth at which the things of the world, whether actual or fancied, are transmuted by the cool heat of the imagination.

—Philip Wheelwright

Metaphor is to the poet what the equation is to the mathematician.

—May Swenson

Poems Related to Chapters 8 and 9

The Silken Tent

She is as in a field a silken tent
At midday when a sunny summer breeze
Has dried the dew and all its ropes relent,
So that in guys it gently sways at ease,
And its supporting central cedar pole,
That is its pinnacle to heavenward
And signifies the sureness of the soul,
Seems to owe naught to any single cord,
But strictly held by none, is loosely bound
By countless silken ties of love and thought
To everything on earth the compass round,
And only by one's going slightly taut
In the capriciousness of summer air
Is of the slightest bondage made aware.

—Robert Frost (1874–1963)

1. Like Marvell's "On a Drop of Dew" this poem is an elaborated simile. What aspects of a love relationship are suggested by the comparison of the beloved to a silken tent?
2. What imagistic details contribute to the effectiveness of the analogy?
3. Why is the poem cast in the form of a single sentence?

Pitcher

His art is eccentricity, his aim
How not to hit the mark he seems to aim at,
His passion how to avoid the obvious,
His technique how to vary the avoidance.
The others throw to be comprehended. He
Throws to be a moment misunderstood.
Yet not too much. Not errant, arrant, wild,
But every seeming aberration willed.
Not to, yet still, still to communicate
Making the batter understand too late.

—Robert Francis (1901–   )

1. What characteristics of a poet are suggested by comparing him to a baseball pitcher?
2. How do you account for the brevity of the poem?

These two songs are from Shakespeare's early play *Love's Labour's Lost.*

Spring

When daisies pied[1] and violets blue,
    And lady-smocks[2] all silver-white,
And cuckoo-buds[3] of yellow hue
    Do paint the meadows with delight,
The cuckoo then, on every tree,
Mocks married men, for thus sings he:
"Cuckoo! cuckoo!" O word of fear,
Unpleasing to a married ear.

When shepherds pipe on oaten straws,[4]
    And merry larks are ploughmen's clocks,
When turtles tread,[5] and rooks, and daws,
    And maidens bleach their summer smocks,
The cuckoo then, on every tree,
Mocks married men, for thus sings he:
"Cuckoo! cuckoo!" O word of fear,
Unpleasing to a married ear.

------

[1] Variegate, of different colors.   [2] Also called cuckoo-flowers.   [3] Buttercups.   [4] Play on musical instruments.   [5] Turtledoves mate.

Winter

When icicles hang by the wall,
    And Dick the shepherd blows his nail,[1]
And Tom bears logs into the hall,
    And milk comes frozen home in pail;
When blood is nipt and ways[2] be foul,
Then nightly sings the staring owl,
"Tu-whit! Tu-who!" A merry note,
While greasy Joan doth keel[3] the pot.

When all aloud the wind doth blow,
    And coughing drowns the parson's saw,[4]
And birds sit brooding in the snow,
    And Marian's nose looks red and raw;
When roasted crabs[5] hiss in the bowl,
Then nightly sings the staring owl,

"Tu-whit! Tu-who!" A merry note,
While greasy Joan doth keel the pot.

—William Shakespeare (1564–1616)

---

¹ Breathes on his fingertips to warm them.   ² Roads.   ³ Cool by stirring
or skimming.   ⁴ Trite proverb.   ⁵ Crab apples.

1. What concrete images bring out the contrast of the two seasons?
2. Is the song of the cuckoo appropriate to the cheerfulness and colorfulness of spring or out of harmony with it? (Because the cuckoo lays its
   eggs in other birds' nests to be hatched and because of its mating cry,
   Elizabethans associated the bird with *cuckold,* a deceived husband.) Is
   the song of the owl in winter really "a merry note"? Explain.
3. What other basic contrasts are to be found in the two poems?
4. What does Shakespeare gain by introducing infidelity in the joyful spring
   poem and a bubbling pot of crabapples in the dreariness of winter?
5. Compare and contrast Shakespeare's "Winter" with Hardy's "The Darkling Thrush" (page 149).

The Soul Selects Her Own Society

The Soul selects her own Society—
Then—shuts the Door—
To her divine Majority—
Present no more—

Unmoved—she notes the Chariots—pausing—
At her low Gate—
Unmoved—an Emperor be kneeling
Upon her Mat—

I've known her—from an ample nation—
Choose One—
Then—close the Valves of her attention—
Like Stone—

—Emily Dickinson (1830–1886)

1. What image of exclusion does the poet use in stanza one? Two? Three?
   In what order are they arranged? How does this arrangement contribute
   to the theme of the poem?
2. What pattern of rhyme does she use? How does this add to the effectiveness of the poem?
3. What change is there in the metrical scheme of the last stanza? Why the
   shift?

Thomas Hardy wrote the following poem during the tragic fighting of World War I.

In Time of "The Breaking of Nations"

1
Only a man harrowing clods
    In a slow silent walk
With an old horse that stumbles and nods
    Half asleep as they stalk.

2
Only thin smoke without flame
    From the heaps of couch-grass;
Yet this will go onward the same
    Though Dynasties pass.

3
Yonder a maid and her wight[1]
    Come whispering by;
War's annals will cloud into night
    Ere their story die.

      —Thomas Hardy (1840–1928)

---

[1] Sweetheart.

1. What two images form the core of the poem? What two immemorial activities of mankind do they represent? What do the images have in common? How do they differ?
2. With what are the two images contrasted? How do these contrasts suggest the theme of the poem?
3. Comment on the poet's use of *silent, half asleep,* and *whispering* in a war poem. Would it have been more effective if Hardy had used hyperbole instead of understatement? Explain.

Holy Sonnet IX

If poisonous minerals, and if that tree,
Whose fruit threw death on (else immortal) us,
If lecherous goats, if serpents envious
Cannot be damn'd, alas! why should I be?
Why should intent or reason, born in me,
Make sins, else equal, in me more heinous?
And, mercy being easy, and glorious
To God, in His stern wrath why threatens He?
But who am I, that dare dispute with Thee?

O God, O! of Thine only worthy blood,
And my tears, make a heavenly Lethean flood,
And drown in it my sin's black memory.
That thou remember them, some claim as debt;
I think it mercy if Thou wilt forget.

—John Donne (1573–1631)

1. In the first eight lines on what principle of order are the images arranged? Are the three questions patterned in the same arrangement? Explain. What does the poem gain by this order?
2. What contrasts are stressed in the poem?
3. The first eight lines are a closely reasoned argument appealing to the intellect; the last six are an emotional appeal for forgiveness through mercy. Does this shift in tone split the poem into two conflicting parts, or is the sonnet artistically unified? Discuss.
4. In lines ten through twelve Donne uses a daring metaphor: a redemptive flood made up of Christ's blood and the repentant tears of the sinner. Does this figure of speech call attention to itself? Is it decorative embellishment in a religious poem, or is it dramatically appropriate in context? Discuss.
5. Explain the antithesis of the concluding couplet.

The following poem was published in England a century ago (1867) when—under the impact of science, industrialism, and a growing materialism—Victorian optimism and religious certainties were being replaced by a disillusioning pessimism and loss of faith.

Dover Beach

The sea is calm tonight,
The tide is full, the moon lies fair
Upon the straits;—on the French coast the light
Gleams and is gone; the cliffs of England stand,
Glimmering and vast, out in the tranquil bay.
Come to the window, sweet is the night-air!
Only, from the long line of spray
Where the sea meets the moon-blanched land,
Listen! you hear the grating roar
Of pebbles which the waves draw back, and fling,
At their return, up the high strand,
Begin, and cease, and then again begin,
With tremulous cadence slow, and bring
The eternal note of sadness in.

Sophocles[1] long ago
Heard it on the Aegean,[2] and it brought

Into his mind the turbid ebb and flow
Of human misery; we
Find also in the sound a thought,
Hearing it by this distant northern sea.

The Sea of Faith
Was once, too, at the full, and round earth's shore
Lay like the folds of a bright girdle[3] furled.
But now I only hear
Its melancholy, long, withdrawing roar,
Retreating, to the breath
Of the night-wind, down the vast edges drear
And naked shingles[4] of the world.

Ah, love, let us be true
To one another! for the world, which seems
To lie before us like a land of dreams,
So various, so beautiful, so new,
Hath really neither joy, nor love, nor light,
Nor certitude, nor peace, nor help for pain;
And we are here as on a darkling plain
Swept with alarms of struggle and flight,
Where ignorant armies clash by night.

—Matthew Arnold (1822–1888)

---

[1] Greek playwright of the fifth century B.C. whose tragedies deal with "the ebb and flow of human misery."   [2] Sea between Greece and Asia Minor.   [3] Colorful sash encircling the waist.   [4] Pebbled beaches.

1. Where is the speaker in the poem? Who is with him? What mood do all the images in the first six lines convey? What mood do the images of the next eight lines suggest? How does this clash suggest the theme of the poem?

2. Why does Arnold bring in the allusion to Sophocles in stanza two? Does this clarify or confuse the theme? Discuss.

3. Explain clearly the metaphorical implications of stanza three. Is the sea figure of speech in this stanza a progressive development of the sea imagery in the preceding stanzas or not? Explain.

4. The last stanza deals with land imagery. How is this related to the preceding three stanzas?

5. In a faithless, meaningless, destructive world, what is the only certainty the speaker can cling to?

6. In the poem is there any progression in the imagery of light and darkness? Explain.

7. Find some concrete examples of the poet's effective use of sound patterns to convey emotion.

8. Can the poet's use of irregular lines, stanzas, and rhyme be justified? If so, on what basis?

"Dover Beach"—A Note to That Poem

The wave withdrawing
Withers with seaward rustle of flimsy water
Sucking the sand down: dragging at empty shells:
The roil after it settling: too smooth: smothered . . .

After forty a man's a fool to wait in the
Sea's face for the full force and the roaring of
Surf to come over him: droves of careening water.
After forty the tug's out and the salt and the
Sea follow it: less sound and violence:
Nevertheless the ebb has its own beauty—
Shells sand and all the whispering rustle.
There's earth in it then and the bubbles of foam gone.

Moreover—and this too has its lovely uses—
It's the outward wave that spills the inward forward
Tripping the proud piled mute virginal
Mountain of water in wallowing welter of light and
Sound enough—thunder for miles back: it's a fine and a
Wild smother to vanish in: pulling down—
Tripping with outward ebb the urgent inward.

Speaking alone for myself it's the steep hill and the
Toppling lift of the young men I am toward now—
Waiting for that as the wave for the next wave.
Let them go over us all I say with the thunder of
What's to be next in the world. It's we will be under it!

—Archibald MacLeish (1892–   )

The poet, in the maturity of his forties, contemplates the onrush of the younger generation. He finds not despair but beauty and exultation in identifying himself with the young men who have absorbed something from him.

1. Around what two basic metaphors is the poem built? How are they interrelated?
2. What do the following images represent: sand and empty shells, bubbles of foam, welter of light and sound?
3. Comment on the poet's use of effective rhythm, alliteration, and onomatopoeia.

The Dover Bitch: A Criticism of Life

So there stood Matthew Arnold and this girl
With the cliffs of England crumbling away behind them,

And he said to her, "Try to be true to me,
And I'll do the same for you, for things are bad
All over, etc., etc."
Well now, I knew this girl. It's true she had read
Sophocles in a fairly good translation
And caught that bitter allusion to the sea,
But all the time he was talking she had in mind
The notion of what his whiskers would feel like
On the back of her neck. She told me later on
That after a while she got to looking out
At the lights across the channel, and really felt sad,
Thinking of all the wine and enormous beds
And blandishments in French and the perfumes.
And then she got really angry. To have been brought
All the way down from London, and then be addressed
As a sort of mournful cosmic last resort
Is really tough on a girl, and she was pretty.
Anyway, she watched him pace the room
And finger his watch-chain and seem to sweat a bit,
And then she said one or two unprintable things.
But you mustn't judge her by that. What I mean to say is,
She's really all right. I still see her once in a while
And she always treats me right. We have a drink
And I give her a good time, and perhaps it's a year
Before I see her again, but there she is,
Running to fat, but dependable as they come.
And sometimes I bring her a bottle of *Nuit d' Amour*.

—Anthony Hecht (1923–   )

1. How do you account for the lack of figurative language in this poem?
    The flatness of rhythm? The colloquial diction?
2. If we characterize the mood of Arnold's poem as pessimistic, MacLeish's
    as optimistic, how would you describe the tone of this poem? Realistic?
    Cynical? Ironic? Or what?

The Hour-Glass

Consider this small dust, here in the glass,
    By atoms moved.
Could you believe that this the body was
    Of one that loved;
And in his mistress' flame playing like a fly,
Was turned to cinders by her eye?
Yes; and in death, as life, unblest,
    To have't expressed,
Even ashes of lovers find no rest.

—Ben Jonson (1573–1637)

1. What two conceits form the basis of this poem? Are they effective or not? Explain.

2. What do the rhymes contribute to the poem? How do the rhymes of the first four lines differ from the others?

3. What is the theme of the poem? Is its mood elegiac or cynical? Discuss.

To Autumn

Season of mists and mellow fruitfulness,
    Close bosom-friend of the maturing sun:
Conspiring with him how to load and bless
    With fruit the vines that round the thatch-eaves run;
To bend with apples the mossed cottage-trees,
    And fill all fruit with ripeness to the core;
        To swell the gourd, and plump the hazel shells
With a sweet kernel; to set budding more,
    And still more, later flowers for the bees,
    Until they think warm days will never cease.
        For Summer has o'er-brimmed their clammy cells.

Who hath not seen thee oft amid thy store?
    Sometimes whoever seeks abroad may find
Thee sitting careless on a granary floor,
    Thy hair soft-lifted by the winnowing wind;
Or on a half-reaped furrow sound asleep,
    Drowsed with the fume of poppies, while thy hook
        Spares the next swath and all its twinèd flowers:
And sometimes like a gleaner thou dost keep,
    Steady thy laden head across a brook;
    Or by a cider-press, with patient look,
        Thou watchest the last oozing hours by hours.

Where are the songs of Spring? Ay, where are they?
    Think not of them, thou hast thy music too,—
While barrèd clouds bloom the soft-dying day,
    And touch the stubble-plains with rosy hue;
Then in a wailful choir the small gnats mourn
    Among the river sallows, borne aloft
        Or sinking as the light wind lives or dies;
And full-grown lambs loud bleat from hilly bourn;
    Hedge-crickets sing and now with treble soft
    The red-breast whistles from a garden-croft;
        And gathering swallows twitter in the skies.

—John Keats (1795–1821)

1. How important is personification in this poem? Is autumn a vague abstraction or given a definite personality? In which stanza is the figure most clearly visualized? By what three vivid pictures?

2. Where does Keats use apostrophe in the poem? What function does it serve?

3. The poem is rich in its appeal to the senses. To what sense—visual, tactile, auditory, gustatory, or olfactory—do the images in stanza one primarily appeal? Stanza two? Stanza three?

4. What references are there to the other seasons of the year? What is their function?

5. The poem suggests that autumn is the season not only of maturing fruitfulness but also of the transience of this rich beauty. Where in stanza one is this implication of dying found? In stanza two? In stanza three? Is there a progression in this concept? Explain.

6. What time of day is suggested in stanza one? Two? Three? How does this time transition help structure the poem? How does it suggest the theme?

7. What is the purpose of Keats in using in stanza one images of ripe fruit, autumn flowers, and plump gourds and nuts? In stanza two harvesting images? In stanza three stubble-plains at sunset? How are these images related to the theme of the poem?

8. What outstanding examples of tone color and onomatopoeia are to be found in the poem? Is the rhythm appropriate to the mood? Explain. What is the rhyme scheme? What is the effect of the final rhyme of each stanza being separated by four lines? Does this in any way contribute to the theme? Explain.

The Cyclists

Spread on the roadway,
With open-blown jackets,
Like black, soaring pinions,
They swoop down the hillside,
    The Cyclists.

Seeming dark-plumaged
Birds, after carrion,
Careening and circling,
Over the dying
    Of England.

She lies with her bosom
Beneath them, no longer
The Dominant Mother,
The Virile—but rotting
    Before time.

The smell of her, tainted,
Has bitten their nostrils.

Exultant they hover,
And shadow the sun with
Foreboding.

—Amy Lowell (1874–1925)

1. What emotions do the two dominant images evoke?

In October 1816 in London Keats and his Enfield friend Charles Cowden Clarke stayed up all night reading aloud selections from Chapman's vigorous Elizabethan translation of *The Iliad* and *The Odyssey*. The profound emotional effect of this literary experience on the young poet is evident in this sonnet.

On First Looking Into Chapman's Homer

Much have I travell'd in the realms of gold,[1]
  And many goodly states and kingdoms seen;
    Round many western islands have I been
Which bards[2] in fealty[3] to Apollo[4] hold.
Oft of one wide expanse had I been told
    That deep-brow'd Homer ruled as his desmesne:[5]
Yet did I never breathe its pure serene[6]
Till I heard Chapman speak out loud and bold:
Then felt I like some watcher of the skies
  When a new planet swims into his ken;[7]
Or like stout Cortez when with eagle eyes[8]
    He star'd at the Pacific—and all his men
Look'd at each other with a wild surmise—
    Silent, upon a peak in Darien.[9]

—John Keats (1795–1812)

---

[1] Spanish and Portuguese conquistadors such as Balboa, Cortez, and Pizarro were primarily interested in the search for gold and other precious treasures. [2] Poets. [3] Swearing oath of loyalty or fidelity. [4] Patron of poetry and sun-god of the Greeks. [5] Domain. [6] Serenity; here used as a noun. [7] Line of vision. [8] Phrase suggested by Titian's portrait of Cortez. [9] On the Isthmus of Panama.

1. By what three images of discovery does Keats communicate his emotion?
2. Are these images arranged in an order of mounting excitement? Discuss.

The Yachts

contend in a sea which the land partly encloses
shielding them from the too heavy blows
of an ungoverned ocean which when it chooses

tortures the biggest hulls, the best man knows
to pit against its beating, and sinks them pitilessly.
Mothlike in mists, scintillant in the minute

brilliance of cloudless days, with broad bellying sails
they glide to the wind tossing green water
from their sharp prows while over them the crew crawls

ant-like, solicitously grooming them, releasing,
making fast as they turn, lean far over and having
caught the wind again, side by side, head for the mark.

In a well guarded arena of open water surrounded by
lesser and greater craft which, sycophant, lumbering
and flittering follow them, they appear youthful, rare

as the light of a happy eye, live with the grace
of all that in the mind is feckless, free and
naturally to be desired. Now the sea which holds them

is moody, lapping their glossy sides, as if feeling
for some slightest flaw but fails completely.
Today no race. Then the wind comes again. The yachts

move, jockeying for a start, the signal is set and they
are off. Now the waves strike at them but they are too
well made, they slip through, though they take in canvas.

Arms with hands grasping seek to clutch at the prows.
Bodies thrown recklessly in the way are cut aside.
It is a sea of faces about them in agony, in despair

until the horror of the race dawns staggering the mind,
the whole sea become an entanglement of watery bodies
lost to the world bearing what they cannot hold. Broken,

beaten, desolate, reaching from the dead to be taken up
they cry out, failing, failing! their cries rising
in waves still as the skillful yachts pass over.

—William Carlos Williams (1883–1963)

1.   Write an allegorical interpretation of this poem.

From *A Coney Island of the Mind,* 15

Constantly risking absurdity
                                        and death
        whenever he performs

above the heads
of his audience
the poet like an acrobat
climbs on rime
to a high wire of his own making
and balancing on eyebeams
above a sea of faces
paces his way
to the other side of day

(än trə ʹshə)

performing entrechats *— a leap in which a ballet dancer crosses his legs and sometimes beats them together*
and sleight-of-foot tricks
and other high theatrics
and all without mistaking
any thing
for what it may not be

For he's the super realist
who must perforce perceive
taut truth
before the taking of each stance or step
in his supposed advance
toward that still higher perch
where Beauty stands and waits
with gravity
to start her death-defying leap

And he
a little charleychaplin man
who may or may not catch
her fair eternal form
spreadeagled in the empty air
of existence

—Lawrence Ferlinghetti (1919–   )

The Glove

In its absence it has become beautiful,
    my black-leather, my rabbit-fur-lined glove,
given over to the foreignness of strangers,

    of mad dogs thieving away to the deep woods
        with my lost glove. I imagine even
the hunger of hobos and the coveted taste

— stew of vegetables, meat, or fish and other ingredients

    of leather in their infamous mulligan stews.
        I consider my lost glove. I consider
the copulation of rabbits, the precise instant

of conception of that hapless [*luckless*] mother's son
    who would inhabit my lost glove. I think
of the busy, unknowable chain of commerce,

    the wholesale and the retail of my lost glove.
    And today I leave my home uncertain
which will effect attention to itself—the one

    gloved hand or the one gloveless. I revisit
    my itinerary [route] of the night before:
Huffy's Sinclair, the Eagle Mart, and Tic-Toc Lounge;

    no one has seen my lost glove. Later I find it
    grease-stained behind the cash register of
the Campus Grill. I pull it on, my slipped skin,

    and it fits like a good metaphor in that
    fortuitous gathering of elements:
cowhide, rabbit fur, the five fingers of my hand.

                   —Harold Bond (1939–   )

fortunate
lucky
accidental
occurring by chance

I made my coat out of old mythologies.

—*William Butler Yeats*

10
Symbol and Myth

A *symbol* is a concrete object, person, or place that represents something other than itself. It differs from a figure of speech such as a
simile or metaphor in that the relationship between the object and
its symbolic significance is not based on some common resemblance.
By constant association and convention we readily accept certain
traditional symbols: the rose for transient beauty, the laurel for victory or honor, the cross for Christianity, the snake for evil, the dove
for peace, Helen of Troy for feminine beauty, Eden for happiness,
a computer for automation, a microscope for scientific research, a
pair of scales for justice.

A symbol in mathematics, physics, chemistry, and phonetics is
really a *sign* representing a specific thing, operation, quantity, or
sound. Such a sign (or combination of signs) is an abbreviated expression of a specific concept that is universally understood. Ein-
stein's famous equation $E=mc^2$ accurately conveys one restricted
meaning to all readers because the terms have been clearly defined:
energy is equal to mass multiplied by the speed of light squared.
A poetic symbol, on the other hand, is the embodiment of emotion
and thought into some object of sensuous experience which then
takes on special significance because of its relationship to other
objects, characters, or events in the poem. The concrete may suggest
the abstract; sense may represent spirit; the particular, the universal;
and the temporal (in Coleridge's phrase), the translucence of the
eternal.

A symbol may have more than one meaning. The lamb in Blake's
"The Tiger" may symbolize gentleness, goodness, and innocence,

but also, because of associative religious connotations, Christ as a sacrificial lamb dying for the salvation of man. Similarly the tiger symbolizes not just abstract evil but the mysterious, demonic power of nature—beauty, strength, and ferocity combined in a terrifying and awe-inspiring creation.

Standing for something different from and greater than itself, a symbol evokes emotional attitudes and implies intellectual concepts that permit the reader to grasp psychological subtleties or elusive nuances of sensibility that he would otherwise miss. An effective symbol, because of its cluster of emotional and mental associations, has the power to raise a poem above the level of logical discourse and can serve as the organizing core of a poem. By its concreteness a symbol permits us to grasp abstractions; by depicting some aspect of the visible world, a symbolic poet can give us glimpses of the invisible; by appealing to our senses, he takes us into a world beyond our senses. Visionary poets such as Dante, Blake, Whitman, Yeats, and Eliot, by their use of symbols, expand our consciousness and permit us to see the ideal in the real, to enjoy transcendental experiences, to capture evanescent moods, and to grasp complex ideas.

Since a poet may draw his symbols from any source—art, nature, music, people (real or mythical), colors, artifacts—he may use the traditional associations or he may construct his own private system. (He may, of course, combine the two.) If he limits himself to the conventional symbols, he has no problem of communication, but he runs the risk of triteness as a creator and a stock response from the reader. He can avoid these poetic defects by giving the conventional symbols a new twist or an original elaboration. If he uses private symbolism, he risks confusing the reader. Blake's long prophetic poems have presented this problem of symbolic obscurity to many readers, in spite of the voluminous explication written to interpret them. Yeats, on the other hand, obviated this difficulty by publishing a prose work, A Vision, which clarified his symbolic system, although his best poems can be understood without reference to it.

In a period of religious faith like the Middle Ages a Dante could use in his Divine Comedy the conventional symbols of Christianity as the framework of his masterpiece. But with the shattering of a unified religious belief and the loss of faith, many modern poets have created their own symbolic systems instead of relying upon those of the past or have revivified traditional symbols by using them in an original way.

A good example of the latter tendency is this poem by Robert Frost.

The Road Not Taken

Two roads diverged in a yellow wood,
And sorry I could not travel both
And be one traveler, long I stood
And looked down one as far as I could
To where it bent in the undergrowth;

Then took the other, as just as fair,
And having perhaps the better claim,
Because it was grassy and wanted wear;
Though as for that the passing there
Had worn them really about the same,

And both that morning equally lay
In leaves no step had trodden black.
Oh, I kept the first for another day!
Yet knowing how way leads on to way,
I doubted if I should ever come back.

I shall be telling this with a sigh
Somewhere ages and ages hence:
Two roads diverged in a wood, and I—
I took the one less traveled by,
And that has made all the difference.

—Robert Frost (1874–1963)

The fork in a road is a familiar symbol of man's need to make choices. But Frost has given this symbol new life, a new twist by not stressing the happy choice he made in taking the "one less traveled by" (i.e., following the unconventional career as a poet) but by using it to suggest the eternal dilemma of the human condition. Satisfactory as our choice may have been, a feeling of uncertainty persistently haunts us. We always wonder whether we would have been happier in choosing the other road. A "sigh" of regret spoils our contentment, for we are forced to make fateful decisions when we are young and inexperienced. Frost has avoided a symbolic cliché by emphasizing the road *not* taken.

Instead of building a poem around a single conventional symbol, many poets utilize several traditional symbols to communicate paradoxical ideas forcefully.

To an Athlete Dying Young

The time you won your town the race
We chaired[1] you through the market-place;

Man and boy stood cheering by,
And home we brought you shoulder-high.

Today, the road all runners come,
Shoulder-high we bring you home,
And set you at your threshold down,
Townsman of a stiller town.

Smart lad, to slip betimes[2] away
From fields where glory does not stay,
And early though the laurel grows
It withers quicker than the rose.

Eyes the shady night has shut
Cannot see the record cut,
And silence sounds no worse than cheers
After earth has stopped the ears:

Now you will not swell the rout[3]
Of lads that wore their honors out,
Runners whom renown outran
And the name died before the man.

So set, before its echoes fade,
The fleet foot on the sill of shade,[4]
And hold to the low lintel[5] up
The still-defended challenge-cup.

And round that early-laureled head
Will flock to gaze the strengthless dead,
And find unwithered on its curls
The garland briefer than a girl's.

—A. E. Housman (1859–1936)

---

[1] Carried triumphantly.   [2] At the proper time, early.   [3] Crowd, mob.
[4] Edge of the grave.   [5] Doorway as entrance to death and the other
world.

The three central metaphors the poet uses symbolically have traditional connotations: life is a *race;* the victor is crowned with *laurel;* transient, feminine beauty is a *rose.* Housman's elaboration of these symbols suggests the theme that, since life inevitably brings frustrations and disappointments, an early death at the height of a person's achievement is not a defeat but a victory and therefore a cause for congratulation instead of lamentation.

By having townsfolk of the "victorious" athlete as the speaker, the poet dramatizes his theme. In the opening stanza we hear the cheers of the crowd watching the triumphal procession of the victorious runner. In the next stanza the silent crowd is honoring the "victor" in the race of life, for he has reached the invisible tape at "the sill of shade," first. The startling, friendly apostrophe "Smart lad" introduces the paradoxical congratulatory note. (This phrase is given particular metrical emphasis by being the only spondee, two successive accents, in the poem.) The third stanza introduces the laurel and rose symbols to suggest that athletic fame is even more transitory than feminine beauty; but since the victor had died at the climax of his career, he will never suffer the inevitable fate of a "has-been." The challenge-cup of victory will be his forever. Line fifteen further echoes the metaphor of victorious "cheers" as the last line reiterates the "rose" garland symbol. The fairly regular rhythm and the exclusive use of masculine rhyme give the poem an appropriate elegiac movement and the beat of finality.

In the preceding poems the symbols, because of frequent use and universal human experience, present no problem in interpretation. However, if a poet uses a created symbol, its meaning may not be explicit or fixed; several interpretations may be valid. The implications are to be felt rather than explained literally. Such a symbol is like a disturbing stone which, cast into a lake, sets up ever-widening circles of meaning and ripples of emotion.

The power of a symbol to suggest a multiplicity of meanings can be illustrated by this short poem of Blake.

The Sick Rose

O Rose, thou art sick!
The invisible worm
That flies in the night,
In the howling storm,

Has found out thy bed
Of crimson joy,
And his dark secret love
Does thy life destroy.

—William Blake (1757–1827)

Clearly this rose, through its relationship to a mysterious "invisible worm," to the darkness of night, and to "the howling storm," stands for something more than transient feminine beauty. By suggesting the destruction of something beautiful by something evil, the poem arouses our pity and shocks us by its horror. Is the rose Eve and the worm Satan? Is the rose with its "crimson joy" blameless?

Is it the moral sickness or depravity of the rose that attracts the devouring worm? Is the worm jealousy, selfishness, deceit, possessive lust? Although we cannot give a single conclusive answer to these disturbing questions, the poem, by the associative power of its oppressive symbols, stirs us imaginatively, emotionally, and intellectually.

Just as a traditional symbol must not be interpreted too explicitly, so a created symbol may evoke multiple reactions; but these are implied by the interaction of image and metaphor within the structural context of the poem. Let us consider the following poem of Yeats which is in great measure built upon his private symbolism.

Sailing to Byzantium[1]

I

That is no country for old men.[2] The young
In one another's arms, birds in the trees
—Those dying generations—at their song,
The salmon-falls, the mackerel-crowded seas,
Fish, flesh, or fowl, commend all summer long
Whatever is begotten, born, and dies.
Caught in that sensual music all neglect
Monuments of unaging intellect.

II

An aged man is but a paltry thing,
A tattered coat upon a stick, unless
Soul clap its hands and sing, and louder sing
For every tatter in its mortal dress,
Nor is there singing school but studying
Monuments of its own magnificence;
And therefore I have sailed the seas and come
To the holy city of Byzantium.

III

O sages standing in God's holy fire[3]
As in the gold mosaic of a wall,
Come from the holy fire, perne in a gyre,[4]
And be the singing-masters of my soul.
Consume my heart away; sick with desire
And fastened to a dying animal
It knows not what it is; and gather me
Into the artifice of eternity.

IV

Once out of nature I shall never take
My bodily form from any natural thing,

But such a form as Grecian goldsmiths make
Of hammered gold and gold enamelling
To keep a drowsy Emperor awake;
Or set upon a golden bough to sing[5]
To lords and ladies of Byzantium
Of what is past, or passing, or to come.

—William Butler Yeats (1865–1939)

---

[1] The holy city of Eastern Christendom (formerly Constantinople, now Istanbul) used by Yeats as a symbol of the immortality of works of art created by the human intellect. He wrote in *A Vision:* "I think if I could be given a month of antiquity and leave to spend it where I chose, I would spend it in Byzantium a little before Justinian opened St. Sophia and closed the Academy of Plato. . . . I think that in early Byzantium, and maybe never before or since in recorded history, religious, aesthetic, and practical life were one; and that architects and artificers . . . spoke to the multitude and the few alike."   [2] The material, sensual world of youth and nature which must die.   [3] The wise men or saints immortalized in the mosaics of the Church of Hagia Sophia (Holy Wisdom), the greatest work of Byzantine architecture. After a series of reincarnations, they come to rest "in the condition of Fire."   [4] Sweeping down in a hawklike spiral motion.   [5] Yeats wrote: "I have read somewhere that in the emperor's palace at Byzantium was a tree made of gold and silver, and artificial birds that sang."

Like Frost in his sonnet "The Oven Bird," Yeats faces the problem of "what to make of a diminished thing," old age. In this visionary poem the aged Yeats imagines himself leaving the natural world, symbolized as a country where sensual youth, singing birds, and spawning fish enjoy physical delights "all summer long" but must die. He sets out on a mystical journey over "the mackerel-crowded seas" for "the holy city of Byzantium," the symbol of immortal works of art created by man's soul and intellect. Beautiful as the world of passion is (the poet praises it by using the word *commend*), it neglects the spiritual and intellectual nature of man, which, as the body decays, should grow stronger. Physically an old man is no better than a scarecrow unless he develops his soul to enjoy the eternal delights that it has created, "monuments of its own magnificence." In stanza three he prays to the sages and martyrs represented in the gold mosaics of Byzantine art to rise phoenixlike from "God's holy fire" and liberate his soul from his dying animal body. Once released from the corruption of mortal flesh, his soul, he hopes, would then be incarnated in the imperishable art form of a golden Byzantine bird singing its timeless song. Only the immortality of art created by man's spirit can triumph over the natural world where everything is "begotten, born, and dies."

In this poem Yeats—by evocative symbols, effective antithesis, and a unifying metaphor of music—has created an "artifice of eternity." By his contrast of body and soul, youth and old age, passion and intellect, losses and gains, nature and art, and time and eternity, he has stimulated our imagination and communicated a complex human experience. This diverse material has been kept under strict artistic control by the use of song in each of the four stanzas. In stanza one we hear the sensual song of all living creatures in the mating season; in stanza two, the strange Blakean music of the mature soul clapping its hands and singing; in stanza three, the poet's soul receiving final musical instruction from supernal singing-masters; and in the concluding stanza, we hear the eternal song of the golden bird "set upon a golden bough."

When symbols are used in a complex of story elements to explain natural phenomena, prevailing social institutions, and lengendary or historical events or personages, we encounter *myth*. As a result of modern studies in linguistics, anthropology, religion, psychology, and literature, today we recognize that myths are not simple childish falsehoods or fantasies of primitive peoples. They are an important expression of man's relationship to the mysterious universe and to his society as well as an explanation of the psychic forces in human life. Because myths reveal the deepest desires, fears, and aspirations of people, they are a natural and universal representation of man's basic compulsions. It is not surprising that these find their embodiment in art, literature, and especially in poetry.

In their primitive forms, myths dealing with the fundamental realities of human experience emanated from anonymous sources but soon attained an aura of religious or traditional sanctity for a homogeneous cultural society. They were readily accepted, for they gave authoritative answers to the eternal mysteries that man faces: the creation of the universe, the life of the gods, the influence of sun, moon, and stars on human destiny, the meaning of life and death, the afterlife, the relation of the sexes. Like folk poetry, myths are the creation of a group rather than of an individual. They survive as long as they satisfy a deep psychological need by giving believers security in an uncertain world, by resolving the age-old problems of human existence in an immense universe, and by serving as spiritual guides to conduct.

By the time a whole cycle of myth has emerged, poets, by their individual modifications and reinterpretations of the stories, use them as literary frameworks to project their personal views. The exploitation of mythical material is helpful to the poet, for it is rich in emotional and intellectual suggestiveness and he can count on the familiarity of his audience with the events and characters. Contemporary readers of the poet may accept the mythology as "true," but later readers can still find it meaningful by viewing it as a symbolic interpretation of universal problems. Thus the Homeric epics—*The Iliad* and *The Odyssey*—had a profund influence on the later Greek tragedies of Aeschylus, Sophocles, and Euripides; and all of these works have moral, philosophic, and aesthetic significance for us today. In the same manner Dante's summation of the medieval Christian ethic in *The Divine Comedy,* Milton's epic of the Protestant Reformation *Paradise Lost,* and Goethe's depiction in *Faust* of Renaissance man's passionate quest for happiness through forbidden knowledge—all have relevance for twentieth-century readers.

Romantic poets such as Keats and Shelley have reinterpreted classic myths for the expression of their personal philosophies. Keats in the unfinished epic *Hyperion* depicts the victory of Apollo and the Olympian gods over Hyperion and the Titans to suggest the triumph of the "eternal law/That first in beauty should be first in might." Shelley modifies the Prometheus myth (in his lyrical drama *Prometheus Unbound*) to affirm the power of man's heroic resistance to conquer the tyranny of an oppressive authoritarian god. Victorian poets such as Tennyson, Arnold, and Swinburne have adapted Greek and Arthurian myths. In *The Dynasts,* an epic-drama, Thomas Hardy uses the Napoleonic legend to project his ironic, deterministic vision of life. To suggest the fragmentation of the modern secular world and its spiritual aridity, T. S. Eliot utilizes in "The Waste Land" myths drawn from many sources: biblical, Greek, Arthurian, and Hindu.

Yeats created his own myth, and Crane searched for a new one— both to give shape and validity to their concepts. This quest for a new mythology to synthesize our contemporary civilization explains the multiplicity of approaches we find in modern poetry. The glorification or denunciation of such symbols of modern life as dynamos, bridges, subways, atom bombs, megalopolis, and automation has produced a proliferation of poetry movements—metaphysical, symbolic, imagist, confessional, antiromantic, surrealist, and projective, all with their attendant critical manifestos. In this age of transition, as old myths die, new ones are being constructed, for man is not only an inveterate tool-making creature but a myth-making one as well.

In our scientific twentieth century it was inevitable that the study of myth would be rigorously examined. Comparative anthropology and psychology proved to be the most fruitful in influencing both poets and critics. The three most important works were J. G. Frazer's *The Golden Bough,* Sigmund Freud's *Symbolism in Dreams,* and particularly Carl G. Jung's *Psychology of the Unconscious.* Jung believed that certain poems move us very profoundly because they contain "primordial images," or "archetypes," which are buried deep in our psyches. These images—basic, general, universal patterns existing in a "collective unconscious" of the human race—we inherit from our ancestors. These primitive ideas, characters, actions, or objects form archetypal recurrent patterns in poetry that stir our deepest emotions. Typical archetypes are our images of the hero, of the eternal wanderer, of the devil, of God; the rivalry of brothers, the conflict of parents and children; the search for a father; the journey to the underworld; sin, expiation, and rebirth; sacrificial death; the culture hero like Prometheus bringing precious gifts to mankind. Around these universal primordial images and archetypal themes, poets of all ages have constructed works that appeal to our deepest instincts and imbedded racial memories.

For Discussion

The schools of poets and philosophers are not more intoxicated with their symbols than the populace with theirs—See the power of national emblems. Some stars, lilies, leopards, a crescent, a lion, an eagle, or other figure which came into credit God knows how, on an old rag of bunting, blowing in the wind on a fort at the ends of the earth, shall make the blood tingle under the rudest or the most conventional exterior. The people fancy they hate poetry, and they are all poets and mystics!

—Ralph Waldo Emerson

In a Symbol there is concealment and yet revelation.

—Thomas Carlyle

Symbols are organic units of consciousness with a life of their own, and you can never explain them away, because their value is dynamic, emotional, belonging to the sense-consciousness of the body and soul, and not simply mental.

—D. H. Lawrence

A poet using archetypes speaks in a voice stronger than his own; he raises the idea he is trying to express above the occasional and transitory into the sphere of the ever-existing. He transmutes personal destiny into the destiny of mankind.

—C. G. Jung

Very deep is the well of the past. Should we not call it bottomless?

—Thomas Mann

In the solar cycle of the day, the seasonal cycles of the year, and the organic cycle of human life, there is a single pattern of significance, out of which myth constructs a central narrative around a figure who is partly the sun, partly vegetative fertility, and partly a god or archetypal human being.

—Northrop Frye

No man needs to *search* for paradox in this world of ours. Let him simply confine himself to the truth, and he will find paradox growing everywhere under his hands as weeds.

—*Thomas DeQuincey*

11
Irony and Paradox

Irony and paradox are used by poets to amuse, stimulate, surprise, and make us aware of the complexities and incongruities of human existence. Their range—from the trivial to the profound, from the comic to the tragic—is unlimited.

Like antithesis, *irony* involves the concept of contrast. The intended meaning is the opposite of the stated one. The outcome of the event is the reverse, as if in mockery, of the one hoped for or expected. Irony appears in many forms; the most common are verbal irony, dramatic (or Sophoclean) irony, irony of situation, and irony of character. These may be found separately or in combination.

Verbal irony is used chiefly for purposes of humor, sarcasm, or ridicule, as when a small car is called a Goliath; an undersized fish, a whale; or a dunce, a scholar. In his funeral oration over Caesar's body, Antony refers to his bitter enemies Brutus, Cassius, and the other conspirators as "honorable men." In *Romeo and Juliet* Mercutio's wry comment on his death-wound is ironic, "No, 'tis not so deep as a well, nor so wide as a church door, but 'tis enough, 'twill serve." A. E. Robinson's sentimental Miniver Cheevy "missed the mediaeval grace of iron clothing."

In the following poem Clough's verbal irony satirizes the Victorian interpretation of the Ten Commandments in order to expose his countrymen's commercialism, false respectability, and desire for material advancement.

The Latest Decalogue *10 commandments*

Thou shalt have one God only; who
Would be at the expense of two?
No graven images may be
Worshipped, except the currency:
Swear not at all; for, for thy curse
Thine enemy is none the worse:
At church on Sunday to attend
Will serve to keep the world thy friend;
Honour thy parents; that is, all
From whom advancement may befall;
Thou shalt not kill; but need'st not strive
Officiously to keep alive:
Do not adultery commit;
Advantage rarely comes of it:
Thou shalt not steal; an empty feat,
When it's so lucrative to cheat:
Bear not false witness; let the lie
Have time on its own wings to fly:
Thou shalt not covet, but tradition
Approves all forms of competition.

—A. H. Clough (1819–1861)

In a similar manner W. H. Auden ironically exposes our modern conformist, automated society which stamps out "faceless zeros."

The Unknown Citizen

*(To JS/07/M/378
This Marble Monument
Is Erected by the State)*

He was found by the Bureau of Statistics to be
One against whom there was no official complaint,
And all the reports on his conduct agree
That, in the modern sense of an old-fashioned word, he was
    a saint,
For in everything he did he served the Greater Community.
Except for the War till the day he retired
He worked in a factory and never got fired,
But satisfied his employers, Fudge Motors Inc.
Yet he wasn't a scab or odd in his views,
For his Union reports that he paid his dues,
(Our report on his Union shows it was sound)
    anyone who goes against the union

And our Social Psychology workers found
That he was popular with his mates and liked a drink.
The Press are convinced that he bought a paper every day
And that his reactions to advertisements were normal in
     every way.
Policies taken out in his name prove that he was fully insured,
And his Health-card shows he was once in hospital but left
     it cured.
Both Producers Research and High-Grade Living declare
He was fully sensible to the advantages of the Installment Plan
And had everything necessary to the Modern Man,
A phonograph, a radio, a car and a frigidaire.
Our researchers into Public Opinion are content
That he held the proper opinions for the time of year;
When there was peace, he was for peace; when there was
     war, he went.
He was married and added five children to the population,
Which our Eugenist says was the right number for a parent
     of his generation, *scientist of heredity*
And our teachers report that he never interfered with
     their education.
Was he free? Was he happy? The question is absurd:
Had anything been wrong, we should certainly have heard.

                   —W. H. Auden (1907–   )

The last two lines are an example of Socratic irony; the poet assumes a pose of ignorance by having the speaker ask simple-minded questions.

    In *dramatic irony* the words of a character in a play or poem express one meaning to the speaker but a different one to the audience or reader, the latter possessing knowledge not available to the speaker. In *Macbeth,* when King Duncan hears of the execution of the rebellious Thane of Cawdor, his comment—

          . . . There's no art
To find the mind's construction in the face:
He was a gentleman on whom I built
An absolute trust—

is ironical for the audience realizes how aptly these words apply to the ambitious Macbeth, the new Thane of Cawdor, who is planning to betray the king in a more tragic action, murder. Outside Macbeth's castle the benignant King Duncan, ignorant of the fact that he is walking into a death trap, blithely comments:

> This castle hath a pleasant seat; the air
> Nimbly and sweetly recommends itself
> Unto our gentle senses.

Dramatic irony is closely related to *irony of situation* whereby the outcome of events is the reverse of what is expected. A classic example is the stubborn persistence of Oedipus to discover the murderer of his father only to learn that he himself is the parricide. The proud, noble king is blind to reality. When Oedipus has his eyesight, only the blind prophet Tiresias sees the truth. In "The Convergence of the Twain," by depicting the destruction of the *Titanic* on her maiden voyage by an iceberg, Hardy shows the futility of man in his vanity attempting to conquer nature. "Crass Casualty" and "dicing Time," these "purblind Doomsters," are the agents of cosmic irony that bring a reversal of man's expectations.

Like Hardy, the American poet E. A. Robinson represented the ironic frustration of man's expectations in some of the inhabitants of his mythical Tilbury Town. The wealthy Richard Cory—the polite, democratic gentleman envied by all the poor—

> . . . one calm, summer night,
> Went home and put a bullet through his head.

Flammonde "with firm address and foreign air" solved many of the difficult personal problems of his townsfolk but could never untie the "small satanic kink" in his own brain. Ironically missing his true destiny of greatness, he became "the Prince of Castaways."

The following two poems are examples of irony of situation. The first is a Scottish folk ballad in which the conventional symbols of loyalty—hawk, hound, and especially lady fair—are suddenly reversed with savage irony by animal instinct and human betrayal. The second, a modern literary ballad, cynically reverses the expectations of canine fidelity.

The Twa Corbies

> As I was walking all alone,
> I heard two corbies[1] making a mane;[2]
> The tane[3] unto t'other say,
> "Where sall we gang and dine to-day?"
>
> "In behint yon auld fail dyke,[4]
> I wot there lies a new slain knight;

And naebody kens[5] that he lies there,
But his hawk, his hound, and lady fair.

"His hound is to the hunting game,
His hawk to fetch the wild-fowl hame,
His lady's ta'en another mate,
So we may mak our dinner sweet.

"Ye'll sit on his white hause-bane,[6]
And I'll pike out his bonny blue e'en.
Wi ae lock o his gowden hair
We'll theek[7] our nest when it grows bare.

"Mony a one for him makes mane,
But nana sall ken where he is gane;
Oer his white banes, when they are bare,
The wind sall blaw for evermair."

—Anonymous

---

[1] Ravens.   [2] Moan.   [3] One.   [4] Turf wall.   [5] Knows.   [6] Neck bone.
[7] Thatch.

"Ah, Are You Digging on My Grave?"

"Ah, are you digging on my grave,
My loved one?—planting rue?"
—"No; yesterday he went to wed
One of the brightest wealth has bred.
'It cannot hurt her now,' he said,
    'That I should not be true.' "

"Then who is digging on my grave?
My nearest dearest kin?"
—"Ah, no: they sit and think, What use!
What good will planting flowers produce?
No tendance of her mound can loose
    Her spirit from Death's gin.' " [1]

"But some one digs upon my grave?
My enemy?—prodding sly?"
—"Nay: when she heard you had passed the Gate
That shuts on all flesh soon or late,
She thought you no more worth her hate,
    And cares not where you lie."

"Then, who is digging on my grave?
Say—since I have not guessed!"
—"O it is I, my mistress dear,
Your little dog, who still lives near,
And much I hope my movements here
    Have not disturbed your rest?"

"Ah, yes! *You* dig upon my grave . . .
Why flashed it not on me
That one true heart was left behind!
What feeling do we ever find
To equal among human kind
    A dog's fidelity!"

"Mistress, I dug upon your grave
To bury a bone, in case
I should be hungry near this spot
When passing on my daily trot.
I am sorry, but I quite forgot
    It was your resting-place."

            —Thomas Hardy (1840–1928)

---

[1] Trap or snare.

    In irony of situation the discrepancy between expectation and fulfillment comes from the unexpected reversal of actions. In *irony of character* either we find a person's traits contrary to what we would normally expect, or the person's self-evaluation is the reverse of what he really is. We expect Falstaff, Shakespeare's greatest comic creation, who is old and fat, gluttonous and bibulous, to be lethargic and dull-witted. He turns out to be the most energetic and wittiest of his companions. A gentleman by birth and education, he is a robber and liar whose lies deceive no one. A war profiteer and coward, he can still be patriotic and courageous on occasion. The folly of his actions is counterbalanced by his earthy common sense. Even though his pretensions are punctured, he never loses his self-possession. It is these ironic incongruities that make him such a rich and delightful character.

    A good example of irony of charatcer is to be found in this famous poem by Browning.

My Last Duchess

Ferrara[1]

That's my last Duchess painted on the wall,
Looking as if she were alive. I call

That piece a wonder, now; Fra Pandolf's hands
Worked busily a day, and there she stands.
Will't please you sit and look at her? I said
"Fra Pandolf"[2] by design, for never read
Strangers like you that pictured countenance,
The depth and passion of its earnest glance,
But to myself they turned (since none puts by
The curtain I have drawn for you, but I)
And seemed as they would ask me, if they durst,
How such a glance came there: so, not the first
Are you to turn and ask thus. Sir, 'twas not
Her husband's presence only, called that spot
Of joy into the Duchess' cheek; perhaps
Fra Pandolf chanced to say, "Her mantle laps
Over my lady's wrist too much," or "Paint
Must never hope to reproduce the faint
Half-flush that dies along her throat": such stuff
Was courtesy, she thought, and cause enough
For calling up that spot of joy. She had
A heart—show shall I say?—too soon made glad,
Too easily impressed: she liked whate'er
She looked on, and her looks went everywhere.
Sir, 'twas all one! My favour at her breast,
The dropping of the daylight in the West,
The bough of cherries some officious fool
Broke in the orchard for her, the white mule
She rode with round the terrace—all and each
Would draw from her alike the approving speech,
Or blush, at least. She thanked men,—good! but thanked
Somehow—I know not how—as if she ranked
My gift of a nine-hundred-years-old name
With anybody's gift. Even had you skill
In speech—(which I have not)—to make your will
Quite clear to such an one, and say "Just this
Or that in you disgusts me; here you miss,
Or there exceed the mark"—and if she let
Herself be lessoned so, nor plainly set
Her wits to yours, forsooth, and made excuse,
—E'en then would be some stooping; and I choose
Never to stoop. Oh, sir, she smiled, no doubt,
Whene'er I passed her; but who passed without
Much the same smile? This grew; I gave commands;
Then all smiles stopped together. There she stands
As if alive. Will't please you rise? We'll meet
The company below, then. I repeat,
The Count your master's known munificence
Is ample warrant that no just pretence
Of mine for dowry will be disallowed;

Though her fair daughter's self, as I avowed
At starting, is my object. Nay, we'll go
Together down, sir. Notice Neptune,[3] though,
Taming a sea-horse, thought a rarity,
Which Claus of Innsbruck[4] cast in bronze for me!

—Robert Browning (1812–1889)

---

[1] A town in Italy noted for its art during the Renaissance.   [2] A fictitious painter.   [3] Roman god of the sea.   [4] A fictitious sculptor.

The speaker in this dramatic poem, a powerful Renaissance duke, sees himself as an art connoisseur, a proud, cultured aristocrat of refined sensibility who was compelled to rid himself of his naive, stupid, and sentimental wife. However, with consummate skill the poet suggests the true nature of the patrician duke and his unhappy last duchess. With his own suave words, the duke reveals his arrogance, snobbishness, avarice, cunning, and cruelty. The duchess emerges as a charming, enthusiastic, democratic, and sensitive young woman.

The use of several forms of irony for the effective communication of theme is illustrated in the following poem by Shelley.

Ozymandias

I met a traveller from an antique land
Who said: Two vast and trunkless legs of stone
Stand in the desert. Near them, on the sand,
Half sunk, a shattered visage lies, whose frown,
And wrinkled lip, and sneer of cold command,
Tell that its sculptor well those passions read
Which yet survive, stamped on these lifeless things,
The hand that mocked them, and the heart that fed;
And on the pedestal these words appear:
"My name is Ozymandias, king of kings:
Look on my works, ye Mighty, and despair!"
Nothing beside remains. Round the decay
Of that colossal wreck, boundless and bare
The lone and level sands stretch far away.

—Percy Bysshe Shelley (1792–1822)

The boastful words of the Egyptian despot, in life so vain of his material power, proclaimed against the vast background of the empty desert reveal how false the tyrant's self-evaluation was. The true character of Ozymandias is seen in the sneering sculptured visage lying beside the trunkless legs of stone. Time has made a mockery of his vanity and his kingdom.

Paradox, like irony, effectively communicates the complexities and contradictions of human existence. A *paradox* is a statement which, on the surface, seems untrue or contradictory but proves, on closer examination, to be valid and meaningful. The apparent clash of concepts vanishes when we resolve the paradox. When Wordsworth tells us "The Child is father to the Man" we grasp the truth in this succinct seeming contradiction by realizing that the traits to be developed by the mature person are all in incipient form embedded in the child. The witches in *Macbeth* chant their creed in the paradoxical statement "Fair is foul and foul is fair." What is "fair" to human beings (sunshine, loyalty, pity) is "foul" to them. What is "foul" to us (storms, treason, cruelty) is "fair" to them. Their perverted concepts of morality expose them as the agents of evil temptation. Shakespeare's "Sonnet 73" (page 145) contains a brilliant paradoxical image of a fire ("Consumed with that which it was nourished by"). Much of the effectiveness of Donne's "A Valediction Forbidding Mourning" (page 153) depends upon its paradoxes.

Verbal and situational paradoxes give us a simultaneous glimpse of two levels of meaning and reveal the complexities, ambiguities, and contrariness of life. Their seeming contradictoriness alerts and startles us. Their terse, enigmatic nature adds to effective communication of meaning.

Let us see how a skillful poet's use of symbol, myth, irony, and paradox communicates a complex sensuous, emotional, and intellectual experience in its totality.

The Garden

How vainly men themselves amaze[1]
To win the palm, the oak, or bays,[2]
And their incessant labors see
Crowned from some single herb or tree,
Whose short and narrow vergèd shade
Does prudently their toils upbraid;
While all flowers and all trees do close
To weave the garlands of repose!

Fair Quiet, have I found thee here,
And Innocence, thy sister dear!
Mistaken long, I sought you then
In busy companies of men.

Your sacred plants, if here below,
Only among the plants will grow;
Society is all but rude
To[3] this delicious solitude.

No white nor red[4] was ever seen
So am'rous as this lovely green.[5]
Fond[6] lovers, cruel as their flame,
Cut in these trees their mistress' name;
Little, alas, they know or heed
How far these beauties hers exceed!
Fair trees, wheresoe'er your barks I wound,
No name shall but your own be found.

When we have run our passion's heat,
Love hither makes his best retreat.
The gods[7] that mortal beauty chase,
Still in a tree did end their race;
Apollo hunted Daphne so,
Only that she might laurel grow;
And Pan did after Syrinx speed,
Not as a nymph, but for a reed.

What wond'rous life is this I lead!
Ripe apples drop about my head;
The luscious clusters of the vine
Upon my mouth do crush their wine;
The nectarine and curious[8] peach
Into my hands themselves do reach;
Stumbling on melons as I pass,
Insnared with flowers, I fall on grass.

Meanwhile the mind, from pleasure less,[9]
Withdraws into its happiness;
The mind, that ocean where each kind[10]
Does straight its own resemblance find;
Yet it creates, transcending these,
Far other worlds and other seas,
Annihilating all that's made
To a green thought in a green shade.

Here at the fountain's sliding foot,
Or at some fruit-tree's mossy root,
Casting the body's vest[11] aside,
My soul into the boughs does glide;
There like a bird it sits and sings,
Then whets,[12] then combs its silver wings,
And till prepared for longer flight,
Waves in its plumes the various light.[13]

Such was that happy garden-state,[14]
While man there walked without a mate;
After a place so pure and sweet,
What other help could yet be meet![15]
But 'twas beyond a mortal's share
To wander solitary there;
Two paradises 'twere, in one,
To live in paradise alone.

How well the skillful gardener drew
Of flowers and herbs this dial new,[16]
Where, from above, the milder sun
Does through a fragrant zodiac run;
And, as it works, th' industrious bee
Computes its time as well as we!
How could such sweet and wholesome hours
Be reckoned but with herbs and flowers?

—Andrew Marvell (1621–1678)

___

[1] Perplex, bewilder.   [2] Victory wreaths woven from the leaves of trees: palm for civic achievement, oak (military), bays (literary).   [3] Compared to.   [4] Colors of feminine beauty.   [5] Garden.   [6] Foolish (as well as affectionate).   [7] In Greek mythology Apollo pursued Daphne, who was turned into a laurel bush; Pan pursued Syrinx, who was turned into a reed from which the god made his musical pipes.   [8] Rare, delicate.   [9] Lesser pleasures, such as society and the senses.   [10] Species.   [11] Vesture, garment.   [12] Preens.   [13] Symbol of created things.   [14] Eden.   [15] Suitable, also a pun with *help*(meet); Eve as a helpmate to Adam.   [16] A sundial, with the signs of the zodiac, made by flowers, often found in formal seventeenth-century gardens.

The poet uses the garden as a symbol of the world and its varied experiences within a framework of time. The speaker, a middle-aged, witty, philosophical person, attempts to justify his way of life—the contemplative as superior to the active—as the one that achieves the richest fulfillment and brings the greatest happiness. In spite of the shifts in mood, the poem is basically unified by the use of trees and garden imagery in each stanza, by the artistic progression of its thought, and by its sustained musical and rhythmic pattern.

In the opening stanza the speaker uses antithesis and a playful paradox to point out the superiority of a life of repose (i.e., contemplation) to the vainglorious hectic bustle of a life of activity. How foolish it is after "incessant labors" to receive the "narrow-verged shade" of the chaplet of *one* tree when by physical inactivity in the garden of life one can enjoy the shade of *all* the trees! In the second stanza the speaker uses personification and irony effectively in describing his futile search for the two dear sisters, fair Quiet and Innocence, to enrich his life. He found them at last not as he expected in the "busy companies of men," in rude society, but in the "delicious solitude" of the garden.

In the third stanza the speaker, not in a misogynic but in a good-natured teasing mood, develops the outrageous paradox that green (a favorite color with Marvell) trees are more beautiful than women. Foolish lovers, by carving their mistresses' names on trees, are destroying the greater beauty to praise the lesser. The only carving he would permit in the garden would be the name of the tree for identification. To sustain his antifeminine, bantering paradox the poet cleverly uses the Greek myth of the metamorphosis of two attractive nymphs, Daphne and Syrinx, from mortals to a higher state, sacred trees.

With stanza five and continuing in six and seven the tone changes from a witty urbanity to a serious, passionate presentation of a mature way of life in natural surroundings. These stanzas are arranged in an ascending order of importance: the delights of the senses (physical), of the mind (philosophical), of the soul (spiritual, religious). The speaker's repudiation of sensuality in line twenty-five—"When we have run our passion's heat"—is replaced in stanza five by an intense enjoyment of the luscious fruits of nature, a stanza as rich in sensuous appeal as the opening stanza of Keats' "To Autumn."

An even greater joy to be found in this pastoral retreat is the use of that marvelous instrument, the human mind, whose activities are described so powerfully in the famous sixth stanza. By philosophical contemplation the mind transcends sensual and sensuous pleasures and achieves an inner happiness, an ecstatic state of enlightenment that we experience when we are intellectually stimulated and our imagination is awakened. By the metaphor that our mind is an ocean, Marvell suggests that, as the mighty ocean reflects and contains all things on earth, so our minds absorb all earthly impressions and experiences. In addition, by the power of the creative imagination, we fashion "other worlds and other seas"; and by intellectually comprehending and evaluating the material world, we reduce everything "to a green thought in a green shade." By philosophical and imaginative contemplation in a bucolic world of nature we reject the false values of life and discover the true realities. Fathomless as the seas, our active, restless minds can give us a transcendent illumination of truth.

Important as mental activity is to the well-being of man, the speaker in the seventh stanza suggests that there is even a higher stage in the development of man's nature—the happiness to be derived from his spiritual potential. By comparing man's soul to a mysterious silver-winged bird gliding into boughs, the poet develops the paradox of man's identification with and separation from nature. This trial flight is simply preparatory to the final departure of the soul from the body at death to enter the timeless eternity of the afterlife. With these delicate religious overtones, the poem completes the cycle of man's life.

Like a musical coda, the last two stanzas bring the poem to a graceful close by returning to the opening tone of witty urbanity. By using biblical imagery the poet ironically suggests that Adam unknowingly enjoyed a double paradise before the creation of Eve disturbed his "happy" solitude. The contemplative life in a pastoral setting is so perfectly ordered that only a timepiece made of "herbs and flowers" can reckon its "sweet and wholesome hours."

By using the poetic resources discussed in the last two chapters, Marvell has fashioned an artistic work that, by a brilliant presentation of a way of life, illustrates Shakespeare's succinct maxim, "Ripeness is all."

For Discussion

Human thought and conduct can only be treated broadly and truly in a mood of tolerant irony.

—J. H. Robinson

The poet, somewhat less spectacularly (than the saint) proves his vision by submitting it to the fires of irony . . . in the hope that the fires will refine it. In other words, the poet wishes to indicate that his vision has been earned, that it can survive reference to the complexities and contradictions of experience.

—Robert Penn Warren

It is the scientist whose truth requires a language purged of every trace of paradox; apparently the truth which the poet utters can be approached only in terms of paradox.

—Cleanth Brooks

Poems Related to Chapters 10 and 11

The Clod and the Pebble

"Love seeketh not Itself to please,
Nor for itself hath any care,
But for another gives its ease,
And builds a Heaven in Hell's despair."

So sung a little Clod of Clay
Trodden with the cattle's feet,
But a Pebble of the brook
Warbled out these metres meet:

"Love seeketh only Self to please,
To bind another to Its delight,
Joys in another's loss of ease,
And builds a Hell in Heaven's despite."

—William Blake (1757–1827)

1. What two types of love are contrasted? How are they alike?
2. Is a clod of clay a good symbol for one? Would a lump of earth be as appropriate? Why or why not?
3. Is a pebble in a brook a good symbol for another type of love? Discuss.
4. Does the poet suggest that one type of love is more fruitful or acceptable than the other? Or is the poem ironical in suggesting a negation of both types? Prove.

Ode on a Grecian Urn

I

Thou still unravish'd bride of quietness,
    Thou foster-child of silence and slow time,
Sylvan historian, who canst thus express
    A flowery tale more sweetly than our rhyme:
What leaf-fring'd legend haunts about thy shape
    Of deities or mortals, or of both,
        In Tempe[1] or the dales of Arcady?[2]
    What men or gods are these? What maidens loth?
What mad pursuit? What struggle to escape?
        What pipes and timbrels?[3] What wild ecstasy?

II

Heard melodies are sweet, but those unheard
    Are sweeter; therefore, ye soft pipes, play on;
Not to the sensual ear, but, more endear'd,
    Pipe to the spirit ditties of no tone:
Fair youth, beneath the trees, thou canst not leave
    Thy song, nor ever can those trees be bare;
        Bold Lover, never, never canst thou kiss,
Though winning near the goal—yet, do not grieve;
        She cannot fade, though thou hast not thy bliss,
    For ever wilt thou love, and she be fair!

III

Ah, happy, happy boughs! that cannot shed
   Your leaves, nor ever bid the Spring adieu;
And, happy melodist, unwearied,
   For ever piping songs for ever new;
More happy love! more happy, happy love!
   For ever warm and still to be enjoy'd,
     For ever panting, and for ever young:
All breathing human passion far above,
   That leaves a heart high-sorrowful and cloy'd,
     A burning forehead, and a parching tongue.

IV

Who are these coming to the sacrifice?
   To what green altar, O mysterious priest,
Lead'st thou that heifer lowing at the skies,
   And all her silken flanks with garlands dressed?
What little town by river or sea shore,
   Or mountain-built with peaceful citadel,
     Is emptied of this folk, this pious morn?
And, little town, thy streets for evermore
   Will silent be; and not a soul to tell
     Why thou art desolate, can e'er return.

V

O Attic[4] shape! Fair attitude! with brede[5]
   Of marble men and maidens overwrought,
With forest branches and the trodden weed;
   Thou, silent form, dost tease us out of thought
As doth eternity: Cold Pastoral!
   When old age shall this generation waste,
     Thou shalt remain, in midst of other woe
Than ours, a friend to man, to whom thou say'st,
Beauty is truth, truth beauty,—that is all
   Ye know on earth, and all ye need to know.

—John Keats (1795–1821)

---

[1] A beautiful valley in Greece, the favorite haunt of Apollo.   [2] Ideally
beautiful part of Greece surrounded by mountains.   [3] Small percussion
instruments such as drums or tambourines.   [4] Grecian.   [5] Decoration.

The poem contrasts the frustrations and disillusionments we suffer as mortals in the real world with the immortal beauty of art which,

by capturing arrested motion in cold clay, can conquer the destructiveness of time.

1. What three bands of decoration are to be found on the urn? What three
   different aspects of human life do they represent?
2. What verses suggest the disappointments of human life? Is the poem
   pessimistic because Keats recognizes their existence? Or does his apostrophizing the urn as a "Cold Pastoral!" influence our evaluation of
   warm, human passion even though it is transient? Discuss.
3. The poet develops his theme by using several effective paradoxes. For
   example, in the first stanza the urn is personified as an "unravished bride
   of quietness," the "foster-child of silence." Yet one of its scenes depicts
   the "wild ecstasy" of a sensual pursuit and a noisy bacchanalian dance
   and revel. What other paradoxes are there in the poem? How are they
   related to the theme?
4. In the first stanza the poet addresses the urn as a "sylvan historian." In
   what stanza does he develop this suggestion? By what images?
5. In the opening stanza why has Keats left us in doubt as to whether it is
   men or gods that are pursuing the maidens? Why in stanza four has he
   not definitely stated where the empty little town is, instead of giving us
   three possible locations?
6. Are the two concluding lines of the poem a didactic tag or a logical
   artistic conclusion that brings the poem to a satisfactory close? Discuss.
7. Compare the urn, a traditional symbol, as an "artifice of eternity" with
   Yeats' created symbol, the golden bird, in "Sailing to Byzantium." How
   are the two poems alike? How do they differ?

Ode to the West Wind

1

O wild West Wind, thou breath of Autumn's being,
Thou, from whose unseen presence the leaves dead
Are driven, like ghosts from an enchanter fleeing,

Yellow, and black, and pale, and hectic[1] red,
Pestilence-stricken multitudes: O thou,
Who chariotest to their dark wintry bed

The wingèd seeds, where they lie cold and low,
Each like a corpse within the grave, until
Thine azure sister of the Spring[2] shall blow

Her clarion o'er the dreaming earth, and fill
(Driving sweet buds like flocks to feed in air)
With living hues and odors plain and hill:

Wild Spirit, which art moving everywhere;
Destroyer and preserver; hear, oh, hear!

2

Thou on whose stream, mid the steep sky's commotion,
Loose clouds like earth's decaying leaves are shed,
Shook from the tangled boughs of Heaven and Ocean,

Angels of rain and lightning: there are spread
On the blue surface of thine aëry surge,
Like the bright hair uplifted from the head

Of some fierce Maenad,[3] even from the dim verge
Of the horizon to the zenith's height,
The locks of the approaching storm. Thou dirge

Of the dying year, to which this closing night
Will be the dome of a vast sepulchre,
Vaulted with all thy congregated might

Of vapours, from whose solid atmosphere
Black rain, and fire, and hail will burst: oh, hear!

3

Thou who didst waken from his summer dreams
The blue Mediterranean, where he lay,
Lulled by the coil of his crystalline streams,

Beside a pumice[4] isle in Baiae's[5] bay,
And saw in sleep old palaces and towers
Quivering within the wave's intenser day,

All overgrown with azure moss and flowers
So sweet, the sense faints picturing them! Thou
For whose path the Atlantic's level powers

Cleave themselves into chasms, while far below
The sea-blooms and the oozy woods which wear
The sapless foliage of the ocean, know

Thy voice, and suddenly grow gray with fear,
And tremble and despoil themselves: oh, hear!

4

If I were a dead leaf thou mightest bear;
If I were a swift cloud to fly with thee;
A wave to pant beneath thy power, and share

The impulse of thy strength, only less free
Than thou, O uncontrollable! If even
I were as in my boyhood, and could be

The comrade of thy wanderings over Heaven,
As then, when to outstrip thy skiey speed
Scarce seemed a vision; I would ne'er have striven

As thus with thee in prayer in my sore need.
Oh, lift me as a wave, a leaf, a cloud!
I fall upon the thorns of life! I bleed!

A heavy weight of hours has chained and bowed
One too like thee: tameless, and swift, and proud.

5

Make me thy lyre, even as the forest is:
What if my leaves are falling like its own!
The tumult of thy mighty harmonies

Will take from both a deep, autumnal tone,
Sweet though in sadness. Be thou, Spirit fierce,
My spirit! Be thou me, impetuous one!

Drive my dead thoughts over the universe
Like withered leaves to quicken a new birth!
And, by the incantation of this verse,

Scatter, as from an unextinguished hearth
Ashes and sparks, my words among mankind!
Be through my lips to unawakened earth

The trumpet of a prophecy! O, Wind,
If Winter comes, can Spring be far behind?

—Percy Bysshe Shelley (1792–1822)

---

[1] Feverish.   [2] South wind.   [3] Frenzied priestess of Bacchus, the god of wine.   [4] Volcanic lava.   [5] Seaside town on the Bay of Naples.

1. How do the first three stanzas differ from the last two? How does the poet connect these two parts to unify the poem?
2. In the first three stanzas the poet describes the activities of the west wind on land, in the sky, and on the seas. What effect does the poet achieve by the use of apostrophe to frame each stanza?
3. What paradox is found in stanza one? How is it resolved? To what extent is it repeated or developed in stanzas two and three? Where in stanzas two and three is the forest image of dead leaves that was used in the first stanza repeated? With what modification? What function does the repetition serve?
4. In stanzas four and five what metaphorical use does Shelley make of the images presented in the first three stanzas? What does the west wind

symbolize? The forest? The dead leaves? The seeds in the ground? Clarion (trumpet)? Winter? Spring?

5. What contrasts in mood are there in stanzas four and five? Are they contradictory, or is there an artistic and emotional modulation from four to five? Discuss.

6. Are the last six lines of stanza four sentimental? Is the poet indulging himself in self-pity? Or do they suggest a realistic appraisal of his own weaknesses and the despair of a rejected prophet, momentary human falterings which he masters in the last stanza? Discuss.

7. What archetypal metaphors of death and regeneration are in the poem? What part do they play in the emotional effectiveness of the poem? How are they related to the central theme?

The Maldive Shark[1]

About the Shark, phlegmatical one,
Pale sot of the Maldive sea,
The sleek little pilot-fish, azure and slim,
How alert in attendance be.
From his saw-pit of mouth, from his charnel of maw
They have nothing of harm to dread,
But liquidly glide on his ghastly flank
Or before his Gorgonian[2] head:
Or lurk in the port of serrated[3] teeth
In white triple tiers of glittering gates,
And there find a haven when peril's abroad,
An asylum in jaws of the Fates!
They are friends; and friendly they guide him to prey,
Yet never partake of the treat—
Eyes and brains to the dotard lethargic and dull,
Pale ravener of horrible meat.

—Herman Melville (1819–1891)

---

[1] Found in the Indian Ocean.   [2] Petrifying, terrifying.   [3] Notched on the edge like a saw.

1. In this poem Melville gives us a vivid description of "The sleek little pilot-fish," the Maldive shark, and their relationship. What contrasts are there in the poem? What paradoxes? How are they related to the theme?

2. Is it possible to read this poem on a symbolic level as the relationship of protected parasites guiding tyrants to their prey (e.g., Polonius as the spy of Claudius, Hamlet's stepfather, or Eichmann seeking out Hitler's victims)? Why or why not?

Soliloquy of the Spanish Cloister

I

Gr-r-r—there go, my heart's abhorrence!
   Water your damned flower-pots, do!
If hate killed men, Brother Lawrence,
   God's blood, would not mine kill you!
What? your myrtle-bush wants trimming?
   Oh, that rose has prior claims—
Needs its leaden vase filled brimming?
   Hell dry you up with its flames!

II

At the meal we sit together:
   Salve tibi![1] I must hear
Wise talk of the kind of weather,
   Sort of season, time of year:
Not a plenteous cork-crop: scarcely
   Dare we hope oak-galls, I doubt:
What's the Latin Name for "parsley"?
   What's the Greek name for Swine's Snout?

III

Whew! We'll have our platter burnished,
   Laid with care on our own shelf!
With a fire-new spoon we're furnished,
   And a goblet for ourself,
Rinsed like something sacrificial
   Ere 'tis fit to touch our chaps—[2]
Marked with L. for our initial!
   (He-he! There his lily snaps!)

IV

Saint, forsooth! While brown Dolores
   Squats outside the Convent bank
With Sanchicha, telling stories,
   Steeping tresses in the tank,
Blue-back, lustrous, thick like horsehairs,
   —Can't I see his dead eye glow,
Bright as 'twere a Barbary corsair's?[3]
   (That is, if he'd let it show!)

V

When he finishes refection,[4]
   Knife and fork he never lays

Cross-wise, to my recollection,
 As do I, in Jesu's praise.
I the Trinity illustrate,
 Drinking watered orange-pulp—
In three sips the Arian[5] frustrate:
 While he drains his at one gulp.

VI

Oh, those melons? If he's able,
 We're to have a feast! so nice!
One goes to the Abbot's table.
 All of us get each a slice.
How go on your flowers? None double?
 Not one fruit-sort can you spy?
Strange!—And I, too, at such trouble,
 Keep them close-nipped on the sly!

VII

There's a great text in Galatians,[6]
 Once you trip on it, entails
Twenty-nine distinct damnations,
 One sure, if another fails:
If I trip him just a-dying,
 Sure of heaven as sure can be,
Spin him round and send him flying
 Off to hell, a Manichee?[7]

VIII

Or, my scrofulous[8] French novel
 On gray paper with blunt type!
Simply glance at it, you grovel
 Hand and foot in Belial's[9] gripe:
If I double down its pages
 At the woeful sixteenth print,
When he gathers his greengages,[10]
 Ope a sieve[11] and slip it in't?

IX

Or, there's Satan!—one might venture
 Pledge one's soul to him, yet leave
Such a flaw in the indenture,
 As he'd miss till, past retrieve,
Blasted lay that rose-acacia
 We're so proud of! *Hy Zy, Hine* . . .[12]

'St, there's Vespers! *Plena gratia*
Ave, Virgo[13] Gr-r-r—you swine!

—Robert Browning (1812–1889)

---

[1] A greeting, "Hail to thee!"   [2] Jaws, lips.   [3] Pirate from northwest coast of Africa.   [4] Light meal.   [5] Arius was a fourth-century heretic who denied the doctrine of the Trinity.   [6] Where there are many difficult passages and curses for disobedience.   [7] Believer in the Manichaean heresy, a concept of two kingdoms, one good, the other evil, both equal in strength. This belief denies God's benevolence and omnipotence.   [8] Morally contaminated.   [9] An evil spirit or the devil.   [10] Plums.   [11] Basket.   [12] Vesper bells (or the beginning of a curse).   [13] Beginning of a prayer, "Hail, Virgin, full of grace."

1. Why is the setting in a Spanish cloister? Is this poem an attack on the monastic life, or is Browning symbolically depicting a universal situation —the inevitable growth and magnification of hatreds and jealousies in people forced into communal living (in offices, factories, armies, colleges, etc.)? Discuss.

2. What use does Browning make of irony in the poem? How does this poem resemble "My Last Duchess" (page 196)?

3. Contrast the character of the speaker with that of Brother Lawrence. What weaknesses of the speaker does he project on Brother Lawrence? What is his purpose?

4. Of which of the seven deadly sins is the speaker guilty? Prove by concrete references. How does he hope to achieve salvation? By what methods does he plan the damnation of Brother Lawrence? In what order are they arranged? How does he plan to outwit Satan? What does this reveal about the speaker's character?

5. By what concrete details does Browning bring out that the speaker is a ritualist? an intellectual monk? a mischief-maker? a sensualist?

6. In Brother Lawrence do we have the portrait of the ideal monk adjusted to the monastic life? Does he possess any traits that could be annoying to his fellow monks? Discuss.

Farewell to Barn and Stack and Tree

"Farewell to barn and stack and tree,
    Farewell to Severn[1] shore.
Terence, look your last at me,
    For I come home no more.

"The sun burns on the half-mown hill,
    By now the blood is dried;
And Maurice amongst the hay lies still
    And my knife is in his side.

"My 'mother thinks us long away;
   'Tis time the field were mown.
She had two sons at rising day,
   To-night she'll be alone.

"And here's a bloody hand to shake,
   And oh, man, here's good-bye;
We'll sweat no more on scythe and rake,
   My bloody hands and I.

"I wish you strength to bring you pride,
   And a love to keep you clean,
And I wish you luck, come Lammastide,[2]
   At racing on the green.

"Long for me the rick will wait,
   And long will wait the fold,
And long will stand the empty plate,
   And dinner will be cold."

      —A. E. Housman (1859–1936)

---

[1] River in Great Britain.　　[2] Beginning of August.

1.　What archetypal theme does this literary ballad treat? How close is it to a similar story in the Bible?
2.　What traditional details are found in the poem? What modern ones?
3.　What new twist has the poet given the story? What concrete details suggest this aspect of the tragedy?
4.　Is the poem faulty because the poet has omitted the motive for the quarrel, or is this unnecessary to the development of the theme? Discuss.

The Second Coming[1]

Turning and turning in the widening gyre[2]
The falcon cannot hear the falconer.[3]
Things fall apart; the centre cannot hold;
Mere anarchy is loosed upon the world,
The blood-dimmed tide is loosed, and everywhere
The ceremony of innocence is drowned:
The best lack all conviction, while the worst
Are full of passionate intensity.

Surely some revelation is at hand;
Surely the Second Coming is at hand.
The Second Coming! Hardly are those words out
When a vast image out of *Spiritus Mundi*[4]

Troubles my sight: somewhere in sands of the desert
A shape with lion body and the head of a man,
A gaze blank and pitiless as the sun,
Is moving its slow thighs, while all about it
Reel shadows of the indignant desert birds.
The darkness drops again: but now I know
That twenty centuries[5] of stony sleep
Were vexed to nightmare by a rocking cradle,
And what rough beast, its hour come round at last,
Slouches towards Bethlehem to be born?

—William Butler Yeats (1865–1939)

---

[1] See Matthew 24 for the Christian prophecy of the second coming.
[2] Revolving cone or vortex.   [3] The falcon, in his ever-widening spiral flight, soars beyond the control of his master, man.   [4] The World Spirit or great racial memory containing all experience and history.   [5] Era of Christianity, now doomed to be replaced by some bestial, anarchic anticivilization.

1. This symbolic prophetic poem was written in January 1919 and published in 1921. What is the poet's impression of the present as depicted in the first stanza? What is his vision of the future as suggested in stanza two?

2. What does the poet mean by ". . . everywhere/The ceremony of innocence is drowned"?

3. The picture of the apocalyptic beast described in stanza two appeared to Yeats in a recurrent dream. In what way is it a primordial image or archetype? What does it symbolize?

4. Compare and contrast the two bird images. What function do they serve in the poem?

5. What is the significance of the reference to Bethlehem? What concept of history is implied in the poem?

6. To what extent have contemporary events confirmed the validity of the poet's pessimistic prophecy?

7. What irony is to be found in the poem?

8. How do you account for the persistent archetypal image of the destruction of the world (by fire, flood, or other agency) found in all mythologies?

At a dinner to celebrate Robert Frost's eighty-fifth birthday, Lionel Trilling made a speech which created a literary furor. On that occasion he made the following comment:

I think of Robert Frost as a terrifying poet. Call him, if it makes things any easier, a tragic poet, but it might be useful every now and then to come out from under the shelter of that literary word.

The universe that he conceives is a terrifying universe. Read the poem called "Design" and see if you sleep the better for it.

Design

I found a dimpled spider, fat and white,
On a white heal-all,[1] holding up a moth
Like a white piece of rigid satin cloth—
Assorted characters of death and blight
Mixed ready to begin the morning right,
Like the ingredients of a witches' broth—
A snow-drop[2] spider, a flower like froth,
And dead wings carried like a paper kite.
What had that flower to do with being white,
The wayside blue and innocent heal-all?
What brought the kindred spider to that height,
Then steered the white moth thither in the night?
What but design of darkness to appall?—
If design govern in a thing so small.

—Robert Frost (1875–1963)

---

[1] Colloquial name for a flower.   [2] White flower that often appears when snow is on the ground.

1. What philosophical belief is Frost attacking in this poem? How do the concrete details of spider, flower, and moth help communicate the theme?
2. Frost uses the adjective *white* five times. In what two different senses is it used?
3. What irony is there in the poem? Symbolism?
4. Does the last line negate the previous questions or affirm them? Discuss.
5. The poem is written in a traditional verse form, the Petrarchan sonnet. Is this appropriate to the subject? Why or why not?

The setting of the following poem is in a blackout during World War II, 1944, in Boston. The statue referred to is that of General "Fighting Joe" Hooker, who commanded the Army of the Potomac in its defeat at Chancellorsville, Virginia, May 2–4, 1863.

Christmas Eve Under Hooker's Statue

Tonight in a blackout. Twenty years ago
I hung my stocking on the tree, and hell's
Serpent entwined the apple in the toe
To sting the child with knowledge. Hooker's heels

Kicking at nothing in the shifting snow,
A cannon and a cairn of cannon balls
Rusting before the blackened Statehouse, know
How the long horn of plenty broke like glass
In Hooker's gauntlets. Once I came from Mass;

Now storm-clouds shelter Christmas, once again
Mars meets his fruitless star with open arms,
His heavy sabre flashes with the rime,[1]
The war-god's bronzed and empty forehead forms
Anonymous machinery from raw men;
The cannon on the Common cannot stun
The blundering butcher as he rides on Time—
The barrel clinks with holly. I am cold:
I ask for bread, my father gives me mould;

His stocking is full of stones. Santa in red
Is crowned with wizened berries. Man of war,
Where is the summer's garden? In its bed
The ancient speckled serpent will appear,
And black-eyed susan with her frizzled head.
When Chancellorsville mowed down the volunteer,
"All wars are boyish," Herman Melville said;[2]
But we are old, our fields are running wild:
Till Christ again turn wanderer and child.

—Robert Lowell (1917–   )

---

[1] White frost.   [2] In his poem "The March Into Virginia" Melville wrote:
"All wars are boyish, and are fought by boys,/The champions and en-
thusiasts of the state."

1. What is the function of the references to childhood in the poem? With
    what images are they contrasted?
2. What is the function of the religious references in the poem?
3. Discuss the poet's use of irony? What comment does the poet make on
    our contemporary civilization? Interpret the symbolic meaning of the
    following metaphors: "the horn of plenty," "anonymous machinery,"
    "the summer's garden," "the ancient speckled serpent."

Ah! Sun-Flower

Ah! Sun-flower, weary of time,
Who countest the steps of the Sun,
Seeking after that sweet golden clime
Where the traveller's journey is done;

Where the youth pined away with desire,
And the pale Virgin shrouded in snow,
Arise from their graves, and aspire
Where my Sun-Flower wishes to go.

—William Blake (1757–1827)

C. M. Bowra interprets this lyric as an expression of Blake's deep compassion for "all young men and women who are robbed of their full humanity because they are starved of love." The sun-flower, rooted in earth, he sees as "Blake's symbol for all men and women whose lives are dominated and spoiled by a longing which they can never hope to satisfy, and who are held down to earth despite their desire for release into some brighter, freer sphere."

Another critic, Harold Bloom, finds a bitter nostalgic irony in the poem:

The Sun-flower desires to go where the sun sets; that heaven is where the Youth and Virgin are resurrected to the rewards of their holy chastity. They arise, and they still aspire to go to their heaven, but that is where they already are. They have not escaped nature, by seeking to deny it; they have become monuments to its limitations. To repress energy is to join the sunset, and yet still to aspire after it. The flower is rooted in nature; the Youth and the Virgin were not, but have become so. To aspire only as the vegetative world aspires is to suffer a metamorphosis into the vegetative existence.

A third reader interprets the sun-flower as a symbol of the poet's soul yearning for heaven, "that sweet golden clime," where the pure youth and the pale virgin, free from sin, are going.

1. Which interpretation of this symbolic poem do you find the most plausible? Justify your choice.
2. A knowledge of a poet's views on the same subject expressed in other poems is sometimes helpful. On the relation of the sexes Blake wrote:

Abstinence sows sands all over
The ruddy limbs and flaming hair,
But Desire Gratified
Plants fruits of life and beauty there.

If you take into consideration this statement, which of the three interpretations would you rule out?

Mythmaking

Beauty is never satisfied
with beauty. Helen,
gazing in the glass,
framed by the lecherous curtains,
the enchanted bed,
knew herself beautiful. Yet she felt life pass
about her. Laughter had been hers
to breed alone. Now mute,
the humdrum pulse run down, she lay
a palpitation of her memory;
a deceitful body and a crumbling smile
where all that love and elixirs had bred.

Men knew her aging odor.
Ravished by the nosings of her fears,
she married. Her fastened gaiety became a jewel
decking a sot. Oh well, we do
with what we have and haven't got;
the pagan cried
against endurance, dressed
and went to dinner at the side
of Menelaus. What would she become, if not her men
would come inside her,
make her whole again!
Each night was Helen
on the reminiscent bed
waiting with spread heart and legs
and willing arch for willing arrowhead.

Sprung from the cracking bow of Troy
he could not notice Helen growing old,
but fitted as a flower, or a toy,
as use to pleasure, went to hold
the woman in his arms.

And were they satisfied, these two,
when afterwards Helen closed her eyes
and slept?
Helen, who turned the too-much heart
to a great dumb shrivelling, could do as much
to any lover.
So squandered Paris in her arms lay dry
and she lay lavish and methodical;
(who offers bread by night may offer mould)
beauty to beauty did not satisfy;

such meetings of perfections cut us, turn us cold
as aging Helen, bittering in her sleep,
and cheat us of desire
by too much hungering.

She must have been glad to wake, not to be satisfied,
to see her husband stir himself and raise a fleet,
and all the world fall shadow
to the crumpling of that sheet.

—Kathleen Spivack (1938–   )

1.   Compare this poem with H. D.'s "Helen" (page 90).

The Approach to Thebes[1]

In the zero of the night, in the lipping hour,
Skin-time, knocking-time, when the heart is pearled
And the moon squanders its uranian[2] gold,
She taunted me, who was all music's tongue,
Philosophy's and wilderness's breed,
Of shifting shape, half jungle-cat, half-dancer,
Night's woman-petaled, lion-scented rose,
To whom I gave, out of a hero's need,
The dolor of my thrust, my riddling answer,[3]
Whose force no lesser mortal knows. Dangerous?
Yes, as nervous oracles foretold
Who could not guess the secret taste of her:
Impossible wine! I came into the world
To fill a fate; am punished by my youth
No more. What if dog-faced logic howls
Was it art or magic multiplied my joy?
Nature has reasons beyond true or false.
We played like metaphysic animals
Whose freedom made our knowledge bold
Before the tragic curtain of the day:
I can bear the dishonor now of growing old.

Blinded and old, exiled, diseased, and scorned—
The verdict's bitten on the brazen gates,
For the gods grant each of us his lot, his term.
Hail to the King of Thebes!—my self, ordained
To satisfy the impulse of the worm,
Bemummied in those famous incestuous sheets,
The bloodiest flags of nations of the curse,
To be hung from the balcony outside the room
Where I encounter my most flagrant source.

Children, grandchildren, my long posterity,
To whom I bequeath the spiders of my dust,
Believe me, whatever sordid tales you hear,
Told by physicians or mendacious scribes,
Of beardless folly, consanguineous lust,
Fomenting pestilence, rebellion, war,
I come prepared, unwanting what I see,
But tied to life. On the royal road to Thebes
I had my luck, I met a lovely monster,
And the story's this: I made the monster me.

                    —Stanley Kunitz (1905–   )

---

[1] This poem is a modern treatment of the famous Oedipus myth best known to us in Sophocles' three plays: *Oedipus Rex, Antigone,* and *Oedipus at Colonus.* [2] Heavenly, celestial. [3] The riddle of the Sphinx was: What goes on four feet, then on two, and finally on three, yet is weakest when it uses the most feet? Oedipus answered, "Man who crawls in his infancy, walks erect in his prime, and uses a cane in his old age."

Money

an introductory lecture

This morning we shall spend a few minutes
Upon the study of symbolism, which is basic
To the nature of money. I show you this nickel.
Icons and cryptograms are written all over
The nickel: one side shows a hunchbacked bison
Bending his head and curling his tail to accommodate
The circular nature of money. Over him arches
UNITED STATES OF AMERICA, and, squinched in
Between that and his rump, E PLURIBUS UNUM,
A Roman reminiscence that appears to mean
An indeterminately large number of things
All of which are the same. Under the bison
A straight line giving him a ground to stand on
Reads FIVE CENTS. And on the other side of our nickel
There is the profile of a man with long hair
And a couple of feathers in the hair; we know
Somehow that he is an American Indian, and
He wears the number nineteen-thirty-six.
Right in front of his eyes the word LIBERTY, bent
To conform with the curve of the rim, appears
To be falling out of the sky Y first; the Indian
Keeps his eyes downcast and does not notice this;
To notice it, indeed, would be shortsighted of him.

So much for the iconography of one of our nickels,
Which is now becoming a rarity and something of
A collectors' item: for as a matter of fact
There is almost nothing you can buy with a nickel,
The representative American Indian was destroyed
A hundred years or so ago, and his descendants'
Relations with liberty are maintained with reservations,
Or primitive concentration camps; while the bison,
Except for a few examples kept in cages,
Is now extinct. Something like that, I think,
Is what Keats must have meant in his celebrated
Ode on a Grecian Urn.
                Notice, in conclusion,
A number of circumstances sometimes overlooked
Even by experts: (*a*) Indian and bison,
Confined to obverse and reverse of the coin,
Can never see each other; (*b*) they are looking
In opposite directions, the bison past
The Indian's feathers, the Indian past
The bison's tail; (*c*) they are upside down
To one another; (*d*) the bison has a human face
Somewhat resembling that of Jupiter Ammon.
I hope that our studies today will have shown you
Something of the import of symbolism
With respect to the understanding of what is symbolized.

                —Howard Nemerov (1920–   )

Theme for English B

The instructor said,

> *Go home and write*
> *a page tonight.*
> *And let that page come out of you—*
> *Then, it will be true.*

I wonder if it's that simple?

I am twenty-two, colored, born in Winston-Salem.
I went to school there, then Durham, then here
to this college on the hill above Harlem.
I am the only colored student in my class.
The steps from the hill lead down into Harlem,
through a park, then I cross St. Nicholas,
Eighth Avenue, Seventh, and I come to the Y,
the Harlem Branch Y, where I take the elevator
up to my room, sit down, and write this page:

It's not easy to know what is true for you or me
at twenty-two, my age. But I guess I'm what
I feel and see and hear, Harlem, I hear you:
hear you, hear me—we two—you, me talk on this page.
(I hear New York, too.) Me—who?
Well, I like to eat, sleep, drink, and be in love.
I like to work, read, learn, and understand life.
I like a pipe for a Christmas present,
or records—Bessie, bop, or Bach.
I guess being colored doesn't make me *not* like
the same things other folks like who are other races.
So will my page be colored that I write?
Being me, it will not be white.
But it will be
a part of you, instructor.
You are white—
yet a part of me, as I am a part of you.
That's American.
Sometimes perhaps you don't want to be a part of me.
Nor do I often want to be a part of you.
But we are, that's true!
As I learn from you,
I guess you learn from me—
although you're older—and white—
and somewhat more free.

This is my page for English B.

—Langston Hughes (1902–1967)

A Way of Life

It's been going on a long time.
For instance, these two guys, not saying much, who slog
Through sun and sand, fleeing the scene of their crime,
Till one turns, without a word, and smacks
His buddy flat with the flat of an axe,
Which cuts down on the dialogue
Some, but is viewed rather as normal than sad
By me, as I wait for the next ad.

It seems to me it's been quite a while
Since the last vision of blonde loveliness
Vanished, her shampoo and shower and general style
Replaced by this lean young lunk-
head parading along with a gun in his back to confess

How yestereve, being drunk
And in a state of existential despair,
He beat up his grandma and pawned her invalid chair.

But here at last is a pale beauty
Smoking a filter beside a mountain stream,
Brief interlude, before the conflict of love and duty
Gets moving again, as sheriff and posse expound,
Between jail and saloon, the American Dream
Where Justice, after considerable horsing around,
Turns out to be Mercy; when the villain is knocked off,
A kindly uncle offers syrup for my cough.

And now these clean-cut athletic types
In global hats are having a nervous debate
As they stand between their individual rocket ships
Which have landed, appropriately, on some rocks
Somewhere in Space, in an atmosphere of hate.

—Howard Nemerov (1920–   )

Plan

My cousin Max is being married
                        on a quiz show.
He is getting a Westinghouse refrigerator
                        a Singer sewing machine
a set of furniture from Sears and Roebuck
                an ant farm
        a General Electric toaster
and a girl.

It is not enough.
He expects babies and happiness
good times and money
and a government that wars on war.

My cousin Max expects too much.

—Rod McKuen (1933–   )

Who Was It Came

Who was it came
Over the mountains bearing
Gifts we did not ask?

—Not the sapience of the thrush
Or the ant's perdurance,
Something a body might use—

Who was it brought
Cerements and a wrinkled skin,
A sour digestion

Over the mountains, offering
Crotchets and a rheumy gaze
And wits gone wandering?

Just when we thought to repossess
The taught frenzies of Chicago jazz
And bridal ardor

Here he comes,
Inexorable gaffer in an old hat
Croaking our names.

     —Daniel Hoffman (1923–   )

The Groundhog

In June, amid the golden fields,
I saw a groundhog lying dead.
Dead lay he; my senses shook,
And mind outshot our naked frailty.
There lowly in the vigorous summer
His form began its senseless change,
And made my senses waver dim
Seing nature ferocious in him.
Inspecting close his maggots' might
And seething cauldron of his being,
Half with loathing, half with a strange love,
I poked him with an angry stick.
The fever arose, became a flame
And Vigour circumscribed the skies,
Immense energy in the sun,
And through my frame a sunless trembling.
My stick had done nor good nor harm.
Then stood I silent in the day
Watching the object, as before;
And kept my reverence for knowledge
Trying for control, to be still,
To quell the passion of the blood;
Until I had bent down on my knees

Praying for joy in the sight of decay.
And so I left; and I returned
In Autumn strict of eye, to see
The sap gone out of the groundhog,
But the bony sodden hulk remained.
But the year had lost its meaning,
And in intellectual chains
I lost both love and loathing,
Mured up in the wall of wisdom.
Another summer took the fields again
Massive and burning, full of life,
But when I chanced upon the spot
There was only a little hair left,
And bones bleaching in the sunlight
Beautiful as architecture;
I watched them like a geometer,
And cut a walking stick from a birch.
It has been three years, now.
There is no sign of the groundhog.
I stood there in the whirling summer,
My hand capped a withered heart,
And thought of China and of Greece,
Of Alexander in his tent;
Of Montaigne in his tower,
Of Saint Theresa in her wild lament.

—Richard Eberhart (1904–   )

1. What do the death and decay of the groundhog symbolize? Explain how the two opening lines of the poem suggest the theme. What is their metrical form? What metrical and rhetorical shift is found in line three? How can it be justified?

2. What lines or phrases suggest the poet's identification with the dead groundhog? Over a period of three years the poet describes his four confrontations with the problem of death. What is ironical and paradoxical about his using only two seasons, summer (three times) and autumn (once)? What changes take place in his attitudes in these four visitations? In his emotional, intellectual, aesthetic, and philosophic reactions is he stating our customary rationalization about death or has he finally accepted the "senseless change" of the physical processes of the universe?

3. In the last four lines is the poet, by his historical and literary allusions, stressing the impermanence of great civilizations and men or the survival of human creative art and spiritual qualities indestructible by ferocious nature? What three important human attributes are symbolized by Alexander, Montaigne, and Saint Theresa?

4. What function is served by the poet's use of contrast: life and death, love and loathing, emotion and reason, chills and fever, "immense energy in the sun" and "sunless trembling," the "angry stick" and the "walking stick"?

I hear ghostly Academics in Limbo screeching about form.

—Allen Ginsberg

12
Structure and Stanza

A good poem, like every living organism, has its own unique pattern which is inevitably an expression of its subject matter. The structure of a poem is just as important as rhythm, imagery, tone, and diction. These elements must be interrelated and organized into a coherent whole. Like the beauty of a blooming flower or the grandeur of a forest tree, a poem (in Wordsworth's phrase)

> Comes not by casting in a formal mould,
> But from its *own* divine vitality.

The form of a poem may be simple or complex, loose or tight, traditional or experimental. Its structure may be based on a logical progression of images or ideas, a psychological relationship of emotions, a connected plot, or coherently shaped by contrast, repetition, or a frame (return) pattern. The success of a poem—short or long— ultimately depends upon the poet's achievement of perfect rapport between its subject matter and the organic form.

Since every good poem is a unique fusion of form and content, it is impossible to enumerate or isolate an arbitrary number of poetic patterns. However, we can distinguish certain forms frequently used by poets. In Yeats' "Sailing to Byzantium" (page 185) we can see how the poet used a logical form of progression in thought development and satisfied the expectation of the reader by a rational conclusion.

A second type of form often employed by poets is the progression, not of logic, but of emotional development. The following dramatic monologue by Browning is an illustration of this structure.

The Laboratory

Ancien Régime[1]

I

Now that I, tying thy glass mask tightly,
May gaze thro' these faint smokes curling whitely,[2]
As thou pliest thy trade in this devil's-smithy—
Which is the poison to poison her, prithee?

II

He is with her, and they know that I know
Where they are, what they do; they believe my tears flow
While they laugh, laugh at me, at me fled to the drear
Empty church, to pray God in, for them!—I am here.

III

Grind away, moisten and mash up thy paste,
Pound at thy powder,—I am not in haste!
Better sit thus, and observe thy strange things,
Than go where men wait me and dance at the King's.

IV

That in the mortar—you call it a gum?
Ah, the brave tree whence such gold oozings come!
And yonder soft phial, the exquisite blue,
Sure to taste sweetly,—is that poison too?

V

Had I but all of them, thee and thy treasures,
What a wild crowd of invisible pleasures!
To carry pure death in an earring, a casket,
A signet, a fan-mount, a filigree basket![3]

VI

Soon, at the King's, a mere lozenge to give,
And Pauline should have just thirty minutes to live!
But to light a pastile, and Elise, with her head
And her breast and her arms and her hands, should drop dead!

VII

Quick—is it finished? The colour's too grim!
Why not soft like the phial's, enticing and dim?
Let it brighten her drink, let her turn it and stir,
And try it and taste, ere she fix and prefer!

VIII

What a drop! She's not little, no minion like me!
That's why she ensnared him: this never will free

The soul from those masculine eyes,—say, "no!"
To that pulse's magnificent come-and-go.

IX

For only last night, as they whispered, I brought
My own eyes to bear on her so, that I thought
Could I keep them one half minute fixed she would fall
Shrivelled; she fell not; yet this does it all!

X

Not that I bid you spare her the pain;
Let death be felt and the proof remain:
Brand, burn up, bite into its grace—
He is sure to remember her dying face!

XI

Is it done? Take my mask off! Nay, be not morose;
It kills her, and this prevents seeing it close:
The delicate droplet, my whole fortune's fee!
If it hurts her, beside, can it ever hurt me?

XII

Now, take all my jewels, gorge gold to your fill,
You may kiss me, old man, on my mouth if you will!
But brush this dust off me, lest horror it brings
Ere I know it—next moment I dance at the King's!

—Robert Browning (1812–1889)

---

[1] Setting is in France during the "Old Order" (before the French Revolution) possibly in the later sixteenth century under the Regency of
Catherine de' Medici. In Renaissance Italy poisoning was developed as
a fine art.   [2] The poison is probably a compound of arsenic.   [3] Devices
used to bring the victim into contact with poison.

The poem is a psychological study of murderous jealousy. The
speaker is a little woman who is willing to sacrifice all her wealth
to secure a deadly poison that will disfigure and destroy her ama-
zonian rival who has "ensnared" her lover. The poem opens with the
murderess, obsessed with hatred, tying on her gas mask. At first,
she speaks calmly; then, as she patiently watches the preparation of
the poison and visualizes her revenge, her eagerness and agitation
mount. The poem ends in an outburst of terrifying excitement stimulated by lust, fear, and murderous hate.

Another variation of progressive form is the reversal of a situation which defeats the expectation of the reader. The reversal may
result in irony, surprise, or a further development of meaning. For

instance, in "Nora Criona" (page 119) the overaffectionate curiosity and possessiveness of the wife does not result in a reciprocated love but in a murder.

A form frequently employed by poets is the antithetical pattern, the construction of a poem to stress a contrast of situations, emotions, characters, or concepts. For instance, the following poem, bipartite in structure, clearly contrasts the noisiness of construction with the quietness of destruction.

The Hammers

Noise of hammers once I heard,
Many hammers, busy hammers,
Beating, shaping, night and day,
Shaping, beating dust and clay
To a palace; saw it reared;
Saw the hammers laid away.

And I listened, and I heard
Hammers beating, night and day,
In the palace newly reared,
Beating it to dust and clay:
Other hammers, muffled hammers,
Silent hammers of decay.

—Ralph Hodgson (1872–1962)

In the poem "In Time of 'The Breaking of Nations' " (page 169) Hardy suggests the reverse contrast: the quiet, creative, permanent activities of man—nourishment from the good earth and love—with the noisy, destructive, transient effects of war.

Consider the following poem written by Wordsworth after his beloved brother John, a captain in the merchant service, lost his life in a shipwreck on February 6, 1805.

Elegiac Stanzas

Suggested by a picture of Peele Castle,
in a storm, painted by Sir George Beaumont

I was thy neighbour once, thou rugged Pile!
Four summer weeks I dwelt in sight of thee:
I saw thee every day; and all the while
Thy Form was sleeping on a glassy sea.

So pure the sky, so quiet was the air!
So like, so very like, was day to day!
Whene'er I looked, thy Image still was there;
It trembled, but it never passed away.

How perfect was the calm? it seemed no sleep;
No mood, which season takes away, or brings:
I could have fancied that the mighty Deep
Was even the gentlest of all gentle Things.

Ah! THEN, if mine had been the Painter's hand,
To express what then I saw; and add the gleam,
The light that never was, on sea or land,
The consecration, and the Poet's dream;

I would have planted thee, thou hoary Pile
Amid a world how different from this!
Beside a sea that could not cease to smile;
On tranquil land, beneath a sky of bliss.

Thou shouldst have seemed a treasure-house divine
Of peaceful years; a chronicle of heaven;—
Of all the sunbeams that did ever shine
The very sweetest had to thee been given.

A Picture had it been of lasting ease,
Elysian quiet, without toil or strife;
No motion but the moving tide, a breeze,
Or merely silent Nature's breathing life.

Such, in the fond illusion of my heart,
Such Picture would I at that time have made:
And seen the soul of truth in every part,
A steadfast peace that might not be betrayed.

So once it would have been,—'tis so no more;
I have submitted to a new control:
A power is gone, which nothing can restore;
A deep distress hath humanised my Soul.

Not for a moment could I now behold
A smiling sea, and be what I have been:
The feeling of my loss will ne'er be old;
This, which I know, I speak with mind serene.

Then, Beaumont, Friend! who would have been the Friend,
If he had lived, of Him whom I deplore,
This work of thine I blame not, but commend;
This sea in anger, and that dismal shore.

O 'tis a passionate Work!—yet wise and well,
Well chosen is the spirit that is here;
That Hulk which labours in the deadly swell,
This rueful sky, this pageantry of fear!

And this huge Castle, standing here sublime,
I love to see the look with which it braves,
Cased in the unfeeling armour of old time,
The lightning, the fierce wind, and trampling waves.

Farewell, farewell the heart that lives alone,
Housed in a dream, at distance from the Kind![1]
Such happiness, wherever it be known,
Is to be pitied; for 'tis surely blind.

But welcome fortitude, and patient cheer,
And frequent sights of what is to be borne!
Such sights, or worse, as are before me here.—
Not without hope we suffer and we mourn.

—William Wordsworth (1770–1850)

---

[1] Human beings, mankind.

The poem is patterned to contrast appearance and reality, the calmness and storminess of the sea, the beneficence and the destructiveness of nature. The first seven stanzas depict the peacefulness and beauty of the sea. In the eighth stanza the poet admits that this view of nature is an illusion. In the last seven stanzas the poet realizes that the painter's vision of the rueful sky, the fierce wind, and the angry sea is the tragic reality. The shock of this discovery and the loss of his brother have humanized the poet's soul. With patience, intensified love, and fortitude, he can now understand and share the common burdens of mankind.

Other poems that are structured by a contrast form are Blake's "The Clod and the Pebble" (page 203), contrasting selfless and selfish love; Donne's "A Valediction Forbidding Mourning" (page 153), contrasting earthly and spiritual love; Browning's "Soliloquy of the Spanish Cloister" (page 210), contrasting the characters of the monks; Keats' "Ode to a Nightingale" (page 133), contrasting the world of mortal man and the world of immortal nature.

Besides progressive and antithetical form a poet may use repetitive form. This consists of communicating a consistent meaning, mood, situation, or character by a slight variation. Such a poem is usually written in regular, patterned stanzas with shifts in imagery and metaphor. It is comparable to a musical composition of a theme and variations. In such a poem the new details must be interesting enough to hold the attention of the reader and must reinforce the theme. A successful poem employing repetitive form fulfills one of the fundamental tenets of all art: unity in variety. The following poem is a representative example.

A Meditation for His Mistress

You are a tulip seen to-day,
But, dearest, of so short a stay
That where you grew scarce man can say.

You are a lovely July-flower,
Yet one rude wind or ruffling shower
Will force you hence, and in an hour.

You are a sparkling rose i' th' bud,
Yet lost ere that chaste flesh and blood
Can show where you or grew or stood.

You are a full-spread, fair-set vine,
And can with tendrils love entwine,
Yet dried ere you distil your wine.

You are like balm enclosèd well
In amber or some crystal shell,
Yet lost ere you transfuse your smell.

You are a dainty violet,
Yet wither'd ere you can be set
Within the virgin's coronet.

You are the queen all flowers among:
But die you must, fair maid, ere long,
As he, the maker of this song.

—Robert Herrick (1591–1674)

Other poems illustrating this pattern are Blake's "London" (page 11), Burns' "A Red, Red Rose" (page 131), and Elizabeth Barrett Browning's "Sonnet XLIII" (page 132).

A poet, for particular effects, may combine these forms or use one of the traditional genres such as the sonnet or dramatic monologue either in the conventional mode or with modification to suit his purpose. The revolt of many modern poets against traditional forms has led to the development of a poetic cult glorifying informality and "antiformality," to use J. V. Cunningham's phrasing. Form can then be defined as "that which remains the same when everything else is changed." Like Whitman these poets are striving to create new forms which are suitable to express the concepts of today's world. A good poem, however, can never be formless.

The relationship of *stanza* to form is important, for stanzas are the essential building blocks that help pattern the construction of a poem. A stanza may vary from a simple couplet of two lines to the complex ten-line stanza of Keats' "Ode to a Nightingale" or to the fourteen-line sonnet. In most traditional poetry a stanza is arranged in a definite metrical and rhyme scheme. A stanza in poetry is similar to a paragraph in prose; by suggesting an advance in thought or a change in tone, it permits us to grasp the relationship of parts to the whole. With the development of printing, poets have begun to pay more attention to the visual appeal of lines and stanzas as they appear on the page in order to combine typographic shape with aural appeal as aids to apprehending poems. The following poem, in which the stanzas are shaped to a form resembling the subject, is an early example of this procedure.

Easter Wings

Lord, Who createdst man in wealth and store,
  Though foolishly he lost the same,
    Decaying more and more,
      Till he became
        Most poore:

        With Thee
       O let me rise,
     As larks, harmoniously,
   And sing this day Thy victories:
Then shall the fall further the flight in me.

My tender age in sorrow did beginne;
  And still with sicknesses and shame
    Thou didst so punish sinne,
      That I became
        Most thinne.

        With Thee
      Let me combine,
    And feel this day Thy victorie;
  For, if I imp[1] my wing on Thine,
Affliction shall advance the flight in me.

—George Herbert (1593–1633)

---

[1] To engraft feathers in a damaged wing to improve the powers of flight.

When there is a direct relationship between a poem's typographic shape and its subject matter, it is called an *emblem poem*. "Skinny Poem" (page 100) is a modern example of this device sometimes employed by Dylan Thomas and e. e. cummings.

The simplest stanza is the *couplet*, which consists of two consecutive lines that are usually rhymed. (The unrhymed couplet is rare in traditional English poetry.) Since Chaucer used the rhyming couplet in *The Canterbury Tales*, it has been popular with poets. In the *closed couplet* there is a pause at the end of the first line and a full stop at the end of the second. Dryden in the seventeenth century and Pope in the eighteenth used this type of couplet skillfully, by fitting syntax and thought neatly into an envelope of meter and rhyme.

> All human things are subject to decay,
> And, when Fate summons, monarchs must obey.
>
> (Dryden's "MacFlecknow")

> Know then thyself, presume not God to scan,
> The proper study of mankind is Man.
>
> (Pope's "Essay on Man")

In the *open couplet* there is no pause at the end of the first line. The thought may flow on for several lines. The romantic poets of the nineteenth century preferred this type.

> A thing of beauty is a joy for ever;
> Its loveliness increases; it will never
> Pass into nothingness; but still will keep
> A bower quiet for us, and a sleep
> Full of sweet dreams, and health, and quiet breathing. . . .
>
> (Keats' "Endymion")

Modern poets have used both effectively: the closed couplet for witty or epigrammatic statements, the open couplet for contemplative and narrative poems.

The most popular form of the couplet metrically has been iambic pentameter, called the *Heroic couplet*, although iambic tetrameter has also been frequently used by English poets. If the two lines of the couplet are different in foot-lengths, they form an *unequal couplet*.

Where the quiet-coloured end of evening smiles,
    Miles and miles
On the solitary pastures where our sheep
    Half-asleep
Tinkle homeward thro' the twilight, stray or stop
    As they crop—
Was the site once of a city great and gay,
    (So they say).

       (Browning's "Love Among the Ruins")

A single couplet or a pair of couplets may form a whole poem, either a witty or paradoxical epigram or an ironic epitaph. The following epigrams are by Donne.

Phryne

Thy flattering picture, Phryne, is like thee,
Only in this, that both painted be.

Hero and Leander

Both robb'd of air, we both lie in one ground;
Both whom one fire had burnt, one water drown'd.

       —John Donne (1573–1631)

These two are by Burns.

On John Bushby of Tinwald Downs

Here lies John Bushby—honest man!
Cheat him, Devil—if you can!

On Wm. Graham of Mossknowe

"Stop thief!" Dame Nature call'd to Death,
As Willie drew his latest breath:
"How shall I make a fool again?
My choicest model thou has taen."

       —Robert Burns (1759–1796)

The last epigram is by Matthew Prior.

Sir, I Admit Your General Rule

Sir, I admit your general rule,
That every poet is a fool:
But you yourself may serve to show it,
That every fool is not a poet.

—Matthew Prior (1664–1721)

Less widely used than the couplet is the *tercet,* a three-line stanza usually containing rhyme. (Unrhymed tercet or a *triplet,* consisting of three consecutive rhyming lines, is very rare in traditional English poetry.) Herrick's "Upon Julia's Clothes" (page 29) is composed of two triplets as is the following poem.

Little Alglae

*To Her Father, on Her Statue Being
Called Like Her*

Father! the little girl we see
Is not, I fancy so like me
You never hold her on your knee.

When she came home, the other day,
You kiss'd her; but I cannot say
She kiss'd you first and ran away.

—Walter Savage Landor (1775–1864)

The most frequently used tercet is the *terza rima* invented by Dante and used as part of his symbolism of the Trinity in *The Divine Comedy.* (His poem consists of three divisions of the other world; three animals terrify him; three holy women intervene for him; three guides lead him, etc.) Terza rima consists of iambic tercets rhyming a b a b c b and so on; the second line is rhymed with the first and third lines of the next stanza. The interlocking rhymes of the stanzas give the poem a continuously forward movement halted at the end of a canto or section by a quatrain or couplet. The following lines from the opening of Browning's "The Statue and the Bust" illustrate his use of terza rima.

There's a palace in Florence, the world knows well,
And a statute watches it from the square,
And this story of both do our townsmen tell,

Ages ago, a lady there,
At the farthest window facing the East
Asked, "Who rides by with the royal air?"

Byron, Shelley, and William Morris in the nineteenth century and W. H. Auden and Archibald MacLeish in the twentieth have made effective use of this stanzaic form.

The favorite English stanza is the *quatrain,* consisting of four lines. The even number of lines permits the poet great flexibility in using rhetorical balance, parallelism, and contrast, and in using little or plentiful rhyme. The quatrain has served as a poem complete in itself, for long narratives, short lyrics, elegies, ballads, hymns, nursery rhymes, and the like.

The simplest and most popular type of quatrain is the *ballad stanza,* which consists of alternating lines of iambic tetrameter and iambic trimeter with the short lines rhyming *a b c b.* An example of a complete poem using this type of quatrain is this famous lyric of the sixteenth century or earlier.

The Lover in Winter Plaineth for the Spring

O Western wind, when wilt thou blow
  That the small rain down can rain?
Christ, that my love were in my arms
  And I in my bed again!

—Anonymous

Another type of quatrain uses alternate rhymes, *a b a b.* Two complete poems of Landor illustrate how this pattern may be appropriate for a concise, epigrammatic statement.

On His Seventy-fifth Birthday

I strove with none; for none was worth my strife,
  Nature I loved, and next to Nature, Art;
I warmed both hands before the fire of life,
  It sinks, and I am ready to depart.

To My Ninth Decade

To my ninth decade I have totter'd on,
  And no soft arm bends now my steps to steady;

> She, who once led me where she would, is gone,
> So when she calls me, Death shall find me ready.
>
> —William Savage Landor (1775–1864)

Another variant of the quatrain is the "In Memoriam" stanza, used by Tennyson in his elegy on the death of Arthur Henry Hallam. This iambic tetrameter stanza rhyming a b b a creates the rhythmic effect of the first and fourth lines enclosing the internal couplet. It is, therefore, sometimes called the "envelope quatrain." Below are four quatrains from "In Memoriam," section LXIII.

> I wage not any feud with Death
>   For changes wrought on form and face;
>   No lower life that earth's embrace
> May breed with him can fright my faith.
>
> Eternal process moving on,
>   From state to state the spirit walks;
>   And these are but the shatter'd stalks,
> Or ruin'd chrysalis of one.
>
> Nor blame I Death, because he bare
>   The use of virtue out of earth;
>   I know transplanted human worth
> Will bloom to profit, otherwhere.
>
> For this alone on Death I wreak
>   The wrath that garners in my heart:
>   He put our lives so far apart
> We cannot hear each other speak.

By varying the length of the line, the kind of feet, and the rhyme pattern, the poet can create many different types of the quatrain stanza adaptable to his particular purpose.

Less common than the quatrain is the five-line stanza, called the *quintain* or *cinquain*. Its most popular use is in the form of humorous limericks (pages 71–72). However, serious poets have occasionally used it, for example, George Herbert (1593–1633) in "The Pulley":

> When God at first made man,
> Having a glass of blessing standing by
>   "Let us," said He, "pour on him all we can:
> Let the world's riches, which dispersèd lie,
>   Contract into a span."

and Edgar Allan Poe in "To Helen":

> Helen, thy beauty is to me
> Like those Nicéan barks of yore
> That gently o'er a perfumed sea
> The weary, way-worn wanderer bore
> To his own native shore.

The *sestet,* a six-line stanza, has been used more frequently than the quintain. William Wordsworth used the sestet in "I Wandered Lonely as a Cloud" (page 4) and Elizabeth Barrett Browning in "Mystery":

> We sow the glebe, we reap the corn,
> We build the house where we may rest,
> And then, at moments, suddenly,
> We look up to the great wide sky,
> Inquiring wherefor we were born . . .
> For earnest, or for jest?

The most famous seven-line stanza or *septet* is *rhyme royal,* which consists of iambic pentameter lines rhyming a b a b b c c. Chaucer used it in his long, psychological narrative poem "Troilus and Criseyde" and in some of *The Canterbury Tales* such as "The Prioresse's Tale" and "The Clerke's Tale." It has been revived by such twentieth-century poets as Robert Graves in his "Rocky Acres" and John Masefield in his narrative of the sea "Dauber." The following stanza is from Shakespeare's early narrative poem "Lucrece."

> Now stole upon the time the dead of night,
> When heavy sleep had closed up mortal eyes:
> No comfortable star did lend his light,
> No noise but owls' and wolves' death-boding cries;
> Now serves the season that they may surprise
> The silly lambs: pure thoughts are dead and still,
> While lust and murder wakes to stain and kill.

The best-known eight-line stanza or *octave* is *ottava rima,* eight iambic pentameter verses rhyming a b a b a b c c. This stanza, developed in Italy, became the favorite of Ariosto, Tasso, and Boccaccio for their epics and romances. Introduced by Wyatt into England, it became popular with English Renaissance poets such as Spenser and Drayton. Shelley used it occasionally, and Byron handled it brilliantly in his satires "Beppo" and "The Vision of Judgment" as well as in his masterpiece, the mock-epic *Don Juan.* Yeats revived it in the twentieth century and wrote three of his best poems in ottava rima: "Sailing to Byzantium" (page 185), "Among School Children," and "The Municipal Gallery Revisited." The following stanza is from the first canto of *Don Juan.*

I

I want a hero: an uncommon want,
   When every year and month sends forth a new one,
Till, after cloying the gazettes with cant,
   The age discovers he is not the true one;
Of such as these I should not care to vaunt,
   I'll therefore take our ancient friend Don Juan—
We all have seen him, in the pantomime,
Sent to the devil somewhat ere his time.

One of the most remarkable innovations in the history of English poetry was the stanza invented by the Elizabethan poet Edmund Spenser. For his long (unfinished) allegory "The Faerie Queene," he used a nine-line stanza, the first eight lines iambic pentameter and the last an iambic hexameter verse (called an alexandrine). The rhyme scheme of the *Spenserian stanza* is a b a b b c b c c. In handling this difficult ingenious stanza, Spenser reveals himself to be as superb a metricist as Milton in his skillful and varied use of blank verse. Particularly suited for descriptive and narrative verse, the Spenserian stanza came into favor with the pre-Romantic poets at the end of the eighteenth century—James Thomson used it in "The Castle of Indolence" and James Beattie in "The Minstrel." Three young romantic poets of the early nineteenth century handled it with varying degrees of skill. Byron used it with moderate success in his poetic travelogue "Childe Harold's Pilgrimage"; Shelley, more effectively in his poignant elegy "Adonais"; and Keats, with remarkable artistry in his "The Eve of St. Agnes."

The One remains, the many change and pass;
Heaven's light forever shines, Earth's shadows fly;
Life, like a dome of many-coloured glass,
Stains the white radiance of Eternity,
Until Death tramples it to fragments.—Die,
If thou wouldst be with that which thou dost seek!
Follow where all is fled!—Rome's azure sky,
Flowers, ruins, statues, music, words, are weak
The glory they transfuse with fitting truth to speak.

(from Shelley's "Adonais")

Although these are the most commonly used stanzaic forms, there is no limit to the number of lines a stanza may have. Many poems written in stanzas of ten, eleven, twelve, and even more lines may be found throughout English poetry.

The most popular poetic form with a fixed number of lines, whether composed as a separate poem or as part of a sequence or cycle, is the *sonnet*—a fourteen-line poem usually in iambic pentameter with a traditional or varied rhyme pattern. Probably Italian in origin during the thirteenth century, it spread rapidly to many European countries and later to the New World. Sir Thomas Wyatt (1503–1542) introduced it into England, and many Elizabethans used it as a lyric or dramatic expression of emotion and thought. In the seventeenth century Donne and Milton made significant contributions to the form. When it fell into disfavor with both critics and poets in the neo-classic eighteenth century, Wordsworth, in a challenging sonnet, defended it.

Scorn Not the Sonnet

Scorn not the Sonnet; Critic, you have frowned,
Mindless of its just honours; with this key
Shakespeare unlocked his heart;[1] the melody
Of this small lute gave ease to Petrarch's wound;[2]
A thousand times this pipe did Tasso[3] sound;
With it Camöens[4] soothed an exile's grief;
The Sonnet[5] glittered a gay myrtle leaf
Amid the cypress with which Dante crowned
His visionary brows: a glow-worm lamp,
It cheered mild Spenser,[6] called from Faeryland
To struggle through dark ways; and when a damp
Fell round the path of Milton, in his hand
The Thing became a trumpet; whence he blew
Soul-animating strains—alas, too few!

—William Wordsworth (1770–1850)

---

[1] Whether Shakespeare's sonnets record profound personal experiences or imaginary ones is still a moot subject.   [2] The grief of Petrarch, a famous Italian poet (1304–1374), at the death of Laura, whose praises he celebrated in his sonnets.   [3] An Italian poet (1554–1595), author of the epic "Jerusalem Delivered," celebrating the First Crusade.   [4] A Portuguese poet (1524–1580).   [5] In addition to *The Divine Comedy* Dante wrote sonnets in his *Vita Nuova* (The New Life) to Beatrice.   [6] Spenser wrote a sonnet cycle called *Amoretti*.

Revived enthusiastically by the Romantic and Victorian poets, the sonnet has since held its ground.

The reason for the sonnet's popularity over the centuries is not difficult to explain. The sonnet is a short poem yet long enough to give the poet room to develop an idea, situation, or emotion in some detail. Within its fourteen lines the poet has considerable freedom in varying his rhyme pattern and utilizing smaller units of couplets and quatrains for the most effective arrangement of his material. He can construct his sonnet as an unbroken unit for a forceful poetic impact. He can use a bipartite pattern: build up tension and then release it; present a problem and suggest its solution; describe a scene or situation and then interpret it. He can contrast two emotions, ideas, or situations by a sudden shift in tone. He can present three related images in three quatrains and then draw a conclusion in a couplet, as in Shakespeare's "Sonnet 73" (page 145). "Within the Sonnet's scanty plot of ground," the poet has, therefore, considerable maneuverability. The sonnet is a perpetual challenge to the skill of a poet. Although countless poets over the centuries have written thousands of sonnets, the number of great or perfect ones that communicate a significant experience is surprisingly small.

Although there are many variant forms of the sonnet, the three most frequently written are the Italian (or Petrarchan), the English (or Shakespearean), and the Miltonic. A sonnet which does not fall into one of these classifications is an irregular sonnet.

An *Italian sonnet* is made up of two parts: the first eight lines form the *octave,* and the last six the *sestet.* Between the two parts there is a definite pause or break indicated by punctuation (period, dash, colon) or a line separation. The octave consists of two interlocking envelope quatrains rhyming *a b b a a b b a.* The rhyme scheme of the sestet varies. This bipartite division is used effectively if the poet presents a problem in the octave and solves it in the sestet, or develops a contrast, or builds up tension and then releases it. Donne's "Holy Sonnet IX," "If Poisonous Minerals" (page 169) is an outstanding example of the effective use of the two-part Petrarchan pattern.

The following sonnet is another example.

The Choice—III

Think thou and act; to-morrow thou shalt die.
   Outstretched in the sun's warmth upon the shore,
   Thou say'st: "Men's measured path is all gone o'er:
Up all his years, steeply, with strain and sigh,
Man clomb until he touched the truth; and I,
   Even I, am he whom it was destined for."

How should this be? Art thou then so much more
Than they who sowed, that thou shouldst reap thereby?
Nay, come up hither. From this wave-washed mound
Unto the furthest flood-brim look with me;
Then reach on with thy thought till it be drown'd.
Miles and miles distant though the grey line be,
And though thy soul sail leagues and leagues beyond,—
Still, leagues beyond those leagues, there is more sea.

—Dante Gabriel Rossetti (1828–1882)

The poem presents in dramatic form a contrast of two attitudes toward life. In the octave the speaker, relaxing "in the sun's warmth upon the shore," justifies his Epicurean philosophy of enjoying the achievements of his predecessors. In the sestet the persona of the poet demolishes this parasitical view of life and by an effective image presents his philosophy of an active life motivated by the endless quest for truth and knowledge.

The *English sonnet* is composed of three separate quatrains of alternating rhyme and a concluding couplet. The rhyme scheme is *a b a b* (first quatrain), *c d c d* (second quatrain), *e f e f* (third quatrain), and *g g* (couplet). Since this sonnet consists of four parts, it permits considerable flexibility in its arrangement. As we have seen, Shakespeare, in his "Sonnet 73," adapts his matter perfectly to its four fold form. One of the delicate problems a poet faces is the handling of the couplet. Standing in the climactic position at the end of the sonnet, it must stress a forceful conclusion or the poem will be weakened.

Let us consider these two sonnets, the first on the nature of love (and friendship) and the second on lust.

Sonnet 116

Let me not to the marriage of true minds
Admit impediments. Love is not love
Which alters when it alteration finds,
Or bends with the remover[1] to remove.[2]
O, no! it is an ever-fixèd mark[3]
That looks on tempests and is never shaken;
It is the star to every wand'ring bark,
Whose worth's[4] unknown, although his height be taken.
Love's not Time's fool, though rosy lips and cheeks
Within his[5] bending sickle's compass come;
Love alters not with his brief hours and weeks,
But bears it out even to the edge of doom.[6]

If this be error, and upon me proved,
I never writ, nor no man ever loved.

—William Shakespeare (1564–1616)

---

[1] Inconstant one.   [2] Depart.   [3] Landmark to guide ships.   [4] Power, influence, value.   [5] Time's.   [6] Judgment day.

Addressed to Shakespeare's young aristocratic friend, this sonnet, in a series of effective images, defines the quality of enduring love and friendship. The theme is developed by alternating negative definition with positive affirmation. In the first quatrain he asserts what true love is *not*: a reaction to a change in one's friend or a separation. These impediments cannot destroy it. In the second quatrain he proclaims the power of love, immeasurable in value, as the guiding light of one's life. In the third quatrain the negative and positive aspects are both present. Love is *not* destroyed by the fading of physical beauty but lasts forever. The concluding couplet, although still preserving the antithetical pattern, adds little to the powerful impact of the preceding lines. It simply confirms the poet's belief.

Sonnet 129

Th' expense[1] of spirit in a waste of shame
Is lust in action: and till action, lust
Is perjur'd, murd'rous, bloody, full of blame,
Savage, extreme,[2] rude, cruel, not to trust:
Enjoy'd no sooner but despised straight;
Past[3] reason hunted, and no sooner had,
Past reason hated, as a swallowed bait
On purpose laid to make the taker mad:
Mad in pursuit and in possession so;
Had, having, and in quest to have, extreme;
A bliss in proof,[4] and prov'd, a very woe;
Before, a joy propos'd,[5] behind, a dream.
    All this the world well knows; yet none knows well
    To shun the heaven that leads men to this hell.

—William Shakespeare (1564–1616)

---

[1] Expenditure, waste.   [2] Violent.   [3] Beyond all.   [4] When experienced.   [5] Anticipated.

The bitter denunciation of lust is an outgrowth of the speaker's involvement with the cruel, faithless "dark lady" of the sonnets. The powerful, hammer-blow adjectives that define lust expose its destruc-

tive effects on man's spirit, and build up to the climax of disillusion-
ment expressed by the ironic antitheses of lines eleven and twelve.
The concluding couplet, however, does more than reaffirm the previous statement. It closes the poem with the disturbing generalization
that man, even with this knowledge, is helpless in the grip of this
powerful passion.

By closing the gap between the octave and the sestet of the
Italian sonnet, Milton introduced an interesting innovation. Thus the
Miltonic sonnet retains the fixed rhyme scheme of the Petrarchan
octave (a b b a a b b a) but by enjambment of the eighth and ninth
lines creates a single, unbroken thought unit. Starting with an effective
verse, the Miltonic sonnet builds up continuous tension and concludes
with a powerful line. A good example is this famous sonnet.

On His Blindness

When I consider how my light is spent,[1]
   Ere half my days, in this dark world and wide
   And that one talent[2] which is death to hide
   Lodged with me useless, though my soul more bent
To serve therewith my Maker, and present
   My true account, lest he returning chide,
   "Doth God exact day-labor, light denied,"
   I fondly[3] ask. But Patience to prevent
That murmur, soon replies, "God doth not need
   Either man's work or his own gifts. Who best
   Bear his mild yoke, they serve him best. His State
Is kingly. Thousands[4] at his bidding speed
   And post o'er land and ocean without rest:
   They also serve who only stand and wait." [5]

           —John Milton (1608–1674)

---

[1] Milton became totally blind at the age of 42.   [2] A unit of money as
well as an ability (see the parable of the talents, Matthew 25:24–30).
[3] Foolishly.   [4] The heavenly angels.   [5] Ready for any heavenly assign-
ment.

A group of sonnets linked by a common theme or related ideas
and sometimes addressed to one person is called a *sonnet sequence.*
Some of the best known English sonnet sequences are Spenser's
Amoretti, Sir Philip Sidney's *Astrophel and Stella,* Shakespeare's *Son-
nets,* Donne's *Holy Sonnets,* Elizabeth Barrett Browning's *Sonnets
from the Portuguese,* Dante Gabriel Rossetti's *The House of Life,*
Robert Bridges' *The Growth of Love,* and Edna St. Vincent Millay's
Fatal Interview.

A poet, of course, is free to construct his own stanza schemes or to write in free verse or units of line measure other than metrical verse. However, there must be some accommodation of sense to shape. Since a poem is a work of art giving us vicarious experiences, it must possess form. If a poet wishes to communicate the chaos and confusion of a world, his poem must not be chaotic and confused. In expressing the boredom of a society, a poet must not bore us.

When certain poetic forms become rigid—because of the precepts of critics or the practice of poets—experimentalists inevitably spring up to challenge the traditionalists. The only constant in the history of English poetry is change. Donne's discordant rhythms and intellectual imagery—"devouring all kinds of experience"—were a revolt against the mellifluous emotionalism of the Elizabethan lyric. In justifying his use of blank verse in *Paradise Lost,* Milton denounced "the troublesome and modern bondage of riming" as "the invention of a barbarous age, to set off wretched matter and lame metre." Wordsworth's Preface to *Lyrical Ballads* was the ringing manifesto of the romantic poets that attacked the subject matter, pattern, and diction of the neo-classic school of criticism and poetry. In America Walt Whitman repudiated the traditional techniques and content of poetry and promulgated new principles of poetic organization. In twentieth-century England Hardy, the later Yeats, T. S. Eliot, and W. H. Auden— attuned to the modern sensibility—reacted against the bucolic conventionalities of the Georgian poets. Again in America Robinson, Masters, and Sandburg destroyed the genteel tradition of polite magazine verse. In our time the "beat" poets and the practitioners of projective, open verse assail the strictly organized poetry of the academic "metaphysicals" and compose their poems in free forms, jazzy or rock rhythms, and a modern American idiom. The poetic pendulum never stops swinging.

For Discussion

Form in literature is an arousing and fulfilment of desires. A work has form insofar as one part of it leads a reader to anticipate another part, to be gratified by the sequence.

—Kenneth Burke

There is a logic of the imagination as well as a logic of concepts. People who do not appreciate poetry always find it difficult to distinguish between order and chaos in the arrangement of images.

—T. S. Eliot

In any poet's poem the shape is half the meaning.

—Louis MacNeice

Form and meaning interactive, become mutually apparent until they are whole.

—Léonie Adams

Form is never more than an extension of content.

—Charles Olson

Poems Related to Chapter 12

The following two irregular sonnets are by contemporary poets.

Am I My Neighbor's Keeper?

The poetry of tragedy is never dead.
If it were not so I would not dream
On principles so deep they have no ending,
Nor on the ambiguity of what things ever seem.

The truth is his and shaped in veils of error,
Rich, unanswerable, the profound caught in plain air.
Centuries after tragedy sought out Socrates
Its inexplicable essence visits us in our lair,

Say here, on a remote New Hampshire farm.
The taciturn farmer disappeared in pre-dawn,
He had beaten his handyman, but no great harm.
Light spoke vengeance and bloodstains on the lawn.
His trussed corpse later under the dam
Gives to this day no answer, says I am.

—Richard Eberhart (1904–   )

1. Discuss the effectiveness of the poet's variation of two famous statements: Keats' "The poetry of earth is never dead" and Cain's "Am I my brother's keeper?"
2. Where is there a shift in tone? How is it achieved? Is it justified?
3. The poem deals with an important question, the responsibility of guilt. Does the poet give a positive answer, or is the question left unresolved in ambiguity? How are the following involved in the tragedy: the handyman, the taciturn farmer, the neighbor or neighbors who murdered him, the poet, the reader?

Sonnet XV

(Sonnets from China)

As evening fell the day's oppression lifted;
Far peaks came into focus; it had rained:
Across wide lawns and cultured flowers drifted
The conversation of the highly trained.

Two gardeners watched them pass and priced their shoes:
A chauffeur waited, reading in the drive,
For them to finish their exchange of views;
It seemed a picture of the private life.

Far off, no matter what good they intended,
The armies waited for a verbal error
With all the instruments for causing pain:

And on the issue of their charm depended
A land laid waste, with all its young men slain,
Its women weeping, and its towns in terror.

—W. H. Auden (1907–   )

1. Why has Eberhart shaped his sonnet into three stanzas and Auden into four?

Cargoes

Quinquireme[1] of Nineveh from distant Ophir,
Rowing home to haven in sunny Palestine,
With a cargo of ivory,
With apes and peacocks,
Sandalwood, cedarwood, and sweet white wine.

Stately Spanish galleon coming from the Isthmus,
Dipping through the Tropics by the palm-green shores,
With a cargo of diamonds,
Emeralds, amethysts,
Topazes, and cinnamon, and gold moidores.[2]

Dirty British coaster with a salt-caked smoke stack
Butting through the Channel in the mad March days,
With a cargo of Tyne coal,
Road-rails, pig-lead,
Firewood, iron-ware, and cheap tin trays.

—John Masefield (1878–1967)

---

[1] A ship with five banks of oars.   [2] Portuguese coins.

1. What is the structural form of the poem: progressive, antithetical, repetitive? Can the tripartite division be justified? Is a fourth stanza necessary? Why or why not?
2. Compare the first two stanzas. Contrast the last one with these. What is the theme of the poem?
3. What parallelism do you find in the poem? Is the stanza appropriate to the content? Is there any rhyme? If so, is it prominent or muffled?

The Cloud

I Bring fresh showers for the thirsting flowers,
    From the seas and the streams;
I bear light shade for the leaves when laid
    In their noonday dreams.
From my wings are shaken the dews that waken
    The sweet buds every one,
When rocked to rest on their mother's breast,
    As she dances about the sun.
I wield the flail of the lashing hail,
    And whiten the green plains under,
And then again I dissolve it in rain,
    And laugh as I pass in thunder.

I sift the snow on the mountains below,
    And their great pines groan aghast;
And all the night 'tis my pillow white,
    While I sleep in the arms of the blast.
Sublime on the towers of my skiey bowers,
    Lightning, my pilot, sits;
In a cavern under is fettered the thunder,
    It struggles and howls at fits;
Over earth and ocean, with gentle motion,
    This pilot is guiding me,
Lured by the love of the genii that move
    In the depths of the purple sea;
Over the rills, and the crags, and the hills,
    Over the lakes and the plains,
Wherever he dream, under mountain or stream,
    The Spirit he loves remains;
And I all the while bask in Heaven's blue smile,
    Whilst he is dissolving in rains.

The sanguine Sunrise, with his meteor eyes,
    And his burning plumes outspread,
Leaps on the back of my sailing rack,
    When the morning star shines dead;
As on the jag of a mountain crag,
    Which an earthquake rocks and swings,

An eagle alit one moment may sit
    In the light of its golden wings.
And when Sunset may breathe, from the lit sea beneath,
    Its ardours of rest and of love,
And the crimson pall of eye may fall
    From the depth of Heaven above,
With wings folded I rest, on mine aëry nest,
    As still as a brooding dove.

That orbèd maiden with white fire laden,
    Whom mortals call the Moon,
Glides glimmering o'er my fleece-like floor,
    By the midnight breezes strewn;
And wherever the beat of her unseen feet,
    Which only the angels hear,
May have broken the woof of my tent's thin roof,
    The stars peep behind her and peer;
And I laugh to see them whirl and flee,
    Like a swarm of golden bees,
When I widen the rent in my wind-built tent,
    Till the calm rivers, lakes, and seas,
Like strips of the sky fallen through me on high,
    Are each paved with the moon and these.

I bind the Sun's throne with a burning zone,
    And the Moon's with a girdle of pearl;
The volcanoes are dim, and the stars reel and swim,
    When the whirlwinds my banner unfurl.
From cape to cape, with a bridge-like shape,
    Over a torrent sea,
Sunbeam-proof, I hang like a roof,—
    The mountains its columns be.
The triumphal arch through which I march
    With hurricane, fire, and snow,
When the Powers of the air are chained to my chair,
    Is the million-coloured bow;
The sphere-fire above its soft colours wove,
    While the moist Earth was laughing below.

I am the daughter of Earth and Water,
    And the nursling of the Sky;
I pass through the pores of the ocean and shores;
    I change, but I cannot die.
For after the rain when with never a stain
    The pavilion of Heaven is bare,
And the winds and sunbeams with their convex gleams
    Build up the blue dome of air,

I silently laugh at my own cenotaph,
   And out of the caverns of rain,
Like a child from the womb, like a ghost from the tomb,
   I arise and unbuild it again.

          —Percy Bysshe Shelley (1792–1822)

1.   What does Shelley gain by using personification throughout the poem? Which line clearly states the theme? What is the poet's attitude toward nature? Death?

2.   What is the form of the poem: progressive, antithetical, repetitive? Are the rhythm, metrical stanza, and rhyme (including internal rhyme) appropriate to the theme? Discuss.

3.   What is the tone of the poem? Is it constant or does it shift? Prove.

The Onset

Always the same, when on a fated night
At last the gathered snow lets down as white
As may be in dark woods, and with a song
It shall not make again all winter long
Of hissing on the yet uncovered ground,
I almost stumble looking up and round,
As one who overtaken by the end
Gives up his errand, and lets death descend
Upon him where he is, with nothing done
To evil, no important triumph won,
More than if life had never been begun.

Yet all the precedent is on my side:
I know that winter death has never tried
The earth but it has failed: the snow may heap
In long storms an undrifted four feet deep
As measured against maple, birch and oak,
It cannot check the peeper's[1] silver croak;
And I shall see the snow all go down hill
In water of a slender April rill
That flashes tail through last year's withered brake
And dead weeds, like a disappearing snake.
Nothing will be left white but here a birch,
And there a clump of houses with a church.

          —Robert Frost (1875–1963)

---

[1] Young frog.

1.   What is the relationship of content to form in this poem? On what basis can the bipartite structure of the poem be justified?

2. What metaphors are common to both parts? What difference is there in the symbol of whiteness in part one and part two? How is this difference related to the theme of the poem?

Get the Gasworks

Get the gasworks into a poem,
and you've got the smoke and smokestacks,
the mottled red and yellow tenements,
and grimy kids who curse with the pungency
of the odor of gas. You've got America, boy.
Sketch in the river and barges,
all dirty and slimy.
How do the seagulls stay so white?
And always cawing like little mad geniuses?
You've got the kind of living
that makes the kind of thinking we do:
gaswork smokestack whistle tooting wisecracks.
They don't come because we like it that way,
but because we find it outside our window each morning,
in soot on the furniture,
and trucks carrying coal for gas,
the kid hot after the ball under the wheel.
He gets it over the belly, all right.
He dies there.

So the kids keep tossing the ball around
after the funeral.
So the cops keep chasing them,
so the mamas keep hollering,
and papa flings his newspaper outward,
in disgust with discipline.

—David Ignatow (1914–   )

1. On what structural principle has this poem been patterned: progression, antithesis, or repetition?

The following poem was inspired by Emerson's reading in Book IV of the *Vishnu Parana,* oldest of the sacred scriptures of the Hindus. Emerson wrote in his Journal for 1845: "These were the verses, Maitreya, which Earth recited and by listening to which ambition fades away like snow before the wind." Vishnu is identified by his worshippers with the supreme deity and regarded as the preserver of the world. *Hamatreya* is a variation of *Maitreya.*

Hamatreya

Bulkeley, Hunt, Willard, Hosmer, Meriam, Flint,
Possessed the land which rendered to their toil
Hay, corn, roots, hemp, flax, apples, wool and wood.
Each of these landlords walked amidst his farm,
Saying, "'Tis mine, my children's and my name's.
How sweet the west wind sounds in my own trees!
How graceful climb those shadows on my hill!
I fancy these pure waters and the flags
Know me, as does my dog: we sympathize;
And, I affirm, my actions smack of the soil."

Where are these men? Asleep beneath their grounds:
And strangers, fond as they, their furrows plough.
Earth laughs in flowers, to see her boastful boys
Earth-proud, proud of the earth which is not theirs;
Who steer the plough, but cannot steer their feet
Clear of the grave.
They added ridge to valley, brook to pond,
And sighed for all that bounded their domain;
"This suits me for a pasture; that's my park;
We must have clay, lime, gravel, granite-ledge,
And misty lowland, where to go for peat.
The land is well,—lies fairly to the south.
'Tis good, when you have crossed the sea and back,
To find the sitfast acres where you left them."
Ah, the hot owner sees not Death, who adds
Him to his land, a lump of mould the more.
Hear what the Earth says:—

Earth-Song

"Mine and yours;
Mine, not yours.
Earth endures;
Stars abide—
Shine down in the old sea;
Old are the shores;
But where are old men?
I who have seen much,
Such have I never seen.

"The lawyer's deed
Ran sure,
In tail,

To them, and to their heirs
Who shall succeed,
Without fail,
Forevermore.

"Here is the land,
Shaggy with wood,
With its old valley,
Mound and flood.
But the heritors?—
Fled like the flood's foam.
The lawyer, and the laws,
And the kingdom,
Clean swept herefrom.

"They called me theirs,
Who so controlled me;
Yet every one
Wished to stay, and is gone,
How am I theirs,
If they cannot hold me,
But I hold them?"

When I heard the Earth-song,
I was no longer brave;
My avarice cooled
Like lust in the chill of the grave.

—Ralph Waldo Emerson (1803–1882)

1. Discuss the form of this poem. On what grounds can the shift in meter be justified?
2. What effect does Emerson create by specifically naming six Concord landowners? What is the theme of the poem?
3. Is the concluding quatrain essential to the poem? Discuss.

The Choice—I

Eat thou and drink; to-morrow thou shalt die.
   Surely the earth, that's wise being very old,
   Needs not our help. Then loose me, love, and hold
Thy sultry hair up from my face; that I
May pour for thee this golden wine, brim-high
   Till round the glass thy fingers glow like gold.
   We'll drown all hours: thy song, while hours are toll'd,
Shall leap, as fountains veil the changing sky.

Now kiss, and think that there are really those,
  My own high-bosomed beauty, who increase
    Vain gold, vain lore, and yet might choose our way!
Through many days they toil; then comes a day
They die not,—never having lived,—but cease;
And round their narrow lips the mould falls close.

—Dante Gabriel Rossetti (1828–1882)

1. Who is speaking in this sonnet? To whom? What is the relationship between the two? What philosophy of life is the speaker defending? What two opposing views is he attacking?
2. What kind of a sonnet is it? Is the form appropriate to the content? Prove. How does the poet's use of *golden* and *gold* in the octave differ from his use of *gold* in the sestet? Is there a shift in tone in the poem? Discuss.

Bright Star, Would I Were Stedfast as Thou Art

Written on a blank page in Shakespeare's Poems,
facing "A Lover's Complaint"

Bright star, would I were stedfast as thou art—
  Not in lone splendour hung aloft the night
And watching, with eternal lids apart,
  Like nature's patient, sleepless Eremite,[1]
The moving waters at their priestlike task
  Of pure ablution round earth's human shores,
Or gazing on the new soft-fallen mask
  Of snow upon the mountains and the moors—
No—yet still stedfast, still unchangeable,
  Pillow'd upon my fair love's ripening breast,
To feel for ever its soft fall and swell,
  Awake for ever in a sweet unrest,
Still, still, to hear her tender-taken breath,
And so live ever—or else swoon to death.

—John Keats (1795–1821)

---

[1] Hermit.

1. What kind of a sonnet is this? Is the tone constant or does it change? Discuss.
2. Evaluate carefully Keats' use of figurative language in the poem. Is there a clash between the religious and sexual imagery, or are they related? Discuss. Is this poem a poignant realistic depiction of humanistic desire or an expression of romantic agony? In what way is the sonnet related to "Ode on a Grecian Urn" (page 204) and "Ode to a Nightingale" (page 133)?

On His Deceased Wife

Methought I saw my late espoused saint[1]
    Brought to me like Alcestis[2] from the grave,
    Whom Jove's great son[3] to her glad husband gave,
    Rescued from death by force, though pale and faint.
Mine, as whom washed from spot of child-bed taint,
    Purification in the Old Law[4] did save,
    And such as yet once more I trust to have
    Full sight of her in Heaven without restraint,
Came vested all in white, pure as her mind.
    Her face was veiled, yet to my fancied sight.
    Love, sweetness, goodness, in her person shined
So clear as in no face with more delight.
    But oh as to embrace me she inclined,
    I waked, she fled, and day brought back my night.[5]

—John Milton (1608–1674)

---

[1] Milton's second wife, Katherine Woodcock, died in 1658, three months after childbirth. The son survived her but a few weeks. [2] Wife of Admetus whose life she preserved by dying in his stead. Hercules brought her back alive from the underworld (Hades). [3] Hercules. [4] In Leviticus, the Mosaic law prescribes the ritual of cleansing women after childbirth. [5] Milton became totally blind in 1652, six years before he wrote this sonnet.

1. In this sonnet is there a shift in tone or is it sustained throughout? Prove. What do the classical and biblical allusions contribute to the poem?

2. Milton was unhappy in his first marriage with Mary Powell. What does this sonnet suggest about his second marriage (which lasted only two years)?

3. What two emotions are expressed in the poem? What poetic effect does Milton create in the last line by using the rhetorical construction of three short independent clauses? What other effective device does he use to bring the sonnet to a powerful conclusion?

Wordsworth and his sister Dorothy spent the month of August 1802 in Calais, France. Here he agreed to meet Annette Vallon, whom he had not seen in ten years. The following sonnet describes a walk the poet took with his daughter, Caroline, along the beach at Calais.

It Is a Beauteous Evening

It is a beauteous evening, calm and free,
The holy time is quiet as a Nun
Breathless with adoration; the broad sun

Is sinking down in its tranquility;
The gentleness of heaven broods o'er the Sea:
Listen! the mighty Being is awake,
And doth with his eternal motion make
A sound like thunder—everlastingly.
Dear Child! dear Girl![1] that walkest with me here,
If thou appear untouched by solemn thought,
Thy nature is not therefore less divine:
Thou liest in Abraham's bosom[2] all the year;
And worshipp'st at the Temple's inner shrine,
God being with thee when we know it not.

—William Wordsworth (1770–1850)

---

[1] Caroline (age ten), daughter of Wordsworth and Annette Vallon.   [2] In God's care (see Luke 16:23).

1. What type of sonnet is this? What is the tone of the octave? The sestet?
2. What is the theme of the poem? Does the child's reaction to the scene differ from the poet's? Discuss. (The relationship of the child and the adult to nature is developed more elaborately in two other famous poems of Wordsworth: "Lines Composed a Few Miles Above Tintern Abbey" and "Ode: Intimations of Immortality from Recollections of Early Childhood.")
3. Are the images and the rhythm appropriate to the mood? Discuss.
4. Compare Wordsworth's attitude toward the sea in this poem and his "Elegiac Stanzas" (page 229).

There Was a Child Went Forth

There was a child went forth every day,
And the first object he look'd upon, that object he became,
And that object became part of him for the day or a
        certain part of the day,
Or for many years or stretching cycles of years.

The early lilacs became part of this child,
And grass and white and red morning-glories, and white and
        red clover, and the song of the phoebe-bird,
And the Third-month lambs and the sow's pink-faint litter,
        and the mare's foal and cow's calf,
And the noisy brood of the barnyard or by the mire of the
        pond-side,
And the fish suspending themselves so curiously below
        there, and the beautiful curious liquid,
And the water-plants with their graceful flat heads, also
        became part of him.

The field-sprouts of Fourth-month and Fifth-month became
    part of him,
Winter-grain sprouts and those of the light-yellow corn, and
    the esculent roots of the garden,
And the apple-trees cover'd with blossoms and the fruit
    afterward, and wood-berries, and the commonest
    weeds by the road,
And the old drunkard staggering home from the outhouse of
    the tavern whence he had lately risen,
And the schoolmistress that pass'd on her way to school,
And the friendly boys that pass'd, and the quarrelsome
    boys,
And the tidy and fresh-cheek'd girls, and the barefoot
    negro boy and girl,
And all the changes of city and country wherever he went.

His own parents, he that had father'd him and she
    that had conceiv'd him in her womb and birth'd him,
They gave this child more of themselves than that,
They gave him afterward everyday, they became part of him.

The mother at home quietly placing the dishes on the
    supper-table,
The mother with mild words, clean her cap and gown, a
    wholesome odor falling off her person and clothes
    as she walks by,
The father, strong, self-sufficient, manly, mean, anger'd,
    unjust,
The blow, the quick loud word, the tight bargain, the
    crafty lure,
The family usages, the language, the company, the furniture,
    the yearning and swelling heart,
Affection that will not be gainsay'd, the sense of what is
    real, the thought if after all it should prove unreal,
The doubts of day-time and the doubts of night-time, the
    curious whether and how,
Whether that which appears so is so, or is it all flashes
    and specks?
Men and women crowding fast in the streets, if they are
    not flashes and specks what are they?
The streets themselves and the facades of houses, and goods
    in the windows,
Vehicles, teams, the heavy-plank'd wharves, the huge crossing
    at the ferries,
The village on the highland seen from afar at sunset, the
    river between,
Shadows, aureola and mist, the light falling on roofs and
    gables of white or brown two miles off,

The schooner nearby sleepily dropping down the tide, the
    little boat slack-tow'd astern,
The hurrying tumbling waves, quick-broken crests, slapping,
The strata of color'd clouds, the long bar of maroon-
    tint away solitary by itself, the spread of purity
    it lies motionless in,
The horizon's edge, the flying sea-crow, the fragrance of
    salt marsh and shore mud,
These became part of that child who went forth every day,
    and who goes, and will always go forth every day.

                —Walt Whitman (1819–1892)

Although this poem lacks a regular stanzaic pattern, meter, and rhyme, it achieves a significant form that encompasses its material.

1. How are the five stanzas—varying in length—alike in their sentence structure? What verb is repeated in each of the stanzas?
2. What is the significance of the word *stretching* in line four? Does it apply to the child? the poem? both?
3. Is the poem built on the pattern of continual expansion or on expansion and contraction? Or on alternation with growth dominant? Prove.
4. What do all the nature images in stanza two have in common? What is their relationship to the child?
5. What new influences are introduced in stanza three? four? five? Does the child simply observe the nature and human elements of his environment, or does he absorb and identify himself with them? Prove. How do you interpret the last line?

Satanic Form

Numerals forkmarks of Satan
Triangles circles squares
hieroglyphs of death
Things invented
abortions smelling of the forge
licked to gruesome smoothness by the lathe
Things metallic or glass
frozen twisted flattened
stretched to agonized bubbles
Bricks beams receptacles vehicles
forced through fire hatched to unwilling form
O blasphemies
Time caught in a metal box
Incongruous the rigid clucking tongue
the needled hands the 12-eyed face
against the open window past which drops the night
like a dark lake on end or flowing hair

Night unanimous over all the city
  The knuckled fist of the heart opening and closing
    Flower and song not cursed with symmetry
      Cloud and shadow not doomed to shape and fixity
        The intricate body of man without rivet or nail
          or the terrible skirl of the screw
            O these are blessed
              Satanic form geometry of death
                The lariat around the neck of space
                The particles of chaos in the clock
                The bottle of the yellow liquor light
                  that circumvents the sifting down of night
                  O love the juice in the green stem growing
                  we cannot synthesize
                    It corrodes in phials and beakers
                      evaporates in the hot breath of industry
                      escapes to the air and the dew
                        returns to the root of the unborn flower
                        O Satan cheated of your power

                                    —May Swenson (1919–   )

Innocence

for Tony White

He ran the course and as he ran he grew,
And smelt his fragrance in the field. Already,
Running he knew the most he ever knew,
The egotism of a healthy body.

Ran into manhood, ignorant of the past:
Culture of guilt and guilt's vague heritage,
Self-pity and the soul; what he possessed
Was rich, potential, like the bud's tipped rage.

The Corps developed, it was plain to see,
Courage, endurance, loyalty and skill
To a morale firm as morality,
Hardening him to an instrument, until

The finitude of virtues that were there
Bodied within the swarthy uniform
A compact innocence, child-like and clear,
No doubt could penetrate, no act could harm.

When he stood near the Russian partisan
Being burned alive, he therefore could behold

The ribs wear gently through the darkening skin
And sicken only at the Northern cold,

Could watch the fat burn with a violet flame
And feel disgusted only at the smell,
And judge that all pain finishes the same
As melting quietly by his boots it fell.

—Thom Gunn (1929–   )

1. What sort of training did the Nazi soldier receive in his Corps? Did it in any way differ from that of a French soldier in Algeria or an American Green Beret in Vietnam? Explain the phrase "the egotism of a healthy body." If the Nazi soldier's training inculcated in him the virtues of "courage, endurance, loyalty, and skill," what was lacking in his military education? Explain the irony in "a morale firm as morality."

2 Since the soldier was a guilty participant in an atrocity against the Russian partisan, why is the poem entitled "Innocence"? Is this an example of irony or a paradoxical truth?

3. Discuss the effectiveness of the poet's imagery in "He ran the course," "the bud's tipped rage," "Hardening him to an instrument."

4. Discuss the appropriateness of the poem's metrical pattern, stanzaic form, and rhyme scheme to its theme.

5. Is the author's purpose to produce an anti-Nazi propaganda poem or to present a comment on the inevitable nature of war?

6. If you were on a jury trying this soldier for a war crime, would you place the blame on him, his officers, the training system, or his government? Justify your answer.

The Meadow Mouse

1

In a shoe box stuffed in an old nylon stocking
Sleeps the baby mouse I found in the meadow,
Where he trembled and shook beneath a stick
Till I caught him up by the tail and brought him in,
Cradled in my hand,
A little quaker, the whole body of him trembling,
His absurd whiskers sticking out like a cartoon-mouse,
His feet like small leaves,
Little lizard-feet,
Whitish and spread wide when he tried to struggle away,
Wriggling like a miniscule puppy.

Now he's eaten his three kinds of cheese and drunk from his
        bottle-cap watering-trough—
So much he just lies in one corner,

His tail curled under him, his belly big
As his head; his bat-like ears
Twitching, tilting toward the least sound.

Do I imagine he no longer trembles
When I come close to him?
He seems no longer to tremble.

2

But this morning the shoe-box house on the back porch is empty.
Where has he gone, my meadow mouse,
My thumb of a child that nuzzled in my palm?—
To run under the hawk's wing,
Under the eye of the great owl watching from the elm-tree,
To live by courtesy of the shrike, the snake, the tom-cat.

I think of the nestling fallen into the deep grass,
The turtle gasping in the dusty rubble of the highway,
The paralytic stunned in the tub, and the water rising,—
All things innocent, hapless, forsaken.

—Theodore Roethke (1908–1963)

A Bat in the Monastery

We killed a bat last night
in our recreation room. Five priests
dropped their masks and newspapers, grasped
each a weapon—broom barrel magazine whatever—
and lunged and flailed the black intruder.
(Poor Luther, I thought) He soared, swooped,
swept the room with vine wings, fluttering
a hum of terror while priests laughed and ducked
and tried to capture him. He settled
finally from exhaustion and despair,
waited on the wall behind the heavy drape.

Big Ned killed him.
With a broom he whaled the hell out of that bat
that never hurt a soul. Cheers like canticles.
A tiny thing, a dirty mouse with wings
crumpled now and scudded to the gutter
like an autumn leaf. Farewell, bat.

The party ended. We picked our way
back to our cells, isolate again, estranged.

Well, anyhow, we got that intruder.

—John L'Heureux (1934–   )

Art necessarily divides itself into three forms progressing from one to the next. These forms are: the lyrical form wherein the artist presents his image in immediate relation to himself; the epical form, the form wherein he presents his image in mediate relation to himself and to others; the dramatic form, the form wherein he presents his image in immediate relation to others.

—*James Joyce*

13

Poetic Genres: Lyric and Epic Poetry

Poetry, as we have seen, is the oldest and most universal of the literary arts. Throughout the centuries and in all lands countless poems in different forms have been written, read, chanted, and sung. Is it possible to group or classify this vast body of poetry into a few traditional types or genres? Or is each poem a unique artistic creation unrelated to previous productions? If over the centuries definite types have developed, what is their relationship to form and what should be the attitude of the poet toward the traditional genres? Should he accept them? Reject them? Modify them? These are some of the questions to be considered in this chapter.

Pioneers in aesthetics, the Greek philosophers Plato and Aristotle suggested the theory of genres which later commentators developed into a three-fold classification of poetry as lyric, epic, and dramatic. In the first century B.C. the Roman satirical poet Horace became the critical arbiter of the Augustan age with the publication of his "Ars Poetica." With the closing of the theaters during the Middle Ages, Greek and Roman dramas were forgotten and generic terms fell into disuse. With the rediscovery of Aristotle's *Poetics* during the Renaissance, commentators elaborated a rigid set of critical rules supposedly derived from Aristotle and grouped and evaluated poems (and drama) by these "classical" standards. Although some critics denounced this genre system, it still prevailed in the seventeenth and eighteenth centuries. The romantics of the nineteenth century rejected what they considered the artificial and restricting categories of the neo-classicists. In the following verses Wordsworth satirizes the timid poet who writes according to the formalized rules of the critic.

A Poet!—He Hath Put His Heart to School

A poet!—He hath put his heart to school,
Nor dares to move unpropped upon the staff
Which Art hath lodged within his hand—must laugh
By precept only, and shed tears by rule.
Thy Art be Nature; the live current quaff,
And let the groveller sip his stagnant pool,
In fear that else, when Critics grave and cool
Have killed him, Scorn should write his epitaph. . . .

In the nineteenth century the German critic Friedrich Schlegel suggested that all genre classifications be abolished, and in the twentieth the Italian critic Benedetto Croce insisted that genres were of no value as aesthetic categories. In this century T. S. Eliot, reverting to the classical theory of representation, subsumed all poetry as the expression of three voices:

> The first is the voice of the poet talking to himself—or to nobody. The second is the voice of the poet addressing an audience, whether large or small. The third is the voice of the poet when he attempts to create a dramatic character speaking in verse; . . .

Under this "imitation" rubric he would classify all poems as (1) lyric, (2) epic or narrative, or (3) dramatic. This classification closely parallels James Joyce's aesthetic as expressed by Stephen Dedalus in *A Portrait of the Artist as a Young Man* (see epigraph to this chapter).

The modern reader of poetry need not become too involved in this battle of the genres. All the great poets, with few exceptions, have avoided the extremes of the slavish imitation of fixed types and the complete rejection of genres. If a poet finds that a traditional poetic form is suitable for his purpose, he will utilize it and not feel any loss of his individuality in the expression of personal emotion and thought. Milton modified every classical genre he used to express his vision of life. In "Lycidas" he followed some of the conventions of the pastoral elegy of Theocritus, Bion, and Moschus (the lament of nature, the procession of mourners, the pastoral consolation); but the Puritan poet introduced new personal elements into this famous poem, such as his discourse on fame and his denunciation of the corrupt clergy. In *Paradise Lost* he Christianized the classical epic and in *Samson Agonistes* Miltonized Greek tragedy. Contemporary poets have altered and adapted the traditional forms of tragedy, the ode, and the elegy without loss of originality, personality, or modernity. In fact, a poet, by associating himself with a literary tradition, gives his work an added dimension and compels us to make a comparative evaluation to see how effective his adoption or modification of a convention has been.

Modern poetry is a combination of tradition and innovation. In reading it we enjoy both the sense of recognition and the sense of novelty. Today there are no literary dictators or critics who prescribe rules that poets must follow. The poet is free to choose any traditional type, combine several genres, modify them to suit his artistic purpose, or reject them all. Today we recognize the uniqueness and originality of every great poem—traditional or unconventional—as long as it expresses the individuality of the poet. Neither the rigid adherence to a familiar genre nor the rejection of it determines the value of a poem.

Since a poet's choice or modification of a genre naturally influences the structure of a poem, the reader will find it helpful to familiarize himself with the chief types of poetry as they have developed over the centuries. It is, of course, impossible to give exact definitions of each type, for often the genres overlap. The world of poetry is so vast and varied that it would be the height of folly to divide it into neat, separate counties. We cannot compartmentalize poetry nor pigeonhole poets.

For the purpose of convenient discussion we can classify poetry into four main types: (1) lyric, (2) epic, (3) narrative, (4) dramatic.

Because of the great diversity of poems included under the rubric *lyric* and because in its long history the term has changed its meaning, it is difficult to give an exact limiting definition.

The lyric includes such disparate poems as epigrams, psalms, sonnets, odes, elegies, and songs. Its content may range from brief imagistic impressions to impassioned emotional effusions, from light-hearted frivolity to metaphysical speculation. The lyric is probably the oldest form of poetry, for in early Egyptian literature (1600 B.C.) we find examples of funeral song, praise to the king, and invocation to gods. Probably the earliest portion of the Bible (1000 B.C.) is the "Song of Deborah" and other Hebrew lyrics. The same holds true for the early literature of India, China, and Japan. In ancient Greece lyrics were composed before *The Iliad* and *The Odyssey*. Before *Beowulf* was written, Old English lyrics such as "The Wanderer" and "The Seafarer" existed. The one characteristic these lyrics all possess is a strong musical quality. They were sung or chanted, with or without instrumental accompaniment. However, after the Renaissance, when printing was developed, the lyric was transformed from a "word-song" composed to be performed by a priest, bard, or troubadour to a written poem to be enjoyed by readers.

Although complete impersonality is impossible in literature, objectivity—to a greater or lesser extent—is possible in epic and narrative poetry. The lyric, on the other hand, is a personal expression of emotion, thought, or vision in a structural pattern of melodious verse. Usually a lyric is a short poem, certainly shorter than an epic and most narratives. In spite of Poe's dictum that a long poem does not exist because it cannot sustain the excitement of "elevating the soul," long lyrics such as Tennyson's elegy "In Memoriam" have been written and have the power to stir readers. Today we associate lyric poetry with a spontaneous, subjective, emotional, and/or intellectual expression of the poet's sensibility in a musical verbal pattern. Lyric poetry, having the widest range of subjects and the greatest flexibility of technique from traditional stanzas and meters to modern free verse, makes up the bulk of English poetry. To categorize, either by content or form, the countless variations of this oldest type of recorded poetry is a futile task. Only the three most common types will be mentioned: the ode, the elegy, and the song.

The *ode* is a lyric usually of considerable length dealing with a serious subject in a complex formal pattern and expressed in an exalted style. The tone of an ode is emotionally intense and reflective in character. Such a lyric is frequently used as a poetic ceremonial utterance on a particular occasion, such as the accession of a ruler or the funeral of a public figure. When used for such a commemorative purpose, it is usually organized on the classic complex pattern of a Pindaric, Horation, or Anacreontic ode. When inspired by the death of an actual person, it is combined with the elegy. Outstanding examples of the elegiac ode are Tennyson's "Ode on the Death of the Duke of Wellington," Whitman's "When Lilacs Last in the Dooryard Bloom'd," Swinburne's "In Memory of Walter Savage Landor," Yeats' "In Memory of Major Robert Gregory," and W. H. Auden's "In Memory of W. B. Yeats." Three famous elegiac odes honoring the dead in our Civil War are James Russell Lowell's "Ode Recited at the Harvard Commemoration" (July 21, 1865), Allen Tate's "Ode to the Confederate Dead," and Robert Lowell's "For the Union Dead," which follows.

For the Union Dead

"Relinquunt omnia servare rem publicam"[1]

The old South Boston Aquarium stands
in a Sahara of snow now. Its broken windows are boarded.
The bronze weathervane cod has lost half its scales.
The airy tanks are dry.

Once my nose crawled like a snail on the glass;
my hand tingled
to burst the bubbles
drifting from the noses of the cowed, compliant fish.

My hand draws back. I often sigh still
for the dark downward and vegetating kingdom
of the fish and reptile. One morning last March,
I pressed against the new barbed and galvanized

fence on the Boston Common. Behind their cage,
yellow dinosaur steam shovels were grunting
as they cropped up tons of mush and grass
to gouge their underworld garage.

Parking lots luxuriate like civic
sand piles in the heart of Boston.
A girdle of orange, Puritan-pumpkin colored girders
braces the tingling Statehouse,

shaking over the excavations, as it faces Colonel Shaw[2]
and his bell-cheeked Negro infantry
on St. Gaudens'[3] shaking Civil War relief,
propped by a plank splint against the garage's earthquake.

Two months after marching through Boston,
half the regiment was dead;
at the dedication,
William James[4] could almost hear the bronze Negroes breathe.

The monument sticks like a fishbone
in the city's throat.
Its Colonel is as lean
as a compass-needle.

He has an angry wrenlike vigilance,
a greyhound's gentle tautness;
he seems to wince at pleasure,
and suffocate for privacy.

He is out of bounds now. He rejoices in man's lovely,
peculiar power to choose life and die—
when he leads his black soldiers to death,
he cannot bend his back.

On a thousand small town New England greens,
the old white churches hold their air
of sparse, sincere rebellion; frayed flags
quilt the graveyards of the Grand Army of the Republic.

The stone statues of the abstract Union Soldier
grow slimmer and younger each year—
wasp-waisted, they doze over muskets
and muse through their sideburns . . .

Shaw's father wanted no monument
except the ditch,
where his son's body was thrown
and lost with his "niggers."

The ditch is nearer.
There are no statues for the last war here;
on Boylston Street, a commercial photograph
shows Hiroshima boiling

over a Mosler Safe, "the Rock of Ages,"
that survived the blast. Space is nearer.
When I crouch to my television set,
the drained faces of Negro school-children rise like balloons.

Colonel Shaw
is riding on his bubble,
he waits
for the blessèd break.

The Aquarium is gone. Everywhere,
giant finned cars move forward like fish;
a savage servility
slides by on grease.

—Robert Lowell (1917–   )

---

[1] They sacrificed all to preserve the Republic.   [2] Robert Gould Shaw
(1837–1863), educated at Harvard. He led the first body of Negro
troops from a free state, 54th Mass. Regt., was killed leading it in the
attack on Ft. Wagner, Charleston, S.C.   [3] Augustus Saint-Gaudens
(1848–1907), one of America's foremost sculptors. His bronze bas-
relief of Colonel Shaw and his regiment stands on Boston Common.
[4] William James (1842–1910), noted American philosopher, brother of
novelist Henry James.

Robert Lowell's elegiac ode, written in seventeen unrhymed, free-verse quatrains, commemorates the civic courage of Colonel Shaw and the sacrificial heroism of his black regiment in the Civil War. The poet contrasts a nineteenth-century individualistic, idealistic America with the "savage servility" of today's mechanized world bent on destroying its historical heritage. It is a somber poem filled with bitter irony in which the poet laments not only the loss of his innocent childhood and the helplessness of contemporary man crouched before his television set but the decline of spiritual values in a commercialistic world dominated by bulldozers, "giant finned cars," and the devastation of atom bombs.

Framed by the image of the ruined Boston Aquarium in the first and last stanza, the poem develops its grim contrast of a decent past with a destructive present by a consistent use of fish imagery. "The bronze weathervane cod has lost half its scales." The "cowed, compliant" bubbling fish of the poet's early memories have escaped from their glass tanks and have become transformed into monstrous, devouring creatures of a dehumanized world. The monument to Colonel Shaw and his regiment "sticks like a fishbone in the city's throat."

The angry, vigilant Robert Shaw—who left his Harvard friends and classmates to lead the black regiment not (in Shakespeare's phrase) to seek the bubble reputation even into the cannon's mouth but to end the curse of slavery in America—is "out of bounds now." Modern materialistic America scorns the ideals of a youth who loves life but chooses death for a noble cause. The insulting remark of a Confederate officer—who, when questioned about the location of Shaw's grave, replied, "We have buried him with his niggers"— became a Union rallying cry.* A century later the poet bitterly muses over our failure to solve the racial problem. On his television set, he sees "the drained faces of Negro school-children rise like balloons." In our violent, technological age the heroic past recedes from us: ". . . frayed flags/quilt the graveyards of the Grand Army of the Republic" and "The stone statues of the abstract Union Soldier/grow slimmer and younger each year—." Our world has shrunk. "Space is nearer" but the ditch of death is closer, and "Hiroshima boiling" foreshadows total annihilation.

Besides death, other serious subjects that odes deal with are music (Dryden's "Alexander's Feast"), poetry (Gray's "The Bard"), art (Keat's "Ode on a Grecian Urn"), immortality (Wordsworth's "Ode: Intimations of Immortality from Recollections of Early Childhood"),

---

* I am indebted to Paul C. Doherty for this information.

and nature (Shelley's "Ode to the West Wind" and Keats' "To Autumn").

An *elegy* is a lyrical poem formal in tone and diction lamenting a person's death or reflecting the views of the poet on the tragic aspects of life. The poet's personal grief is usually tempered by expressions of praise or consolation in some form of immortality. Some of the great elegies in English literature are Shelley's "Adonais," lamenting and glorifying Keats; Tennyson's "In Memoriam," honoring his closest college friend, Arthur Henry Hallam; and Arnold's "Rugby Chapel," commemorating the character and achievements of his father. Gray's famous "Elegy" is not a lament for a particular person but a sorrowful meditation on the poor unknown dead in a country churchyard, who, hampered by poverty and obscurity, were denied the opportunities to develop their latent powers and to win fame in the world.

A poignant modern example of the personal elegy or monody is this poem by Roethke.

Elegy for Jane

My Student, Thrown by a Horse

I remember the neckcurls, limp and damp as tendrils;
And her quick look, a sidelong pickerel smile;
And how, once startled into talk, the light syllables
    leaped for her,
And she balanced in the delight of her thought,
A wren, happy, tail into the wind,
Her song trembling the twigs and small branches.
The shade sang with her;
The leaves, their whispers turned to kissing,
And the mould sang in the bleached valleys under the rose.

Oh, when she was sad, she cast herself down into such a
    pure depth,
Even a father could not find her:
Scraping her cheek against straw;
Stirring the clearest water.

My sparrow, you are not here,
Waiting like a fern, making a spiney shadow.
The sides of wet stones cannot console me,
Nor the moss, wound with the last light.

If only I could nudge you from this sleep,
My maimed darling, my skittery pigeon.

Over this damp grave I speak the words of my love:
I, with no rights in this matter,
Neither father nor lover.

— Theodore Roethke (1908–1963)

In a *pastoral elegy* the poet represents himself and his dead friend as shepherds and pictures nature herself as mourning her loss. During the Renaissance the classical conventions of this type of poetry established by the Greek poets of Sicily—Theocritus, Bion, and Moschus—were revived. The traditional components of the pastoral elegy consisted of an invocation, a lament, an inquiry into the causes of death, the sympathy and weeping of nature, a procession of mourners, and consolation. With slight variations Spenser followed this pattern in his "Astrophel," commemorating the death of Sir Philip Sidney; Milton, in his "Lycidas," honoring Edward King; and Shelley, in "Adonais," grieving for Keats.

A *song* is a short lyric usually expressing a unified strong emotion in melodic verse. The distinguishing features of a good song—amorous, convivial, devotional, or martial—are an emphatic, fluid rhythm; simplicity of language; an elemental, universal emotion; and brevity. Shakespeare, Herrick, Burns, and Blake have written some of our best poetic songs.

Even though a lyric is a subjective expression of a poet's emotions and thoughts, the reader is not justified in evaluating the poem on the basis of its biographical truth or the writer's "sincerity." The situation the poet responds to may be real or imaginary. The reader must experience the poem as an artistic creation in which all the interrelated elements function harmoniously. Furthermore, a poet is not to be denigrated as contradictory if his lyrics express different feelings or ideas on the same subject. A poet's work, expressing many moods and attitudes, encompasses a wide range of human experiences. Donne's love lyrics, for instance, evoke an amazing variety of responses from the simple to the complex, from the cynical to the passionately serious, from the sensual to the spiritual. Hardy insisted that his lyrics were simply "questionings in the exploration of reality . . . a series of fugitive impressions." The speaker in a lyric may be a *persona,* a voice substituting for but not identifiable as the poet. Poets are not only myth makers but protean characters who, like Shakespeare and Yeats, don many masks and speak with different tongues. The "I" in Whitman's poems is not always the poet but often the voice of various inarticulate Americans. He becomes their spokesman. Whitman's blunt assertion applies to all lyric poets.

> Do I contradict myself?
> Very well then I contradict myself.
> (I am large, I contain multitudes.)

Almost as old as the lyric is the *epic,* a long narrative poem presenting the adventures of a hero in a dignified style. Early lyrics were sung but ancient epics were chanted by legendary bards. Epic poetry, serious in tone, deals with man's relationship to higher supernatural beings and reveals the whole truth of a culture as the poet sees it.

There are two types of epics, the folk epic and the literary epic, and both have become almost extinct in modern literature. The *folk epic,* sometimes the work of one man of genius, is a poem expressing the mores and philosophy of a nation in a particular age. It is based on folk material that has existed for many generations—history, legends, myths of heroes and demigods who achieved great victories over tribal enemies, monsters, or natural forces. The marvelous deeds of a hero, first glorified by separate poems, are gradually magnified by tradition so that, when the great epic poet appears, his task is to unify this material, shape it into a connected story, and present it in an elevated style suitable to the heroic proportions of his theme. These early poetic narratives dealing with violent action and strong emotions have great rhythmic power, for they were designed to be recited by bards. The folk epics, furthermore, have a grandeur and dignity which delighted listeners impressed by the noble deeds of their traditional heroes immortalized in expressive verse, heroes that become archetypes of a people.

Based on legend and myth as well as history, the folk epic includes the intervention of gods and goddesses in human affairs and other supernatural elements, such as conflicts with demons and strange monsters and adventures in the afterlife. The passions celebrated are strong, primitive, and elemental rather than subtle or sophisticated, with reverence and fear of the gods and the forces of nature. The virtues that are glorified are physical courage, prowess in battle, patriotism, loyalty, cunning, and strength. Showing respect for the customs and traditions of a particular people, an epic poet, the voice of a community, stirs us not only by an exciting story of marvelous feats of valor and a strong emotional appeal, but also by his power to reanimate the past, to depict a culture and a civilization that has vanished.

Some of the outstanding examples of the national folk epic are the following: *Gilgamesh* (the Babylonian epic written about 2000 B.C. by an unknown author); *Kalevala* (Finnish epic; old folklore compiled in nineteenth century); *Beowulf* (Old English epic about 700

A.D.); *Song of Roland* (French, about 1080 A.D.); *The Cid* (Spanish, of 1150 A.D.); and *Nibelungenlied* (German, about 1200 A.D.).

The *Iliad* and *The Odyssey* are almost universally considered to be the greatest examples of the folk epic. These Homeric poems have exerted the profoundest influence upon succeeding poets, who, like Virgil and Milton, have creatively imitated and modified the epic genre. As a result of this Homeric influence, certain subsidiary characteristics have become associated with the epic tradition and later poets have incorporated them into their works. Some of these are an invocation to the muse; the epic question; the statement of the theme; opening the narrative in the middle of the action (in *medias res*); episodes which explain the antecedent action (similar to flashbacks in the novel); digressions for variety of mood; ill-omens, dreams, or prophecies to prepare the reader for future events; a long enumeration of warriors, ships, supernatural beings (the epic catalog); battle scenes; and a feast. To add dignity to the style, the epic poet employs extended comparisons (the epic or Homeric simile) and proper names for their romantic and historical associations.

The *literary epic,* a stately narrative about important historical or legendary events, is written by a more artful and sophisticated poet whose work is designed to be read, not recited. Employing the epic genre, such a poet produces a work that is more subtle and intellectual, rather than primitive and direct. Since the personality of the poet is more dominant in the literary epic, his poem is more the expression of an individual than the impersonal representation of the spirit of a people. Some of the important literary epics are Virgil's *Aeneid* (written in Latin 19 B.C.); Firdusi's *Shah Namah* (Persian, about 1000 A.D.), one episode of which Arnold used for his epic fragment *Sohrab and Rustum;* Tasso's *Jerusalem Delivered* (Italian, 1575); and Milton's *Paradise Lost* (1667), the greatest English epic.

There are other famous poems possessing some of the characteristics of the epic which are loosely classified in this category. Dante's *Divine Comedy* lacks two of the prime essentials of the epic, a hero and a related narrative of his exploits. Spenser's long poem *The Faerie Queene* tells several different stories. Each book has a different hero, and the attempt to unify the poem by presenting Prince Arthur as the central unifying figure is not successful. The poem is really an unfinished allegory. Tennyson's *Idylls of the King,* though completed, for the same reasons violates the traditional canons of the epic. Stephen Vincent Benét's impressive Civil War poetic chronicle *John Brown's Body,* shifting from John Brown to Lincoln, to Northern and Southern romantic protagonists, lacks a central integrating hero as well as a unified poetic style.

Since Milton's achievement no English poet has written an equally satisfactory epic. Many reasons have been advanced for the abandonment of this poetic genre: disbelief in the supernatural, the loss of religious faith, the diminution of man's heroic stature, the growth of science, the increasing complexity and rapid changes of modern civilization, the development of the novel as a literary art form to replace the epic, and so forth. Some modern poets, reacting against the classical concept of a strict separation of the genres, have created a hybrid literary form, the epic-drama, which incorporates some of the epic conventions but adds dialogue, frequent changes of setting, actors, and other features of the drama. Goethe's *Faust* and Hardy's *The Dynasts* are outstanding examples of philosophic epic-dramas.

For Discussion

Man's pleasure in a literary work is compounded of the sense of novelty and the sense of recognition. . . . The genre represents, so to speak, a sum of aesthetic devices at hand, available to the writer and already intelligible to the reader. The good writer partly conforms to the genre as it exists, partly stretches it.

—René Wellek and Austin Warren

Poems Related to Chapter 13

Of A' the Airts[1]

I
Of a' the airts the wind can blaw
   I dearly like the west,
For there the bonie lassie lives,
   The lassie I lo'e best.
There wild woods grow, and rivers row,
   And monie a hill between,
But day and night my fancy's flight
   Is ever wi' my Jean.

II
I see her in the dewy flowers—
   I see her sweet and fair.
I hear her in the tunefu' birds—
   I hear her charm the air.

There's not a bonie flower that springs
   By fountain, shaw,[2] or green,
There's not a bonie bird that sings,
   But minds me o' my Jean.

     —Robert Burns (1759–1796)

---

[1] Directions.   [2] Wood.

So, We'll Go No More a Roving

So, we'll go no more a roving
   So late into the night,
Though the heart be still as loving,
   And the moon be still as bright.

For the sword outwears its sheath,
   And the soul wears out the breast,
And the heart must pause to breathe,
   And love itself have rest.

Though the night was made for loving,
   And the day returns too soon,
Yet we'll go no more a roving
   By the light of the moon.

     —George Gordon, Lord Byron (1788–1824)

Lines: "When the Lamp Is Shattered"

I

When the lamp is shattered
The light in the dust lies dead—
   When the cloud is scattered
The rainbow's glory is shed.
   When the lute is broken,
Sweet tones are remembered not;
   When the lips have spoken
Loved accents are soon forgot.

II

As music and splendour
Survive not the lamp and the lute,
   The heart's echoes render
No song when the spirit is mute: —
   No song but sad dirges,

Like the wind through a ruined cell,
  Or the mournful surges
That ring the dead seaman's knell.

III
When hearts have once mingled
Love first leaves the well-built nest;
  The weak one is singled
To endure what it once possessed.
  O Love! who bewailest
The frailty of all things here,
  Why choose you the frailest
For your cradle, your home, and your bier?

IV
Its passions will rock thee
As the storms rock the ravens on high;
  Bright reason will mock thee,
Like the sun from a wintry sky.
  From thy nest every rafter
Will rot, and thine eagle home
  Leave thee naked to laughter,
When leaves fall and cold winds come.

—Percy Bysshe Shelley (1792–1822)

Silence

There is a silence where hath been no sound,
  There is a silence where no sound may be,
  In the cold grave—under the deep deep sea,
Or in the wide desert where no life is found,
Which hath been mute, and still must sleep profound;
  No voice is hush'd—no life treads silently,
  But clouds and cloudy shadows wander free,
That never spoke, over the idle ground:
But in green ruins, in the desolate walls
  Of antique palaces, where Man hath been,
Though the dun fox, or wild hyena, calls,
  And owls, that flit continually between,
Shriek to the echo, and the low winds moan,
There the true Silence is, self-conscious and alone.

—Thomas Hood (1799–1845)

Little Rock Arkansas 1957

Dedicated to the Nine Children

Clasping like bucklers to their bodies, books,
nine children move through blasts of killing looks.
Committed to this battle each child dares,
deliberately, the fusillades of jeers.
Their valor iron in their ironed clothes
they walk politely in their polished shoes
down ambushed halls to classrooms sown with mines
to learn their lesson. Obviously nine's
a carefully calculated number, odd
not even, a suave size that can be added to, discreetly, later, or culled now
should one child break not bend; or fail to bow
sufficiently his bloody head . . . a rule
to heed, child, be you black and going to school.

—Isabella Gardner (1915–   )

Ex-Basketball Player

Pearl Avenue runs past the high school lot,
Bends with the trolley tracks, and stops, cut off
Before it has a chance to go two blocks,
At Colonel McComsky Plaza. Berth's Garage
Is on the corner facing west, and there,
Most days, you'll find Flick Webb, who helps Berth out.

Flick stands tall among the idiot pumps—
Five on a side, the old bubble-head style,
Their rubber elbows hanging loose and low,
One's nostrils are two S's, and his eyes
An E and O. And one is squat, without
A head at all—more of a football type.

Once, Flick played for the high school team, the Wizards.
He was good: in fact, the best. In '46,
He bucketed three hundred ninety points,
A county record still. The ball loved Flick.
I saw him rack up thirty-eight or forty
In one home game. His hands were like wild birds.

He never learned a trade; he just sells gas,
Checks oil, and changes flats. Once in a while,

As a gag, he dribbles an inner tube,
But most of us remember anyway.
His hands are fine and nervous on the lug wrench.
It makes no difference to the lug wrench, though.

Off work, he hangs around Mae's Luncheonette.
Grease-grey and kind of coiled, he plays pinball,
Sips lemon cokes, and smokes those thin cigars;
Flick seldom speaks to Mae, just sits and nods
Beyond her face towards bright applauding tiers
Of Necco Wafers, Nibs, and Juju Beads.

—John Updike (1932–   )

Provide, Provide

The witch that came (the withered hag)
To wash the steps with pail and rag,
Was once the beauty Abishag,

The picture pride of Hollywood.
Too many fall from great and good
For you to doubt the likelihood.

Die early and avoid the fate.
Or if predestined to die late,
Make up your mind to die in state.

Make the whole stock exchange your own!
If need be occupy a throne,
Where nobody can call *you* crone.

Some have relied on what they knew,
Others on being simply true.
What worked for them might work for you.

No memory of having starred
Atones for later disregard
Or keeps the end from being hard.

Better to go down dignified
With boughten friendship at your side
Than none at all. Provide; provide!

—Robert Frost (1874–1963)

The Oven Bird

There is a singer everyone has heard,
Loud, a mid-summer and a mid-wood bird,
Who makes the solid tree trunks sound again.
He says that leaves are old and that for flowers
Mid-summer is to spring as one to ten.
He says the early petal-fall is past
When pear and cherry bloom went down in showers.
On sunny days a moment overcast;
And comes that other fall we name the fall.
He says the highway dust is over all.
The bird would cease and be as other birds
But that he knows in singing not to sing.
The questions that he frames in all but words
Is what to make of a diminished thing.

—Robert Frost (1874–1963)

Ultima Ratio Regum[1]

The guns spell money's ultimate reason
In letters of lead on the Spring hillside.
But the boy lying dead under the olive trees
Was too young and too silly
To have been notable to their important eye.
He was a better target for a kiss.

When he lived, tall factory hooters never summoned him.
Nor did restaurant plate-glass doors revolve to wave him in.
His name never appeared in the papers.
The world maintained its traditional wall
Round the dead with their gold sunk deep as a well,
Whilst his life, intangible as a Stock Exchange rumour,
        drifted outside.

O too lightly he threw down his cap
One day when the breeze threw petals from the trees.
The unflowering wall sprouted with guns,
Machine-gun anger quickly scythed the grasses;
Flags and leaves fell from hands and branches;
The tweed cap rotted in the nettles.

Consider his life which was valueless
In terms of employment, hotel ledgers, news files.
Consider. One bullet in ten thousand kills a man.

Ask. Was so much expenditure justified
On the death of one so young, and so silly
Lying under the olive trees, O world, O death?

—Stephen Spender (1909–   )

---
[1] The ultimate argument of kings.

At the Slackening of the Tide

Today I saw a woman wrapped in rags
Leaping along the beach to curse the sea.
Her child lay floating in the oil, away
From oarlock, gunwale, and the blades of oars.
The skinny lifeguard, raging at the sky,
Vomited sea, and fainted on the sand.

The cold simplicity of evening falls
Dead on my mind,
And underneath the piles the water
Leaps up, leaps up, and sags down slowly, farther
Than seagulls disembodied in the drag
Of oil and foam.

Plucking among the oyster shells a man
Stares at the sea, that stretches on its side.
Now far along the beach, a hungry dog
Announces everything I knew before:
Obliterate naiads weeping underground,
Where Homer's tongue thickens with human howls.

I would do anything to drag myself
Out of this place:
Root up a seaweed from the water,
To stuff it in my mouth, or deafen me,
Free me from all the force of human speech;
Go drown, almost.

Warm in the pleasure of the dawn I came
To sing my song
And look for mollusks in the shallows,
The whorl and coil that pretty up the earth,
While far below us, flaring in the dark,
The stars go out.

What did I do to kill my time today,
After the woman ranted in the cold,
The mellow sea, the sound blown dark as wine?

After the lifeguard rose up from the waves
Like a sea-lizard with the scales washed off?
Sit there, admiring sunlight on a shell?

Abstract with terror of the shell, I stared
Over the waters where
God brooded for the living all one day.
Lonely for weeping, starved for a sound of mourning,
I bowed my head, and heard the sea far off
Washing its hands.

—James Wright (1927–   )

Black Jackets

In the silence that prolongs the span
Rawly of music when the record ends,
The red-haired boy who drove a van
In weekday overalls, but, like his friends,

Wore cycle boots and jacket here
To suit the Sunday hangout he was in,
Heard, as he stretched back from his beer,
Leather creak softly round his neck and chin.

Before him, on a coal-black sleeve
Remote exertion had lined, scratched, and burned
Insignia that could not revive
The heroic fall or climb where they were earned.

On the other drinkers bent together,
Concocting selves for their impervious kit,
He saw it as no more than leather
Which, taut across the shoulders grown to it,

Sent through the dimness of a bar
As sudden and anonymous hints of light
As those that shipping give, that are
Now flickers in the Bay, now lost in night.

He stretched out like a cat, and rolled
The bitterish taste of beer upon his tongue,
And listened to a joke being told:
The present was the things he stayed among.

If it was only loss he wore,
He wore it to assert, with fierce devotion,

Complicity and nothing more.
He recollected his initiation,

And one especially of the rites.
For on his shoulders they had put tattoos:
    The group's name on the left, The Knights,
And on the right the slogan Born To Lose.

—Thom Gunn (1929–   )

There is a place for classification in criticism, as in any other discipline which is more important than an elegant accomplishment of some mandarin caste. The strong emotional repugnance felt by many critics toward any form of schematization in poetics is again the result of a failure to distinguish criticism as a body of knowledge from the direct experience of literature, where every act is unique, and classification has no place.

—*Northrop Frye*

14
Narrative and Dramatic Poetry

Another type of narrative poetry shorter than the epic is the ballad, either of popular origin transmitted orally or the work of a known poet. The former is a *folk ballad,* the latter, a *literary ballad.*

Every country has its folk ballads or story-songs, and ballad-making is a continual process. Our collection of English popular balladry goes back to the late Middle Ages.

This oral literature was not the exclusive possession of any one class but belonged to the whole people at a time when there was no formal division between the literate and the illiterate. Folk poetry, transmitted by word of mouth for hundreds of years, has therefore a variety of sources reflected in the broad range of subject matter. Some of the ballads are riddle poems; some deal with the adventures of Robin Hood as a folk hero; some are based on historical events; some reflecting medieval superstitions deal with the supernatural; some handle tragic themes simply and powerfully; and some are humorous. Since this poetry was the emotional expression in a narrative framework of a homogeneous group rather than the creative expression of one individual, many versions of the same story, experience, or tradition exist. In oral transmission over periods of time and in changes of locale, verses were modified, added, or dropped. As a result of these changes and improvisations we often do not have one definitive text but several versions of the same material.

Varied as the subject matter of the ballad is, the treatment possesses certain characteristics that readily identify the folk ballad as a distinct literary type. It always tells a story in simple language (often in the colloquial speech or dialect of a region). The central focus is on some dramatic event or the consequences of some crucial episode. We see events enacted rather than explained. Since many of the stories are traditional and therefore familiar to the listeners, a detailed, connected plot is not essential. Little attention is given to setting. Figurative language is scarce. The opening is usually abrupt and the story advances by *leaping and lingering,* that is, the transitions are sudden, and the poet touches briefly on some parts and elaborates others. The listener or reader, by the use of his stimulated imagination, readily fills in the gaps in the story. Dialogue plays an important part in creating tone and revealing character. The author, adapter, or singer does not express his reactions to the narrative but preserves an attitude of objectivity. This impersonality, coupled with the use of vivid oral language that appeals directly to the senses of sight and hearing, gives the popular ballad its distinctive flavor as the expression of a folk group rather than of an individual.

The folk ballad, emerging before the invention of printing and the rise of sophisticated and cultured audiences, naturally appealed more to the ear of the listener than the eye of the reader. As a result, repetition plays an important part. This takes the form of repeating words or phrases in stanzas or the use of a rhythmic *refrain* (probably chanted by the group) after each stanza. Some ballads use *incremental repetition,* a slight variation in a significant word or phrase to link stanzas together, to emphasize important details, to bring out contrasts, and to create suspense and mounting tension in the story. Since the folk ballad is probably more the creation of a group held together by communal tradition than the work of one individual, similar verses or stanzas are frequently found in different ballads. These ready-made lines taken from a common poetic storehouse are called *commonplaces.*

In addition to repetition the balladeer utilizes other poetic devices to communicate emotion and to shape his material into an artistic form. He uses a simple but effective rhythm appropriate to his subject and almost always employs rhyme. The most common stanzaic pattern is the *ballad stanza,* easy to compose and easy to memorize.

The vigor, spontaneity, and dramatic power of the early folk ballads dealing with the elemental passions of humanity—love, hatred, faith, revenge, courage, and loyalty—have had a profound influence on the English poets of the Romantic, Victorian, and modern eras. Bare of imagery, primitive in emotional expression, and simple in diction, these folk poems have delighted listeners and readers for centuries. Scholars such as Bishop Thomas Percy and Sir Walter Scott in the eighteenth and nineteenth centuries have been diligent in collecting the traditional ballads of England and Scotland. The definitive collection of 305 ballads (some in as many as 25 versions) was published at the end of the nineteenth century by Professor Francis James Child of Harvard.

A good example of the traditional folk ballad is this famous poem.

Sir Patrick Spence

The king sits in Dumferling toune,
    Drinking the blude-reid wine:
"O whar will I get guid sailor,
    To sail this schip of mine?"

Up and spak an eldern knicht,
    Sat at the kings richt kne:
"Sir Patrick Spence is the best sailor,
    That sails upon the se."

The king has written a braid[1] letter,
    And signd it wi his hand,
And sent it to Sir Patrick Spence,
    Was walking on the sand.

The first line that Sir Patrick red,
    A loud lauch lauched[2] he;
The next line that Sir Patrick red,
    The teir blinded his ee.[3]

"O wha is this has don this deid,
    This ill deid don to me,
To send me out this time o' the yeir,
    To sail upon the se!

"Mak haste, mak haste, my mirry men all
    Our guid schip sails the morne:"
"O say na sae, my master deir,
    For I feir a deadlie storme.

"Late, late yestreen I saw the new moone,
    Wi the auld[4] moone in hir arme,
And I feir, I feir, my deir master,
    That we will cum to harme."

O our Scots nobles wer rich laith[5]
   To weet their cork-heild schoone;[6]
Bot lang owre[7] a' the play wer playd,
   Thair hats they swam aboone.[8]

O lang, lang may their ladies sit,
   Wi thair fans into their hand,
Or eir they se Sir Patrick Spence
   Cum sailing to the land.

O lang, lang, may the ladies stand,
   Wi thair gold kems[9] in thair hair
Waiting for thair ain deir lords,
   For they'll se thame no mair.

Haf owre,[10] half owre to Aberdour,
   It's fiftie fadom deip,
And their lies guid Sir Patrick Spence,
   Wi the Scots lords at his feit.

            —Anonymous

---

[1] Broad.   [2] Laughed.   [3] Eye.   [4] Old.   [5] Loath, reluctant.   [6] Shoes.
[7] Before.   [8] Above them.   [9] Combs.   [10] Over.

The narrative consists of five separate scenes without transitions: (1) the events in the king's court at Dumferling, the choice of Sir Patrick for the mission, and the dispatch of the king's letter; (2) on the seashore, the reactions of Sir Patrick to the letter and the preparations, despite forebodings for the dangerous journey; (3) the shipwreck suggested by the floating hats of the doomed passengers and crew; (4) back to land where the aristocratic ladies are waiting for the triumphal return of their "ain deir lords"; and (5) the bottom of the sea where the victims of the disaster lie.

The concrete details a poet includes in his work must be functional, that is, they must be justified in terms of character revelation, plot motivation, or illumination of theme. If they serve no necessary literary purpose, they simply clutter up the poem and confuse or distract the reader. In this ballad all the details are essential. "The blude-reid wine" the king drinks foreshadows the tragic disaster. Through folly or carelessness in ordering this doomed expedition, he becomes a canniballike destroyer. For advice the young king turns to his trusted old counselor, the "eldern knicht" (Is the latter perhaps an enemy of Sir Patrick?). The king's "braid" letter signed with his own hand indicates the importance of the mission. The image of "the new moone,/ Wi the auld moone in hir arme" is the second example of a foreshadowing. The imported "corkheild schoone" of the Scots nobles reveals their wealth and high rank as do the fans and "gold kems" of their wives.

The three concrete details of the last stanza are of particular significance. The fact that the storm struck the ship when it was "half owre to Aberdour" reveals that it had reached the point of no return, where the water was "fiftie fadom deep." Therefore there were no survivors from this national disaster. The concluding picture of the Scots lords at the feet of Sir Patrick Spence forcefully suggests the theme of the poem: the glory and tragedy of loyalty. In the days of feudalism people of lesser rank swore allegiance to those above them. In the poem the dead Scots lords, though superior in rank, show their fealty to the faithful Sir Patrick Spence by the reversal of positions. The anonymous poet suggests not only Sir Patrick's loyalty to the king (as a symbol of his country) but also the loyalty of the crew to their captain and the fidelity of the wives to their husbands.

The poet's use of contrast and irony—separate or combined—functions with similar effectiveness. The hero's first reaction to the king's missive, a joyous laugh at the flattering opening words (or disbelief at the proposed dangerous voyage?), is quickly shifted to weeping as the tragic nature of this suicidal mission is revealed. His characterization of his men as "mirry" (really depressed) and his ship as "guid" (really doomed) are examples of verbal irony. The reluctance of the nobles to wet their expensive shoes is bitterly ironical, as is the expectation of their well-dressed wives awaiting the return of their husbands. The faithful noblewomen will have to exchange their colorful garments for somber widows' weeds.

The *literary ballad,* written by a specific poet with a definitive published text, imitated many of the characteristics of the popular ballad but added subtle variations in rhythm and psychology as well as sophistication and symbolism. A typical modern example is this poem by W. H. Auden.

O What Is That Sound

O what is that sound which so thrills the ear
  Down in the valley drumming, drumming?
Only the scarlet soldiers, dear,
  The soldiers coming.

O what is that light I see flashing so clear
  Over the distance brightly, brightly?
Only the sun on their weapons, dear,
  As they step lightly.

O what are they doing with all that gear;
    What are they doing this morning, this morning?
Only the usual maneuvers, dear,
    Or perhaps a warning.

O why have they left the road down there;
    Why are they suddenly wheeling, wheeling?
Perhaps a change in the orders, dear.
    Why are you kneeling?

O haven't they stopped for the doctor's care;
    Haven't they reined their horses, their horses?
Why, they are none of them wounded, dear,
    None of these forces.

O is it the parson they want, with white hair;
    Is it the parson, is it, is it?
No, they are passing his gateway, dear,
    Without a visit.

O it must be the farmer who lives so near.
    It must be the farmer, so cunning, cunning;
They have passed the farm already, dear,
    And now they are running.

O where are you going? stay with me here!
    Were the vows you swore me deceiving, deceiving?
No, I promised to love you, dear,
    But I must be leaving.

O it's broken the lock and splintered the door,
    O it's the gate where they're turning, turning;
Their feet are heavy on the floor
    And their eyes are burning.

                                        —W. H. Auden (1907–   )

The modern poet uses many of the traditional devices of the folk ballad, such as an abrupt opening, a four-line rhymed stanza, melodic repetition, simple diction, a question-answer pattern to advance an exciting plot, and the like. But the total effect of this literary ballad is quite different. Its sophisticated artfulness reveals the hand of a distinct poet, and its conscious ambiguity suggests symbolic overtones. The poem opens quietly with a wary man and woman in a house observing a troop of "scarlet soldiers" coming down a highway. Gradually the tension of the watchers mounts. Vague suspicion shifts to fear, fear rises to terror as they realize the soldiers are here to arrest the man (perhaps as a subversive, spy, or informer), terror turns to despair as the woman sees her faithless lover desert her, and the poem ends in a nightmare of panic. The poet has intentionally introduced an atmosphere of hallucinatory vagueness in the events, characters, and setting to universalize a betrayal situation. (Readers of Bernard Shaw's *The Devil's Disciple* may think of a dramatic parallel in the British redcoats coming to arrest the "rebel" minister, Anthony Anderson; and the readers of Sean O'Casey's *Juno and the Paycock* will perhaps recall the terrified prayer of Johnny Boyle as the Irish Irregulars drag him out to be shot as an informer; others will recall sudden arrests in the totalitarian regimes of our own times.)

W. H. Auden has intensified the excitement by accelerating the action. In line eight the soldiers step "lightly," in line fourteen they are "suddenly wheeling," and in line twenty-eight "they are running." Within the framework of the general symbolic action, the poet has compressed some minor unresolved dramatic episodes which stimulate the imagination. What are the emotional implications of the man's evocative question, "Why are you kneeling?" (Fright? Pleading? Prayer?) Who is the farmer characterized as "so cunning, cunning"? (Is he the betrayer of the betrayed, a double-agent?) Her quick, eager, frightened questions are contrasted with his slow, evasive, false reassurances.

In this poem the prosodic and rhetorical variations on the conventional form of the folk ballad are equally interesting. Instead of using the popular ballad quatrain of "Sir Patrick Spence" (alternating lines of four and three stresses with only the short lines rhyming), Auden constructs a stanza with a powerful rhythmic beat, consisting of three four-stress lines and a clipped two-stress final line. The powerful marching rhythm is emphasized by the alternation of masculine rhymes of the first and third lines and feminine rhymes of the second and fourth lines (i.e., ending in an added unaccented repetition syllable). The dramatic effect of the ballad is heightened by beginning each stanza with an emotional *O* and intensified by the ominous repetition of the woman's words at the end of every second line. In the concluding stanza the poet suggests the disorder of violence and the panic of the terrified "patriot" not only by the images of the broken lock and the splintered door but by shattering the previous pattern he has so carefully constructed. In the final quatrain there are two despairing *O's* and no questions because the false lover has fled, as has his courage. Betrayed and deserted she is left alone to face her fate.

Many of the folk ballads brought to America by English settlers were modified by their descendants as they adjusted to their new environment. Names were changed, the diction was Americanized, the supernatural was often rationalized, and local new-world customs were superimposed on or substituted for the old. Alongside the traditional British folk songs, native American ballads were composed by anonymous poets. Some of these ballads written before the American Revolution reflect the patriotic sentiments of the colonists protesting the "hellish plan" of taxing tea and glorifying their rebellious heroes. One authentic New England ballad, "The Yankee's Return from Camp" (1775), sung to the tune of "Yankee Doodle," became a popular marching song during the Revolution. In the nineteenth century, as the American frontier expanded rapidly to the Pacific, popular ballads and folk songs expressed the moods and attitudes of otherwise inarticulate groups. Many of these emotional poems reflected the prevailing tone of a romantic nationalism or exalted the common man and his democratic ideals. Through the alchemy of poetic folklore, real people were transformed into mythical characters. Davy Crockett, the Tennessee bear hunter elected to Congress in 1827, was built up as an invincible champion who defeated all adversaries, performed prodigious feats of valor, and even controlled the elements of nature. After his heroic death he became the legendary hero of many ballads.

In a similar fashion we read in popular ballads of the apotheosis of Mike Fink, "the King of the Keelboatmen"; of Casey Jones, the railroad engineer; and of John Henry, "that steel-drivin' man with his twelve poun' hammer." John Chapman planted nurseries and apple orchards in his trek westward and became Johnny Appleseed, the symbol of American fertility.

On the western frontier, three robbers and lawless desperadoes, all betrayed by Judaslike informers, were glorified by popular legend, and many a folk ballad recounted the deeds and "sad" fates of Jesse James, Billy the Kid, and Sam Bass. On the wide prairies the cowboys, while herding their cattle or sitting around campfires, sang their sentimental ballads. On the seven seas American sailors intoned their sea chanteys as they pulled in rhythm on the halyards or hunted whales. In the industrial centers the growing labor movement created its own songs celebrating its efforts to organize and eulogizing the death of its martyrs. From the slave plantations of the South came our richest heritage of folk poetry and music in the form of the noble and moving black spirituals. In 1860 one of our greatest poets could proudly proclaim the following.

I Hear America Singing

I hear America singing, the varied carols I hear,
Those of mechanics, each one singing his as it should
    be blithe and strong,
The carpenter singing his as he measures his plank or beam,

The mason singing his as he makes ready for work, or
    leaves off work,
The boatman singing what belongs to him in his boat,
    the deck-hand singing on the steamboat deck,
The shoemaker singing as he sits on his bench, the hatter
    singing as he stands,
The wood-cutter's song, the ploughboy's, on his way in
    the morning, or at the noon intermission or at
    sundown,
The delicious singing of the mother, or of the young
    wife at work, or of the girl sewing or washing,
Each singing what belongs to her and to none else,
The day what belongs to the day—at night the party of
    young fellows, robust, friendly,
Singing with open mouths their strong melodious songs.

—Walt Whitman (1819–1892)

This tradition of American folk balladry has inspired the work of twentieth-century poets such as Vachel Lindsay, Carl Sandburg, Stephen Vincent Benét, Robert Penn Warren, and "Woody" Guthrie. The popularity of this genre is attested to by the countless number of folk singers and rock groups performing on the contemporary scene.

Today we are witnessing a renaissance of the bardic tradition. Poets such as Bob Dylan, Leonard Cohen, Rod McKuen, Paul Simon, and Arlo Guthrie are singing rather than just printing their verses. Rock groups utilizing guitars, sitars, and other plucked, picked, and strummed as well as percussion instruments are experimenting with new rhythms and sound effects aided by electrical amplification. New song and ballad forms with shifting rhythms, radical stanzaic patterns, and a rock beat are emerging as an expression of the revolution of modern youth.

Since violence and lawlessness have been an integral part of our historical tradition, it is no wonder that Jesse James has become an archetype of the outlaw, glorified in spite of the robberies and murders, as a romantic American Robin Hood. The melodramatic nature of his depredations, the wide publicity he and his gang received, and his death at the age of 35 after nineteen years of sensational exploits naturally made him a legendary figure in dime-novel literature and folk ballads.

Jesse James

It was on a Wednesday night, the moon was shining bright,
    They robbed the Danville train.

And the people they did say, for many miles away,
    'Twas the outlaws Frank and Jesse James.

Refrain

Jesse had a wife to mourn him all her life,
    The children they are brave.
'Twas a dirty little coward shot Mister Howard,[1]
    And laid Jesse James in his grave.

Jesse was a man was a friend to the poor,
    He never left a friend in pain.
And with his brother Frank he robbed the Chicago bank
    And then held up the Glendale train.

It was Robert Ford, the dirty little coward,
    I wonder how he does feel,
For he ate of Jesse's bread and he slept in Jesse's bed,
    Then he laid Jesse James in his grave.

It was his brother Frank that robbed the Gallatin Bank,
    And carried the money from the town.
It was in this very place that they had a little race,
    For they shot Captain Sheets to the ground.

They went to the crossing not very far from there,
    And there they did the same;
And the agent on his knees he delivered up the keys
    To the outlaws Frank and Jesse James.

It was on a Saturday night, Jesse was at home
    Talking to his family brave,
When the thief and the coward, little Robert Ford,
    Laid Jesse James in his grave.

How people held their breath when they heard of Jesse's death,
    And wondered how he ever came to die.
'Twas one of the gang, dirty Robert Ford,
    That shot Jesse James on the sly.

Jesse went to rest with his hand on his breast;
    He died with a smile on his face.
He was born one day in the county of Clay,
    And came from a solitary race.

                        —Anonymous

---

[1] The name assumed by Jesse James when living unarmed in St. Joseph, Mo.

Like many people throughout history suffering from oppression, the black man in America found hope and encouragement in the ancient example of Moses delivering his people from bondage. The following spiritual handles this theme with beautiful simplicity and sincerity.

Go Down, Moses

When Israel was in Egypt's land,
    Let my people go;
Oppressed so hard dey could not stand,
    Let my people go.

Go down, Moses,
    Way down in Egypt's land,
Tell ole Pha-roh,
    Let my people go.

Thus saith the Lord, bold Moses said,
    Let my people go;
If not I'll smite your first-born dead,
    Let my people go.

Go down, Moses, etc.

No more shall dey in bondage toil,
    Let my people go;
Let dem come out wid Egypt's spoil,
    Let my people go.

Go down, Moses, etc.

—Anonymous

Related to the literary ballad but usually longer is the *metrical romance,* a colorful story of love and heroic deeds of aristocratic adventurers. The poet allows his fancy free play; the narrative is rather leisurely and discursive. Addressed primarily to a literate aristocratic audience, the metrical romance stresses chivalry, love (sacred and profane), extraordinary events, and frequently the supernatural. Brought to England by the Normans, this type of narrative poetry was popularized by French minstrels and court poets. Many of the early Arthurian stories, such as "Sir Gawain and the Green Knight," were metrical romances. In the nineteenth century Scott, in "The Lay of the Last Minstrel," "The Lady of the Lake," and "Marmion," and Byron in his melodramatic oriental narratives "The Giaour" and "The Corsair," revived the popularity of the metrical romance. In the twentieth century Edwin Arlington Robinson in modern blank verse reinterpreted the Arthurian story in his "Merlin," "Lancelot," and "Tristram."

The *poetic tale* is a verse narrative of varying length. Examples of this most popular narrative genre are Chaucer's *Canterbury Tales*, William Morris' stories in *The Earthly Paradise*, Burns' "Tam o' Shanter," Wordsworth's "Ruth," Keats' "Lamia," Tennyson's "Enoch Arden," John Masefield's "Dauber," and Frost's "The Death of the Hired Man."

Every poetic tale contains a plot, setting, and characters; whether the poet emphasizes one of these elements or all depends upon his artistic purpose. If he is interested primarily in presenting a picture of pastoral or courtly life, subordinating character and action to pictorial setting, he produces an *idyll* such as Burns' "A Cotter's Saturday Night," Whittier's "Snowbound," or Tennyson's "The Gardener's Daughter."

Lyric poetry expressing the poet's emotions and thoughts is the most subjective literary genre; dramatic poetry expressing the moods and views of characters created by the poet is the most objective. The most important type of dramatic poetry is the monologue.

A *dramatic monologue* is a prolonged poetic utterance of a single character (not the author) addressed to another person, or it is a meditation revealing the thoughts and feelings of the speaker. Thus a dramatic monologue may be heard or, if a soliloquy, overheard. A dramatic monologue reveals some details of the speaker's life, his character, and his philosophy. Frequently the poet represents the character at some critical moment in his career and by revealing motivation of action, inner conflict, and emotional states brings the character alive.

The speaker created by the author may be a fictitious, legendary, or historical person; the monologue may be an exterior one (spoken to someone present) or an inner one. In either case, the author must present the character with objectivity; the poet cannot simply impersonate the character or put a mask on his own face and express his own views thinly disguised. Poetic ventriloquism is acceptable in the lyric, but it is ineffective in the dramatic monologue.

The greatest master of the dramatic monologue is Robert Browning. A failure as a playwright, he developed the genre of the one-man little drama by writing many superb dramatic monologues that revealed the souls of real and imagined characters who are surpassed in range and depth only by Shakespeare's incomparable gallery of humanity. Although Browning did not invent the dramatic monologue, he perfected it as a poetic art form, and it has been utilized by many important poets in the twentieth century: Robinson, Masters, Hardy, Yeats, Pound, Eliot, Stevens, and Frost.

The development of this genre in our literature covers many centuries. The beautiful Old English poems "The Wanderer," "The Seafarer," and "The Wife's Lament" are dramatic monologues as are many religious poems of the Middle Ages. The prologues to some of Chaucer's *Canterbury Tales,* such as the Pardoner's and the Wife of Bath's, are other examples. The wily Pardoner, in confessing boastfully to his fellow pilgrims how he dupes the naive religious rustics by his use of fake relics, reveals his avarice, hypocrisy, and cunning. The lusty Wife of Bath in her garrulous apologia vigorously defending her five marriages and the supremacy of wife over husband frankly reveals her sensuality, her worldliness, and her restlessness. Many of the soliloquies in the plays of Shakespeare and other Elizabethan dramatists contributed to the development of the poetic monologue. Its popularity in our time as a vehicle of poetic expression results from our interest in Freudian psychology and the unconscious as well as the use of the stream-of-consciousness and "free association" technique found in the contemporary novel since James Joyce's *Ulysses.* Modern poets have further refined the use of the dramatic monologue to illuminate the dark recesses of the human phyche, to dramatize a situation, and to expose the complex ironies of life and character.

Let us examine one of Browning's shorter and simpler examples of this genre.

Instans Tyrannus[1]

I
Of the million or two, more or less,
I rule and possess,
One man, for some cause undefined,
Was least to my mind.

II
I struck him, he grovelled of course—
For, what was his force?
I pinned him to earth with my weight
And persistence of hate:
And he lay, would not moan, would not curse,
As his lot might be worse.

III
"Were the object less mean, would he stand
At the swing of my hand!
For obscurity helps him and blots
The hole where he squats."
So, I set my five wits on the stretch
To inveigle the wretch.

All in vain! Gold and jewels I threw,
Still he couched there perdue;[2]
I tempted his blood and his flesh,
Hid in roses my mesh,
Choicest cates[3] and the flagon's best spilth:[4]
Still he kept to his filth.

IV

Had he kith now or kin, were access
To his heart, did I press:
Just a son or a mother to seize!
No such booty as these.
Were it simply a friend to pursue
'Mid my million or two,
Who could pay me in person or pelf
What he owes me himself!
No: I could not but smile through my chafe:
For the fellow lay safe
As his mates do, the midge and the nit,
—Through minuteness, to wit.

V

Then a humour more great took its place
At the thought of his face,
The droop, the low cares of the mouth,
The trouble uncouth
'Twixt the brows, all that air one is fain
To put out of its pain.
And, "no!" I admonished myself,
"Is one mocked by an elf,
Is one baffled by toad or by rat?
The gravamen's[5] in that!
How the lion, who crouches to suit
His back to my foot,
Would admire that I stand in debate!
But the small turns the great
If it vexes you,—that is the thing!
Toad or rat vex the king?
Though I waste half my realm to unearth
Toad or rat, 'tis well worth!"

VI

So, I soberly laid my last plan
To extinguish the man.
Round his creep-hole, with never a break
Ran my fires for his sake;
Over-head, did my thunder combine
With my underground mine:

Till I looked from my labour content
To enjoy the event.

VII
When sudden . . . how think ye, the end?
Did I say "without friend"?
Say rather, from marge to blue marge
The whole sky grew his targe[6]
With the sun's self for visible boss,
While an Arm ran across
Which the earth heaved beneath like a breast
Where the wretch was safe prest!
Do you see? Just my vengeance complete,
The man sprang to his feet,
Stood erect, caught at God's skirts, and prayed!
—So, I was afraid!

—Robert Browning (1812–1889)

---

[1] The threatening tyrant.   [2] In concealment or hiding.   [3] Delicacies.
[4] Outpourings.   [5] The heart of a grievance or complaint.   [6] Shield.

The title of the poem and the theme were suggested by Horace's "Ode on the Just Man" (the third ode in Book III) and perhaps by the persecution of the early Christians. A prose translation of the relevant passage from Horace would read: "The just man, firm of purpose, is not to be shaken from his fixed resolve by the fury of an impious mob nor by the frown of a threatening tyrant." (When the Dutch statesman DeWitt was tortured to death by a mob in the seventeenth century, it was said that he quoted these lines.)

The poem, in portraying the conflict of physical force and spiritual faith, explores the psychology of a despot corrupted by power. It also brings out the poet's evangelical belief that one with God is in the majority. The speaker is an unnamed absolute ruler of an anonymous kingdom. By not being specific, Browning universalizes this experience and makes it symbolize an ever-recurring conflict in human history.

The authoritarian king, moved by whim, takes a dislike to one of his humble subjects and strikes him down. The victim, using the powerful weapon of passive resistance, does not give the tyrant the satisfaction of active opposition. Physical violence proving futile, the despot tries to break the man's spirit by cajolery, bribery, and cunning temptations. When these fail, he determines to resort to the usual cowardly pressures of a dictator—hostages and reprisals. Frustrated to learn that his insignificant victim has neither friends, parents, nor children, the sadistic tyrant arranges an elaborate execution plan to rid himself of this uncomplaining but annoying nonentity. In a powerful cosmic image, the poet reveals the sudden reversal of the situation and the eventual triumph of courageous spiritual faith.

In the brilliant dramatic monologues "The Bishop Orders His Tomb at St. Praxed's Church," "Fra Lippo Lippi," and "Saul," Browning reveals not only the personalities of the speakers but also the spirit of the age in which they lived. However, when he sometimes fails to preserve the objectivity demanded by the dramatic genre, we hear the voice of the poet instead of that of the speaker. In "Rabbi Ben Ezra" Browning does not give us a realistic portrait of the great Spanish astronomer, physician, poet, and biblical commentator but simply uses the medieval rabbi as a mouthpiece of his own favorite doctrines—success through failure, the necessity for spiritual development, faith in God and immortality, unbounded optimism, and so forth. Missing are the rabbi's scientific and scholarly contributions, his wry humor ("If I sold shrouds, none would die. If candles were my wares, the sun would not set till the day of my death"), and the tragedy of his exile from Spain because of an outbreak against the Jews.

The poetic monologue is a miniature drama which presents a character portrait in verse. Because of its concentrated power, the dramatic monologue demands close attention from the reader. Especially important is the identification of the speaker and the situation in which he finds himself. The central character is not always the speaker. For instance, in the following poem the wealthy Richard Cory is portrayed by the voice of the poor people in a New England community.

Richard Cory

Whenever Richard Cory went down town,
We people on the pavement looked at him:
He was a gentleman from sole to crown,
Clean favored, and imperially slim.

And he was always quietly arrayed,
And he was always human when he talked;
But still he fluttered pulses when he said,
"Good-morning," and he glittered when he walked.

And he was rich—yes, richer than a king—
And admirably schooled in every grace:
In fine, we thought that he was everything
To make us wish that we were in his place.

So on we worked, and waited for the light,
And went without the meat, and cursed the bread;
And Richard Cory, one calm summer night,
Went home and put a bullet through his head.

—Edwin Arlington Robinson (1869–1935)

In the *Spoon River Anthology* Edgar Lee Masters gives us a cross-section of the inhabitants of a small Midwestern town by having the dead speak from their graves. One of the most admirable characters is the subject of the following poem.

Lucinda Matlock

I went to the dances at Chandlerville,
And played snap-out at Winchester.
One time we changed partners,
Driving home in the moonlight of middle June,
And then I found Davis.
We were married and lived together for seventy years,
Enjoying, working, raising the twelve children,
Eight of whom we lost
Ere I had reached the age of sixty.
I spun, I wove, I kept the house, I nursed the sick,
I made the garden, and for holiday
Rambled over the fields where sang the larks,
And by Spoon River gathering many a shell,
And many a flower and medicinal weed—
Shouting to the wooded hills, singing to the green valleys.
At ninety-six I had lived enough, that is all,
And passed to a sweet repose.
What is this I hear of sorrow and weariness,
Anger, discontent and drooping hopes?
Degenerate sons and daughters,
Life is too strong for you—
It takes life to love Life.

—Edgar Lee Masters (1869–1950)

For Discussion

It is hard to tell at any given moment what is relevant. . . . The question is not that of the topicality of a subject. It is that of the writer's own grounding in his time, the relation of his sensibility to his time, and paradoxically enough, of his resistance to his time.

—Robert Penn Warren

Poems Related to Chapter 14

The Twa Brothers

There were two brethren in the north,
   They went to school thegithar;
The one unto the other said,
   Will you try a warsle[1] afore?

They wrestled up, they wrestled down,
   Till Sir John fell to the ground
And there was a knife in Sir Willie's pouch,
   Gied him a deadlie wound.

"Oh brither dear, take me on your back,
   Carry me to your burn[2] clear,
And wash the blood from off my wound,
   And it will bleed nae mair."

He took him up upon his back,
   Carried him to yon burn clear,
And washd the blood from off his wound,
   And aye it bled the mair.

"Oh brother dear, take me on your back,
   Carry me to yon kirk-yard,
And dig a grave baith wide and deep,
   And lay my body there."

He's taen him up upon his back,
   Carried him to yon kirk-yard
And dug a grave both deep and wide,
   And laid his body there.

"But what will I say to my father dear,
   Should he chance ta say, Willie, whar's John?"
"Oh say that he's to England gone,
   To buy him a cask of wine."

"And what shall I say to my mother dear,
   Should she chance to say, Willie, whar's John?"
"Oh say that he's to England gone,
   To buy a new silk gown."

"And what will I say to my sister dear,
   Should she chance to say, Willie, whar's John?"
"Oh say that he's to England gone,
   To buy her a wedding ring."

"What will I say to her you loe[3] dear,
    Should she cry, Why tarries my John?"
"Oh tell her I lie in fair Kirk-land,
    And home will never come."

—Anonymous

---

[1] Wrestle.   [2] Brook.   [3] Love.

1. What characteristics of a typical folk ballad are revealed in this poem?
2. What two types of repetition are to be found in the poem?
3. How does the last stanza differ from the three preceding ones? Why?

The following humorous folk ballad is based on a traditional story found in the East and in Italian folklore. This battle of the sexes ends with the woman triumphant.

Get Up and Bar the Door

It fell about the Martinmas time,[1]
    And a gay time it was then,
When our goodwife got puddings[2] to make,
    And she's boild them in the pan.

The wind sae cauld blew south and north,
    And blew into the floor;[3]
Quoth our goodman to our goodwife,
    "Gae out and bar the door."

"My hand is in my hussyfskap,[4]
    Goodman, as ye may see;
An it should nae be barrd this hundred year,
    It's no be barrd for me."

They made a paction[5] tween them twa,
    They made it firm and sure,
That the first word whaeer shoud speak,
    Shoud rise and bar the door.

Then by there came two gentlemen,
    At twelve o'clock at night,
And they could neither see house nor hall,
    Nor coal nor candle-light.

"Now whether is this a rich man's house,
    Or whether is it a poor?"
But neer a word wad ane of them speak,
    For barring of the door.[6]

And first they ate the white puddings,
  And then they ate the black;
Tho muckle thought the goodwife to herself,
  Yet neer a word she spake.

Then said the one unto the other,
  "Here, man, tak ye my knife;
Do ye tak aff the auld man's beard,
  And I'll kiss the goodwife."

"But there's nae water in the house,[7]
  And what shall we do than?"
"What ails ye at the pudding-broo,
  That boils into the pan?"

O up then started our goodman,
  An angry man was he:
"Will ye kiss my wife before my een,
  And scad me wi pudding-bree?"

Then up and started our goodwife,
  Gied three skips on the floor:
"Goodman, you've spoke the foremost word,
  Get up and bar the door."

—Anonymous

---

[1] November 11.   [2] Sausages.   [3] Room.   [4] Housewifery (here making puddings).   [5] Agreement.   [6] For fear of having to bar the door.   [7] Hot water for shaving.

Compare the following American folk ballad with "Jesse James" (page 291).

Jessey James

Whilst living in Missouri was a great, bold man,
He was known from Seattle 'way down to Birmingham,
From Boston, Massachusetts and across the states,
From Denver, Colorado to the Golden Gate.

You people all have heard of some famous men,
In every nook and corner you have heard of Jessey James.
We used to read about him in our homes by candlelight,
The wind came down the chimney and made us shake
    with fright.

Jessey said one morning, "Boys, some coin we need."
He polished up his shotgun and he got a trusty steed.
He mounted to his horse and rode down to brother Frank's,
Says, "We've got to get some money from the Pittsville bank."

They rode to town next morning, around at ten o'clock;
The cashier of the bank, he got an awful shock;
While Jessey kept him covered with his trusty forty-four,
The cashier counted out a half a million or more.

Jessey in his cabin one day all alone,
His wife had left him to straighten up the room.
She was scrubbing up the kitchen when the doorbell rang
And in stepped forty members of the outlaw gang.

The photograph of Jessey's wife was hanging on the wall;
Jessey says, "I'm going to put that picture in the hall."
Says, "Tonight the western mail is coming into town,
But I'll have time to put back the picture I took down."

He got up and started to put the picture near the stair,
He reached to put it up, had to stand up on a chair.
Then Robert with his forty-four took aim at Jessey's head,
The news flew over the country, "Jessey James is dead!"

The news went over the country that Jessey James was dead.
And on his tombstone they carved these simple words that read:
"If you're going to be a bandit, live a single man's life,"
For Jessey wouldn't have been killed, but for that picture
    of his wife.

—Anonymous

1. How does this poem differ from the previous poem about Jesse James?
    Which do you prefer? Why?

The following literary ballad is based on the events in biblical
history recounted in II Chronicles, 19:35. Sennacherib, King of Assyria
(705–681 B.C.), invaded Palestine in the reign of Hezekiah, King of
Judah (c727–c698 B.C.). A pestilence that broke out in the Assyrian
army forced Sennacherib to retire.

The Destruction of Sennacherib

The Assyrian came down like the wolf on the fold,
And his cohorts were gleaming in purple and gold;
And the sheen of their spears was like stars on the sea,
When the blue wave rolls nightly on deep Galilee.

Like the leaves of the forest when Summer is green,
That host with their banners at sunset were seen:
Like the leaves of the forest when Autumn hath blown,
That host on the morrow lay wither'd and strown.

For the Angel of Death spread his wings on the blast,
And breathed in the face of the foe as he pass'd;
And the eyes of the sleepers wax'd deadly and chill,
And their hearts but once heaved, and for ever grew still!

And there lay the steed with his nostril all wide,
But through it there roll'd not the breath of his pride:
And the foam of his gasping lay white on the turf,
And cold as the spray of the rock-beating surf.

And there lay the rider distorted and pale,
With the dew on his brow and the rust on his mail;
And the tents were all silent, the banners alone,
The lances unlifted, the trumpet unblown.

And the widows of Ashur[1] are loud in their wail,
And the idols are broke in the temple of Baal;[2]
And the might of the Gentile, unsmote by the sword,
Hath melted like snow in the glance of the Lord!

—George Gordon, Lord Byron (1788–1824)

---

[1] A city in Assyria.   [2] One of the chief gods of the Assyrians.

1. Is this ballad primarily narrative or descriptive? Prove. Where is there a shift in tone? Why?

2. Compare the amount of figurative language in this literary ballad with that in one of the Scottish folk ballads. What figure of speech is dominant?

3. What is the meter of the poem? Characterize the rhythm. Is it appropriate to subject and tone?

4. What sound-pattern devices does Byron employ? Are they effective? Discuss.

5. Does the poet stir any sympathy for the Gentile invaders? Or is the poem a song of triumph for those faithful to Jehovah? Discuss.

Browning was only twenty-four years old when he wrote the following dramatic monologue, a study in abnormal psychology.

Porphyria's Lover

The rain set early in to-night,
   The sullen wind was soon awake,

It tore the elm-tops down for spite,
   And did its worst to vex the lake:
   I listened with heart fit to break.
When glided in Porphyria; straight
   She shut the cold out and the storm,
And kneeled and made the cheerless grate
   Blaze up, and all the cottage warm;
   Which done, she rose, and from her form
Withdrew the dripping cloak and shawl,
   And laid her soiled gloves by, untied
Her hat and left the damp hair fall,
   And, last, she sat down by my side
   And called me. When no voice replied,
She put my arm about her waist,
   And made her smooth white shoulder bare,
And all her yellow hair displaced,
   And, stooping, made my cheek lie there,
   And spread, o'er all, her yellow hair,
Murmuring how she loved me—she
   Too weak, for all her heart's endeavour,
To set its struggling passion free
   From pride, and vainer ties dissever,
   And give herself to me for ever.
But passion sometimes would prevail,
   Nor could to-night's gay feast restrain
A sudden thought of one so pale
   For love of her, and all in vain:
   So, she was come through wind and rain.
Be sure I looked up at her eyes
   Happy and proud; at last I knew
Porphyria worshipped me; surprise
   Made my heart swell, and still it grew
   While I debated what to do.
That moment she was mine, mine, fair,
   Perfectly pure and good: I found
A thing to do, and all her hair
   In one long yellow string I wound
   Three times her little throat around,
And strangled her. No pain felt she;
   I am quite sure she felt no pain.
As a shut bud that holds a bee,
   I warily oped her lids: again
   Laughed the blue eyes without a stain.
And I untightened next the tress
   About her neck; her cheek once more
Blushed bright beneath my burning kiss:
   I propped her head up as before,
   Only, this time my shoulder bore

Her head, which droops upon it still:
　　The smiling rosy little head,
So glad it has its utmost will,
　　That all it scorned at once is fled.
　　And I, its love, am gained instead!
Porphyria's love: she guessed not how
　　Her darling one wish would be heard.
And thus we sit together now,
　　And all night long we have not stirred,
　　And yet God has not said a word!

—Robert Browning (1812–1889)

1. If you were on the jury and heard the prisoner's account of the crime, would you consider the murderer sane or insane? Justify your opinion.

2. What do we learn of the past relationship of Porphyria and her lover? What kept them apart?

3. What function does the description of the storm serve in the poem? Where was Porphyria before she came to the lover's cottage? Was her departure a premeditated or impulsive act? Was his crime premeditated or impulsive?

4. How does he justify the murder? Was it motivated primarily by love, jealousy, hatred, or self-sacrifice? Discuss. When he commits the murder, is he in an excited emotional state or does he act with deliberate rationality, that is, with a method to his madness? In this connection consider the simile "As a shut bud that holds a bee,/I warily oped her lids."

5. How do you interpret the last line? Its ambiguity can be resolved in at least three ways: (1) by not punishing him, God approves the speaker's sacrificial act of risking damnation for Porphyria's salvation; (2) by not giving a sign of approval, God condemns his act as a brutal, sinful murder; (3) God is completely indifferent to his act.

6. What do the meter and rhyme scheme contribute to the effect of the poem? Why does not Browning pattern the poem into separate stanzas?

7. Contrast the characters of Porphyria and her lover. What tragic irony is found in the poem?

　　Tennyson found the plot of this dramatic monologue in a "penny dreadful," a cheap periodical that featured morbidly sensational stories, comparable to our American "dime novels." In the eighteenth century a Brighton youth was hanged for a highway robbery he had committed. His body was left hanging on the gallows until the clothes and flesh were gone. As the bones dropped to the ground, his grief-stricken mother during stormy nights gathered up his bones and buried them "in the hallowed enclosure of old Shoreham Churchyard."

When the poem opens, the religious grief-crazed mother is on her death-bed talking to an evangelist sister of mercy who has come to pray with her.

Rizpah

I

Wailing, wailing, wailing, the wind over land and sea—
And Willy's voice in the wind, "O mother, come out to me."
Why should he call me to-night, when he knows that I cannot
    go?
For the downs are as bright as day, and the full moon
    stares at the snow.

II

We should be seen, my dear; they would spy us out of the town.
The loud black nights for us, and the storm rushing
    over the down,
When I cannot see my own hand, but am led by the
    creak of the chain,
And grovel and grope for my son till I find myself
    drenched with the rain.

III

Anything fallen again? nay—what was there left to fall?
I have taken them home, I have number'd the bones,
    I have hidden them all.
What am I saying? and what are *you*? do you come as a spy?
Falls? what falls? who knows? As the tree falls so must it lie.

IV

Who let her in? How long has she been? you—what
    have you heard,
Why did you sit so quiet? you never have spoken a word.
O—to pray with me—yes—a lady—none of their spies—
But the night has crept into my heart, and begun to
    darken my eyes.

V

Ah—you, that have lived so soft, what should *you*
    know of the night,
The blast and the burning shame and the bitter frost
    and the fright?
I have done it, while you were asleep—you were only
    made for the day.
I have gather'd my baby together—and now you may go
    your way.

VI

Nay—for it's kind of you, Madam, to sit by an old dying wife.
But say nothing hard of my boy, I have only an hour of life.
I kiss'd my boy in the prison, before he went out to die.
"They dared me to do it," he said, and he never has told me a lie.
I whipt him for robbing an orchard once when he was
      but a child—
"The farmer dared me to do it," he said; he was always so wild—
And idle—and couldn't be idle—my Willy—he never could
      rest.
The King should have made him a soldier,
      he would have been one of his best.

VII

But he lived with a lot of wild mates, and they
      never would let him be good;
They swore that he dare not rob the mail, and
      he swore that he would;
And he took no life, but he took one purse,
      and when all was done
He flung it among his fellows—"I'll none of it," said my son.

VIII

I came into court to the Judge and the lawyers.
      I told them my tale,
God's own truth—but they kill'd him, they
      kill'd him for robbing the mail.
They hang'd him in chains for a show—we
      had always borne a good name—
To be hang'd for a thief—and then put away
      —isn't that enough shame?
Dust to dust—low down—let us hide! but they set him so high
That all the ships of the world could stare at him, passing by.
God 'ill pardon the hell-black raven and horrible fowls of the air,
But not the black heart of the lawyer who
      kill'd him and hang'd him there.

IX

And the jailer forced me away. I had bid him my last goodbye;
They had fasten'd the door of his cell. "O
      mother!" I heard him cry.
I couldn't get back tho' I tried, he had something further to say,
And now I never shall know it. The jailer forced me away.

X

Then since I couldn't but hear that cry of my boy that was dead,
They seized me and shut me up: they fasten'd
      me down on my bed.

"Mother, O mother!"—he call'd in the dark
    to me year after year—
They beat me for that, they beat me—you
    know that I couldn't but hear;
And then at the last they found I had grown so stupid and still
They let me abroad again—but the creatures
    had worked their will.

XI

Flesh of my flesh was gone, but bone of my bone was left—
I stole them all from the lawyers—and you,
    will you call it a theft?—
My baby, the bones that had suck'd me, the
    bones that had laughed and had cried—
Theirs? O No! they are mine—not theirs—
    they had moved in my side.

XII

Do you think I was scared by the bones?
    I kiss'd em, I buried 'em all—
I can't dig deep, I am old—in the night by the churchyard wall.
My Willy 'ill rise up whole when the trumpet
    of judgment 'ill sound,
But I charge you never to say that I laid him in holy ground.

XIII

They would scratch him up—they would
    hang him again on the cursed tree.
Sin? O yes—we are sinners, I know—let all that be,
And read me a Bible verse of the Lord's good will toward men—
"Full of compassion and mercy, the Lord"—let me hear it again;
"Full of compassion and mercy—long-suffering." Yes, O yes!
For the lawyer is born but to murder—the
    Saviour lives but to bless.
He'll never put on the black cap except for the worst of the worst,
And the first may be last—I have heard it
    in church—and the last may be first.
Suffering—O long-suffering—yes, as the Lord must know,
Year after year in the mist and the wind and
    the shower and the snow.

XIV

Heard, have you? what? they have told you
    he never repented his sin.
How do they know it? are *they* his mother? are *you* of his kin?
Heard! have you ever heard, when the storm on the downs
    began,
The wind that 'ill wail like a child and the
    sea that'll moan like a man?

XV

Election, Election and Reprobation—it's all very well.
But I go to-night to my boy, and I shall not find him in Hell.
For I cared so much for my boy that the
          Lord has look'd into my care,
And He means me I'm sure to be happy with
          Willy, I know not where.

XVI

And if *he* be lost—but to save *my* soul, that is all your desire:
Do you think that I care for *my* soul if my boy be gone to the
          fire?
I have been with God in the dark—go, go,
          you may leave me alone—
You never have borne a child—you are just as hard as a stone.

XVII

Madam, I beg your pardon! I think that you mean to be kind,
But I cannot hear what you say for my
          Willy's voice in the wind—
The snow and the sky so bright—he used but to call in the dark,
And he calls to me now from the church and
          not from the gibbet—for hark!
Nay—you can hear it yourself—it is coming
          —shaking the walls—
Willy—the moon's in a cloud—Good-night. I am going. He
          calls.

                              —Alfred, Lord Tennyson (1809–1892)

1. Has the poet succeeded in transmuting the melodramatic material into tragic or pathetic poetry? Why or why not?
2. What do we learn of Willie's past? Characterize the boy. What do we learn of the mother's past? Characterize her.
3. What defense does she make of her son? Why did not the court accept it? What is her attitude toward the law? Is it justified? Discuss.
4. What clash does she find in her ethical values as derived from her religion and those propounded by the law?
5. Compare the type of love revealed in this poem with that in "Porphyria's Lover."

The Three Ravens

There were three ravens sat on a tree,
    Down a downe, hay down, hay downe,
There were three ravens sat on a tree,
    With a downe,

There were three ravens sat on a tree,
They were as blacke as they might be.
   With a downe, derrie, derrie, derrie,
     downe, downe.

The one of them said to his mate,
"Where shall we our breakfast take?"

"Downe in yonder greene field,
There lies a knight slain under his shield.

"His hounds they lie downe at his feete,
So well they can their master keepe.

"His haukes they flie so eagerly,
There's no fowle dare him come nie."[1]

Downe there comes a fallow doe,
As great with yong as she might goe.

She lift up his bloudy hed,
And kist his wounds that were so red.

She got him up upon her backe,
And carried him to earthen lake.[2]

She buried him before the prime,[3]
She was dead herselfe ere even-song time.[4]

God send every gentleman,
Such haukes, such hounds, and such a leman.[5]

—Anonymous

---

[1] Near. [2] Pit, cavity. [3] First of the daytime canonical hours. [4] Vespers, evening prayer. [5] Beloved (wife or sweetheart).

Compare and contrast this folk ballad with "The Twa Corbies" (page 194).

The Demon Lover

"O where have you been, my long, long love,
   This long seven years and mair?"
"O, I'm come to seek my former vows
   Ye granted me before."

"O hold your tongue of your former vows,
　For they will breed sad strife;
O hold your tongue of your former vows,
　For I am become a wife."

He turned him right and round about,
　And the tear blinded his ee;
"I wad never hae trodden on Irish ground,
　If it had not been for thee.

"I might hae had a king's daughter,
　Far, far beyond the sea;
I might have had a king's daughter,
　Had it not been for love o thee."

"If ye might have had a king's daughter,
　Yer sel ye had to blame;
Ye might have had taken the king's daughter,
　For ye kend[1] that I was nane.[2]

"If I was to leave my husband dear,
　And my two babes also,
O what have you to take me to,
　If with you I should go?"

"I hae seven ships upon the sea—
　The eighth brought me to land—
With four-and-twenty bold mariners,
　And music on every hand."

She has taken up her two little babes,
　Kissed them baith[3] cheek and chin:
"O fair ye weel, my ain[4] two babes,
　For I'll never see you again."

She set her foot upon the ship,
　No mariners could she behold;
But the sails were o the taffetie,
　And the masts o the beaten gold.

She had not sailed a league, a league,
　A league but barely three,
When dismal grew his countenance,
　And drumlie[5] grew his ee.

They had not sailed a league, a league,
　A league but barely three,
Until she espied his cloven foot,
　And she wept right bitterlie.

"O hold your tongue of your weeping," says he,
  "Of your weeping now let me be;
I will shew you how the lilies grow
  On the banks of Italy."

"O what hills are yon, yon pleasant hills,
  That the sun shines sweetly on?"
"O yon are the hills of heaven," he said,
  "Where you will never win."

"O whaten a mountain is yon," she said,
  "All so dreary wi frost and snow?"
"O yon is the mountain of hell," he cried,
  "Where you and I will go."

He strack the tap-mast wi his hand,
  The fore-mast wi his knee,
And he brake that gallant ship in twain,
  And sank her in the sea.

                                —Anonymous

---

¹ Knew.   ² None.   ³ Both.   ⁴ Own.   ⁵ Dark.

Edward

"Why dois your brand¹ sae² drap wi bluid,
    Edward, Edward,
Why dois your brand sae drap wi bluid,
    And why sae sad gang³ yee O?"
"O I hae killed my hauke⁴ sae guid,
    Mither, mither,
O I hae killed my hauke sae guid,
    And I had nae mair bot hee O."

"Your haukis bluid was nevir sae reid,
    Edward, Edward,
Your haukis bluid was nevir sae reid,
    My deir son I tell thee O."
"O I hae killed my reid-roan steid,⁵
    Mither, mither,
O I hae killed my reid-roan steid,
    That erst was sae fair and frie O."

"Your steid was auld,⁶ and ye hae gat mair,⁷
    Edward, Edward,

Your steid was auld, and ye hae gat mair,
   Sum other dule[8] ye drie O."
"O I hae killed my fadir[9] deir,
   Mither, mither,
O I hae killed my fadir deir,
   Alas, and wae is mee O!"

"And whatten penance wul ye drie[10] for that,
   Edward, Edward?
And whatten penance will ye drie for that?
   My deir son, now tell me O."
"Ile set my feit in yonder boat,
   Mither, mither,
Ile set my feit in yonder boat,
   And Ile fare ovir the sea O."

"And what wul ye doe wi your towirs and you ha,[11]
   Edward, Edward?
And what wul ye doe wi your towirs and your ha,
   That were sae fair to see O?"
"Ile let thame stand tul they doun fa,
   Mither, mither,
Ile let thame stand tul they doun fa,
   For here nevir mair maun I bee O."

"And what wul ye leive to your bairns[12] and your wife,
   Edward, Edward?
And what wul ye leive to your bairns and your wife,
   Whan ye gang ovir the sea O?"
"The warldis[13] room, late them beg thrae life,
   Mither, mither,
The warldis room, late them beg thrae life,
   For thame nevir mair wul I see O."

"And what wul ye leive to your ain mither deir,
   Edward, Edward?
And what wul ye leive to your ain mither deir?
   My deir son, now tell me O."
"The curse of hell frae me sall[14] ye beir,
   Mither, mither,
The curse of hell frae me sall ye beir,
   Sic[15] counseils[16] ye gave to me O."

—Anonymous

---

[1] Sword. [2] So. [3] Go. [4] Hawk. [5] Steed. [6] Old. [7] More. [8] Grief.
[9] Father. [10] Undergo. [11] Hall, manor house. [12] Children. [13] World's.
[14] Shall. [15] Such. [16] Advice.

Down in Dallas

Down in Dallas, down in Dallas
Where the shadow of blood lies black
Lee Oswald nailed Jack Kennedy up
With the nail of a rifle crack.

Every big bright Cadillac stompled its brakes,
Every face in the street fell still,
While the slithering gun like a tooth of sin
Recoiled from the window sill.

In a white chrome room on a table top,
Oh, they tried all a scalpel knows
But they couldn't spell stop to that drop-by-drop
Till it bloomed to a rigid rose.

Down on the altar, down on the altar
Christ is broken to bread and wine
But each asphalt stone where the blood dropped down
Prickled into a cactus spine.

Oh down in Dallas, down in Dallas
Where the wind has to cringe tonight
Lee Oswald nailed Jack Kennedy up
On the cross of a rifle sight.

—X. J. Kennedy (1929–   )

Waist Deep in the Big Muddy

It was back in nineteen forty-two,
I was part of a good platoon.
We were on maneuvers in Loozianna,
One night by the light of the moon.
    The captain told us to ford a river,
    and that's how it all begun.
    We were knee deep in the Big Muddy,
    but the big fool said to push on.

The sergeant said, Sir, are you sure
This is the best way back to the base?
Sergeant, go on; I've forded this river
Just a mile above this place.
    It'll be a little soggy but just keep slogging
    We'll soon be on dry ground.
    We were waist deep in the Big Muddy
    And the big fool said to push on.

The sergeant said, Sir, with all this equipment
No man'll be able to swim.
Sergeant, don't be a nervous nellie
The captain said to him.
  All we need is a little determination
  Men, follow me, I'll lead on.
  We were neck deep in the Big Muddy
  And the big fool said to push on.

All at once, the moon clouded over
We heard a gurgling cry
A few seconds later, the captain's helmet
Was all that floated by.
  The sergeant said, turn around men
  I'm in charge from now on
  And we just made it out of the Big Muddy
  With the captain dead and gone.

We stripped and dived and found his body
Stuck in the old quicksand.
I guess he didn't know that the water was deeper
Than the place he'd once before been
  Another stream had joined the Big Muddy
  Just a half mile from where we'd gone.
  We were lucky to escape from the Big Muddy
  When the big fool said to push on.

Well, I'm not going to draw any moral,
I'll leave that to yourself
Maybe you're still walking, you're still talking,
And you'd like to keep your health
  But every time I read the papers
  That old feeling comes on:
  We're waste deep in the Big Muddy
  And the Big Fool says to push on.

—Peter Seeger (1919–   )

La Belle Dame Sans Merci[1]

O what can ail thee, knight at arms,
  Alone and palely loitering?
The sedge has withered from the lake,
  And no birds sing!

O what can ail thee, knight at arms,
   So haggard and so woe-begone?
The squirrel's granary is full,
   And the harvest's done.

I see a lily on thy brow,
   With anguish moist and fever dew;
And on thy cheeks a fading rose
   Fast withereth too. —

I met a lady in the meads,
   Full beautiful, a faery's child;
Her hair was long, her foot was light,
   And her eyes were wild.

I made a garland for her head,
   And bracelets, too and fragrant zone;[2]
She looked at me as she did love,
   And made sweet moan.

I set her on my pacing steed,
   And nothing else saw, all day long;
For sidelong would she bend, and sing
   A faery's song.

She found me roots of relish[3] sweet,
   And honey wild, and manna[4] dew;
And sure in language strange she said,
   "I love thee true."

She took me to her elfin grot[5]
   And there she wept and sighed full sore;
And there I shut her wild, wild eyes
   With kisses four.

And there she lullèd me asleep,
   And there I dreamed, ah woe betide!
The latest dream I ever dreamt,
   On the cold hillside.

I saw pale kings, and princes too,
   Pale warriors, death-pale were they all,
Who cried, "La belle dame sans merci
   Thee hath in thrall!"[6]

I saw their starved lips in the gloam
   With horrid warning gapèd wide—
And I awoke, and found me here,
   On the cold hill's side.

And this is why I sojourn here,
   Alone and palely loitering;
Though the sedge is withered from the lake,
   And no birds sing.

          —John Keats (1795–1821)

---

[1] The beautiful lady without pity.   [2] Belt or sash.   [3] Taste or flavor.
[4] Food miraculously supplied to the Israelites when they wandered in the wilderness.   [5] Grotto, small cave.   [6] Enslavement, bondage.

Booker T. and W. E. B.

(Booker T. Washington and W. E. B. Du Bois)

"It seems to me," said Booker T.,
"It shows a mighty lot of cheek
To study chemistry and Greek
When Mister Charlie needs a hand
To hoe the cotton on his land,
And when Miss Ann looks for a cook,
Why stick your nose inside a book?"

"I don't agree," said W. E. B.
"If I should have the drive to seek
Knowledge of chemistry or Greek,
I'll do it. Charles and Miss can look
Another place for hand or cook.
Some men rejoice in skill of hand,
And some in cultivating land,
But there are others who maintain
The right to cultivate the brain."

"It seems to me," said Booker T.,
"That all you folks have missed the boat
Who shout about the right to vote,
And spend vain days and sleepless nights
In uproar over civil rights.
Just keep your mouths shut, do not grouse,
But work, and save, and buy a house."

"I don't agree," said W. E. B.,
"For what can property avail
If dignity and justice fail?
Unless you help to make the laws,
They'll steal your house with trumped-up clause.
A rope's as tight, a fire as hot,
No matter how much cash you've got.

Speak soft, and try your little plan,
But as for me, I'll be a man."

"It seems to me," said Booker T.—

"I don't agree,"
Said W. E. B.

—Dudley Randall (1914–   )

Crazy Jane Talks with the Bishop

I met the Bishop on the road
And much said he and I.
"Those breasts are flat and fallen now,
Those veins must soon be dry;
Live in a heavenly mansion,
Not in some foul sty."

"Fair and foul are near of kin,
And fair needs foul," I cried.
"My friends are gone, but that's a truth
Nor grave nor bed denied,
Learned in bodily lowliness
And in the heart's pride.

"A woman can be proud and stiff
When on love intent;
But Love has pitched his mansion in
The place of excrement;
For nothing can be sole or whole
That has not been rent."

—William Butler Yeats (1865–1939)

An Ex-Judge at the Bar

Bartender, make it straight and make it two—
One for the you in me and the me in you.
Now let us put our heads together: one
Is half enough for malice, sense, or fun.

I know, Bartender, yes, I know when the Law
Should wag its tail or rip with fang and claw.
When Pilate washed his hands, that neat event
Set for us judges a Caesarean precedent.

What I shall tell you now, as man is man,
You'll find in neither Bible nor Koran.
It happened after my return from France
At the bar in Tony's Lady of Romance.

We boys drank pros and cons, sang *Dixie;* and then,
The bar a Sahara, we pledged to meet again.
But lo, on the bar there stood in naked scorn
The Goddess Justice, like September Morn.

Who blindfolds Justice on the courthouse roof
While the lawyers weave the sleight-of-hand of proof?
I listened, Bartender, with my heart and head,
As the Goddess Justice unbandaged her eyes and said:

"To make the world safe for Democracy,
You lost a leg in Flanders fields—*oui, oui?*
To gain the judge's seat, you twined the noose
That swung the Negro higher than a goose."

Bartender, who has dotted every *i?*
Crossed every *t?* Put legs on every *y?*
Therefore, I challenged her: "Lay on, Macduff,
And damned be him who first cries, 'Hold, enough!' "

The boys guffawed, and Justice began to laugh
Like a maniac on a broken phonograph.
Bartender, make it straight and make it three—
One for the Negro . . . one for you and me.

                    —Melvin B. Tolson (1898–1966)

The Bishop Orders His Tomb at Saint Praxed's Church[1]

Rome, 15–

Vanity, saith the preacher,[2] vanity!
Draw round my bed: is Anselm keeping back?
Nephews—sons mine . . . ah God, I know not! Well—
She, men would have to be your mother once,
Old Gandolf[3] envied me, so fair she was!
What's done is done, and she is dead beside,
Dead long ago, and I am Bishop since,
And as she died so must we die ourselves,
And thence ye may perceive the world's a dream.
Life, how and what is it? As here I lie
In this state-chamber, dying by degrees,
Hours and long hours in the dead night, I ask

"Do I live, am I dead?" Peace, peace seems all.
Saint Praxed's ever was the church for peace;
And so, about this tomb of mine. I fought
With tooth and nail to save my niche, ye know:
—Old Gandolf cozened me, despite my care;
Shrewd was that snatch from out the corner South
He graced his carrion with, God curse the same!
Yet still my niche is not so cramped but thence
One sees the pulpit o' the epistle-side,
And somewhat of the choir, those silent seats,
And up into the aery dome where live
The angels, and a sunbeam's sure to lurk:
And I shall fill my slab of basalt there,
And 'neath my tabernacle take my rest,
With those nine columns round me, two and two,
The odd one at my feet where Anselm stands:
Peach-blossom marble all, the rare, the ripe
As fresh-poured red wine of a mighty pulse
—Old Gandolf with his paltry onion-stone,
Put me where I may look at him! True peach,
Rosy and flawless: how I earned the prize!
Draw close: that conflagration of my church
—What then? So much was saved if aught were missed!
My sons, ye would not be my death? Go dig
The white-grape vineyard where the oil-press stood,
Drop water gently till the surface sinks,
And if ye find . . . ah God, I know not, I! . . .
Bedded in store of rotten fig-leaves soft,
And corded up in a tight olive-frail,[4]
Some lump, ah God, of *lapis lazuli,*
Big as a Jew's head cut off at the nape,
Blue as a vein o'er the Madonna's breast—
Sons, all have I bequeathed you, villas, all,
That brave Frascati villa with its bath—
So, let the blue lump poise between my knees,
Like God the Father's globe on both his hands
Ye worship in the Jesu Church so gay,
For Gandolf shall not choose but see and burst!
Swift as a weaver's shuttle fleet our years;[5]
Man goeth to the grave, and where is he?
Did I say basalt for my slab, sons? Black—
'Twas ever antique-black I meant! How else
Shall ye contrast my frieze to come beneath?
The bas-relief in bronze ye promised me,
Those Pans and Nymphs ye wot of, and perchance
Some tripod, thyrsus, with a vase or so,
The Saviour at his sermon on the mount,

St. Praxed in a glory, and one Pan
Ready to twitch the Nymph's last garment off,
And Moses with the tables[6] . . . but I know
Ye mark me not! What do they whisper thee,
Child of my bowels, Anselm? Ah, ye hope
To revel down my villas while I gasp
Bricked o'er with beggar's moldy travertine
Which Gandolf from his tomb-top chuckles at!
Nay, boys, ye love me—all of jasper, then!
'Tis jasper ye stand pledged to, lest I grieve
My bath must needs be left behind, alas!
One block, pure green as a pistachio-nut,
There's plenty jasper somewhere in the world—
And have I not St. Praxed's ear to pray
Horses for ye, and brown Greek manuscripts,
And mistresses with great smooth marbly limbs?
—That's if ye carve my epitaph aright,
Choice Latin, picked phrase, Tully's every word,
No gaudy ware like Gandolf's second line—
Tully, my masters? Ulpian[7] serves his need!
And then how I shall lie through centuries,
And hear the blessèd mutter of the mass,
And see God made and eaten all day long,
And feel the steady candle-flame, and taste
Good strong thick stupefying incense-smoke!
For as I lie here, hours of the dead night,
Dying in state and by such slow degrees,
I fold my arms as if they clasped a crook,
And stretch my feet forth straight as stone can point
And let the bedclothes for a mortcloth drop
Into great laps and folds of sculptor's-work:
And as yon tapers dwindle, and strange thoughts
Grow, with a certain humming in my ears,
About the life before I lived this life,
And this life too, popes, cardinals and priests,
Saint Praxed at his sermon on the mount,
Your tall pale mother with her talking eyes,
And new-found agate urns as fresh as day,
And marble's language, Latin pure, discreet,
—Aha, ELUCESCEBAT[8] quoth our friend?
No Tully, said I, Ulpian at the best!
Evil and brief hath been my pilgrimage.
All lapis, all, sons! Else I give the Pope
My villas: will ye ever eat my heart?
Ever your eyes were as a lizard's quick,
They glitter like your mother's for my soul,
Or ye would heighten my impoverished frieze,

Piece out its starved design, and fill my vase
With grapes, and add a vizor and a Term,
And to the tripod ye would tie a lynx
That in his struggle throws the thyrsus down,
To comfort me on my entablature
Whereon I am to lie till I must ask
"Do I live, am I dead?" There, leave me, there!
For ye have stabbed me with ingratitude
To death—ye wish it—God, ye wish it! Stone—
Gritstone, a-crumble! Clammy squares which sweat
As if the corpse they keep were oozing through—
And no more lapis to delight the world!
Well, go! I bless ye. Fewer tapers there,
But in a row: and, going, turn your backs
—Ay, like departing altar-ministrants,
And leave me in my church, the church for peace,
That I may watch at leisure if he leers—
Old Gandolf, at me, from his onion-stone,
As still he envied me, so fair she was!

—Robert Browning (1812–1889)

---

[1] St. Praxed's is in Rome, but the bishop and the tomb are imaginary.
[2] Ecclesiastes 1:2.   [3] His predecessor.   [4] An olive basket.   [5] Job 7:6.
[6] Exodus 24–34.   [7] A Roman jurist with a fine Ciceronian style.   [8] "He was famous," but the bishop prefers the classic form *elucebat*.

The Patriot

An Old Story

I

It was roses, roses, all the way,
    With myrtle mixed in my path like mad;
The house-roofs seemed to heave and sway,
    The church-spires flamed, such flags they had,
A year ago on this very day.

II

The air broke into a mist with bells,
    The old walls rocked with the crowd and cries.
Had I said, "Good folk, mere noise repels—
    But give me your sun from yonder skies!"
They had answered, "And afterward, what else?"

III

Alack, it was I who leaped at the sun
    To give it my loving friends to keep!

Nought man could do, have I left undone;
   And you see my harvest, what I reap
This very day, now a year is run.

IV

There's nobody on the house-tops now—
   Just a palsied few at the windows set;
For the best of the sight is, all allow,
   At the Shambles' Gate—or better yet,
By the very scaffold's foot, I trow.

V

I go in the rain, and, more than needs,
   A rope cuts both my wrists behind;
And I think, by the feel, my forehead bleeds,
   For they fling, whoever has a mind,
Stones at me for my year's misdeeds.

VI

Thus I entered, and thus I go!
   In triumphs, people have dropped down dead.
"Paid by the world, what dost thou owe
   Me?"—God might question; now instead,
'Tis God shall repay: I am safer so.

          —Robert Browning (1812–1889)

The following three poems are from the *Spoon River Anthology.*

Reuben Pantier

Well, Emily Sparks, your prayers were not wasted,
Your love was not all in vain.
I owe whatever I was in life
To your hope that would not give me up,
To your love that saw me still as good.
Dear Emily Sparks, let me tell you the story.
I pass the effect of my father and mother;
The milliner's daughter made me trouble
And out I went in the world,
Where I passed through every peril known
Of wine and women and joy of life.
One night, in a room in the Rue de Rivoli,
I was drinking wine with a black-eyed cocotte,
And the tears swam into my eyes.
She thought they were amorous tears and smiled
For thought of her conquest over me.

But my soul was three thousand miles away,
In the days when you taught me in Spoon River.
And just because you no more could love me,
Nor pray for me, nor write me letters
The eternal silence of you spoke instead.
And the black-eyed cocotte took the tears for hers,
As well as the deceiving kisses I gave her.
Somehow, from the hour, I had a new vision—
Dear Emily Sparks!

Emily Sparks

Where is my boy, my boy—
In what far part of the world?
The boy I loved best of all in the school?—
I, the teacher, the old maid, the virgin heart,
Who made them all my children.
Did I know my boy aright,
Thinking of him as spirit aflame,
Active, ever aspiring?
Oh, boy, boy, for whom I prayed and prayed
In many a watchful hour at night,
Do you remember the letter I wrote you
Of the beautiful love of Christ?
And whether you ever took it or not,
My boy, wherever you are,
Work for your soul's sake,
That all the clay of you, all the dross of you,
May yield to the fire of you,
Till the fire is nothing but light! . . .
Nothing but light!

Judge Selah Lively

Suppose you stood just five feet two,
And had worked your way as a grocery clerk,
Studying law by candle light
Until you became an attorney at law?
And then suppose through your diligence,
And regular church attendance,
You became attorney for Thomas Rhodes,
Collecting notes and mortgages,
And representing all the widows
In the Probate Court? And through it all
They jeered at your size, and laughed at your clothes

And your polished boots? And then suppose
You became the County Judge?
And Jefferson Howard and Kinsey Keene,
And Harmon Whitney, and all the giants
Who had sneered at you, were forced to stand
Before the bar and say "Your Honor"—
Well, don't you think it was natural
That I made it hard for them?

—Edgar Lee Masters (1869–1950)

These three characters are from Robinson's New England Tilbury Town.

How Annandale Went Out

"They called it Annandale—and I was there
To flourish, to find words, and to attend:
Liar, physician, hypocrite, and friend,
I watched him; and the sight was not so fair
As one or two that I have seen elsewhere:
An apparatus not for me to mend—
A wreck, with hell between him and the end,
Remained of Annandale; and I was there.

"I knew the ruin as I knew the man;
So put the two together, if you can,
Remembering the worst you know of me.
Now view yourself as I was, on the spot—
With a slight kind of engine. Do you see?
Like this . . . You wouldn't hang me? I thought not."

Cliff Klingenhagen

Cliff Klingenhagen had me in to dine
With him one day; and after soup and meat,
And all the other things there were to eat,
Cliff took two glasses and filled one with wine
And one with wormwood. Then, without a sign
For me to choose at all, he took the draught
Of bitterness himself, and lightly quaffed
It off, and said the other one was mine.

And when I asked him what the deuce he meant
By doing that, he only looked at me
And smiled, and said it was a way of his.

And though I know the fellow, I have spent
Long time a-wondering when I shall be
As happy as Cliff Klingenhagen is.

Charles Carville's Eyes

A melancholy face Charles Carville had,
But not so melancholy as it seemed,
When once you knew him, for his mouth redeemed
His insufficient eyes, forever sad:

In them there was no life-glimpse, good or bad,
Nor joy nor passion in them ever gleamed;
His mouth was all of him that ever beamed,
His eyes were sorry, but his mouth was glad.

He never was a fellow that said much,
And half of what he did say was not heard
By many of us: we were out of touch
With all his whims and all his theories
Till he was dead, so those blank eyes of his
Might speak them. Then we heard them, every word.

—Edwin Arlington Robinson (1889–1935)

Caboose Thoughts

It's going to come out all right—do you know?
The sun, the birds, the grass—they know.
They get along—and we'll get along.

Some days will be rainy and you will sit waiting
And the letter you wait for won't come,
And I will sit watching the sky tear off gray and gray
And the letter I wait for won't come.

There will be ac-ci-dents.
I know ac-ci-dents are coming.
Smash-ups, signals wrong, washouts, trestles rotten,
Red and yellow ac-ci-dents.
But somehow and somewhere the end of the run
The train gets put together again
And the caboose and the green tail lights
Fade down the right of way like a new white hope.

I never heard a mockingbird in Kentucky
Spilling its heart in the morning.

I never saw the snow on Chimborazo.
It's a high white Mexican hat, I hear.

I never had supper with Abe Lincoln,
Nor a dish of soup with Jim Hill.

But I've been around.
I know some of the boys here who can go a little.
I know girls good for a burst of speed any time.

I heard Williams and Walker
Before Walker died in the bughouse.

I knew a mandolin player
Working in a barber shop in an Indiana town,
And he thought he had a million dollars.

I knew a hotel girl in Des Moines.
She had eyes; I saw her and said to myself
The sun rises and the sun sets in her eyes.
I was her steady and her heart went pit-a-pat,
We took away the money for a prize waltz at a Brotherhood
        dance.
She had eyes; she was safe as the bridge over the
        Mississippi at Burlington; I married her.

Last summer we took the cushions going west.
Pike's Peak is a big old stone, believe me.
It's fastened down; something you can count on.

It's going to come out all right—do you know?
The sun, the birds, the grass—they know.
They get along—and we'll get along.

—Carl Sandburg (1878–1967)

The Lifeguard

In a stable of boats I lie still,
From all sleeping children hidden.
The leap of a fish from its shadow
Makes the whole lake instantly tremble.
With my foot on the water, I feel
The moon outside

Take on the utmost of its power.
I rise and go out through the boats.
I set my broad sole upon silver,

On the skin of the sky, on the moonlight,
Stepping outward from earth onto water
In quest of the miracle

This village of children believed
That I could perform as I dived
For one who had sunk from my sight.
I saw his cropped haircut go under.
I leapt, and my steep body flashed
Once, in the sun.

Dark drew all the light from my eyes.
Like a man who explores his death
By the pull of his slow-moving shoulders,
I hung head down in the cold,
Wide-eyed, contained, and alone
Among the weeds.

And my fingertips turned into stone
From clutching immovable blackness.
Time after time I leapt upward
Exploding in breath, and fell back
From the change in the children's faces
At my defeat.

Beneath them, I swam to the boathouse
With only life in my arms
To wait for the lake to shine back
At the risen moon with such power
That my steps on the light of the ripples
Might be sustained.

Beneath me is nothing but brightness
Like the ghost of a snowfield in summer.
As I move toward the center of the lake,
Which is also the center of the moon,
I am thinking of how I may be
The savior of one

Who has already died in my care.
The dark trees fade from around me.
The moon's dust hovers together.
I call softly out, and the child's
Voice answers through blinding water.
Patiently, slowly,

He rises, dilating to break
The surface of stone with his forehead.
He is one I do not remember

Having ever seen in his life.
The ground that I stand on is trembling
Upon his smile.

I wash the black mud from my hands.
On a light given off by the grave,
I kneel in the quick of the moon
At the heart of a distant forest
And hold in my arms a child
Of water, water, water.

—James Dickey (1923–   )

We live but a fraction of our life. Why do we not let on the flood, raise the gates, and set all our wheels in motion? He that hath ears to hear, let him hear.

—Henry David Thoreau

15
Comparing and Contrasting Poems

In the history of mankind, poets have dealt with every aspect of human experience. In every age poets have dealt with certain universal themes—love, war, nature, beauty, mortality—reinterpreting them in the light of their contemporary vision and in the language of their period. For the interested reader it is profitable to consider the treatment that different poets give similar subject matter. Such a study will enable one to broaden his range of enjoyment, to differentiate good from lesser poems, to respond to the total experience of a poem, and to clarify some of the principles of poetic art.

To some extent this comparative approach to the study of poetry has already been presented in previous chapters. The *carpe diem* motif ("seize and enjoy the day") has been treated by Herrick in his "To the Virgins, to Make Much of Time" (page 77) and by Marvell in his "To His Coy Mistress" (page 137). Emily Dickinson and Stephen Spender have presented contrasting views of the railroad in their respective poems "I Like to See It Lap the Miles" (page 35) and "The Express" (page 34). The theme of the reaction to the death of a child is handled sentimentally in "Dead Cousin" (page 130) and brilliantly in "Bells for John Whiteside's Daughter" (page 130). In effective but different ways Karl Shapiro, Robert Frost, and Thomas Hardy have treated the theme of accident as a tragic fact in human existence.

To provide further opportunity to pursue this approach to the understanding and enjoyment of poetry, the following groups of poems dealing with related themes are included: (1) Man and Nature,

(2) Snow, (3) Time and Beauty, (4) Mother, (5) Success and Failure, (6) The Oppressed, (7) War, (8) Death, (9) Tributes to Milton, (10) Music, (11) Art, (12) Science, and (13) The End of the World. As a final exercise, it is suggested that the reader structure his own approach in his study and comparison of these poems.

Nature and Man

Lines Written in Early Spring

I heard a thousand blended notes
While in a grove I sate reclined,
In that sweet mood when pleasant thoughts
Bring sad thoughts to the mind.

To her fair works did Nature link
The human soul that through me ran;
And much it grieved my heart to think
What man has made of man.

Through primrose tufts, in that sweet bower,
The periwinkle trailed its wreaths;
And 'tis my faith that every flower
Enjoys the air it breathes.

The birds around me hopped and played,
Their thoughts I cannot measure,—
But the least motion which they made,
It seemed a thrill of pleasure.

The budding twigs spread out their fan
To catch the breezy air;
And I must think, do all I can,
That there was pleasure there.

If this belief from heaven be sent,
If such be Nature's holy plan,
Have I not reason to lament
What man has made of man?

                —William Wordsworth (1770–1850)

In Harmony with Nature

To a Preacher

"In harmony with Nature?" Restless fool,
Who with such heat dost preach what were to thee,

When true, the last impossibility—
To be like Nature strong, like Nature cool!

Know, man hath all which Nature hath, but more,
And in that *more* lie all his hopes of good.
Nature is cruel, man is sick of blood;
Nature is stubborn, man would fain adore;

Nature is fickle, man hath need of rest;
Nature forgives no debt, and fears no grave;
Man would be mild, and with safe conscience blest.

Man must begin, know this, where Nature ends;
Nature and man can never be fast friends.
Fool, if thou canst not pass her, rest her slave!

—Matthew Arnold (1822–1888)

In a Wood

Pale beech and pine so blue,
    Set in one clay,
Bough to bough cannot you
    Live out your day?
When the rains skim and skip,
Why mar sweet comradship,
Blighting with poison-drip
    Neighbourly spray?

Heart-halt and spirit-lame,
    City-opprest,
Unto this wood I came
    As to a nest;
Dreaming that sylvan peace
Offered the harrowed ease—
Nature a soft release
    From men's unrest.

But, having entered in,
    Great growths and small
Show them to men akin—
    Combatants all!
Sycamore shoulders oak,
Bines the slim sapling yoke,
Ivy-spun halters choke
    Elms stout and tall.

Touches from ash, O wych,[1]
    Sting you like scorn!

You, too, brave hollies, twitch
 Sidelong from thorn.
Even the rank poplars bear
Lothly a rival's air,
Cankering in black despair
 If overborne.

Since, then, no grace I find
 Taught me of trees,
Turn I back to my kind,
 Worthy as these.
There at least smiles abound,
There discourse trills around,
There, now and then, are found
 Life-loyalties.

—Thomas Hardy (1840–1928)

---

¹ A species of elm.

Foxtail Pine

bark smells like pineapple: Jeffries
cones prick your hand: Ponderosa

nobody knows what they are, saying
"needles three to a bunch."

          turpentine tin can hangers
          high lead riggers

"the true fir cone stands straight,
the doug fir cone hangs down."

—wild pigs eat acorns in those hills
cascara cutters
tanbark oak bark gatherers
myrtlewood burl bowl-makers
little cedar dolls,
               baby girl born from the split crotch
                    of a plum
               daughter of the moon—

foxtail pine with a
clipped curve-back cluster of tight
          five-needle bunches
     the rought red bark scale

and jigsaw pieces sloughed off
               scattered on the ground.
—what am I doing saying "foxtail pine"?

those conifers whose home was ice
age tundra, taiga, they of the
          naked sperm
do whitebark pine and white pine seem the same?

      a sort of tree
      its leaves are needles
      like a fox's brush
(I call him fox because he looks that way)
      and call this other thing, a
          foxtail pine.

               —Gary Snyder (1930–   )

Snow

The Snow-Storm

Announced by all the trumpets of the sky,
Arrives the snow, and, driving o'er the fields,
Seems nowhere to alight: the whited air
Hides hills and woods, the river, and the heaven,
And veils the farm-house at the garden's end.
The sled and traveller stopped, the courier's feet
Delayed, all friends shut out, the housemates sit
Around the radiant fireplace, enclosed
In a tumultuous privacy of storm.

      Come see the north wind's masonry.
Out of an unseen quarry evermore
Furnished with tile, the fierce artificer
Curves his white bastions with projected roof
Round every windward stake, or tree, or door.
Speeding, the myriad-handed, his wild work
So fanciful, so savage, nought cares he
For number or proportion. Mockingly,
On coop or kennel he hangs Parian wreaths;
A swan-like form invests the hidden thorn;
Fills up the farmer's lane from wall to wall,
Maugre the farmer's sighs; and at the gate
A tapering turret overtops the work.
And when his hours are numbered, and the world
Is all his own, retiring, as he were not,

Leaves, when the sun appears, astonished Art
To mimic in slow structures, stone by stone,
Built in an age, the mad wind's night-work,
The frolic architecture of the snow.

—Ralph Waldo Emerson (1803–1882)

Snow in the Suburbs

Every branch big with it,
Bent every twig with it;
Every fork like a white web-foot;
Every street and pavement mute:
Some flakes have lost their way, and grope back upward, when
Meeting those meandering down they turn and descend again.
The palings are glued together like a wall,
And there is no waft of wind with the fleecy fall.

A sparrow enters the tree,
Whereon immediately
A snow-lump thrice his own slight size
Descends on him and showers his head and eyes.
And overturns him,
And near inurns[1] him,
And lights on a nether twig, when its brush
Starts off a volley of other lodging lumps with a rush.

The steps are a blanched slope,
Up which, with feeble hope,
A black cat comes, wide-eyed and thin;
And we take him in.

—Thomas Hardy (1840–1928)

---

[1] Buries.

Snow

The room was suddenly rich and the great bay-window was
Spawning snow and pink roses against it
Soundlessly collateral and incompatible:
World is suddener than we fancy it.

World is crazier and more of it than we think,
Incorrigibly plural. I peel and portion
A tangerine and spit the pips and feel
The drunkenness of things being various.

And the fire flames with a bubbling sound for world
Is more spiteful and gay than one supposes—
On the tongue on the eyes on the ears in the palms of
     your hands—
There is more than glass between the snow
     and the huge roses.

                —Louis MacNeice (1907–   )

Time and Beauty

Discordants—III

Dead Cleopatra lies in a crystal casket,
Wrapped and spiced by the cunningest of hands.
Around her neck they have put a golden necklace,
Her tatbebs,[1] it is said, are worn with sands.

Dead Cleopatra was once revered in Egypt,
Warm-eyed she was, this princess of the South.
Now she is very old and dry and faded,
With black bitumen they have sealed up her mouth.

O sweet clean earth, from whom the green blade cometh!
When we are dead, my best belovèd and I,
Close well above us, that we may rest forever,
Sending up grass and blossoms to the sky.

                Conrad Aiken (1889–   )

------

[1] Sandals.

Blue Girls

Twirling your blue skirts, travelling the sward
Under the towers of your seminary,
Go listen to your teachers old and contrary
Without believing a word.

Tie the white fillets then about your lustrous hair
And think no more of what will come to pass
Than bluebirds that go walking on the grass
And chattering on the air.

Practise your beauty, blue girls, before it fail;
And I will cry with my loud lips and publish
Beauty which all our power shall never establish,
It is so frail.

For I could tell you a story which is true;
I know a lady with a terrible tongue,
Blear eyes fallen from blue,
All her perfections tarnished—and yet it is not long
Since she was lovelier than any of you.

—John Crowe Ransom (1888–   )

Mother

To My Mother

Because I feel that, in the Heavens above,
    The angels, whispering to one another,
Can find, among their burning terms of love,
    None so devotional as that of "Mother",
Therefore by that dear name I long have called you—
    You who are more than mother unto me,
And fill my heart of hearts, where Death installed you
    In setting my Virginia's spirit free.
My mother—my own mother, who died early,
    Was but the mother of myself; but you
Are mother to the one I loved so dearly,
    And thus are dearer than the mother I knew
By that infinity with which my wife
    Was dearer to my soul than its soul-life.

—Edgar Allan Poe (1809–1849)

Sonnet to My Mother

Most near, most dear, most loved and most far,
Under the window where I often found her
Sitting as huge as Asia, seismic with laughter,
Gin and chicken helpless in her Irish hand,
Irresistible as Rabelais but most tender for
The lame dogs and hurt birds that surround her,—
She is a procession no one can follow after
But be like a little dog following a brass band.

She will not glance up at the bomber or condescend
To drop her gin and scuttle to a cellar,
But lean on the mahogany table like a mountain
Whom only faith can move, and so I send
O all my faith and all my love to tell her
That she will move from mourning into morning.

—George Barker (1913–   )

My Mother

My mother writes from Trenton,
a comedian to the bone
but underneath, serious
and all heart. "Honey," she says,
"be a mensch and Mary too,
its no good to worry, you
are doing the best you can
your Dad and everyone
thinks you turned out very well
as long as you pay your bills
nobody can say a word
you can tell them to drop dead
so save a dollar it can't
hurt—remember Frank you went
to highschool with? he still lives
with his wife's mother, his wife
works while he writes his books and
did he ever sell a one
the four kids run around naked
36 and he's never had,
you'll forgive my expression
even a pot to piss in
or a window to throw it,
such a smart boy he couldnt
read the footprints on the wall
honey you think you know all
the answers you dont, please try
to put some money away
believe me it wouldn't hurt
artist shmartist life's too short
for that kind of, forgive me,
horseshit, I know what you want
better than you, all that counts
is to make a good living
and the best of everything,
as Sholem Aleichem said
he was a great writer did
you ever read his books dear,
you should make what he makes a year
anyway he says some place
Poverty is no disgrace
but its no honor either
that's what I say,
                    love,
                       Mother"

—Robert Mezey (1935–   )

Success and Failure

Success Is Counted Sweetest

Success is counted sweetest
By those who ne'er succeed.
To comprehend a nectar
Requires sorest need.

Not one of the purple Host
Who took the Flag today
Can tell the definition
So clear of Victory

As he defeated—dying—
On whose forbidden ear
The distant strains of triumph
Burst agonized and clear!

—Emily Dickinson (1830–1886)

Life in a Love

Escape me?
Never—
Beloved!
While I am I, and you are you,
So long as the world contains us both,
Me the loving and you the loth,
While the one eludes, must the other pursue.
My life is a fault at last, I fear:
It seems too much like a fate, indeed!
Though I do my best I shall scarce succeed.
But what if I fail of my purpose here?
It is but to keep the nerves at strain,
To dry one's eyes and laugh at a fall,
And, baffled, get up and begin again,—
So the chase takes up one's life, that's all.
While, look but once from your farthest bound
At me so deep in the dust and dark,
No sooner the old hope goes to ground
Than a new one, straight to the self-same mark,
I shape me—
Ever
Removed!

—Robert Browning (1812–1889)

The Last Word

Creep into thy narrow bed,
Creep, and let no more be said!
Vain thy onset! all stands fast.
Thou thyself must break at last.

Let the long contention cease!
Geese are swans, and swans are geese.
Let them have it how they will!
Thou art tired; best be still.

They out-talk'd thee, hiss'd thee, tore thee?
Better men fared thus before thee;
Fired their ringing shot and pass'd,
Hotly charged—and sank at last.

Charge once more, then, and be dumb!
Let the victors, when they come,
When the forts of folly fall,
Find thy body by the wall!

    —Matthew Arnold (1822–1888)

To a Friend Whose Work Has Come to Nothing

Now all the truth is out,
Be secret and take defeat
From any brazen throat,
For how can you compete,
Being honour bred, with one
Who, were it proved he lies,
Were neither shamed in his own
Nor in his neighbours' eyes?
Bred to a harder thing
Than Triumph, turn away
And like a laughing string
Whereon mad fingers play
Amid a place of stone,
Be secret and exult,
Because of all things known
That is most difficult.

—William Butler Yeats (1865–1939)

The Oppressed

Song to the Men of England

I

Men of England, wherefore plough
For the lords who lay ye low?
Wherefore weave with toil and care
The rich robes your tyrants wear?

II

Wherefore feed, and clothe, and save,
From the cradle to the grave,
Those ungrateful drones who would
Drain your sweat—nay, drink your blood?

III

Wherefore, Bees of England, forge
Many a weapon, chain, and scourge,
That these stingless drones may spoil
The forced produce of your toil?

IV

Have ye leisure, comfort, calm,
Shelter, food, love's gentle balm?
Or what is it ye buy so dear
With your pain and with your fear?

V

The seed ye sow, another reaps;
The wealth ye find, another keeps;
The robes ye weave, another wears;
The arms ye forge, another bears.

VI

Sow seed,—but let no tyrant reap;
Find wealth,—let no imposter heap;
Weave robes,—let not the idle wear;
Forge arms,—in your defence to bear.

VII

Shrink to your cellars, holes, and cells;
In halls ye deck another dwells.
Why shake the chains ye wrought? Ye see
The steel ye tempered glance on ye.

VIII

With plough and spade, and hoe and loom,
Trace your grave, and build your tomb,
And weave your winding-sheet, till fair
England be your sepulchre.

—Percy Bysshe Shelley (1792–1822)

(Harlem)

What happens to a dream deferred?

Does it dry up
like a raisin in the sun?

Or fester like a sore—
And then run?
Does it stink like rotten meat?
Or crust and sugar over—
like a syrupy sweet?

Maybe it just sags
like a heavy load.

Or does it explode?

—Langston Hughes (1902–1967)

Same in Blues

I said to my baby,
Baby, take it slow.
I can't, she said, I can't!
I got to go!

> *There's a certain*
> *amount of traveling*
> *in a dream deferred.*

Lulu said to Leonard,
I want a diamond ring.
Leonard said to Lulu,
You won't get a goddamn thing!

> *A certain*
> *amount of nothing*
> *in a dream deferred.*

Daddy, daddy, daddy,
All I want is you.
You can have me, baby—
but my lovin' days is through.

> *A certain*
> *amount of impotence*
> *in a dream deferred.*

Three parties
On my party line—
But that third party,
Lord, ain't mine!

> *There's liable*
> *to be confusion*
> *in a dream deferred.*

From river to river,
Uptown and down,
There's liable to be confusion
when a dream gets kicked around.

—Langston Hughes (1902–1967)

War

Anthem for Doomed Youth

What passing-bells for these who die as cattle?
Only the monstrous anger of the guns.
Only the stuttering rifles' rapid rattle
Can patter out their hasty orisons.
No mockeries for them; no prayers nor bells,
Nor any voice of mourning save the choirs,—
The shrill, demented choirs of wailing shells;
And bugles calling for them from sad shires.

What candles may be held to speed them all?
Not in the hands of boys, but in their eyes
Shall shine the holy glimmers of good-byes.
The pallor of girls' brows shall be their pall;
Their flowers the tenderness of patient minds,
And each slow dusk a drawing-down of blinds.

—Wilfred Owen (1893–1918)

The Man He Killed

"Had he and I but met
    By some old ancient inn,
We should have sat us down to wet
    Right many a nipperkin!

"But ranged as infantry,
    And staring face to face,
I shot at him as he at me,
    And killed him in his place.

"I shot him dead because—
    Because he was my foe,
Just so: my foe of course he was;
    That's clear enough; although

"He thought he'd 'list, perhaps,
    Off-hand like—just as I;
Was out of work, had sold his traps—
    No other reason why.

"Yes; quaint and curious war is!
    You shoot a fellow down
You'd treat if met where any bar is,
    Or help to half-a-crown."

—Thomas Hardy (1840–1928)

A Refusal to Mourn the Death, by Fire, of a Child in London

Never until the mankind making
Bird beast and flower
Fathering and all humbling darkness
Tells with silence the last light breaking
And the still hour
Is come of the sea tumbling in harness

And I must enter again the round
Zion of the water bead
And the synagogue of the ear of corn
Shall I let pray the shadow of a sound
Or sow my salt seed
In the least valley of sackcloth to mourn

The majesty and burning of the child's death.
I shall not murder
The mankind of her going with a grave truth
Nor blaspheme down the stations of the breath
With any further
Elegy of innocence and youth.

Deep with the first dead lies London's daughter,
Robed in the long friends,
The grains beyond age, the dark veins of her mother,
Secret by the unmourning water
Of the riding Thames.
After the first death, there is no other.

—Dylan Thomas (1914–1953)

On a Child Burned to Death in Vietnam

(man' ə)
manna – Bible food
miraculously provided
for the Israelites in
the wilderness /
divine aid /
anything badly needed
which comes miraculously

This is a child that was burned by napalm that fell down
on her village out of a clear sky at evening
It fell as freely as the manna that is said to have fallen
from heaven on the Israelites perplexed in the desert
The analogy is of course incorrect for manna is said to nourish
both spirit and flesh and is believed to come from Jehovah
whereas napalm burns at 1200° Fahrenheit and sticks to the
skin which it causes to melt or to turn to an ashy and brittle
crust And it is known to come from America

Here then Look at the child where she lies still on a cot
in a hot ramshackle hospital long on good will devoid of supplies
Her mother beside her is waving a sheet of tired newsprint
as though waving farewell and farewell She is trying to keep off
the flies The child's eyes are brown they stare straight up It took
20 hours to get her here to lie on this cot with nothing but pity
to help her No antibiotics no plasma nothing but vaseline jelly
The flesh of her chin has flowed down on her chest her mouth
is unable to close Her still body

is pitted and raked like the moon's face or a cold battlefield
after the guns Yes her father was killed It is clear she too will
die before long The spokesmen hired to express official
regret promise inquiries and recite the usual quote from General
Sherman will then pay the widow a condolence payment or is it
a prize of 66 dollars in Vietnamese money Not what you might
call
an assessed valuation but a gesture literally profane
" 'Imagine' said Ivan 'that you are creating a fabric of human
destiny with the object of making men

happy in the end but that it was necessary and inevitable
to torture to death only one tiny creature and to found that edi-
fice on its unavenged tears Would you consent to be the architect
on those conditions Tell me and tell the truth'   'No
I wouldn't consent' said Alyosha softly" But the American people
consent If not actively then by default with silence if not in
words out of ignorance apathy self-love and fear Compassion
and courage in danger of being drowned in the warm oil
of consent the consent of Americans

neither quiet nor ugly just drifting who watch at eleven in their
ghost living rooms the exciting war films from Vietnam
8000 light years away and consent to the death of the child for
These people must be burned to be saved from the Communist
        heresy
And wait through the newscast with opium eyes for the weather
magician to come on with glass map horn-rims and chalk-talk
to tell what they "truly desire to know" which is that it will be
sunny and warmer on Sunday the high in the 40's and only a
10% chance of rain falling down from the sky

                              —Rudolph von Abele (1922–   )

To a Commencement of Scoundrels

My boys, they lied to you.
The world by definition stinks
of Cain, no matter what
your teachers told you. Heroes
and the fools of God may rise
like accidental green
on gray saharas, but the sand
stays smotheringly near.

Deny me if you can. Already
you are turning into personnel,
manpower, figures on a list
of earners, voters, prayers,
soldiers, payers, sums
of population tamed with forms:
last name, middle name, first name—
telephone—date of birth—

home address—age—hobbies—
experience. Tell them the truth.
Your name is legion. You
are aged a million. Tell

them that. Say you breathe
between appointments: first day,
last day. The rest is no
one's business. Boys, the time

is prime for prophecy.
Books break down their bookends.
Paintings burst their frames.
The world is more than reason's
peanut. Homer sang it real.
Goya painted it, and Shakespeare
staged it for the pelting rinds
of every groundling of the Globe.

Wake up! Tonight the lions
hunt in Kenya. They
can eat a man. Rockets
are spearing through the sky.
They can blast a man to nothing.
Rumors prowl like rebellions.
They can knife a man. No one
survives for long, my boys.

Flesh is always in season,
lusted after, gunned, grenaded,
tabulated through machines,
incinerated, beaten to applause,
anesthetized, autopsied, mourned.
The blood of Troy beats on
in Goya's paintings and the truce
of Lear. Reason yourselves

to that, my buckaroos,
before you march for God,
country and siss-boom-bah!
You won't, of course. Your schooling
left you trained to serve
like cocksure Paul before
God's lightning smashed
him from his saddle. So—

I wish you what I wish
myself: hard questions
and the nights to answer them,
the grace of disappointment
and the right to seem the fool
for justice. That's enough.
Cowards might ask for more.
Heroes have died for less.

—Samuel Hazo (1928–   )

Death

The Cross of Snow

In the long, sleepless watches of the night,
A gentle face—the face of one long dead—
Looks at me from the wall, where round its head
The night-lamp casts a halo of pale light.
Here in this room she died; and soul more white
Never through martyrdom of fire was led
To its repose; nor can in books be read
The legend of life more benedight.
There is a mountain in the distant West,
That, sun-defying, in its deep ravines
Displays a cross of snow upon its side.
Such is the cross I wear upon my breast
These eighteen years, through all the changing scenes
And seasons, changeless since the day she died.

—Henry Wadsworth Longfellow (1807–1882)

After Great Pain a Formal Feeling Comes

After great pain a formal feeling comes—
The nerves sit ceremonious like tombs;
The stiff Heart questions—was it He that bore?
And yesterday—or centuries before?

The feet mechanical go round
A wooden way
Of ground or air or Ought,
Regardless grown,
A quartz contentment like a stone.

This is the hour of lead
Remembered if outlived
As freezing persons recollect
The snow—
First chill, then stupor, then
The letting go.

—Emily Dickinson (1830–1886)

The Going

Why did you give no hint that night
That quickly after the morrow's dawn,

And calmly, as if indifferent quite,
You would close your term here, up and be gone
        Where I could not follow
        With wing of swallow
To gain one glimpse of you ever anon!

        Never to bid good-bye,
        Or lip me the softest call,
Or utter a wish for a word, while I
Saw morning harden upon the wall,
        Unmoved, unknowing
        That your great going
Had place that moment, and altered all.

Why do you make me leave the house
And think for a breath it is you I see
At the end of the alley of bending boughs
Where so often at dusk you used to be;
        Till in darkening dankness
        The yawning blankness
Of the perspective sickens me!

        You were she who abode
        By those red-veined rocks far West,
You were the swan-necked one who rode
Along the beetling Beeny Crest,
        And, reining nigh me,
        Would muse and eye me,
While Life unrolled us its very best.

Why, then, latterly did we not speak,
Did we not think of those days long dead,
And ere your vanishing strive to seek
That time's renewal? We might have said,
        "In this bright spring weather
        We'll visit together
Those places that once we visited."

        Well, Well! All's past amend,
        Unchangeable. It must go.
I seem but a dead man held on end
To sink down soon. . . . O you could not know
        That such swift fleeing
        No soul foreseeing—
Not even I—would undo me so!

                —Thomas Hardy (1840–1928)

Do Not Go Gentle Into That Good Night

Do not go gentle into that good night,
Old age should burn and rave at close of day;
Rage, rage against the dying of the light.

Though wise men at their end know dark is right,
Because their words had forked no lightning they
Do not go gentle into that good night.

Good men, the last wave by, crying how bright
Their frail deeds might have danced in a green bay,
Rage, rage against the dying of the light.

Wild men who caught and sang the sun in flight,
And learn, too late, they grieved it on its way,
Do not go gentle into that good night.

Grave men, near death, who see with blinding sight
Blind eyes could blaze like meteors and be gay,
Rage, rage against the dying of the light.

And you, my father, there on the sad height,
Curse, bless, me now with your fierce tears, I pray.
Do not go gentle into that good night.
Rage, rage against the dying of the light.

—Dylan Thomas (1914–1953)

Tributes to Milton

London 1802

Milton! thou shouldst be living at this hour:
England hath need of thee: she is a fen
Of stagnant waters: altar, sword, and pen,
Fireside, the heroic wealth of hall and bower,
Have forfeited their ancient English dower
Of inward happiness. We are selfish men;
Oh! raise us up, return to us again;
And give us manners, virtue, freedom, power.
Thy soul was like a Star, and dwelt apart;
Thou hadst a voice whose sound was like the sea:
Pure as the naked heavens, majestic, free,
So didst thou travel on life's common way,
In cheerful godliness; and yet thy heart
The lowliest duties on herself did lay.

—William Wordsworth (1770–1850)

Milton

Alcaics[1]

O Mighty-Mouth'd inventor of harmonies,
O skill'd to sing of Time or Eternity,
   God-gifted organ-voice of England,
      Milton, a name to resound for ages;
Whose Titan angels, Gabriel,[2] Abdiel,[3]
Starr'd from Jehovah's gorgeous armouries,
   Tower, as the deep-domed empyrean
      Rings to the roar of an angel onset—
Me rather all that bowery loneliness,
The brooks of Eden mazily murmuring,
   And bloom profuse and cedar arches
      Charm, as a wanderer out in ocean,
Where some refulgent sunset of India
Streams o'er a rich ambrosial ocean isle,
   And crimson-hued the stately palm-woods
      Whisper in odorous heights of even.

     —Alfred, Lord Tennyson (1809–1892)

---

[1] A Greek meter invented by Alceus, a lyric poet, about 600 B.C.
[2] "Chief of the angelic guards" in *Paradise Lost*. [3] The faithful angel
who opposed Satan's revolt.

To the Ghost of John Milton

If I should pamphleteer twenty years against royalists,
With rewards offered for my capture dead or alive,
And jails and scaffolds always near,

And then my wife should die and three ignorant daughters
Should talk about their father as a joke, and steal the
Earnings of books, and the poorhouse always reaching for me,
If I then lost my eyes and the world was all dark and I
Sat with only memories and talk—

I would write "Paradise Lost", I would marry a second wife
And on her dying I would marry a third pair of eyes to
Serve my blind eyes, I would write "Paradise Regained", I
Would write wild, foggy, smoky, wordy books—

I would sit by the fire and dream of hell and heaven,
Idiots and kings, women my eyes could never look on again,
And God Himself and the rebels God threw into hell.

     —Carl Sandburg (1878–1967)

Music

A Toccata¹ of Galuppi's²

Oh Galuppi, Baldassare, this is very sad to find!
I can hardly misconceive you; it would prove me deaf and
      blind;
But although I take your meaning, 'tis with such a heavy mind!

II
Here you come with your old music, and here's all the good it
      brings.
What, they lived once thus at Venice where the merchants were
      the kings,
Where Saint Mark's is, where the Doges used to wed the sea
      with rings?³

III
Ay, because the sea's the street there; and 'tis arched by . . .
      what you call
. . . Shylock's bridge with houses on it, where they kept the
      carnival:
I was never out of England—it's as if I saw it all.

IV
Did young people take their pleasure when the sea was warm
      in May?
Balls and masks begun at midnight, burning ever to midday,
When they made up fresh adventures for the morrow, do you
      say?

V
Was a lady such a lady, cheeks so round and lips so red,—
On her neck the small face buoyant, like a bellflower on its bed,
O'er the breast's superb abundance where a man might base
      his head?

VI
Well, and it was graceful of them—they'd break talk off and
      afford
—She, to bite her mask's black velvet—he, to finger on his
      sword,
While you sat and played Toccatas, stately at the clavichord?⁴

VII
What? Those lesser thirds so plaintive, sixths diminished, sigh
      on sigh,

Told them something? Those suspensions, those solutions—
   "Must we die?"
Those commiserating sevenths—"Life might last! we can but
   try!"

VIII

"Were you happy?"—"Yes."—"And are you still as happy?"—
   "Yes. And you?"
—"Then, more kisses!"—"Did *I* stop them, when a million
   seemed so few?"
Hark, the dominant's persistence till it must be answered to!

IX

So, an octave struck the answer. Oh, they praised you, I dare
   say!
"Brave Galuppi! that was music! good alike at grave and gay!
I can always leave off talking when I hear a master play!"

X

Then they left you for their pleasure: till in due time, one by
   one,
Some with lives that came to nothing, some with deeds as well
   undone,
Death stepped tacitly and took them where they never see the
   sun.

XI

But when I sit down to reason, think to take my stand nor
   swerve,
While I triumph o'er a secret wrung from nature's close reserve,
In you come with your cold music till I creep thro' every nerve.

XII

Yes, you, like a ghostly cricket, creaking where a house was
   burned:
"Dust and ashes, dead and done with, Venice spent what Venice
   earned.
The soul, doubtless, is immortal—where a soul can be
   discerned.

XIII

"Yours for instance: you know physics, something of geology,
Mathematics are your pastime; souls shall rise in their degree;
Butterflies may dread extinction,—you'll not die, it cannot be!

XIV

"As for Venice and her people, merely born to bloom and drop,
Here on earth they bore their fruitage, mirth and folly were the
   crop:
What of soul was left, I wonder, when the kissing had to stop?

XV

"Dust and ashes!" So you creak it, and I want the heart to
scold.
Dear dead women, with such hair, too—what's become of all
the gold
Used to hang and brush their bosoms? I feel chilly and grown
old.

—Robert Browning (1812–1889)

---

[1] A technical musical composition ("touch-piece"), an overture or pre-
lude, stressing freedom of improvisation rather than the more formal
organization of a sonata. Bach was the first to make the toccata an
important kind of composition. [2] Baldassare Galuppi (1706–1785)
was a famous Venetian musician who composed many light operas. He
also resided and performed in London and in Russia at the court of
Catherine II. In 1768 he became the organist at St. Mark's, Venice. His
music is rarely performed today. [3] When Venice was a republic, the
Doge was the chief magistrate of the city. In an annual ceremony he
flung a ring into the Adriatic to symbolize the wedding of the city with
the sea and the city's domination of the Adriatic. [4] A keyboard instrument superseded by the piano.

Bound No'th Blues

Goin' down the road, Lawd,
Goin' down the road.
Down the road, Lawd,
Way, way down the road.
Got to find somebody
To help me carry this load.

Road's in front o' me,
Nothin' to do but walk.
Road's in front o' me,
Walk . . . an' walk . . . an' walk.
I'd like to meet a good friend
To come along an' talk.

Hates to be lonely,
Lawd, I hates to be sad.
Says I hates to be lonely,
Hates to be lonely an' sad,
But ever' friend you finds seems
Like they try to do you bad.

Road, road, road, O!
Road, road . . . road . . . road, road!
Road, road, road, O!

On the no'thern road.
These Mississippi towns ain't
Fit fer a hoppin' toad.

—Langston Hughes (1902–1967)

Jazz Fantasia

Drum on your drums, batter on your banjos, sob on the long
    cool winding saxophones. Go to it, O jazzmen.

Sling your knuckles on the bottoms of the happy tin pans, let
    your trombones ooze, and go husha-husha-hush with the
    slippery sandpaper.

Moan like an autumn wind high in the lonesome treetops, moan
    soft like you wanted somebody terrible, cry like a racing
    car slipping away from a motorcycle cop, bang-bang! you
    jazzmen, bang altogether drums, traps, banjos, horns,
    tin cans—make two people fight on the top of a stairway
    and scratch each other's eyes in a clinch tumbling down
    the stairs.

Can the rough stuff. . . . Now a Mississippi steamboat
    pushes up the night river with a hoo-hoo-hoo-oo . . .
    and the green lanterns calling to the high soft stars . . .
    a red moon rides on the humps of the low river hills. . . .
    Go to it, O jazzmen.

—Carl Sandburg (1878–1967)

Guitar

Ma six string guitar with the lonesome sound
Can't hold its own against a Georgia hound.

O mamma when the sun goes the downstairs way
And the night spreads out an the moon make day,

I sits with ma feet raised to the rail
And sings the song bout ma buddy in jail:

    In the red-dirt land,
    And the pine tree high,
    Gonna find me peace
    By-an-by.

Gonna find me a baby
Some pretty-eye gal
To be ma mother
Ma wife an pal.

Ain't had nobody
To call me home
From the electric cities
Where I roam.

Yes, I been travelin
Over all
To find a place
What I could call
Home, baby,
Sweet cotton-field home. . . .

When I gets to the place where a cracker got mad,
Struck ma fine buddy, struck all I had,
The hound start howlin till the stars break down
An make ma song like a boat what's drown.

Ma six string guitar with the lonesome sound
Can't hold its own against that Georgia hound.

—Owen Dodson (1914–   )

Art

On Seeing the Elgin Marbles

My spirit is too weak—mortality
   Weighs heavily on me like unwilling sleep,
   And each imagin'd pinnacle and steep
Of godlike hardship, tells me I must die
Like a sick Eagle looking at the sky.
   Yet 'tis a gentle luxury to weep
   That I have not the cloudy winds to keep,
Fresh for the opening of the morning's eye.
Such dim-conceived glories of the brain
   Bring round the heart an undescribable feud;
So do these wonders a most dizzy pain,
   That mingles Grecian grandeur with the rude
Wasting of old Time—with a billowy main—
   A sun—a shadow of a magnitude.

—John Keats (1795–1821)

Lapis Lazuli[1]

for Harry Clifton

I have heard that hysterical women say
They are sick of the palette and fiddle-bow,
Of poets that are always gay,
For everybody knows or else should know
That if nothing drastic is done
Aeroplane and Zeppelin will come out,
Pitch like King Billy[2] bomb-balls in
Until the town lie beaten flat.

All perform their tragic play,
There struts Hamlet, there is Lear,
That's Ophelia, that Cordelia;
Yet they, should the last scene be there,
The great stage curtain about to drop,
If worthy their prominent part in the play,
Do not break up their lines to weep.
They know that Hamlet and Lear are gay;
Gaiety transfiguring all that dread.
All men have aimed at, found and lost;
Black out; Heaven blazing into the head:
Tragedy wrought to its uttermost.
Though Hamlet rambles and Lear rages,
And all the drop-scenes drop at once
Upon a hundred thousand stages,
It[3] cannot grow by an inch or an ounce.

On their own feet they came, or on shipboard,
Camel-back, horse-back, ass-back, mule-back,
Old civilisations put to the sword.
Then they and their wisdom went to rack:
No handiwork of Callimachus,[4]
Who handled marble as if it were bronze,
Made draperies that seemed to rise
When sea-wind swept the corner, stands;
His long lamp-chimney shaped like the stem
Of a slender palm, stood but a day;[5]
All things fall and are built again,
And those that build them again are gay.

Two Chinamen, behind them a third,
Are carved in lapis lazuli,
Over them flies a long-legged bird,
A symbol of longevity;
The third, doubtless a serving-man,
Carries a musical instrument.

Every discoloration of the stone,
Every accidental crack or dent,
Seems a water-course or an avalanche,
Or lofty slope where it still snows
Though doubtless plum or cherry-branch
Sweetens the little half-way house
Those Chinamen climb towards, and I
Delight to imagine them seated there;
There, on the mountain and the sky,
On all the tragic scene they stare.
One asks for mournful melodies;
Accomplished fingers begin to play.
Their eyes mid many wrinkles, their eyes,
Their ancient, glittering eyes, are gay.

—William Butler Yeats (1865–1939)

---

[1] Harry Clifton had given Yeats a lapis lazuli medallion, with an azure-blue stone on which was carved "the semblance of a mountain with temple, trees, paths, and an ascetic and pupil about to climb a mountain" (Yeats' letter to Dorothy Wellesley).   [2] King William III (of Orange) defeated James II at the Battle of the Boyne in 1690 by bombardment, and Kaiser Wilhelm's Zeppelins bombed London near the end of World War I.   [3] Tragedy.   [4] Fifth-century B.C. Greek sculptor.   [5] Mentioned by Pausanias, second-century traveler and geographer, in his *Description of Greece*.

Musée des Beaux Arts

About suffering they were never wrong,
The Old Masters: how well they understood
Its human position; how it takes place
While someone else is eating or opening a window or
        just walking dully along;
How, when the aged are reverently, passionately waiting
For the miraculous birth, there always must be
Children who did not specially want it to happen, skating
On a pond at the edge of the wood:
They never forgot
That even the dreadful martyrdom must run its course
Anyhow in a corner, some untidy spot
Where the dogs go on with their doggy life and the tor-
        turer's horse
Scratches its innocent behind on a tree.

In Breughel's[1] *Icarus,* for instance; how everything turns
        away
Quite leisurely from the disaster; the ploughman may
Have heard the splash, the forsaken cry,
But for him it was not an important failure; the sun shone

As it had to on the white legs disappearing into the green
Water; and the expensive delicate ship that must have seen
Something amazing, a boy falling out of the sky,
Had somewhere to get to and sailed calmly on.

—W. H. Auden (1907–)

---

[1] Peter Breughel the elder (1525–1569), Flemish painter whose *Land-scape with the Fall of Icarus* and *The Numbering at Bethlehem* are in the Museum of Fine Arts in Brussels.

From *A Coney Island of the Mind,* 1

In Goya's greatest scenes we seem to see
                   the people of the world
    exactly at the moment when
      they first attained the title of
              "suffering humanity"
    They writhe upon the page
          in a veritable rage
             of adversity
    Heaped up
      groaning with babies and bayonets
            under cement skies
  in an abstract landscape of blasted trees
    bent statues bats wings and beaks
         slippery gibbets
  cadavers and carnivorous cocks
  and all the final hollering monsters
    of the
        "imagination of disaster"
  they are so bloody real
        it is as if they really still existed

And they do

     Only the landscape is changed

They still are ranged along the roads
   plagued by legionaires
      false windmills and demented roosters

They are the same people
      only further from home
  on freeways fifty lanes wide
    on a concrete continent
    spaced with bland billboards
  illustrating imbecile illusions of happiness

The scene shows fewer tumbrils
                but more maimed citizens
                                in painted cars
    and they have strange license plates
        and engines
                that devour America

—Lawrence Ferlinghetti (1919–   )

Museum Tour

The children are coming down
the corridor. Their tall, apple-thighed
art student-teacher
positions them alongside

the painting. The French. Seurat,
and *Sunday Afternoon on the Island
of La Grande Jatte.*
Pell-mell, the children upend

the silence. Portable chairs
tip open in their hands like switchblades.
The museum guard
insouciantly draws the shades,

hungering for the cigarette
he cannot have. Children, the teacher
says, notice the greens,
and notice the way the river

disappears from the painting.
One little henry bobs from his chair.
He's got it, saying,
Vanishing perspective, where

the eye follows a line of sight.
Beside him another, less precocious
henry listens to
his radio and the Coasters

singing "Soul Pad." The teacher
tugs at her watch now to bid them go,
past the guard, knowing
how, outside, it is Chicago.

—Harold Bond (1939–   )

Science

Mock On

Mock on, Mock on Voltaire, Rousseau:
Mock on, Mock on: 'tis all in vain!
You throw the sand against the wind,
And the wind blows it back again.

And every sand becomes a Gem
Reflected in the beams divine;
Blown back they blind the mocking Eye,
But still in Israel's paths they shine.

The Atoms of Democritus[1]
And Newton's Particles of light[2]
Are sands upon the Red sea shore,
Where Israel's tents do shine so bright.

—William Blake (1757–1857)

---

[1] Fifth-century B.C. philosopher who believed atoms were the ultimate constituents of all things. [2] Newton had written a treatise on light.

Sonnet—To Science

Science! true daughter of Old Time thou art!
Who alterest all things with thy peering eyes.
Why preyest thou thus upon the poet's heart,
Vulture, whose wings are dull realities?
How should he love thee? or how deem thee wise?
Who wouldst not leave him in his wandering
To seek for treasure in the jewelled skies,
Albeit he soared with an undaunted wing?
Hast thou not dragged Diana from her car?
And driven the Hamadryad from the wood
To seek a shelter in some happier star?
Hast thou not torn the Naiad from her flood,
The Elfin from the green grass, and from me
The summer dream beneath the tamarind tree?

—Edgar Allan Poe (1809–1849)

Faith

"Faith" is a fine invention
When Gentlemen can *see*—

But *Microscopes* are prudent
In an Emergency.

—Emily Dickinson (1830–1886)

The Happy Encounter

I saw sweet Poetry turn troubled eyes
    On shaggy Science nosing in the grass,
  For by that way poor Poetry must pass
On her long pilgrimage to Paradise.
He snuffled, grunted, squealed; perplexed by flies,
    Parched, weatherworn, and near of sight, alas,
    From peering close where very little was
In dens secluded from the open skies.

But Poetry in bravery went down,
    And called his name, soft, clear, and fearlessly;
Stooped low, and stroked his muzzle overgrown;
Refreshed his drought with dew: wiped pure and free
    His eyes! and lo! laughed loud for joy to see
In those grey deeps the azure of her own.

              —Walter de la Mare (1873–1956)

The Prophets Really Prophesy as Mystics
The Commentators Merely by Statistics

With what unbroken spirit naïve science
Keeps hurling our Promethean defiance
From this atomic ball of rotting rock
At the Divine Safe's combination lock.

In our defiance we are still defied.
But have not I, as prophet, prophesied:
Sick of our circling round and round the sun
Something about the trouble will be done.

Now that we've found the secret out of weight,
So we can cancel it however great.
Ah, what avail our lofty engineers
If we can't take the planet by the ears,

Or by the poles or simply by the scruff,
And saying simply we have had enough
Of routine and monotony on earth,
Where nothing's going on but death and birth.

And man's of such a limited longevity,
Now in the confidence of new-found levity
(Our gravity has been our major curse)
We'll cast off hawser for the universe

Taking along the whole race for a ride
(Have I not prophesied and prophesied?)
All voting *viva voce* where to go,
The noisier because they hardly know

Whether to seek a scientific sky
Or wait and go to Heaven when they die,
In other words to wager their reliance
On plain religion or religious science.

They need to crash the puzzle of their lot
As Alexander crashed the Gordian knot,
Or as we crashed the barrier of sound
To beat the very world's speed going round.

Yet what a charming earnest world it is,
So modest we can hardly hear it whizz,
Spinning as well as running on a course
It seems too bad to steer it off by force.

—Robert Frost (1874–1963)

Radar

Distance is swept by the smooth
Rotations of power, whose staring
Feelers multiply our eyes for us,
Mark objects' range and bearing.

Linked to them, guns rehearse
Calculated obedience; echoes of light
Trigger the shadowing needle, determine
The flaring arrest of night.

Control is remote: feelings, like hands,
Gloved by space. Responsibility is shared, too:
And destroying the enemy by radar,
We cannot see what we do.

—Alan Ross (1922–   )

The End of the World

Darkness

I had a dream, which was not all a dream.
The bright sun was extinguish'd, and the stars
Did wander darkling in the eternal space,
Rayless, and pathless, and the icy earth
Swung blind and blackening in the moonless air;
Morn came and went—and came, and brought no day,
And men forgot their passions in the dread
Of this their desolation; and all hearts
Were chill'd into a selfish prayer for light.
And they did live by watch fires—and the thrones,
The palaces of crowned kings—the huts,
The habitations of all things which dwell,
Were burnt for beacons; cities were consumed,
And men were gather'd round their blazing homes
To look once more into each other's face.
Happy were those who dwelt within the eye
Of the volcanos, and their mountain-torch:
A fearful hope was all the world contain'd;
Forests were set on fire—but hour by hour
They fell and faded—and the crackling trunks
Extinguish'd with a crash—and all was black.
The brows of men by the despairing light
Wore an unearthly aspect, as by fits
The flashes fell upon them; some lay down
And hid their eyes and wept; and some did rest
Their chins upon their clenched hands, and smiled;
And others hurried to and fro, and fed
Their funeral piles with fuel, and look'd up
With mad disquietude on the dull sky,
The pall of a past world; and then again
With curses cast them down upon the dust,
And gnash'd their teeth and howl'd. The wild birds shriek'd,
And, terrified, did flutter on the ground,
And flap their useless wings; the wildest brutes
Came tame and tremulous; and vipers crawl'd
And twined themselves among the multitude,
Hissing, but stingless—they were slain for food.
And War, which for a moment was no more,
Did glut himself again;—a meal was bought
With blood, and each state sullenly apart
Gorging himself in gloom. No love was left;
All earth was but one thought—and that was death,
Immediate and inglorious; and the pang

Of famine fed upon all entrails—men
Died, and their bones were tombless as their flesh;
The meagre by the meagre were devour'd,
Even dogs assail'd their masters, all save one,
And he was faithful to a corpse, and kept
The birds and beasts and famish'd men at bay,
Till hunger clung them, or the dropping dead
Lured their lank jaws. Himself sought out no food,
But with a piteous and perpetual moan,
And a quick desolate cry, licking the hand
Which answer'd not with a caress—he died.
The crowd was famish'd by degrees; but two
Of an enormous city did survive,
And they were enemies. They met beside
The dying embers of an altar-place,
Where had been heap'd a mass of holy things
For an unholy usage; they raked up,
And shivering scraped with their cold skeleton hands
The feeble ashes, and their feeble breath
Blew for a little life, and made a flame
Which was a mockery. Then they lifted up
Their eyes as it grew lighter, and beheld
Each other's aspects—saw, and shriek'd, and died—
Even of their mutual hideousness they died,
Unknowing who he was upon whose brow
Famine had written Fiend. The world was void,
The populous and the powerful was a lump,
Seasonless, herbless, treeless, manless, lifeless—
A lump of death—a chaos of hard clay.
The rivers, lakes, and ocean all stood still,
And nothing stirr'd within their silent depths;
Ships sailorless lay rotting on the sea;
And their masts fell down piecemeal; as they dropp'd
They slept on the abyss without a surge—
The waves were dead; the tides were in their grave,
The Moon, their mistress, had expired before;
The winds were wither'd in the stagnant air,
And the clouds perish'd; Darkness had no need
Of aid from them—She was the Universe.

—George Gordon, Lord Byron (1788–1824)

Blind Date

No more the swanboat on the artificial lake
its paddled path through neon light shall take;

the stars are turned out on the immortal ferris wheel,
dark and still are the cars of the Virginia Reel.
Baby, it is the last of all blind dates,
and this we keep with the keeper of the golden gates.

For the last time, my darling, the chute-the-chutes,
the Tunnel of Love, the cry "all men are brutes,"
the sweaty dance-hall with the juke-box playing,
pretzels and beer, and our young love a-Maying:
baby, it is the last of all blind dates,
and this we keep with the keeper of the golden gates.

The radios in a thousand taxis die;
at last man's music fades from the inhuman sky;
as, short or long, fades out the impermanent wave
to find in the ether or the earth its grave.
Baby, it is the last of all blind dates,
and this we keep with the keeper of the golden gates.

Hold hands and kiss, it will never come again,
look in your own eyes and remember the deep pain,
how hollow the world is, like a bubble burst,
yes, and all beauty by some wretchedness accursed!
Baby, it is the last of all blind dates,
and this we keep with the keeper of the golden gates.

Love now the footworn grass, the trampled flowers,
and the divided man of crowds, for he is ours—
love him, yes, love him now, this sundered being,
who most himself seeks when himself most fleeing—
baby, it is the last of all blind dates,
and this we keep with the keeper of the golden gates.

But look—the scenic railway is flashed from red to green—
and swiftly beneath our feet as this machine
our old star plunges down the precipitous sky,
down the hurrahs of space! So soon to die!—
But baby, it is the last of all blind dates;
and we shall keep it with the keeper of the golden gates.

                              —Conrad Aiken (1889–   )

Fire and Ice

Some say the world will end in fire,
Some say in ice.
From what I've tasted of desire

I hold with those who favor fire.
But if it had to perish twice,
I think I know enough of hate
To say that for destruction ice
Is also great
And would suffice.

—Robert Frost (1874–1963)

The End of the World

Quite unexpectedly as Vasserot
The armless ambidextrian was lighting
A match between his great and second toe
And Ralph the lion was engaged in biting
The neck of Madame Sossman while the drum
Pointed, and Teeny was about to cough
In Waltz-time swinging Jocko by the thumb—
Quite unexpectedly the top blew off:

And there, there overhead, there, there, hung over,
Those thousands of white faces, those dazed eyes,
There in the starless dark the poise, the hover,
There with vast wings across the canceled skies,
There in the sudden blackness the black pall
Of nothing, nothing, nothing,—nothing at all.

—Archibald MacLeish (1892–   )

The Event Itself

A curious reticence afflicts my generation, faced with the
    holocaust;
We speak seldom of the event itself, but only of what will be
    lost;
We, having betrayed our fathers and all our silent grandfathers,
    cannot cry out for ourselves, the present and tempest-
    tossed.

But many things and all manner of things will be hurled
In a force like dawnlight breaking, and the billion bagpipes of
    our screams will be skirled
Stupendously month after month, the greatest pain ever known
    in the world.

There will be some instantly indistinguishable from the molten
    stone;
But most will have bleeding, burning, gangrene, the sticking-
    out bone;
Men, women, and little children will be made pregnant of the
    nipping crab whose seed will be universally sown.

In the screaming and wallowing one thought will make each
    eye stare,
And that thought will be the silence pressing down at the
    end of the air,
Soon to smother the last scream forever and everywhere.

For the last man in the world, dying, will not know that he is
    the last,
But many will think it, dying; will think that in all the vast
And vacant universe they are the final consciousness, going
    out, going out, going out, with nothing to know it has
    passed.

                      —Hayden Carruth (1921–　)

Annotated Bibliography

ABRAMS, M. H. (ed.). *English Romantic Poets: Modern Essays in Criticism.* New York: Oxford University Press, 1960.

    Three general essays on English romanticism and essays on Blake, Wordsworth, Coleridge, Byron, Shelley, and Keats by contemporary critics.

————. *The Mirror and the Lamp: Romantic Theory and the Critical Tradition.* New York: Oxford University Press, 1953.

    A scholarly treatment of the English romantic theory of poetry in the first four decades of the nineteenth century.

ADAMS, HAZARD. *The Contexts of Poetry.* Boston: Little, Brown and Co., 1963.

    Study of the poem as a work of art produced at a particular stage of literary history, with emphasis on genre development.

ADAMS, ROBERT ADAM. *Milton and the Modern Critics.* Ithaca: Cornell University Press, 1955.

    A reevaluation of Milton's poetry in the light of modern criticism.

BAILEY, J. O. *The Poetry of Thomas Hardy: A Handbook and Commentary.* Chapel Hill: University of North Carolina Press, 1970.

    Factual data of sources, identification of persons and places, and events in the life of Hardy as aids to an understanding of his poems.

BEATY, JEROME and WILLIAM H. MATCHETT. *Poetry: From Statement to Meaning.* New York: Oxford University Press, 1965.

    Discussion of poetry as verbal communication between poem and reader and the relation of poetic statement to form and meaning.

BLACKMUR, R. P. *Form and Value in Modern Poetry.* New York: Doubleday & Co., 1957.

    Seventeen essays discussing works of poets from Thomas Hardy to e.e. cummings, with stress on technical analysis.

BLOOM, HAROLD. *The Visionary Company: A Reading of English Romantic Poetry.* New York: Doubleday & Co., 1963.

    A modern interpretation by an acute critic of the major English romantic poets from Blake to Keats.

ANNOTATED BIBLIOGRAPHY

———. *Yeats.* New York: Oxford University Press, 1970.

A reevaluation of the poetry of Yeats as a twentieth-century continuation of the tradition of English romanticism.

BODKIN, MAUD. *Archetypal Patterns in Poetry: Psychological Studies of Imagination.* New York: Vintage Books, 1958.

A study of Jungian archetypes in poetry: rebirth, heaven and hell, the image of woman, images of the devil, hero, and God.

BROOKS, CLEANTH. *The Well Wrought Urn: Studies in the Structure of Poetry.* New York: Harcourt, Brace & World, 1947.

Eleven essays by a pioneer of the "new criticism."

BURKE, KENNETH. *The Philosophy of Literary Form: Studies in Symbolic Action* (rev. ed.). New York: Vintage Books, 1957.

Speculations on the general problems of internal structure in literary works, semantic and poetic meaning, and Freud's analysis of poetry.

BUSH, DOUGLAS. *Science and English Poetry: A Historical Sketch, 1590–1950.* New York: Oxford University Press, 1950.

The influence of developing scientific concepts on the works of poets.

———. *Mythology and the Romantic Tradition in English Poetry.* New York: W. W. Norton & Co., 1937.

A scholarly account of the use of myth by English and American poets from the eighteenth century to the present.

CADDEN, JOHN J. and PATRICK R. BROSTOWIN (eds.). *Science and Literature: A Reader.* Lexington, Mass.: D. C. Heath and Co., 1964.

Prose selections and poems showing the impact of scientific thought on English and American literature, with discussion of conflicts in faith, mysticism, agnosticism, skepticism.

CARROLL, PAUL. *The Poem in Its Skin.* Chicago: Follett/Big Table Books, 1968.

Essays on ten poems, one from each of the following contemporary poets: John Ashbery, Robert Creeley, James Dickey, Isabella Gardner, Allen Ginsberg, John Logan, W. S. Merwin, Frank O'Hara, W. D. Snodgrass, and James Wright.

DAY-LEWIS, CECIL. *The Poetic Image.* New York: Oxford University Press, 1947.

Lectures by a modern poet on the nature, patterns, and use of images.

———. *The Poet's Way to Knowledge.* Cambridge: Cambridge University Press, 1957.

How a poet's apprehension of truth and reality differs from other approaches.

DEUTSCH, BABETTE. *Poetry in Our Time: A Critical Survey of Poetry in the English-speaking World, 1900–1960* (2d ed.). New York: Doubleday & Co., 1963.

A modern reappraisal of the important poetic movements and poets.

DREW, ELIZABETH. *Poetry: A Modern Guide to Its Understanding and Enjoyment*. New York: Dell Publishing Co., 1959.
A popular treatment of the poetic process, with stress upon recurrent themes of human experience.

ELIOT, T. S. *Selected Essays: 1917–1932*. New York: Harcourt, Brace & World, 1932.
Important essays on tradition in English poetry and revival of interest in "metaphysical poets" such as Donne and Marvell.

————. *On Poetry and Poets*. New York: Farrar, Straus and Giroux, 1961.
A reevaluation of some of Eliot's earlier criticism (e.g., of Milton) and additional essays of the 40s and 50s.

ENGLE, PAUL and JOSEPH LANGLAND. *Poet's Choice*. New York: Dell Publishing Co., 1962.
One hundred and four contemporary poets choose their favorite poem from their own work and give the reasons for their choices.

FRY, NORTHROP. *Anatomy of Criticism: Four Essays*. Princeton: Princeton University Press, 1937.
Attempts to establish a science of poetic criticism based on archetype and ritual, developing a theory of modes, symbols, myths, and genres.

FUSSELL, PAUL JR. *Poetic Meter and Poetic Form*. New York: Random House, 1965.
Technical study of modern theories of meter and form.

GROSS, HARVEY (ed.). *The Structure of Verse: Modern Essays on Prosody*. Greenwich, Conn.: Fawcett Publications, 1966.
Essays by modern critics on the definition and history of prosody and theories of meter.

HEMPHILL, GEORGE (ed.). *Discussions of Poetry: Rhythm and Sound*. Lexington, Mass.: D. C. Heath and Co., 1961.
Essays on metrics from the Elizabethans to John Crowe Ransom.

HOLLANDER, JOHN (ed.). *Modern Poetry: Essays in Criticism*. New York: Oxford University Press, 1968.
Twenty-five essays by modern poets and critics comprising a cross-section of the various approaches to an understanding of twentieth-century poetry in English.

HOLMES, JOHN. *Writing Poetry*. Boston: The Writer, Inc., 1960.
In three sections: (1) five essays by Holmes on the craft of writing poetry, (2) essays on poetry and poetry writing by nine contemporary poets and critics, and (3) more than four hundred quotations on the art of poetry.

HOWARD, RICHARD. *Alone with America: Essays on the Art of Poetry in the United States Since 1950*. New York: Atheneum, 1969.
A comprehensive work on the publication and development of forty-one contemporary American poets, with acute critical comments.

HUBLER, EDWARD. *The Sense of Shakespeare's Sonnets.* New York: Hill & Wang, 1952.
A critical discussion of the problems of Shakespeare's sonnets: form, matter, and obscurity.

JEFFARES, A. NORMAN. *A Commentary on the Collected Poems of W. B. Yeats.* Stanford: Stanford University Press, 1968.
A valuable source of information on Yeats' sources, reading, and life as related to his poetry.

LANGBAUM, ROBERT. *The Poetry of Experience: The Dramatic Monologue in Modern Literary Tradition.* New York: Random House, 1957.
The development of the dramatic monologue and its use in contemporary poetry.

LINENTHAL, MARK (ed). *Aspects of Poetry: Modern Perspectives.* Boston: Little, Brown and Co., 1963.
Essays by contemporary poets and critics on the sources, interpretations, and functions of poetry.

MARITAIN, JACQUES. *Creative Intuition in Art and Poetry.* New York: Meridian Books, 1955.
Lectures on the aesthetics of poetry and beauty and their relationship to art and music.

MARTZ, LOUIS L. *The Poem of the Mind: Essays on Poetry/English and American.* New York: Oxford University Press, 1966.
Essays on poetry of the interior life of such poets as John Donne, Edward Taylor, T. S. Eliot, and Wallace Stevens.

MAZZARO, JEROME (ed.). *Modern American Poetry: Essays in Criticism.* New York: McKay, 1970.
Fifteen critics discuss the works of poets from Walt Whitman to W. D. Snodgrass.

MURPHY, FRANCIS (ed.). *Discussions of Poetry: Form and Structure.* Lexington, Mass.: D. C. Heath and Co., 1964.
Thirteen essays by contemporary critics discussing the problems of fixed forms and rhetorical structures in poetry.

NEMEROV, HOWARD (ed.). *Poets on Poetry.* New York: Basic Books, 1966.
The views of poets, in prose and poetry, on the nature and purpose of their art.

OSTROFF, ANTHONY (ed.). *The Contemporary Poet as Artist and Critic.* Boston: Little, Brown and Co., 1964.
Explications of eight modern poems by various critics with comments by the poets Richard Eberhart, Stanley Kunitz, Robert Lowell, Richard Wilbur, Theodore Roethke, John Crowe Ransom, W. H. Auden, and Karl Shapiro.

PERRY, JOHN OLIVER (ed.). *Approaches to the Poem: Modern Essays in the Analysis and Interpretation of Poetry.* San Francisco: Chandler Publishing Co., 1965.
Twenty modern critics analyze the basic concepts they use in interpreting poetry.

POTTLE, FREDERICK. *The Idiom of Poetry.* Ithaca: Cornell University Press, 1946.
A scholarly discussion of how the changing language of poetry reveals a shift in the sensibility of an age.

PREMINGER, ALEX (ed.). *Encyclopedia of Poetry and Poetics.* Princeton: Princeton University Press, 1965.
An invaluable, comprehensive reference work dealing with all aspects of poetry: history, types, movements, prosody, and critical terminology.

PRESS, JOHN. *The Chequer'd Shade: Reflections on Obscurity in Poetry.* New York: Oxford University Press, 1963.
An analysis and explanation of poetic obscurity in diction, syntax, allusion, and imagery.

RICHARDS, I. A. *Practical Criticism: A Study of Literary Judgment.* New York: Harcourt, Brace & World, 1929.
A pioneering book that exposed the inability of students to understand and evaluate poetry and led to the introduction of the "new criticism."

ROSENTHAL, M. L. *The New Poets: American and British Poetry Since World War II.* New York: Oxford University Press, 1967.
An account of "confessional poetry," the "projectivist" movement, and contemporary British and Irish poetry.

SHAPIRO, KARL. *In Defense of Ignorance* New York: Random House, 1960.
Polemical essays attacking the "modernist" school of Ezra Pound and T. S. Eliot as well as the "new criticism."

———— (ed.). *Prose Keys to Modern Poetry.* Evanston: Row, Peterson and Co., 1962.
Chief prose documents upon which modern classical and romantic poetry is based.

———— and ROBERT BEUM. *A Prosody Handbook.* New York: Harper & Row, 1965.
A clear, informal, practical manual for the general poetry reader.

UNTERMEYER, LOUIS (ed.). *National Poetry Festival Proceedings: October 22–24, 1962.* Washington, D.C.: Library of Congress, 1964.
Talks, discussions, and readings by contemporary American poets that present a panoramic view of the state of poetry in the 60s.

VAN DOREN, MARK. *Introduction to Poetry: Commentaries on Thirty Poems* New York: Hill & Wang, 1966.
Explications of favorite works by a poet and famous teacher.

WAGGONER, HYATT H. *American Poets from the Puritans to the Present.* Boston: Houghton Mifflin Co., 1968.

A chronological treatment of representative American poets from Anne Bradstreet to Robert Creeley, stressing the centrality of Ralph Waldo Emerson as thinker and poet.

WALCUTT, CHARLES and J. EDWIN WHITESELL (eds.). *The Explicator Cyclopedia* (Vol. I, Modern Poetry; Vol. II, Traditional Poetry: Medieval to Late Victorian). Chicago: Quadrangle Books, 1966, 1968.

Poems explicated by many critics of various schools.

Author and Title Index*

---

* Entries are limited to poems printed in their entirety.

Subject Index